ETHICAL ISSUES IN THE CARE OF THE DYING AND BEREAVED AGED

John D. Morgan, Ph.D.

King's College Center for Education
about Death and Bereavement

Death, Value and Meaning Series
Series Editor: John D. Morgan

Baywood Publishing Co., Inc.
AMITYVILLE, NEW YORK

Library of Congress Catalog Number: 96-4565
ISBN: 0-89503-136-1 (Cloth)

Library of Congress Cataloging-in-Publication Data

Ethical issues in the care of the dying and bereaved aged / edited by
    John D. Morgan
        p.   cm. - - (Death, value and meaning series)
    Includes bibliographical references and index.
    ISBN 0-89503-136-1 (cloth)
    1. Terminal care- -Moral and ethical aspects. 2. Aged- -Medical
care- -Moral and ethical aspects. 3. Bereavement- -Psychological
aspects. 4. Aged- -Death. I. Morgan, John D., 1933- .
II. Series.
R726.8.E87 1996
174' .2- -dc20   96-4565
                                       CIP

DEDICATION

To
Dorothy Ley, M.D., F.R.C.P.(C)., F.A.C.P.
(1924 to 1994)
who enriched all our lives by her example

Acknowledgments

I wish to take this opportunity to thank King's College and its Principal, Dr. Philip J. Mueller, whose support has made the Center for Education about Death and Bereavement a reality. In spite of great financial pressures in the academic world, King's College has maintained a commitment to offer courses, seminars, and conferences in non-traditional areas which have as their sole purpose the improvement of the quality of life of those in need. I also wish to thank Mr. Michael Lacy whose editorial assistance has made the *Death, Value and Meaning* series more than just a possibility. Mr. Lacy's work is especially evident in this volume. Finally, I wish to extend thanks to Mr. Stuart Cohen of Baywood Publishing Company who continues to offer encouragement to this series of books. Baywood must be one of the few publishers which thinks of its role primarily as the advancement of knowledge.

Table of Contents

Introduction

The philosopher Jean-Paul Sartre has said that the human is the only animal that can fail [1, p. 26]. Only persons have to ask themselves what they must do in order to have a successful life, to be a good person. Indeed, it is precisely this need to create ourselves in our actions that constitutes us as humans [2, p. 6]. Persons have been engaged in his process of self discovery, a definition of ethics, since at least the fifth century before the common era. As we examine questions of right and wrong, good and evil, we still stand on the shoulders of the giants of the past: Plato, Aristotle, Aquinas, Augustine, Mill, and Kant. However, the problems that we face are radically different from those faced by our ancestors. While the philosophers mentioned above differed among themselves about the nature of the good, and how it came about in practice, they all assumed the existence of common goals in a stable community [3, p. 286]. They assumed the basic predictability of life and death. None of them knew of or faced the problems of an aging population in societies of diverse cultures.

It is a truism that we live in an aging society. Age-adjusted life expectancy grew from eighteen years at the time of Socrates, to twenty-four in the Middle Ages. At the beginning of the twentieth century, life expectancy was forty-nine years, as we approach the end of the same century it is eighty. While the greatest part of the shift comes from the fact that fewer women die in childbirth, and fewer children die of childhood illnesses, part of the longer life span is due to the fact that the diseases which killed most of our forefathers and mothers are now controlled by antibiotics. As a result we are living longer lives, and what is important for this book, we are dying longer deaths. The purpose of this book is to examine the status of the aged at the end of the twentieth century, and examine the ethical issues faced by them and those who care for them. As the history of thought has borne out, ethical problems grow more rapidly than does our ability to solve those problems. This volume is meant to advance the quality of life of the

1

aged by examining some of the issues that affect them in the closing days of the twentieth century.

Through these chapters there is a continuous thread of concern about the rightness of the manner in which we treat one another. Since Plato, philosophers and theologians have debated the theoretical, or metaethical criteria by which decisions are to be made. Metaethical views such as "seek happiness in community through virtue" [4, p. 1108], "act in conformity with the natural and eternal law" [5, p. 777], "seek the greatest balance of good over evil" [6, p. 357; 3, p. 286], or "act so as to create a kingdom of ends" [7, p. 54] have guided human understanding over the centuries and are presupposed in this volume. Even the more commonly asserted principles of medical ethics: non-malfeasance, autonomy, and beneficence, are not discussed here. What are discussed in this volume are the very practical problems which the aged, dying and bereaved, and those who care for them, face everyday, and principles by which these problems can be understood and acted upon.

This task is particularly important in the closing years of the second millennium. The need to rationalize resources comes at the same time as we have a larger population of aged in need of greater resources. This problem calls upon all our collective wisdom: those who are aging today are precisely the ones to whom we are indebted for our present culture and standard of living.

The volume is presented into five sections. The first deals with some general issues of the aged. Dr. Dorothy Ley, to whom this book is dedicated, challenges us to see the aged as a resource and not as a burden. Neil Thompson challenges us to reflect about "ageism." Are we truly committed to eradicating ageism, or is it simply another social fad? Eric Tappenden asks us to consider the values we are espousing as we create, or deny, funeral rituals and the effects of these decisions on the aged. Judith van Heerden tells of the particular problems of the aged dying in South Africa and a modest proposal for help. Finally Victor Marshall calls on gerontologists to actively incorporate the idea of death into a theory of ageing, rather than leaving it as an unexplored barrier.

The second section is, in a way, the main part of the book. Here we examine specific issues that the aged and the dying, and those who care for them face beginning with illness, moving through dying, to the ensuing grief. Mary Austrom and Hugh Hendrie speak of the problems which patients with Alzheimer's disease and their families face. Pearl Langer examines the specific dynamics of adult children who have aging parents. Miriam and Sydney Moss take the argument further to the anticipation of the death of those parents. Steven Connor has us examine the ethical aspects of giving hope and confronting denial in a hospice situation. Colin Parkes, whose book *Bereavement: Studies of Grief in Adult Life* is the classic in the field of grief, examines some of the basic principles of bereavement care. Peter Hill has us look at how we help the bereaved face physical and psychical "sites and objects" that are painful. Finally, Dennis Klass examines the ways in which the bereaved remember the dead and the resulting spiritual issues.

The third section deals with some ethical problems specific to the twentieth century. Esther Gjertsen and Cand Polit examine the tragedy of the various ways in which the abuse of the elderly occurs. Flora MacDonald, the former Canadian Ambassador to the United Nations, reminds us that many people of the world do not have the luxury of living to be aged, or to enjoy the benefits of hospice and bereavement services. Finally, Margaret Somerville gives a well reasoned exploration of the language of euthanasia and asks us what we are saying about ourselves when we advocate euthanasia.

In the fourth section, we look at some specific problems to which health care providers must attend. Phyllis Palgi examines the importance of physicians attending to their own needs as well as the sources of strength for health care professionals. Patrice O'Connor shows how health care professionals can be educated to cope with issues of death and bereavement. Connie Holden examines whether patient autonomy is always a blessing and whether or not lifting some of the burden of autonomy might be the more noble thing to do. Ben-Joshua Jaffee reminds us that not only is the human the only animal that is aware of death, the human is also the only animal that can use humor as an antidote to grief. Finally, Elizabeth Latimer reminds us of the importance of physician training.

In the final section Rabbi Roberts and Doug Graydon reflect us with on the importance of religious traditions in issues of aging, death, and bereavement. There are, of course, many issues not covered in this volume. I believe, however, that this book does contribute to our understanding of what it is like to be aged, to be dying, and to be bereaved in the closing days of the twentieth century.

REFERENCES

1. J. P. Sartre, Existentialism, in *Existentialism and Human Emotions,* J. P. Sartre (ed.), B. Frechtman (trans.), Citadel, Seacus, New Jersey, 1957.
2. L. Stevenson, *Seven Theories of Human Nature,* Oxford, New York, 1974.
3. J. S. Mill, Utilitarianism, in *Mill's Ethical Writings,* J.B. Schneewind (ed.), Collier, New York, 1965.

4. Aristotle, Nicomachean Ethics, in *The Basic Works of Aristotle,* R. McKeon (ed.), Random House, New York, 1941.
5. St. Thomas Aquinas, Treatise on Law, in *Basic Writings of Saint Thomas Aquinas,* A. C. Pegis (ed.), Random House, New York, 1945.
6. S. E. Stumpf, *Socrates to Sartre: A History of Philosophy,* McGraw Hill, New York, 1966.
7. I. Kant, *Fundamental Principles of the Metaphysic of Morals,* T. K. Abbot (trans.), Bobbs-Merrill, Indianapolis, 1949.

John D. Morgan, Ph.D.
King's College Center for Education
about Death and Bereavement
London, Canada

PART I

General Issues of the Aged

In this section we examine some of the specific issues that the aged, and those who work with the aged must address. Dorothy Ley, who died soon after the first chapter was written, reminded us that being old is a state of mind. She maintained her *joie de vivre*: a love of life and living until her death. Our culture tends to regard the elderly as uniform; however, the aging population is not homogenous, exhibiting wide socio-economic and cultural differences. In increasingly multi-cultural and pluralistic societies such as Canada and the United States, it is essential that caregivers recognize the different attitudes toward the elderly within different cultures and ethnic backgrounds.

The elderly are caught between the cold harsh realities of major demographic changes, and economic plans demanding reassessments of social networks. The elderly in the Canadian population has been risen from just under 10 percent in 1980 and is expected to rise to a peak of about 27 percent in 2031. In 1991, the increase was 12 percent. There will be a particularly dramatic rise in so-called frail elderly, those over eighty-five. For example, it is anticipated that between 1981 and 2001, a proportion of those aged eighty-five or older will increase by 130 percent.

The demographic changes in North America are not alarming per se. Many European countries have lived with 18 percent of their population over sixty-five for the last twenty years. Until recently, Canada and the United States had some of the lowest proportions of elderly in the Western world. It is the rapidity with which it is taking place which gives cause for concern because we are not ready for them.

Mandatory retirement, its associated loss of power, economic depen-dence, and a system of care that limits the ability to make decisions all diminish the freedom and responsibility of the elderly. It is clear that the majority would prefer to remain in their own communities with support, even at some inconvenience to themselves. The tension that exists between them and their families and caregivers is a direct result of a failure to recognize the elderly as autonomous human beings with rights and responsibilities.

Thompson reminds us that ageism shows itself in subtle ways. The term "ageism" is recent compared with concepts such as "racism" and "sexism." It refers to a negative and demeaning attitude toward older people and the discrimination that such attitudes both reflect and engender. Ageism must be recognized as a significant force in society and a major barrier to good care of older people. The awareness of ageism is evidenced by the growing literature on the subject and the increasing tendency for such matters to be included in training programs. The fact that such awareness remains uneven is evidenced by the continuing proliferation of examples of poor practice.

For workers in the health care field there is little understanding of the cultural and structural ageism based on ideology, power, and oppression. For example, the fact that discriminatory language reflects the workings of an underlying ageist ideology which marginalizes and demeans older people is not appreciated. As long as staff awareness of ageism does not extend to the cultural dimension of age discrimination, it seems likely that any commitment to anti-ageist practice will remain superficial because of a lack of understanding of the ideological underpinnings.

Thompson indicates that ageism is not simply a lack of respect for older people. It reflects a serious underestimation of the extent and intensity of oppression experienced by older people in barriers to medical treatment, infantilization, denial of sexuality, elder abuse, stereotypes, medicalization, and disablism.

Tappenden believes that changes in burial practice have affected the quality of life of the aged and the bereaved. The first, and one of the most marked changes, is the rapid rise in the cremation rate. While this is not entirely a global phenomenon, it is happening in many parts of the world. In Sweden, the rate is as high as 62.7 percent. The second change is an increase in "scattering" of cremated remains or "doing nothing" with cremated remains. Is it ethical to "do nothing" with cremated remains or is it important to scatter, or inter them and place some form of memorial with them for future generations as a focal point of remembrance? Third, there are more closed casket ceremonies. Funeral directors, and some clergy and psychologists, believe that an open casket at visitation is important in order for family and friends to accept the reality of death. There are even fewer funeral services. More memorial services without the body present are being conducted. The rising cost of traditional funerals and greater availability of low-cost services makes the traditional funeral almost out of reach for many persons. There are fewer religious services and fewer services in places of worship.

The questions that Tappenden challenges are: Do our practices help the grieving process and grieving person or hinder them? Is what we're doing reinforcing or changing our death-denying culture? Is what we're doing dignified? Does what we're doing recognize the value of rituals, however familiar or unfamiliar, however traditional or unique? Is what we're doing consistent with our other deeply held beliefs and values, spiritual or otherwise, or is it in conflict? Are we considering what family or other survivors need and want?

Marshall believes that a theory of aging and dying should deal with the lived experience of aging and dying. It should try to get at the phenomenology of aging and dying, at the ways in which aging phenomena interweave with age-related death of others in the social experience of an individual, and with that individual's own experience of finitude. We also need a understanding of aging and dying in terms of social institutions and social structure. He seeks a greater understanding of the ways in which mortality affects the organization of society and on the ways in which this organization around death and dying issues in turn influences the ways in which individuals in later life will experience their process of dying.

The theory that he proposes should incorporate the following theoretical propositions about aging and dying: 1) the shift in the typical age of death to the later years, where it is seen as the normal or typical end of a life course; 2) the longer duration of dying increases the need for institutionalized organizational arrangements for those who are old and dying; 3) the importance of shared meanings for dying as a process, and for death as an outcome or state; 4) the greater desire to exercise control over the "contingencies" of death and dying, such as its timing, association with pain, and social characteristics; and 5) the "cultural lag" in the legitimation potential of culture in highly modernized societies to "explain" death.

Van Heerden points out the injustices of the care for the aged black and the care for the aged white in South Africa. Even in integrated facilities social mixing did not occur between live-in patients (usually black) and local daycare (mostly colored) groups. This was due to the fact that daily activities were in full swing by the time live-in patients returned from hospital treatment clinics. Live-in patients were strangers in the community and socially isolated. They carried the burden of their illness alone and become withdrawn and depressed.

The patients felt trapped in treatment decisions and wanted more information to participate in management decisions.

I believe that these chapters will be useful in setting the stage for a discussion of the care of the aged, the dying, and the bereaved in the years to come.

CHAPTER 1

Palliative Care and the Aged in Canada

Dorothy C. H. Ley

I am reminded of Alexander Dumas' reply to an admirer who asked, "How do you grow old so gracefully?" "Madam," he replied, "I give all my time to it." And now so do I, and so do we all.

Being old is a state of mind. There are many of us over sixty-five who have a *joie de vivre*: a love of life and living that is far greater than some of our younger friends. Perhaps for some, our enjoyment is accentuated by the knowledge that the time we have remaining is shorter and therefore sweeter and more valuable. A famous Toronto surgeon who has been dead for many years once said to me, "Dorothy, life is for the living, and it's for living. You can't get it in the bank and get interest on it, you can't pass it on to your children. You can't lend it to anyone. All you can do is live it." How right he was.

There is a widespread, although not universal perception that the elderly are a problem group in society. Certainly there are figures from many countries, including both the United States and Canada that could be interpreted to support this pessimistic view. But equally there are figures that support the contrary view. The elderly are not a problem, but a valuable resource. They are not a burden, but a challenge. Many of the issues surrounding the care of the elderly are uniquely Western in their origin. The status of the elderly varies widely in different primitive societies. In a matriarchal society, the elderly man may be considered useless, whereas the elderly woman is revered for her knowledge and for her position as the mother of the tribe. In hunting and gathering times, the elderly may have been cast off as impediments for the movement of the tribe and therefore its survival. In underdeveloped countries, the average life expectancy may be in the forties, for example forty-eight in Tanzania. (I would not hazard a guess as to what it is in Somalia and Uganda.) In contrast, it is seventy-nine in Canada. Our concern with the care of people over the age of sixty-five and, in particular, with the frail elderly, is seen by the Third World at best as incomprehensible, at worst, a waste of scarce resources. However, in many primitive societies where an elder is living, they are treated with care and concern as a responsibility of the extended family.

We tend to think of the elderly as uniform; however, the aging population is not homogenous. It exhibits wide socio-economic and cultural differences. In an increasingly multicultural and pluralistic society such as Canada and the United States, it is essential that caregivers recognize the different attitudes toward the elderly within different cultures and ethnic backgrounds.

Until recently, in Canada there was a white European culture predominantly of Judeo-Christian religious orientation. That is rapidly changing, particularly in our large urban centers. In Toronto, for example, some 11 percent of the population is Italian, predominantly Roman Catholic, predominantly male dominated. This can pose problems, for example, for a young female Anglo-Saxon Protestant physician who is trying to administer palliative care.

North American society is still having great difficulty coming to terms with the fact that it is aging rapidly. Simonne de Beavoir commented on the position of the elderly in society some years ago when she wrote "It is the tendency for every society to live and to go on living. It extols the strength and fecundity that are so closely linked with youth. It dreads the worn-out stability and the decrepitude of age." Nowhere has the philosophy of youth been more extolled than on this continent; in a competitive and materialistic society we put a premium on dominance and power. It is not surprising that our perception of aging is one of decline in productivity and potential, increasing dependency and powerlessness, and increasing need for protective intervention in the lives of the elderly. This has led to benign paternalism on the part of families, of caregivers, of governments. It has affected public policy and private attitudes, and is largely responsible for the pessimistic interpretation of the demographic changes that we face in the next two decades. Ageism has now joined sexism and racism on a list of attitudes that offend against human rights. The values that should guide our relationships with the elderly and provide us with provision of care for them, whether that would be care in the early decades of old age or care of the terminally ill elderly, are familiar ones of justice, freedom, and responsibility. Too often however, when we care for the aging it is motivated more by a justification of our own existence as caregivers, than by the expressed needs of the elderly. Do we in fact know or care what they really need or want? We have created a system in most of the rest of the world that has medicalized, segregated, and institutionalized their care, and as William May has pointed out, one has to wonder if by such actions we are not protecting ourselves from reminders of our own vulnerability and of our fear—putting our personal responsibility on the shoulders of competent professionals. At the same time, we impose the power and influence of the community at large on a segment of our society that has been rendered relatively powerless. Before we can have a meaningful discussion of palliative care for the elderly in the Canadian context, I believe we must examine their place in the Canadian health care system.

The elderly are caught in the middle, between the cold harsh realities of major demographic changes and an economic plan that is leading the demands for a reassessment of a Canadian social network. To understand the nature and extend to the potential problems, let me briefly describe two studies that were commissioned by the Canadian Medical Association.

The first was the Watson Task Force which was initiated in 1983. It studied the impact of health care phenomena, the rapid expansion of high technology, and the demographic changes that would take place between 1980 and 2021. Projections were startling, and the financial implications for the health care systems were even more startling. It was anticipated that there would have to be a 75 percent increase in public expenditures, both operating and capital to maintain the *status quo*. The current admission rate of the elderly to chronic care beds is at 100 percent. There will have to be an increase of those beds of somewhere between 100 and 225 percent of the existing number of beds. In Canada, the *status quo* is a relatively high level of institutionalization, something over 9 percent. This compares to Great Britain, for example, where the institutionalization of the elderly, people over sixty-four, is at about 5 percent.

In response to the Watson Task Force, the Canadian Medical Association established a committee in 1985 to study the health care of the elderly. I had the privilege of chairing that committee which was composed of physicians from across Canada. The mandate was to examine the existing system of care as it related to the elderly and to make broad recommendations for changes that would improve the quality of that care and would meet anticipated needs as the number of elderly increased. It was almost immediately apparent that clinical issues could not be the only concern. The committee, in fact examined health care, not medical care. Social, economic, and political considerations had to be of equal importance.

The projections for the increase in the number of elderly in the Canadian population has been consistent: from just under 10 percent in 1980 to a peak of about 27 percent in 2031. In 1991, the increase was 12 percent. To date, these projections have been correct. There will be a particularly dramatic rise in so-called frail elderly, those over eighty-five. For example, it is anticipated that between 1981 and 2001, a proportion of those aged eighty-five or older will increase by 130 percent. At this point we are right in the middle of that increase, the number of people in Canada has increased by 81 percent in the last decade, those over seventy-five, at 22 percent. However, we are not all going to be old and in wheelchairs and receiving palliative care, because in 2001 the rate of growth in those who are very old, over seventy-five, will slow down. However, the baby boomers are aging, and the number in the sixty-five to seventy-four year old cohort will increase.

The importance of these figures is the effect on health care planning policies, including policies for the care of the terminally ill, because short-term policies for the care of the frail elderly (that 120%) and long-term policies for the care of the 2,031 are needed now and must be interrelated.

The demographic changes in Canada are not alarming per se. Many European countries have lived with 18 percent of their population over sixty-five for the last twenty years. Until recently, Canada had one of the lowest proportions of elderly in the Western world. It is the rapidity with which it is taking place which gives cause for concern because we are not ready for it.

There are certain characteristics of the aging Canadian population in the last decade of the twentieth century that distinguish it from previous cohorts. First, it is the first generation in which the majority of people can expect to live to old age. It is the first generation in which the average life expectancy equals or exceeds the age of mandatory retirement. Future cohorts will expect retirement and will be better prepared both mentally and financially for that retirement, if the economy stabilizes or improves and if private pension plans become increasingly more common. As more women enter the work force, more of them will contribute to such plans, reducing their reliance on government transfer payments. When the committee did its study, one in four of women over sixty-four were living below the poverty line; in 1991 that figure had been reduced to 38 percent. Second, more of tomorrow's elderly will live alone, rather than with a spouse, reflecting higher numbers of divorced and single people now in the younger age groups of "never married." (I love that phrase, it's a heck of a lot better than old maids.)

There's a gender difference in both Canada and the United States, with a preponderance of women over age sixty-five, and that preponderance is predicted to become more marked. Who are they? Roughly 50 percent of women over the age of sixty-five are widowed, 40 percent are married; 15 percent of men are widowers, 75 percent are married. This makes a tremendous difference in hospice programs and palliative care programs. At the hospice with which I am associated, the majority of people receiving care are women. The majority of whom (over 65) are widowed. This presents great problems, because frequently these people have no primary caregivers. The absence of a primary caregiver in the home is not only reflected in the difficulty of hospice programs to prepare for these people, but in the fact that somewhere between 67 and 75 percent of the elderly in care institutions are women.

Finally, informal care, now provided mostly by women may decrease because of their increasing role in the work force. At present, 80 percent of care for the elderly in the community comes from the voluntary sector or from family. That will decrease. Conversely, the expectation is that community support systems will increase, and there will be a cry for daycare and a cry for subsidized elder care.

Old age is not a disease, and the majority of the elderly are not sick, despite the fact that 40 percent of health care expenditures are accounted for by the elderly. Where do they live? Where are they? Well, there are two distinct cohorts of elderly: the early years of old age, and the years of advanced age (the frail elderly over 85). The years between sixty-five and seventy-five are generally characterized by good health and independence, but 90 percent of these elderly live in private households, 70 percent alone or with a spouse. Roughly 10 percent are institutionalized at any one time. Two percent of people between sixty-five and seventy-five are in long-term care facilities. Whereas, one-third of the frail elderly over seventy-five require chronic institutionalization.

There is not one system of care for the elderly in Canada. Each province has a range of medical and social services for the elderly that is funded by federal, provincial, and local governments. The range of services provided in any community varies and depends on the availability of financial and human resources, on the philosophy of care in that community, and on the direction of care in that particular province.

Over the years we have identified and commented on the fragmentation of care. There is an arbitrary division in the responsibility of care for everyone but particularly the elderly between competing ministries, agencies, and departments at all levels of government. It is called "turf syndrome" and there is a general lack of coordination within the health care system as well as between health and social services. This is a major hinderance to the continuity of care, whether that care be geriatric care or palliative care. There is evidence right across this country of bureaucratic self-interest and defensive turf, not only in large public institutions, but in many autonomous non-governmental organizations. Patients may and do often receive uncoordinated care from professionals who are not communicating with each other and who are confused concerning their professional role and responsibility, particularly in the community. We educate our health care professionals in a tertiary care system, we turn them out expecting to work within that system, then we wonder why they cannot function in the community where the system does not exist.

The fragmentation and the lack of coordination of care in Canada is aggravated by inappropriate financing. There is a maldistribution of resources to some services and incentives created by the methods of financing professional, institutional, and community care. We have in Canada, by both government policies and public attitude, perpetuated an institutionally-based acute interventionist medical model of care. This has been perpetuated by the way we pay for it, and by health expenditures across the country. The *Canada Health Act* provides for payment of health services, but, in fact, health insurance covers the cost of care within the medical model and provides payment for "medical acts." The move, in some provinces, is to de-insure some of our services as a cost-cutting effort. This is a reflection of the failure to recognize that health care is not medical care. Health is dependant on a person's total environment, be it physical, financial, social, or spiritual. Although, generally, it should be noted that Canadians are well served by our medical services.

Public expectations are reflected in public policy: at the present time, there is little evidence of political will to alter the pattern of funding to allocate increased resources to the community, to long-term care, or to palliative care. Ontario is taking the first steps to revitalize the delivery of long-term care and, for the first time, to recognize that palliative care does exist and to provide funding for that care. However, in a budget of several billion dollars, palliative care received 1.8 million, primarily for education. The Canadian public is much more enamoured of new intensive care units than of the allocation of large funds of money to community services. Such a decision to move that money from acute care institutions into the community may or may not be politically attractive. If politicians are astute about anything, it is about what gets them re-elected. For example, in the middle of the last election campaign in Ontario, the government announced that it intended to charge the elderly for certain home support services of our home care system based on a means test. There was little notice before the announcement, there has been little implemented, and as far as I know the elderly are not marching up and down the streets. Ideally, a system of community care for the elderly shall embrace private homes, residential, extended care, nursing facilities, acute care hospital beds, geriatric assessments, day hospitals, day care centers, rest beds, palliative care units, palliative care teams, and palliative care programs. There should be free movement between all types of this system.

The emphasis in legislation and practice in the Canadian health care system has been on medical care—the physician being the gate-keeper to such services. To change this, the method of payment for health professionals, particularly physicians, is going to have to be altered. We have a traditional fee for service method of payment and as such it does not encourage time consuming payment activities such as team meetings. It is generally accepted that the assessment for the elderly, particularly the terminally ill elderly, is best carried out in their own environment. In the present system of reimbursement for physicians and other health care workers, professionals do not encourage home visits, particularly if they are lengthy or in rural areas. Proposed legislation in the Ontario legislature is going to limit those home visits even further. Governments, medical, and other professional associations are going to have to be prepared to design more appropriate remuneration structures for people practicing palliative care and for people caring for the elderly.

As a society we exercise great control over the elderly's environment. We are all guilty of the benevolent paternalism I mentioned in the beginning. The elderly themselves have come to expect such an attitude and only recently have begun to react to it. The competent elderly must be free to choose and to take the consequences of their actions. They must be allowed to live at risk. A relative of mine once said to me when I took her arm to help her across the street "Don't do that." I asked, "Why not?" She replied, "Because if I get hit by a bus, it's my life and I'm going to take the responsibility for it." So I took my hand off her elbow.

Mandatory retirement, its associated loss of power, economic dependence, and a system of care that limits the ability to make decisions, all diminish the freedom and responsibility of the elderly. The arguments about euthanasia highlight our removal of responsibility from that group in society. It is clear that the majority would prefer to remain in their own communities with support, even at some inconvenience to themselves. The tension that exists between them and their families and caregivers is a direct result of a failure to recognize the elderly as autonomous human beings with rights and responsibilities. It is essential, as Winkler notes, "[t]hat society recognize the elderly as bearers of certain responsibilities as well as rights." Thus, we must take them seriously as moral agents, not merely dependant publics of social policy, however benevolently motivated such policy might be. To put it very simply, it is a two-way street. The freedom to live at risk is intimately associated with the responsibility to participate in society to the fullest extent possible, then to take the results with that participation.

It has been said that it is the philosophy of care, not the place that makes the hospice unique. Palliative care is universal in its application, it applies to all age groups. However, in St. Christopher's hospice in 1987, only 38 percent of patients admitted were seventy-five or older. At the same time in the United States, 70 percent of hospice patients were over sixty-five. In Canada in 1986, 72 percent of new cancers were in men, and 51 percent of women were diagnosed after the age of sixty. Those figures are increasing. So on this continent at least, there appears to be a growing need to address the issues surrounding palliative care for people over age sixty-five. There are both specific and subtle differences in palliative care for the young or the middle aged, and palliative care for the aged. Hospice or palliative care is firmly rooted in the holistic approach to people who are dying and rejection of the disease oriented model of care. Nowhere is this more important or more difficult than in palliative care of the terminally ill elderly, particularly the very old. The presence of multiple pathologies and the multiplicity of symptoms frequently makes dying a diagnosis of disclusion. This severely limits the time available to have good palliative care. The average length of stay at St. Christopher's hospice in 1987 was ten days. This compared to two days of pre-death dependency in a geriatric unit. It could be argued that the so called "old old" are slowly dying, and thus merit palliative care for some longer period of time before their actual demise. This begs the question of when and where to initiate such care, and how and by whom it should be carried out. I hear my friends who run palliative care units complaining that many of them should be running long-term care units because of the age of the people in them. It does, however, underline the change in a recent attitude toward the care of the elderly, to place the emphasis on holistic care. It also suggests the need for a closer link between palliative care and term care. Will the ladder be provided in a community or in an institution? Palliative care is dependant on effective communication for its successful implementation.

In studies of the terminally ill geriatric patients, the report is that 40 percent may be confused with impaired perception of their continuing state and impending death. About one-half were demented. This compares with 27 percent of patients at St. Christopher. This makes communication difficult. Further, the elderly may have major communication problems related to cardiovascular disease and strokes: difficulty speaking or reading, impaired vision, impaired hearing, and poor memory. Apart from the impact of patient compliance with a plan of care, the inability to communicate freely makes it difficult for caregivers not only to assess a person's overall comfort, but also to provide the spiritual and emotional support that is such an essential component of palliative care.

Patients, families, and friends are considered to be the unit of care in palliative care or hospice care. Who are they for an elderly widow in a nursing home who has no family in that community? Who are the patient's family and friends? The people in the nursing home, they become a surrogate family. Caregivers sometimes forget that when people from nursing homes are put into acute care institutions for the last two or three days of care, they are being torn away from their family and friends.

Although today 80 percent of the care of the elderly is provided by family and voluntary groups, in the future the pool of care will decrease. What are we going to do as people age? The probability of their living alone increases. Although aging people have pets, neither a dog nor a cat is a very good primary caregiver. Even if close relatives, such as a spouse, are alive, they may themselves be in care. Some 90 percent of Canadians have expressed a desire to die at home; however, fewer than 30 percent do so. The frail terminally ill elderly at home requires one person's full-time commitment to coordinate care and be present at night. That one person, what I call a "surrogate head nurse in the home" is needed, as are regular home visits from the physician, the nurse, other regular home workers, and home support staff. In some jurisdictions, the absence of the primary caregiver in the home disqualifies the dying person from receiving any hospice care at all. To meet the needs of the elderly at home who are dying, as well as the elderly in general, is going to require a major shift in resources. In fact, community-based palliative care in Canada has been inhibited by the limited, fragmented, and poorly funded home health and social services in all of the provinces. To satisfy the need in Canada for palliative care outside the institution, there has been a rapid increase taking place in the number of non-governmental community palliative care programs staffed by a mix of trained volunteers and professionals: a 200 percent increase in the mid 1980s.

These community hospices provide care and support in the home and, for many elderly, become a surrogate family. They cooperate with the existing home care professionals and with the family physicians in the community. Effective pain and symptom control is the hallmark of good palliative care, but the medical management of terminally ill elderly patients is complicated by their age and the frequent presence of multiple medical problems. The use of narcotics or other drugs to control symptoms is modified by their interaction with coexisting medication and by the changes in drug metabolism that accompany aging. Moreover, the pattern of perception of symptoms by the elderly is frequently different. In fact, shortness of breath, restlessness, and agitation are more common symptoms in the dying elderly than is pain. Counseling, particularly psychosocial counseling, is another important component of palliative care, although it has unique characteristics for each age group. Frequently, the elderly have already had to cope with multiple losses: the loss of a job at retirement, the change in the nature of their role in the family, and the change of physical capacity. They have often experienced the death of a spouse or other family members or friends. Because of this, most older people have come to the recognition and acceptance of the finitude of life and their own mortality. Sociologists tell us that the elderly are much more likely than the young to accept responsibly of their lives as lived; to accept their lives, successful or not, as having meaning; and to come to terms with death itself. In general, they are concerned with maintaining independent living and physical function, but are more fearful of becoming a burden to their family or society than they are of dying. According to Marshall, a vast majority come to a point where death and their own dying make more sense to them than continuing to live forever. Generally, the elderly are less concerned with the time left to live than with the quality of that life. Spiritual care of the elderly also has somewhat different dimensions. In the process of coming to terms with their own lives, they have had time to concentrate their spirituality. That spirituality must be reinforced and the religious ties that so many elderly people have must be strengthened. The wide gap and life experience between young caregivers and the very old make it difficult to provide appropriate spiritual care.

In an increasingly multicultural and pluralistic society, ethnic values and practices with the elderly may be at odds, not only at the present generation in their own culture, but with the setting in which their care is provided. Frequently, there can be a critical need following the death of an elderly patient to identify family members who will require bereavement support. The loss of a partner or close companion of many years may be a devastating experience for an elderly person and may precipitate his or her own institutionalization. The social situation and the intergenerational conflicts may be complex and the need for support and counseling acute.

This will become increasingly true, as the number of elderly increase in society to the point (and this has already happened for caregivers) where children are also elderly. The ethical issues with respect to the terminally ill elderly are multiple and complex. Many health care professionals are caught between the philosophy of care espoused by the hippocratic oath and the need for triage of scarce resources. A situation is being forced upon them by the economic constraints within both the Canadian and the American systems. The spectre of age-related aspects of care is in the background of all planning exercises In fact, economic constraints may force all those concerned with the care of the elderly, in particular the frail or the terminally ill, to make decisions concerning care that by default are based ultimately on the age of the recipients. In our consideration of the just and equitable distribution of limited resources, we must find a way to resolve the ethical conflicts that develop between the claims of the individual and those of society.

An issue that is frequently overlooked is that of research on the elderly. Maggie Coon once wrote,

> On persons who are old, poor, and stigmatized by society, they become objects of gerontological research, they are seen as problems by society rather than of persons experiencing problems created by society. Neither medicine or gerontology has democratized research. They have made the elderly subjects or respondents rather than participants.

It has been strongly stated that gerontological research is actually unethical because it reflects and perpetuates the socially structured inadequacy of older adults in the wider society.

The other, more obvious issue is that of research on the non-competent elderly. It is particularly relevant, for example, in the research of the cause and treatment of Alzheimer disease. It is unethical to conduct research on demented patients to solve the problems of a disease that causes dementia because research can only be carried out on people who are unable to give informed consent to its conduct. The simple application of at least three principles of biomedical research, penephisen, autonomy, and justice will not provide solutions. The first two are in conflict with demented elderly. Finally, the meaning of one's dying should be a final expression of personal dignity under the meaning one is put to life and to love. The reality can make the application of such a philosophy complex and difficult. We are faced today with technological advances that have outstripped our ability to make rational, ethical decisions about palliative care, and how to respect the dignity of unconscious or incompetent patients. Margaret Somerville asked, "What does dying with dignity mean?" What is dignity? We are faced with different choices in caring for the comatose and the demented. What is the difference between so-called "passive" and "active" euthanasia? When is one justified in withdrawing food? Is one ever justified in killing someone? What is morally justified, what is legally acceptable? Dying with dignity has become a slogan used against useless technological elongation of life. Unfortunately, it has also become a cry for killing patients who fail to die fast enough for the convenience or economics of the system. To quote David Roy, "This reveals levels of desperation that mark profound societal discord about important matters."

The way we deal with the dying, the terminally ill, and those that medicine can save but not cure, are in question. The controversy is about life, not just the ideas. Should society give the power to kill to medicine or any other profession? Or on the other hand, should we recognize that such situations exist and act accordingly avoiding discussions and legalities. Increasing demand for euthanasia by the elderly is an indictment of society's ability to use high technology wisely—in anticipation of long-term results of that use and our failures of caregivers, our failures to recognize the distinction of microethics of care, and the legalities surrounding the provision of care. The increasing demand for living wills on the part of the elderly reflects the fact that they trust neither health caregivers or the system. Hospice, or palliative care is not a panacea for all the problems of the terminally ill elderly. However, it must be agreed that the proper medical care of the patient with the terminal illness may not necessarily be prolongation of life with every modern technique available. Rather, aid the patient with concurrence of the family to die with dignity, and without unnecessary pain and suffering.

Over the centuries the attitude to death has changed. As Aries points out, in the beginning death was accepted without fear as part of the natural progression of life. We now live in a society where most deaths occur in aging populations and in institutions. It is not surprising that society is ambivalent in its reaction to death. The philosophy of palliative care brings to the care of the terminally ill elderly a reinforcement of the belief that life is of value, that treatment, which prolongs pain and suffering is unacceptable, and that the physician has a duty to relieve suffering and to maintain respect for human dignity. Hospice also brings to the competent and informed elderly the right of choice, and the enhancement of personal control over their dying. To quote Roy again:

> Aging challenges the ethos, morality and ethics of the community. Though we share a common humanity, persons are unique, often remarkably different in what they value most highly in life. As we strive to build a clinical ethic, on the basis of our common humanity, the danger to be avoided is the production of an establishment ethics that leaves little freedom for moral minorities. As you strive to build an ethic capable of originality, the danger to be aware of was the seduction of a facile relativism that ignores the bonds and possibility of our shared humanity.

These bonds are the foundation for the ethics of the aged. With all the attendant difficulties of modern society in providing effective palliative care for the elderly, there is still a promise of care that reinforces the meaning of the dying person's life. Dillon Thomas wrote to his father, "Old age should burn and wave at close of day, rage, rage, against the dying of a life." Perhaps with palliative care we can convert that raging to the attitude described by William Code Ryan in his lines from *Thanatos*, "Sustain and soothe by an unfaltering thrust, approach thy grave like one that wraps the drapery of his coat about him, and lies down to pleasant dreams."

CHAPTER 2

Tackling Ageism— Moral Imperative or Current Fad?

Neil Thompson

Anti-discriminatory policy and practice in health and social welfare have developed significantly in recent years. However, doubts remain as to whether a genuine philosophy of equality and empowerment has been embraced. The question is posed as to whether apparent advances in developing anti-ageist practice represent a fundamental shift in attitudes, values and practices or, more superficially, a token-istic and fashionable response to the emerging critique of traditional approaches.

The central argument of this chapter is that a genuine commitment to anti-ageist practice must be premised on an understanding of ageism within the framework of:

1. the broader context of cultural and structural factors; and
2. the inter-relationship of ageism and other forms of oppression such as sexism and racism.

Anti-ageism is presented as a moral imperative—an essential aspect of good practice in the care of older people.

The past decade has seen a considerable growth of interest in the field of what has become known as "anti-discriminatory practice." Generally the focus of anti-discriminatory practice has been on racism and sexism: in particular, the ways in which these forms of oppression have previously been given inadequate attention in health and social welfare theory and practice [1]. However, we are now increasingly seeing the development of a much stronger and clearer theory base and practice wisdom with regard to these areas as the concept of equality of

23

opportunity is being recognized more and more as a service delivery issue, rather than merely as a matter of employment rights.

Far less attention has been given to other areas of discrimination and oppression such as disability or age, although there are signs that attention is increasing [2]. As these issues achieve a firmer footing on the policy and practice agenda for the caring professions, we need to ask the question: Is anti-discriminatory practice genuinely a moral imperative or is it simply a matter of academic, professional, or political fashion?

This chapter will address this question with regard to one specific area of discrimination, that of ageism. Considerable progress has been made in recent years in challenging the marginalization of older people and their needs. Social gerontology has become a more established academic discipline and health and welfare practice with older people has been given a much higher profile in the United Kingdom and many other countries due, in no small part, to the demographic "rising tide" of older people. This growth of interest in older people raises a number of questions:

- Is there a genuinely new attitude toward older people or are we simply seeing a rhetorical commitment to anti-ageist practice?
- Can ageism widely be seen as an issue just as worrying and worthy of our attention as racism and sexism or will it continue to be seen as secondary to them?
- What is the relationship between sexism, racism, and ageism?
- What are the pitfalls we must avoid if anti-ageist practice is to become established as a central part of good practice and not dismissed as a fad or fashion?

ANTI-AGEISM: BREAKTHROUGH OR BANDWAGON?

The term "ageism" is relatively recent compared with concepts such as racism and sexism. However, it has been over twenty-five years since Butler introduced the concept of "ageism" to describe a negative and demeaning attitude toward older people and the discrimination that such attitudes both reflect and engender [3]. Butler's insights have taken a long time to make a serious impact on health and social welfare practice. Even now the recognition of ageism as a significant force in society and a potentially major barrier to good practice in the care of older people has yet to have an impact on substantial numbers of people in the caring professions. Awareness of ageism—and the need to develop anti-ageist practice—would appear to be on the rise. However, the awareness remains variable and inconsistent. The growth of awareness is evidenced by the growing literature on the subject and the increasing tendency for such matters to be included in training programs at both the qualifying and post-qualifying level. The fact that such a growth of awareness remains uneven is evidenced by the continuing proliferation of examples of poor practice. For example, it is not uncommon for older social work clients to be referred to in such patronizing terms as "old dear." Hughes and Mtezuka echo this observation in the context of working with older women:

> . . . at the level of communicating with older women, the way in which the practitioner approaches and talks to the older woman will reflect a belief in her right to respect and autonomy. There can be no place, then, for addressing older women by their first name without their permission; for using infantilizing or stereotypical labels such as "granny" or "old dear"; for treating or speaking to the person in any way which symbolically reflects an abuse of power or an invasion of their privacy or rights [4, p. 236].

The same authors define ageism as:

> . . . the social process through which negative images of and attitudes towards older people, based solely on the characteristics of old age itself, result in discrimination [4, p. 220].

They then go on to argue that: "Social work has not only failed to challenge ageism and its implicit assumptions of assumed homogeneity, it appears to have embraced these values" [4, p. 233].

The situation therefore remains one in which considerable progress remains to be made before we can genuinely claim to have developed anti-ageist practices. However, at a superficial level at least, we do seem to have made major strides forward in recent years. For example, the concept of elder abuse, although still receiving far less attention than child abuse, is now receiving much more serious consideration than in previous years. This is exemplified by the fact that, despite the absence of a legislative base or a national policy framework, many local authorities in the United Kingdom now have guidelines on how to deal with elder abuse or are in the process of developing them [5]. This can be seen as part of the development of anti-ageist practice for, as Wright and Ogg point out: "In its widest context, elder abuse can be seen as the way society marginalizes and discriminates against older people" [6, p. 16].

The situation could therefore be summarized as one in which there are signs of progress having been made, but also signs that the establishment of anti-ageist practice as a professional norm is a longer term goal rather than an immediate one. This raises a significant question: Are we witnessing a genuine and far-reaching, albeit gradual, change in social work and health care practice with older people, or are the apparent changes simply superficial adjustments to what remains a paternalistic approach? This brings us, in effect, to the central question to be addressed in this chapter: Is anti-ageism a moral imperative or can it more accurately be seen as simply a current fad or fashion?

I have argued elsewhere that good practice must be anti-discriminatory practice:

> a social work practice which does not take account of oppression and discrimination cannot be seen as good practice, no matter how high its standards may be in other respects. For example, a social work intervention with a disabled person which fails to recognize the marginalized position of disabled people in society runs the risk of providing the client with more of a disservice than a service [2, pp. 10-11].

It is in this sense that anti-ageist practice can be seen as a moral imperative. That is, once it is recognized that older people are an undervalued, disadvantaged, and oppressed group, there can be no moral justification for continuing to practice in a way which reinforces or condones the marginalized position of older people in society.

Unfortunately, tackling ageism suffers from many of the problems encountered in the struggles against racism and sexism. Primary among these is the tendency to view the situation in individualistic terms. To the refrains of "I'm not racist . . ." and "I'm not sexist . . ." can now be added "I'm not ageist . . ." For many workers in the social welfare field there is little understanding of discrimination beyond the level of personal prejudice, little awareness of the cultural and structural dimensions relating to ideology, power, and oppression. For example, the link between discriminatory language and the dominant ideology of ageism is one that is often not appreciated. Marshall comments on the depersonalizing language commonly used: "Usage of the term 'the elderly' is a way of distancing ourselves from them: they become dehumanized" [7, p. 119]. But, of course, this is not simply a matter of an unfortunate choice of terminology—it also reflects the workings of an underlying ageist ideology which marginalizes and demeans older people. Bytheway argues that this ideology is also apparent in the literature relating to older people, a fact which adds some degree of legitimacy to its negative portrayal of elders:

> evidence does support the proposition that popular attitudes and beliefs about old age are based, to a considerable extent, upon the vocabularies and images found in currently available literature, and that there is in the production of literature a powerful regenerative element which serves to maintain dominant ideological perspectives and understandings as new generations of students come to undertake their work [8, p. 154].

This ideological representation of older people takes the issue of age discrimination beyond the simplistic analysis of personal prejudice and locates it within the broader context of cultural norms, images, and values. Individual negative perceptions and constructions of older people can therefore be seen as manifestations of the stereotypical images of elders implicit within culturally codified conceptions of normality.

It is this cultural/ideological level of analysis that is so often missing from the commonly held views (among the general public and, more specifically, among health and social welfare staff). Negative attitudes are seen primarily as a matter of individual pathology, the negative excesses of a prejudiced minority. This conception of ageism is one which fails to take account of the significant role of wider cultural values, as exemplified by media representations, which marginalize, stigmatize, and oppress older people [9].

While staff awareness of the complexities of ageism does not extend to take cognizance of the cultural dimension of age discrimination, it seems likely, if not inevitable, that any commitment to anti-ageist practice will remain superficial (more rhetorical than real) because of a lack of understanding of the ideological underpinnings. However, there is even a further step that will need to be taken if anti-ageist practice is to be more than rhetorical. This relates to the structural level of ageism:

> Phillipson adopts a "political economy" approach to understanding the position of older people in society . . . He links negative attitudes towards older people to the structural requirements of the capitalist quest for profit. He argues that old age is seen as "nonproductive" and a "period of social redundancy" [10, p. 7]. But this is no coincidence—this negative and dismissive ideology is pervasive because it is linked inextricably with the economic requirements of capitalism [2, p. 94].

Old age is a "social division"—one of the dimensions, together with those of class, "race" and gender, along which society is structured. As such, it has significant implications in terms of economics and politics. In particular, old age has close links with the labor market, specifically with respect to compulsory retirement and policies for removing older workers from the workforce [10, 11]. In this way, the structural level informs and reinforces the cultural or ideological level where the notion that older people are unproductive and a drain on national resources [12, 13] enjoys common currency.

An understanding of ageism, purely at the level of personal prejudice, therefore neglects significant dimensions of this important aspect of human services. It is a *reductionist* approach—it reduces a complex, multifaceted phenomenon to a simple matter of individual attitude. And, as such, it likely to be superficial at best—influenced more by current trends and bandwagons than a genuine understanding of the issues or a commitment to a more deep-rooted and far-reaching change in the marginalized position of older people.

AGEISM AS A SOCIAL PROBLEM

Ageism as a cause for social and political concern has yet to approach the extent and intensity of concern generated by the more firmly established social problems of racial and sexual oppression. However, as Townsend suggests, "There are forms of discrimination against the elderly which are as deep as forms of discrimination against women and ethnic minorities" [14, p. 15]. Similarly, the Board for Social Responsibility argue that ageism is a problem just as urgent and important as sexism and racism [15]. There are, therefore, indications that ageism is being increasingly recognized as a major source of oppression and therefore significant social problem.

In contrast to this, however, there remains some resistance to ageism being addressed as a major concern alongside racism and sexism. For example, McNay argues that

> [w]hile other forms of discrimination need to be addressed, they are
> not central to the structured inequality essential for the profit base
> of our current economic relations, as are the divisions of gender,
> race and class [16, p. 53] .

Clearly, McNay is underplaying the structural dimension of ageism by not taking account of the role of age as a significant dimension of the political economy. She appears to be relegating ageism (and other forms of discrimination, such as disablism) to a secondary position and, in so doing, is subscribing to the destructive myth of a "hierarchy of oppressions" in which some forms of discrimination are seen as "more important" than others. Bytheway and Johnson take this critique a step further by arguing that:

> The issue of ageism should not be seen simply to be one in a series of "isms" through which different sections of the population suffer various forms of deprivation and prejudice. This approach fosters the absurd league table mentality, typified by crass questions such as "which group is most oppressed—women, ethnic minorities, the elderly or the disabled?" (see Blakemore [18]). More pragmatically, if ageism is perceived simply to be an idea formulated in the mode of sexism and racism, then it can be dismissed as no more than joining a bandwagon [17, p. 30].

The notion which needs to be challenged and set aside, therefore, is that ageism is less important than sexism and racism or is simply, as Bytheway and Johnson imply, an attempt to jump on a bandwagon, to become part of a fad or fashion.

Ageism is not simply a lack of respect for older people and, indeed, such a view reflects a serious underestimation of the extent and intensity of oppression experienced by older people as a result of ageist structures, attitudes, and practices. De Beauvoir captures this in her argument that: "It is common knowledge that the condition of old people today is scandalous . . . we must try to understand how it comes about that society puts up with it so easily" [19, p. 243]. More specifically, the following examples of ageist oppression can be seen in our society:

- *Barriers to medical treatment.* Older people are often denied access to medical treatment and facilities "presumably because they have less life expectancy, and therefore less to gain from such treatments" [20, p. 22];
- *Infantilization.* Older people are frequently treated like children—a process Leonard [21] describes as "infantilization"—and thereby marginalized and disempowered;
- *Dependency creation.* Ageist ideology promotes a view of older people as frail, dependent and in need of welfare support. Townsend [14] argues that dependency is created by:

> the imposition and acceptance of earlier retirement; the legitimation of low income; the denial of rights to self determination in institutions; and the construction of community services for

recipients assumed to be predominantly passive (quoted in Stevenson [22, p. 15]).

- *Denial of sexuality.* Sexuality in older people is assumed not to exist and, where it is evidenced, tends to be seen as unnatural and disgusting [23]. Older people are therefore discouraged from enjoying a sex life or are made to feel guilty about it;
- *Elder abuse.* We are increasingly recognizing the extent and severity of the abuse of older people [24] and dispelling the myth of older people always being safe and cared for.

These are examples of some of the many ways in which older people are subjected to discrimination and oppression. They are, of course, not the only ones but are sufficient to support the point that anti-ageism is not an attempt to jump on the equal opportunities bandwagon but, rather, a genuine attempt to tackle a social problem of major proportions.

THE RELATIONSHIP OF AGEISM TO SEXISM AND RACISM

The relationship of ageism to sexism is a particularly significant one for, as Peace points out, the world of the old is, for demographic reasons, predominantly a woman's world [25]. However, the interaction of ageism and racism is also not without significance, especially in the United Kingdom where the influx of workers from the New Commonwealth in response to the post-war labor shortage is now producing a new generation of black elders.

To take the position of older women in society first, the comments of Hughes and Mtezuka are apt:

Ageism and sexism are connected in two ways. First, the impact of ageing on women has implications for the extent to which old women can conform to the image of womanhood propagated by sexism. A woman not only loses the physical attractiveness ascribed to the ideal woman, but also the prescribed social roles of caring for the family. Indeed, she may need care herself and, as the carer becomes the cared-for, a role reversal underlines the failure of the older woman to conform to the stereotype of womanhood. Thus, passage into old age increases the potential for dissonance with social norms of womanhood and femininity.

Second, an old woman evokes primeval images of women as mystics and witches, derived from woman's proximity to (and men's alienation from) the processes of nature [4, p. 223].

This raises important issues in terms of commitment to anti-ageist practice for, in effect, this means that anti-ageism must be premised on anti-sexism. Given the close linkages between age and gender, health and welfare practice that reinforces or fails to challenge patriarchal relations will not contribute to the empowerment of older people.

Norman's [26] notion of "triple jeopardy" is an important one in so far as it describes the interaction of age, ethnicity and class—a potent combination which leaves black elders experiencing discrimination and oppression at a number of levels:

> Older black people tend to suffer socio-economic disadvantage relative to other groups. Just like elderly people in the dominant culture, ethnic minority elders tend to be marginalized and devalued but they are doubly disadvantaged compared with older white people as a direct result of their ethnic minority—and frequently also for this generation, immigrant-status. They often live in deprived inner-city areas (quoted in Fennell et al. [27, p. 120]).

The interaction of racism and ageism is therefore a serious issue for social policy, unless the needs and circumstances of ethnic minority elders are taken into account, there is a danger that health and welfare practice will be based on stereotypical assumptions of the "they look after their own" variety. Once again, a commitment to anti-ageist practice that does not take cognizance of broader factors such as ethnicity and racism is a shallow commitment more in tune with the rhetoric of anti-discriminatory practice than the reality of it.

TOWARD ANTI-AGEIST PRACTICE

An underlying theme of this chapter is that attempts to bring about anti-discriminatory practice that do not recognize the complexity of the issues involved run the risk of becoming superficial and ineffectual solutions that generate more problems than they solve. A reductionist approach can not only distort the issues but also alienate people from them. One of the first steps toward anti-ageist practice, therefore, is to recognize the magnitude of the task and be wary of superficial and simplistic solutions.

Indeed, the tendency in some quarters to see tackling ageism as simply a matter of treating older people with kindness is itself a major barrier to genuine progress, a significant pitfall to be avoided. This is one among many such pitfalls that lie in the path of the development of anti-ageist practice. Other such pitfalls include:

- *Stereotypes.* A central part of the maintenance of ageist ideology is the reliance on stereotypical characterizations of older people as represented, for example, in comic humor. Such stereotypes can be so deeply ingrained that staff may not realize that they are using them;
- *Medicalization.* A further aspect of ageist ideology is the tendency for old age to be seen as a medical problem. Scrutton comments:

> The medicalization of ageing is consistent with an image of old age as a process of inevitable physiological and biological decline. It suggests that the process can be temporarily halted only by skilled intervention by professional medical staff. These claims and the fatalism of dominant attitudes towards elderly health need to be seriously examined [20, p. 21].

Again, such beliefs tend to be deeply ingrained and can readily be reproduced in the theory and practice of health and social welfare workers if not actively challenged;

- *Denial of citizenship.* One of the recurring themes in working with older people is the tension between rights and risk [26]. There is a danger that concerns to protect older people from risk can have the effect of undermining citizenship rights [2];
- *Disablism.* While it is a mistake to equate old age with disability, it is important to note that the incidence of disability among the older population is higher than in the population as a whole. One consequence of this is that many older people are also subject to disablism—discrimination on the grounds of physical impairment [28]. This reinforces the earlier point, namely that it is necessary to take a wider view of ageism and appreciate how it articulates with other forms of oppression.

Such potential pitfalls to the development of anti-ageist practice serve to underline the central thesis of the chapter—that a superficial commitment to anti-ageism is an inadequate response which fails to recognize that "[t]he challenge . . . which confronts us is formidable" [22, p. 8].

CONCLUSION

This chapter has addressed the question of whether the increasing attention given to issues of age and ageism reflects a genuine commitment to anti-ageism or, more superficially, simply a current fad or fashion. The basic answer proposed is that, for anti-ageism to be more than a token nod in the direction of anti-discriminatory practice, understanding must run much more deeply than the level of personal values and individual concerns—it must also take account of wider cultural and structural issues. Without this broader perspective, health and social welfare staff will not be able to grasp, and engage with, anything but the surface manifestations of the underlying processes of age discrimination and oppression. Adjusting our focus to accommodate a wider perspective also involves locating ageism within the context of other forms of discrimination such as sexism, racism, and disablism. It involves recognizing that older people can experience discrimination on a number of fronts simultaneously. What is needed, therefore, is an approach to health and social welfare which acknowledges, and responds constructively to, the position of older people as an oppressed group, marginalized from mainstream society by processes of stereotyping and stigmatization. This presents a challenge to all involved in the care of older people—practitioners, managers, and educators—to develop methods of working which seek to undermine ageist practices and replace them with an ethos of empowerment.

The empowerment of older people as a strategy of anti-ageist practice must be seen as a moral imperative—an essential part of a principled approach to the care of older people—for, as was emphasized earlier, good practice must be anti-discriminatory practice. To avoid issues of discrimination or to deal with them at the superficial level of a fad or fashion, is to condone the oppression such discrimination engenders. On such important matters there can be no morally neutral ground—to fail to tackle ageism is to subscribe to its continuation, to allow it to flourish unchallenged.

REFERENCES

1. F. Williams, *Social Policy: A Critical Introduction*, Polity, London, 1989.
2. N. Thompson, *Anti-Discriminatory Practice*, Macmillan, London, 1993.
3. R. N. Butler, Ag-ism: Another Form of Bigotry, *The Gerontologist*, 9, 1969.
4. B. Hughes and M. Mtezuka, Social Work and Older Women: Where have Older Women Gone?, in *Women, Oppression and Social Work: Issues in Anti-Discriminatory Practice*, M. Langan and L. Day (eds.), Routledge, London, 1992.
5. M. A. Hildrew, *Guidelines on Elder Abuse*, British Association of Social Workers, United Kingdom, 1991.
6. M. Wright and J. Ogg, Challenging Stereotypes, *Community Care*, 17:24, December 1992.
7. M. Marshall, The Sound of Silence: Who Cares about the Quality of Social Work with Older People, in *The Haunt of Misery: Critical Essays in Social Work and Helping*, C. Rojek, G. Peacock, and S. Collins (eds.), Routledge, London, 1989.

8. W. R. Bytheway, *The Later Part of Life: A Study in the Concept of Old Age,* Occasional Paper No. 10, School of Social Studies, University College, Swansea, Wales, United Kingdom, 1985.
9. C. Victor, *Old Age in Modern Society,* Croom Helm, London, 1987; M. Featherstone and M. Hepworth, Images of Ageing, in *Ageing in Society: An Introduction to Social Gerontology,* J. Bond and P. Coleman (eds.), Sage, London, 1990.
10. C. Phillipson, *Capitalism and the Construction of Old Age,* Macmillan, London, 1982.
11. X. Gaullier, What Failure for Older Workers?, *Ageing International,* June 1990.
12. D. Redding, Problematic Term, *Community Care, 25,* May 1989.
13. A. Walker, The Economic 'Burden' of Ageing and the Prospect of Inter-generational Conflict, *Ageing and Society, 10*:4, 1990.
14. P. Townsend, Ageism and Social Policy, in Ageing and Social Policy: A *Critical Assessment,* C. Phillipson and A. Walker (eds.), Gower, Aldershot,1986.
15. Board for Social Responsibility, *Ageing,* Church House Publishing, London, 1990.
16. M. McNay, Social Work and Power Relations: Towards a Framework for Integrated Practice, in *Women, Oppression and Social Work: Issues in Anti-Discriminatory Practice,* M. Langan and L. Day (eds.), Routledge, London, 1992.
17. B. Bytheway and J. Johnson, On Defining Ageism, *Critical Social Policy, 29,* 1990.
18. K. Blakemore, Does Age Matter? The Case of Old Age in Minority Ethnic Groups, in *Becoming and Being Old,* B. Bytheway et al. (eds.), Sage, London, 1989.
19. S. de Beauvoir, *Old Age,* Penguin, Harmondsworth, 1970.
20. S. Scrutton, *Counselling Older People,* Edward Arnold, London, 1989.
21. P. Leonard, *Personality and Ideology: Towards a Materialist Under-standing of the Individual,* Macmillan, London, 1984.
22. O. Stevenson, *Age and Vulnerability,* Edward Arnold, London, 1989.
23. T. Gibson, *Love, Sex and Power in Later Life,* Freedom Press, London, 1992.
24. C. Phillipson and S. Biggs, *Understanding Elder Abuse,* Longman, London, 1992.
25. S. Peace, The Forgotten Female: Social Policy and Older Women, in *Ageing and Social Policy: A Critical Assessment,* C. Phillipson and A. Walker (eds.), Gower, Aldershot, 1986.
26. A. Norman, Overcoming an Old Prejudice, *Community Care, 29,* January 1987.
27. G. Fennell, C. Phillipson, and H. Evers, *The Sociology of Old Age,* Open University Press, Milton Keynes, 1988.
28. M. Oliver, *The Politics of Disablement,* Macmillan, London, 1990.

CHAPTER 3

Ethical Questions in Changing Funeral and Burial Practices

Eric C. Tappenden

The subject of funeral and burial practices is one which is not often discussed in our death-denying culture. However, in a collection of essays on "Ethical Issues in the Care of the Dying and the Bereaved Aged" we would be remiss if we didn't address it. I would like to suggest three assumptions as the basis for my discussion in this chapter:

1. The first is that funeral and burial practices in our society are changing significantly.
2. The second assumption is that these issues are inherently of an ethical nature because of the spiritual and emotional values which our society attaches to death and associated rituals.
3. The third assumption, is that although an issue is an ethical one if you believe it to be so, given the definitional problems with the word "ethics," I will use the following definition of the word "ethics" to focus our attention. Ethics is:

> the science of morals, moral principles, rules of conduct; relating to morals, treating of moral questions, morally correct, honourable, whole field of moral science . . . [1].

There are a number of changing funeral and burial practices in our society today, with ethical issues arising out of them. These practices are driven by forces of change and resistance, and the ethical positions taken by a variety of groups including churches and religious groups, the funeral industry, environmental and heritage groups, memorial societies, and families.

WHAT SIGNIFICANT CHANGES ARE OCCURRING IN FUNERAL, BURIAL, AND CREMATION PRACTICES?

The first, and one of the most marked changes, is the rapid rise in the cremation rate. While this is not entirely a global phenomenon, it is happening in many parts of the world. In England, the number of cremations as a percentage of deaths is now over 70 percent. In other European countries, particularly where Roman Catholicism is strong and other burial practices such as entombment in a mausoleum crypt are preferred, the cremation rate remains low (see Table 1). However, in countries such as Sweden, the rate is as high as 62.7 percent.

In North America, the cremation rate varies significantly. Overall in the United States the rate was 18.5 percent in 1991, or roughly half of what it was in Canada (34.25%). Interestingly, the general trend tends to be a stronger preference for cremation on the west coast in both countries (43.2% in California and 70% in British Columbia—see Table 2). Cremation is also generally more common in urban areas for a variety of reasons.

Table 1. Selected Cremation Rates 1990-1991
(Percent, by Country)

Canada	34.25
United States	18.50
Great Britain	69.90
Sweden	62.70
The Netherlands	45.28
Italy	1.50
Japan	97.40
Australia	47.20
China	31.00
Confederation of Independent States	34.62
Switzerland	59.72
Spain	2.83
France	7.17

Source: *Pharos International Magazine,* Cremation Society of Britain, United Kingdom, p. 144, Winter 1992.

Table 2. Selected Cremation Rates
in North America 1991-1992
(Percent)

California	43.21
New York State	14.32
Michigan	20.01
Mississippi	2.41
Oregon	42.24
Florida	35.50
Washington, D.C.	0.39
British Columbia[a]	70.00
Quebec[a]	42.00
Ontario[a]	34.00
Metropolitan Toronto	47.30

[a]Estimates
Source: Cremation Association of North America, *Cremation Magazine, 27*:4, pp. 16-17, 1991; and Cremation Association of North America, *Projections to the Year 2010,* 1993.

Urban areas typically have more crematoria, making access easier. They also tend to have less inclination to maintenance of traditions, and a greater degree of secularization. Furthermore, they tend to have a greater concentration of ethnic and religious groups, some of which practice cremation exclusively, such as Hindus and Buddhists. Urban areas also tend to have significantly higher prices for graves, because of the value of land, making traditional ground burial more expensive than cremation, and thereby making cremation attractive to those who do not wish to spend a great deal of money.

In the area where I live and work, the greater Toronto area, the cremation rate was 5 percent in 1970, and it had risen to 47.4 percent in 1992. As Table 3 demonstrates, it has risen by an average of 2.2 percent percentage points in each of the last four years, and is expected to be over 50 percent by 1995. In Ontario, the rate is now over 30 percent, and in Quebec it is over 40 percent.

The rapid growth of cremation in Quebec is interesting in an ethical context. Quebec is a province which is largely Roman Catholic. The Roman Catholic Church did not approve of cremation until 1963, when the Vatican II allowed it, with two qualifiers: first, that the motive of choosing cremation was not to deny the doctrine of the bodily resurrection and, second, that the cremated remains be interred appropriately

Table 3. Cremation Growth in Toronto Area

Year	No. of Deaths	No. of Cremations	Cremation Rate
1989	20,473	8,355	40.8%
1990	20,404	8,656	42.4%
1991	20,602	9,160	44.5%
1992	20,690	9,810	47.4%

Source: Registrar General of Ontario, Ontario Chief Coroner's Office.

[2]. As a result, the cremation rate in Quebec was low until the 1960s. During the "Quiet Revolution" of that decade, many Quebecers rebelled against the teachings and traditions of the church which had so dominated the Quebec culture since its early settlement. The effect of this so-called revolution on Quebec society is such that the province has gone from having the highest birth rate in the country to the lowest, from the lowest divorce rate to the highest, the highest incidence of common-law relationships in lieu of marriage [3] and, interestingly enough, the second highest cremation rate in the country, in only a few short decades.

In British Columbia, the high cremation rate appears to be due in part to the relative absence of strong historical traditions of burial, the western "tradition" of reaction against "eastern" traditions, a strong Memorial Society,[1] and a combination of the other reasons why people choose cremation. I have heard families and individuals give the following reasons for choosing cremation: concern about the use of valuable urban land for burial space, environmental issues such as concerns with embalming fluid leaking into groundwater,[2] and a desire among some for simpler funerals with less emphasis on the body of the deceased.

---

[1] Memorial societies are consumer groups which educate the public and negotiate with funeral homes on behalf of members to encourage simple, inexpensive funerals. The Memorial Society of British Columbia has over 140,000 members, and is growing by over 1,000 per year.

[2] Although many have speculated about this potential environmental problem, the only major scientific study carried out of which I am aware concludes that it is neither a problem, nor a significant risk. See Beak Consultants Ltd., *Soil and Groundwater Quality Study of the Mount Pleasant Cemetery*, July 1992 (for a copy contact Commemorative Services of Ontario in Toronto, Canada (416) 696-7866, attention: Louise Winton).

WHAT ARE THE ETHICAL ISSUES
THAT ARISE?

Well, what of the ethical questions? What ethical questions arise as a result of the increase in cremation rates? Is cremation an ethical option? Clearly these questions must be answered in the context of belief and value systems. For an orthodox Jew or a Muslim, whose religions or cultures find cremation repugnant, cremation may not be an ethical alternative. For Hindus and Buddhists it may be the only ethical alternative. For many others, however, whose faith are not particularly directive about methods of disposition of human remains, the ethical questions are more complex and not easily answered.

Many view the choice of cremation versus traditional ground burial in the context of ethics. Is it right or is it wrong? Is it dignified? Others look on it as an issue of preference: what will the impact on the family be? Will they (or I) find it offensive, or will I think it is the most environmentally responsible form of disposition? I have heard Christians of virtually every denomination take just about every side of this issue: "I don't see any reference to cremation in the Bible"; "It's just a return of the body to its natural elements more quickly—dust to dust and ashes to ashes"; "That's not the way Christ's body was buried" (note, of course, that Christ's body was entombed, not buried).

But the ethics of these issues are broader than just a particular religious or cultural viewpoint. When assessing funeral and burial practices in an ethical context it is important to have a framework for doing so. Hopefully the framework I present will assist in thinking through not only the issue of cremation versus traditional burial, but the multitude of other choices we face in making funeral arrangements because of the changing funeral and burial practices.

A FRAMEWORK FOR ASSESSING FUNERAL
AND BURIAL PRACTICES IN
AN ETHICAL CONTEXT

1. Do our practices help the grieving process and grieving person or hinder them? Is what we're doing helping survivors resolve or, as Alan Wolfelt calls it, "reconcile" their grief, or does it make it more difficult?
2. Is what we're doing reinforcing or changing our death-denying culture? I, for one, think that the taboo associated with death in our culture is both unusual in the global context and unhealthy, and that practices which help us learn to be less death-denying should be encouraged.

3. Is what we're doing dignified? While definitions of dignity differ, it seems apparent that we must, to be ethical, both deal with the body and have rituals which afford a measure of dignity.
4. Does what we're doing recognize the value of rituals, however familiar or unfamiliar, however traditional or unique?
5. Are we being judgmental in deciding what is "ethical" for others? Is part of being "ethical" being non-judgmental?
6. Is what we're doing consistent with our other deeply held beliefs and values, spiritual or otherwise, or is it in conflict?
7. Are we considering what family or other survivors need and want? After all, the entire commemorative process, including the funeral, is for them (meaning us), not for the deceased.

This framework can be used to assess funeral and burial practices. Other changes in these practices in recent years include:

- *An increase in "scattering" of cremated remains.*
- *"Doing nothing" with cremated remains.* Many families see cremation as an end in itself and do not realize or are not informed that there are cremated remains to be dealt with. Is it ethical to "do nothing" with cremated remains or is it important to scatter or inter them and place some form of memorial with them, for future generations as a focal point of remembrance?
- *More closed caskets.* Funeral directors and some clergy and psychologists believe that an open casket at visitation, with the body embalmed and cosmetized, is important, in order for family and friends to accept the reality of death. Rev. John Wilton, an Anglican clergyman from Brampton, Ontario has suggested that without this practice, people will hallucinate [4]. Of course, since open caskets and embalming are not practiced by most cultures in the world, he may be suggesting that 90 percent of the world's peoples are prone to hallucinations. In contrast, others, like *Toronto Star* columnist on Ethics, and former Anglican clergyman Tom Harpur, suggest that open caskets are "barbaric" [5]. Sometimes, to make a point, I ask funeral directors the question: "If it is so important to have an open casket in order that families accept the *reality* of death, why do you go to so much trouble to make the body look life-like, use euphemisms like "resting," and talk to families about the preservative qualities of various caskets and burial vaults?"
- *Fewer funeral services.* An increasing number of people are not having funeral services at all. In some cases, this is related to a person being pre-deceased by friends and family, but in others it is

a rejection of the value of rituals. The ethical issues here include: do we respect others' views enough not to be judgmental if a family does not want a service (i.e., they may be grieving in a healthy way without rituals—there are exceptions to any rule)? Or do we encourage the almost universally accepted practice that death and grieving may be dealt with best through ritual? Perhaps our society is pluralistic enough that we at least need to broaden our definition of rituals to go well beyond what we think of as "traditional funerals."

• *More memorial services without the body present.* Again, there is the issue of the importance of emphasis on the body versus the memory of the person. Very few would argue that dignified treatment of the body is not important, but the significant emphasis on the presence and visibility of the body in a funeral ritual is being challenged more and more. For example, former Bishop Lewis S. Garnsworthy of the Anglican Church of Canada did not mince words in his *Diocesan Directive and Suggestions*:

> We do not honour the dead, any more than we honour the living by ostentation. Above all, practices which are designed to conceal the reality of death by attempting to give the body a life-like appearance or which serve to retard the natural processes of dissolution are to be deplored and avoided; deception can find no place in Christian practice. Coffins and other funeral arrangements should be simple . . . extravagant expenditures at the time of death are not a valid indication of our love and concern for the deceased, but in many cases place an unnecessary burden on the bereaved.
>
> The accent on costly methods and paraphernalia—in fact, any undue concern about the body—is a worldly and pagan emphasis, not a Christian one [6].

• *Less embalming.* While many funeral directors imply that embalming must be done by law, or at least presume that families want it, it is, at least in Ontario, against the law to embalm a body without permission of the executor or family. Our funeral industry's preoccupation with embalming in North America is, to say the least, peculiar in a global context. In Britain and most of Europe it is the exception rather than the rule. And while embalming may be required, e.g., by an air carrier for shipping, or by a receiving country when a body is transported, there are many cases where it just isn't necessary. It is, of course, tied to the other components of a traditional funeral, such as an open casket and a period of visitation with the body present. Ethical issues and opinions range from embalming being important to facilitate open caskets and for hygienic/health reasons, to embalming being a barbaric, undignified, or unnecessary procedure.

- *More environmentally friendly caskets.* Casket manufacturers have been slow to change, but gradually environmental authorities and activists, and crematorium operators are convincing them to remove metals, non-combustible linings, and toxic glues and finishes which are particularly harmful when burned in a crematorium retort. The ethical issues here focus on our responsibility to the environment, in this, yet another part of our life, where in the past we never thought about it.

- *Rising cost of traditional funerals and greater availability of low-cost services.* In Canada, as low-cost services become more widely available, traditional funeral costs go up, well beyond inflation levels. Is it ethical to raise the price of a $7,000 funeral to $8,000 to maintain profit margins because more and more people are choosing the $1,500 funeral? Without questioning the role of free enterprise in a sector where people being served are more emotionally and financially vulnerable than in any other transaction in their life, the ethical issue relates to the family choosing the traditional funeral. Are they being taken advantage of? Treated fairly? Surely it is only ethical to ensure that every family is presented with the full range of choices and not made to feel guilty if they choose a $1,000 funeral over a $7,000 one. And perhaps it is also ethical to examine the economics of an industry where price elasticity has seemingly known no bounds and bankruptcy is almost unknown.

- *Memorial donations instead of flowers.* This rapidly changing practice has to do with donations that last, or accomplish something meaningful for the living. On the other hand, some find flowers a comfort, a symbol of life, and a meaningful part of the funeral ritual. While funeral flowers are "disposable," they often see double use in decorating a church sanctuary or a gravesite.

- *Fewer religious services and fewer services in places of worship.* While fewer religious services are a reflection of an increasingly secular culture (at least rejecting institutional religion, if not spirituality), it is quite amazing how many people request a religious service "just in case there is an afterlife" or because "well, it is traditional." Fewer services in a place of worship is a different issue. Over time, more and more services are held in funeral home chapels and fewer in churches. Some cynics cite the chapel rental revenue or the reduction in costs to the funeral home, while others suggest it is often just more convenient for families. Some clergy have expressed the need to "take back control of the funeral." In their view, funeral directors have taken ownership and leadership of funeral planning and the ceremony itself, and it is time that the community of faith and family take back control of what is a rite of passage, like baptism, confirmation, and marriage. Some, if not many clergy, however, must be content with the number of funerals in funeral homes, or changes would be taking place. Or would they?

• *Prearranging and prepaying are becoming more common.* Although research indicates that only 1 to 3 percent of the adult population in North America has made any prearrangements at all for funeral or burial, it is becoming more common, and seen as a good idea by many in surveys. While it does save a family considerable expense and emotional stress at having to make a lot of detailed arrangements at the time of death, and can be financially sound, it raises an ethical question. Whose wishes should be followed, the family's or the deceased's? Laws vary in states and provinces. In some, a written will or prepaid funeral contract is binding. In Ontario, and other jurisdictions, the executor has the final say and may dispose of the body in the manner he or she sees fit.

This latter position is helpful to families who say "the funeral is for us, the survivors, not him." But where the deceased has specifically requested or arranged something different than they feel is appropriate, it can cause long-term unresolved family tensions and grief. In the organization in which I work, we encourage people to prearrange or prepay, but only after discussing preferences with their families or loved ones, and finding some measure of consensus that will not cause unresolved grief later on.

• *Leasing of burial rights.* In North America we have a tradition of not disturbing gravesites once a burial has taken place. We call this purchasing "perpetual burial rights." The notion of re-using a grave after a period of time is considered repugnant by some and just never thought of by others.

Due to the vast amount of land and burial space we have been used to, this has become somewhat sacred to us here in North America. However, in most of Europe, and many other parts of the world, burial rights are purchased for a fixed period of time, ten, twenty-five, or fifty years. After that period, unless a local heritage committee deems otherwise, or unless the family renews the term, the grave is re-used and the marker or memorial is moved to another part of the cemetery for storage. If this practice had not occurred in Europe, its entire land mass would be a burial ground by now.

What about our urban areas in North America which are rapidly running out of burial space? Is the European model of leasing interment rights appropriate? Should people have a choice? Will *not* moving to this practice force some who prefer burial to choose cremation, because of cost or lack of space? While this is an ethical issue, it is also a practical and pressing one.

- *Funeral service becoming "big business" with family firms giving way to multinational corporations.* In many ways, this is just part of a changing industry structure, and not relevant to ethics. But changing business practices, worries about restricting competition, vertical integration and market domination on one hand, and lack of local family or community character on the other, are concerns that have been expressed by regulators, consumer groups, and the media.
- *People (some) are discussing funeral arrangements more openly.* While we still live in a society where death has replaced sex as the ultimate cultural taboo, there are signs of people becoming more accepting of talking about death as a natural culmination and fact of life. Death and bereavement education at all levels, professional and self-help groups and agencies, and an increasingly sensitized media are all helping this to happen.

Although this brief chapter cannot fully discuss each of the changes in these practices, let alone all of the ethical issues arising, I hope that the framework I have presented will assist the reader in assessing these issues and coming to a fuller and more comfortable understanding of the ethics of burial and funeral choices for oneself and others.

REFERENCES

1. *The Concise Oxford Dictionary*, Oxford University Press, Oxford, 1987.
2. *Vatican Council II*, 1963; and *Revised Code of Common Law*, 1983 (see also L. Winton (ed.), *Burial Rites Handbook*, Commemorative Services of Ontario, Toronto, p. 8, 1985).
3. Statistics Canada, *1991 Census*.
4. Quoted from Alternative Funeral Service Raises Concern, *The Anglican*, p. 2, January 1991.

5. T. Harpur, Showing Body in Open Coffin Barbaric and Embarrassing, *The Toronto Star*, p. B7, September 22, 1991.
6. As quoted from the Canadian Association of Memorial Societies pamphlet *Church Comment on Funerals,* 1978.

CHAPTER 4

Applying Hospice Principles in South Africa

Judith van Heerden

The hospice philosophy was an important medical development of the seventies and eighties. As a convert, I make no apology for my enthusiasm for a philosophy that puts the patient back in the picture admitting that there is a patient behind every diagnosis. It is disappointing that the desired effect of humanizing medicine has not permeated the entire discipline. Nonetheless, South Africans can proudly reflect on the growth of hospice over the past fourteen years.

In the major South African cities, excellent hospice programs have been established to cater primarily to the needs of the suburbs (privileged whites). More recently this care has extended to rural towns. Hospice in South Africa has followed the traditional method of training a large number of volunteers and of contributing to the teaching and training of nurses. The focus is now centered on an outreach to the impoverished (black) townships where the need for hospice care is critical. In spite of these commendable developments, hospice in South Africa has neglected to establish a research base with which to achieve academic credibility. Now, firmly rooted, the hospice philosophy has an important role to play in our changing political climate. Unless attitudes change, removing apartheid from the statute books will have no significant impact. *All* South Africans need to be invested with their full worth and dignity as individuals, before change will occur.

47

COURSE PROPOSAL (1992)

In order to facilitate attitudinal change, the University of Cape Town initiated a practical course whereby medical and paramedical students were introduced to communities unfamiliar to them. The academic handbook for medical students describes the first year Human Biology course as follows:

> The Human Biology course as a whole has the objective of trying to demonstrate to students that the context of humanity is not only biological, but also historical, ecological and social.

An eight-week *Field Studies* program forms the practical component of this course. It focuses on the concept of "community," giving students the opportunity to:

1. study various aspects of a given community in Cape Town, and
2. observe at first hand the relevant social services which medical practitioners consult.

The purpose of the field study is to sensitize students to the fact that appropriate health care is based on an understanding of a community and its resources. A variety of physical, social, economic, and medical aspects were included to foster personal understanding of the term "community." This program forms the basis for the future development of a community based medical curriculum.

BACKGROUND

Housing

Although the formal structures of apartheid have been eliminated, we continue to live with the heritage of a racist system. Grand apartheid was based on classification by race: White, "coloured," Indian, and African. In terms of the Group Areas Act, each group was restricted to a racially designated region of South Africa. As people were forcibly removed from their homes, sprawling sub-economic housing communities were established on the outskirts of the major cities. Although communities are still largely divided along racial lines, segregation is now illegal. The following geographical terminology has become accepted in the greater Cape Town:

- privileged whites live in the *suburbs,*
- the "coloured" community reside in the *Cape Flats,*

• the African labor force lives in shacks (tin shanties) in *townships* or in squatter settlements.

Schooling

Unlike North America, where students obtain a basic under-graduate degree before starting medical training, South African students enroll at medical school directly after completing high school. Consequently, they may have finely-tuned academic minds, but in many instances they are socially and emotionally unprepared. In recent years, the University of Cape Town has adopted an affirmative action policy for educationally disadvantaged students (drawn from "coloured" and Bantu education systems). Academic Support Programs were introduced to narrow the gap between a disadvantaged education and the rigorous demands of tertiary education. I believe that privileged white students have also been disadvantaged by their isolation in the suburbs. Introducing students to a different (colored) community serves to build bridges on both sides.

FIELD STUDIES PROGRAM

General Outline

The 1992 class of 260 first-year medical, physiotherapy, and occupational therapy students was divided into eighteen tutorial groups of fifteen students each. Each group was to research various aspects of an allocated community.

In the eight weeks assigned to the field study, two four-week projects were completed. The first project, was to explore the structure and function of an allocated community and its health and welfare services. In the second project, various aspects of a specific service organization in detail were considered.

Each tutorial group was evaluated on a fifteen-minute presentation to the class. A poster demonstrating key findings was used to illustrate the talk. Groups thus shared what they had learned. In addition, each group submitted a comprehensive report for which marks were allocated.

The discussion which follows is based on the work of tutorial groups in the Athlone community and at the Eikenhof Interim Home, Athlone for out-of-town cancer patients.

Course Preparation

Community excursions were carefully planned and closely monitored. Long-standing links with progressive networks facilitated the planning of the program. Consequently, students were able to study several community outreach initiatives related to all levels of education, child care, and support for the frail and elderly. With one exception, all the organizations approached were pleased and enthusiastic to make contact and increase understanding between themselves and the students.

One difficulty was ensuring that students were as enthusiastic as their instructors about the community field trips. Among thirty students (2 tutorial groups), seven had attended traditional, exclusive schools. They were perceptibly discomforted by the thought of exploring the unfamiliar colored areas of the city. As the program progressed and they got to know the place and its people, students relaxed. Several students found the field trips an insightful experience.

Athlone Community Profile

Athlone is a large middle-class "coloured" community close to Cape Town. Due to its size, two tutorial groups (30 students) were assigned to the area. The students split into ten units of three. Each unit explored an aspect of community life in general and a particular health service (as shown in Table 1).

Table 1. Athlone Community Profile

General Aspects	Health Services
Housing	Child care/creches
Estate agents	Old age service (Cape Peninsula
Police, crime, and violence	Organization for the Aged)
Legal firms and aid	Youth health service
Grassroots and civic organizations	Progressive Primary Health Care
Entertainment	and AIDS Training, Information &
Busines, formal/informal	Counselling Centre
Muslim religion	Alcoholic treatment unit
Christian religion	Cerebral palsy
Schools and Careers Research and	Day Hospital
Information Centre	Private hospital/clinic
	Baby Clinics
	Child Welfare

Students obtained information through personal interviews. Provided with contact names and numbers, they arranged appointments and interviewed contact people in the community. At report-back sessions the dramatic impact of the exercise became apparent. Here only housing is reviewed as, next to unemployment, it is the most pressing problem within the disadvantaged communities.

Housing in Athlone

Athlone is a stable, middle-class, "coloured" community, where some have lived for generations. In 1948 the Nationalist Government introduced Apartheid, and denied people-of-color the right to own property. The first State-owned council houses, erected in 1949, fell under the control of the Cape Town City Council. Housing is either economic (with bath) or sub-economic, with one (SE1), two (SE2), or three (SE3) rooms. The first flats were provided with water and lights, but had one major drawback: an enclosed staircase which provided shelter for vagrants resulting in pollution and leading to many incidents of sexual violence and drug abuse. The council housing backlog in Cape Town is about 42,000 units. Because of inordinate delays, the waiting list is expressed in years (not numbers). It varies with the desirability of the area. For the least desirable housing, the waiting list dates back to 1985, while in the most sought after areas it varies from 1969 to 1972. Rent office employees are under constant pressure from frustrated applicants, who perceive them to be the bureaucrats in control of housing.

At hospital clinics serving the Cape Flats, one finds that, on average, six to eight people live in a house with two rooms, a kitchen and a bathroom. It is not uncommon to find twelve to sixteen people and occasionally as many as twenty-two living in one house, often with shacks in the yard. According to a survey conducted by the rent office, there are five to six "legal" occupants per dwelling, with up to two families living "illegally." The three students who explored housing were horrified by what they saw. In one house they found unemployed youths, members of the "Young Americans" gang, ironing their stars-and-stripes while upstairs a frail and ailing grandmother was completely ignored. They found the marks of squashed bedbugs on the walls of dwellings disturbing. On one cold winter day, they arrived at a one-bedroom flat, with twenty occupants. It was furnished with one single and two double beds. Only three of the eight adults living there were employed. Those not at work sat huddled over an open fire. One of them had tuberculosis.

This experience made an indelible impression on the students, who suggested that:

> students should see for themselves what the living conditions were like. Otherwise, how will they ever understand what patients are talking about.

Facts about Black Housing

The situation is much worse in the townships. Influx control laws did away with the provision of housing for black people in 1966. In the ten years that followed about 4000 family units were built for blacks in Cape Town (Guguletu).

These legal restrictions and the resultant housing shortages led to a dramatic increase in the number of squatters. In the mid-eighties when the government conceded the need for black housing, the sand dunes (35 kilometers out of town) were flattened and small cheaply-built houses were erected in the bleakest of settings at Khayelitsha. Tin shantles of squatters have appeared all around. By 1993 there was an estimated backlog of 1.4 million houses and 1.1 million serviced sites in South Africa (see Table 2).

EIKENHOF INTERIM HOME, A SERVICE ORGANIZATION

The study of a service organization, in this case a half-way house for cancer patients, was a challenge for both the facilitator and the students. A way had to be found to approach the emotionally-laden subject of cancer sufferers with young students. My tutorial group (15 students) was one of two allocated to a cancer care facility; we visited the Eikenhof Interim Home, while the other group visited St. Luke's Hospice in the suburbs.

The group that visited St. Luke's concentrated on the management and facilities offered by the hospice. The reluctance to allow students

Table 2. Housing Facts in South Africa

	Cape "Homelands"	Western Cape	Khayelitsha
Population	2,549,185	889,467	371,470
Formal housing	1,013,486 (40%)	260,990 (29%)	66,480 (18%)
Site and service	632,213 (25%)	221,655 (25%)	164,990 (44%)
Squatter camps	903,486 (35%)	406,822 (46%)	140,000 (38%)

interaction with hospice patients can be attributed to time constraints. In a facility catering to the terminally ill, two afternoons were insufficient time to deal with the emotional issues related to care of the dying.

To prepare students for their first encounter with cancer patients at Eikenhof, they were given preliminary readings on the history, needs, purpose, and function of a hospice. At the first meeting these issues were discussed, and the benefits of hospice care for both patients and their families emphasized. The humanizing ripple effect of hospice management was stressed. Students were given an outline of the need that Eikenhof meets in the community. Because Eikenhof caters to ambulant "well" patients, it was decided that the students would benefit most by getting to know the patients. In one student's view:

> The main purpose of the study was to introduce students to cancer sufferers and to illustrate their needs. Students had the opportunity of talking to patients, finding out about their problems, and to investigate the facilities offered by the Interim Home.

REPORT ON EIKENHOF INTERIM HOME

In 1975, George Borwick donated his home and property in Athlone to the National Cancer Association (NCA). This met the need for an interim home to house upcountry black and colored cancer patients attending Groote Schuur Hospital for treatment. Known as Eikenhof Interim Home, it fulfills this function by offering free accommodation for up to twenty individuals. The NCA are responsible for the running, maintenance, and upkeep of the home.

Eikenhof also serves as a day care venue. A bus collects and returns patients from around the Peninsula who attend either the Monday or the Wednesday morning activities. Entertainment (dance, music, and games), or more serious demonstrations and discussions (talks and videos) are arranged. The center thus provides a place to socialize. Here patients find mutual support among individuals with similar problems as well as receiving professional help from nurses or social workers.

During their first visit, students were shown around and introduced to the staff of the home. Mrs. Dreyer, the house mother, cooks and cares for the upcountry patients, coordinates day care activities, and ministers to the patients. At first, the students were nervous about mixing with cancer patients:

> Initially quiet standoffish, and unsure of what to ask, we were quickly pleasantly surprised. A more positive group of people one

could not have hoped to have met. We were warmly welcomed and soon joined in the jovial small talk.

Amusing comments from the patients put the students at ease:

Then I was in my prime, now I sit behind my knees with arthritis.

Once you are 40 your joints dry up. That is why you must drink a spoonful of castor oil with orange juice every week. It wets the joints.

By joining the bus service, students had hoped to see patients' homes and living conditions, and thus to assess what type of intervention could be recommended. However, they found that patients were already outside waiting impatiently for the bus. The bus driver, though untrained, made several insightful comments about working with patients:

What these people need, mam, is love.

If they want to get in by themselves, I let them in. It gives them courage.

Respect for the value of personal independence was an important lesson for students.

The day-patients were a cohesive group. One man was severely reprimanded for even considering attending an alternative venue. Among similarly afflicted people, the group were able to speak openly:

I look forward to Wednesdays, it's nice to get away and talk freely. We talk among each other about our illness. I have learnt a lot that way.

This mutual support helped patients to cope with their disease and the friendly atmosphere did much to relieve their social isolation. Some felt that they were a burden at home, that they had to put on a brave face, but that here they could relax and talk freely. It also gave those at home a break. Through comments like these, the students became aware that irrespective of wealth, color, or politics, all share the same hopes, dreams, and joys; the same disappointments, frustration, and anger; the same concerns, sadness, and fears. It must be borne in mind that although these are basic hospice principles, they were the observations of students with no hospice training or experience.

Despite the important role that Eikenhof fulfills in the cancer community, students made the following recommendations:

1. Social mixing did not occur between live-in patients (usually black) and local day care (mostly colored) groups. This was due to the fact that daily activities were in full swing by the time live-in patients returned from hospital treatment clinics. A Xhosa-speaking social worker/volunteer could encourage integration and participation in daily activities.
2. Live-in patients were strangers in the community and socially isolated. They carried the burden of their illness alone and became withdrawn and depressed. If the NCA bus was available over weekends, the housekeeper would be able to take boarders on outings. It would alleviate their boredom, isolation, and loneliness.
3. Patients were unhappy about the impersonal treatment they received from hospital staff. They felt trapped in treatment decisions and wanted more information to participate in management decisions. They asked that a Xhosa-speaking nurse act as interpreter at the hospital.
4. After radio and chemotherapy treatment, delays in transport back to Eikenhof resulted in patients waiting for hours in discomfort. For the comfort of patients a better system of communication between patients, staff, and the driver was recommended to reduce the waiting time.

In conclusion, the students felt that these problems did not overshadow the positive role Eikenhof played in the cancer community. The eagerness of the day care patients reflected the success of the service. Students learned that the treatment of cancer involves more than medical intervention: that coming to terms with emotional stress and social isolation is as important for the well-being of patients. They found that the personal commitment and willingness of the Eikenhof and NCA staff played a major part in the effective running of the whole organization.

As the facilitator I would like to make two last comments.

1. It was good that the students did more than simply "look at" the role of the Interim Home. The problems they identified were submitted with recommendations to the management committee of the NCA for consideration. If the NCA acts on them, it will give meaning to the time the students devoted to their task. Knowing that they are able to make a difference to the way people are treated, encourages students to take a more active part in patient care in the community.
2. I hope that, on a personal level, the students gained some understanding of how the stresses in the home and at work impact on health, and how this is magnified by protracted illness. That with

better insight, they will have a clearer understanding of what can be done to help patients.

CONCLUSION

By using the hospice model of humanizing medicine, we have introduced a first year community program at medical school which aims to increase the understanding and sensitivity of students and to change attitudes, an essential component for the success of a new South Africa.

Note: As the standards of the projects improved between 1992 and 1995, this program expanded to incorporate a theoretical component. Since 1995 the theoretical and practical work together form a full course credit for first-year medical students. The course Health and Society aims to provide students with a better understanding of the many factors which impact on health: class, race, and gender; historical developments; economics; ethics; and the philosophy of Primary Health Care.

CHAPTER 5

Death, Bereavement, and the Social Psychology of Aging and Dying

Victor W. Marshall

The second era in the development of death and dying studies was the period in which Kübler-Ross published her book, *On Death and Dying* [1], and the sociologists Glaser and Strauss published *Time for Dying* [2]. The first had been defined by Feifel when he published his edited collection, *The Meaning of Death* in 1959 [3]. Fulton, a sociologist, published an edited collection, *Death and Identity*, in 1965 [4], but the social psychology in it was largely the work of psychiatrists and psychologists. It was also in that year that Glaser and Strauss' landmark sociological study, *Awareness of Dying* [5], appeared. Despite these now-classic works, the social sciences have contributed little to our understanding of aging and dying. This chapter will focus on the social sciences and, in particular, in the social psychology area, since that is my own background and the focus of my own work since I first developed my research interest in the sociology of aging and dying twenty-five years ago. We have now, as we did not have then, a very large number of research studies conducted by social scientists, and a much larger pool of data based on clinical and case reports of care of the dying which can be adapted for analyses dealing with aging and dying. We do not, however, have very much in the way of generalizable knowledge or theory in this area.

I argue that we might benefit from an effort to develop explicit theory in the area of aging and dying and first note the conditions which a theory of aging and dying should meet. I then review a selection of theoretical contributions, including my own—concluding with some theoretical generalizations and research questions which I think deserve future attention.

WHAT SHOULD WE LOOK FOR IN A THEORY OF AGING AND DYING?

Formally, we could say that a theory is a set of logically related statements that purports to describe the relationship between variables. However, theories need not be stated in formal, deductive logic. Much theorizing in the social sciences rests on the development of typologies which allow events to be classified and placed in some wider frame of reference. The Linnean classification of species in biology, or the periodic table in chemistry are examples of this kind of theorizing outside the social sciences [6, p. 8]. Much theorizing, as Geertz has indicated, involves making analogies: ". . . the earth is a magnet, the heart is a pump, light is a wave, the brain is a computer . . ." [7, pp. 22-23]. Good theorizing will invoke analogies, or perhaps metaphors, that are both insightful and precise. There are therefore many ways to theorize and there is nothing mysterious about theory. It may be argued that, at a general level, the term theory can be used to refer to *any disciplined* process of describing events in the world [8].

What would a disciplined process of describing aging and dying events have to provide? Aging and dying encompass a huge domain of life experience, and I have to narrow my focus considerably to the *linkage* between aging and dying. A lot of other important topics in gerontology and in thanatology cannot be dealt with here, as we focus on the connections, the interweaving, of aging and dying. Thus, only brief attention is given to widowhood and bereavement, even though these are age-related and death-related events, or to the medical care of the aged who are dying, which is a topic of enormous importance and which no doubt influences the meaning of aging and dying for those who are doing it (for excellent recent examples of this literature see Field [9], Kellehear [10], Kelner and Bourgeault [11], and Moller [12]).

A theory of aging and dying should deal with the lived experience of aging and dying. It should try to get at the phenomenology of aging and dying, at the ways in which aging phenomena interweave with age-related death of others in the social experience of an individual, and with that individual's own experience of finitude. We need to place the aging and dying individual in social context. We also need a macro-level understanding of aging and dying in terms of social institutions and social structure. Judith Levy and I have called this the "social organization of death and dying" [13]. We seek a greater understanding of the ways in which mortality affects the organization of society and of the ways in which this organization around death and dying issues in turn influences the ways in which individuals in later life will experience their process of dying. The sociologist Georg Simmel stated the area for investigation well in 1908:

> We are, from birth on, beings that will die. We are this, of course, in different ways. The manner in which we conceive this nature of ours and its final effect, and in which we react to this conception, varies greatly. So does the way in which this element of our existence is interwoven with its other elements (quoted in Wolff [14]).

Let me then introduce just a few macro-level considerations as context for a social psychology of aging and dying. The term "social organization of death and dying" refers to a society's set of values, beliefs, behavior, and institutional arrangements concerning death, including societal forces and cultural arrangements for managing death and the potential of death to create disruptiveness.

The age at which death typically occurs in a society is an important feature of the social context in which people do their aging and dying. Death has lost its unpredictability and is now typically located, in modern or postmodern societies, in very advanced years [15]. This shift in the age location of mortality is due to dramatic declines in infant and childhood mortality and, to a lesser extent, reduction in age-specific mortality in late middle age. Three-fourths of children born today in the United States and other advanced industrial nations are likely to die after the age of sixty-five [16]. Therefore, for most persons, death—the experience of it, the awareness of it, the anticipation of it—is an important aspect of the experience of aging, and much less an aspect of childhood and young adulthood.

Another contextual feature is cause of death which, for about 70 percent of Americans, is from heart attack, cancer, and stroke [17, 18], in other words, from or following chronic illness. The age at which people die is becoming later, but the duration of dying may well be longer than in earlier times.

The social organization of death and dying cannot be fully understood without considering the impact of mortality on the maintenance and survival of a society. A first set of problems posed for social organization by death is that death creates disruption for a group or community by removing one of its members, and ultimately death threatens the very capacity of a society to survive. Among tribal societies, for example, the loss of even a single individual enormously affects community functioning due to their small population size [19, 20].

Death is particularly disruptive for a society when the person who dies is actively engaged in or symbolically important to the family, community, or institution (e.g., the death of a parent, political leader, company president, or celebrity). In pre-industrial societies, death and role replacement occur disproportionately among infants, children, and young adults actively engaged in social roles associated with early stages of the life course. This contrasts with industrial and post-industrial societies where death typically occurs in later life. The social institution of retirement can be seen as a means of diminishing the disruptiveness to society of the death of a member, by removing that member from important economic roles in an orderly scheduled way. Retirement becomes, in the words of French sociologist Anne-Marie Guillemard, a "social death"—"une mort sociale" [21].

Just as untimely, early death can disrupt society, so can untimely, late death. In the Royal Navy of Britain, and in the Royal Canadian Navy, there is a separate toast for each day, to be said in the officers' mess or wardroom. One of these toasts is "To a bloody war or a sickly season." This expressed wish for seeming misfortune is explained by the younger officers' desire for promotion. Only a bloody war or a sickly season will eliminate the high-ranking officers, creating vacancies and upward occupational mobility. I am not aware of ritualized expressions of the same hope in the family context, but we are all aware of how the lives of adult children or of spouses are influenced by the prolonged duration of later life, including unduly prolonged life extension through medical technology. Moller describes the "roller coaster journey of dying," with ups and downs of hope and despair, as "a pilgrimage defined by the management of dying patients through technology" [12, p. 93].

At a mundane level, dying and death create bodies—sick bodies and dead bodies. Contemporary dying takes longer because of medical technology. This requires that sick bodies be transported to and maintained at specific locations such as nursing homes and hospitals. Today, dying most frequently occurs in formal settings, and the dead are almost always taken care of by specialized agencies called funeral homes. As Blauner suggests, "Modern societies control death through bureaucratization, our characteristic form of social structure" [22, p. 384]. He further notes that, "When the dying are segregated among specialists for whom contact with death has become routine and even somewhat impersonal, neither their presence while alive nor as corpses interferes greatly with the mainstream of life" [22, p. 384]. With the bureaucratization of death, dying and body preparations for burial in contemporary societies typically occur within formal institutions under the control of paid functionaries. People today have fewer opportunities to learn about death and dying through direct observation [23, p. 3].

Death can threaten the legitimacy of a society's meaning system. Mortality may call into question shared cultural assumptions, since the search for meaning in death simultaneously raises questions about the meaning of life [24, p. 101]. Malinowski observes that death ". . . breaks the normal course of life and shakes the moral foundations of society" [19, pp. 52-53]. Every religious belief system includes an explanation for why people die. These rationales suggest a universal quest to render death more acceptable. With the rise of science, religion no longer provides the sole framework of meanings through which to understand death. Secular explanations increasingly compete with religious interpretations. As Cassell explains, in such societies "death is a technical matter, a failure of technology in rescuing the body" [25, pp. 31-32].

Ritual is a way that people work with meanings and apply religious or other beliefs to try to explain or "make right" disruptions such as death. However, formal ritual has declined in industrial societies under the pressures of modernization. For example, mourning rites and bereavement leave in the United States have become less lengthy and are shaped by the temporal norms of the business world [26].

SOME THEORETICAL CONTRIBUTIONS

The field of aging and dying, so defined, has not been totally neglected by social theorists. At this point a few such contributions will be noted (see Riley [27] for a similar approach).

Talcott Parsons

Talcott Parsons devoted considerable attention to a sociology of aging and dying in two essays [28, 29]. Parsons and Lidz argue that the meaning of death in American society is consonant with dominant values of activism and our faith in science [29]. Demographic changes have placed death, typically, at the completion of a normal life cycle. The meaning of death is now tied to old age, and quite different from that in earlier periods when death could occur at any point in the life course. The idea that death was "unnatural" does not apply when it occurs predictably at the end of a long life. People do not think they should control death per se; however, "conditional" aspects of death such as its precise timing and its quality are seen as legitimate objects for control efforts.

Parsons and Lidz see death as always having been a matter of consequence within the sphere of the family. However, within large-scale societies, in contrast to smaller societies which were more common in the past, the family is a relatively smaller unit. Thus, the impact of death on the society as a whole is less strong than in former times. This, they argue, accounts for the fact that the ritual marking of death is less elaborate in contemporary societies than it has been in the past. The argument is profoundly sociological in relating attitudes and behavior concerning death to historical changes in demographic patterns and in culture.

Parsons and Lidz argue that both the dying person and the survivors are expected to approach dying within the "active" orientation of contemporary society: they should "face up" to death realistically and their grief work should be done efficiently (see Riley [27, p. 211]).

Robert Blauner

Blauner has taken a similar view in an essay which has become something of a classic in the field. He notes:

> Modern societies . . . have largely succeeded in containing mortality and its social disruptiveness. Yet the impact of mortality on a society is not a simple matter of such demographic considerations as death rates and the size of the group. Also central is the manner in which a society is organized, the way it manages the death crisis, and how its death practices and mortuary institutions are linked to the social structure [22, p. 379].

Perhaps indicating Blauner's judgment of the congruity between death-related practices and other aspects of contemporary society, Blauner refers to North American death practices and beliefs as the "bureaucratization" of death—practices in which the treatment of death is removed from the family and placed in the hands of experts and social institutions such as hospitals and the funeral industry (see James and Field [30] for a discussion of bureaucratization of hospice care).

Blauner explicitly links his analysis of death and social structure to aging issues. He suggests that:

The disengagement of the aged in modern societies enhances the continuous functioning of social institutions and is a corollary of social structure and mortality patterns. Disengagement, the transition period between the end of institutional functioning and death, permits the changeover of personnel in a planned and careful manner, without the inevitably disruptive crises of disorganization and succession that would occur if people worked to the end and died on the job [22, p. 383].

Blauner thus describes a major link between aging and dying. Death can disrupt the smooth functioning of society, as Malinowski [19] and Hertz [31, p. 85] had earlier noted. This can happen by unpredictably removing a functioning member of the society or, even if the death is predictable, by causing problems of succession. Reducing the social status of those who are about to die decreases the potential disruption that might be caused by their death; hence, the devaluation of the aging and the near-dead. The argument is a version of the disengagement theory of aging. It is also well grounded in some classical anthropological theory.

Cumming and Henry

The disengagement theory of aging is the only major sociological theory of aging explicitly to consider death and dying. It holds that older people are "given permission" by society to disengage from active participation in society so that their death will not be disruptive and that the position they vacate can be filled smoothly [32]. From the individual's perspective, disengagement is held to be voluntary. Initiated by the growing awareness of finitude, psychological disengagement is a withdrawal of attention and affect from the external social world and an increasing focus on the self.

Disengagement theory is highly speculative about the nature and timing of the heightened awareness of finitude which is held to initiate disengagement from the perspective of the individual. This makes the theory difficult to test [33; 34, pp. 80-81]. Disengagement theory was postulated as a universal theory, but the claim to universality is clearly not supportable. The conditions under which disengagement of the form specified by the theory does occur remain to be addressed by theorists. Regrettably, despite the hundreds of papers addressing disengagement theory, the majority of these deal with the relationship between activity levels and life satisfaction, while very few address the components of the theory which deal with awareness of finitude and the self as aging and dying. Cumming and Henry themselves have little to say about death and dying, other than to include awareness of finitude as a "starting mechanism" for the process of disengagement. They are unconcerned in their work with other aspects of dying.

Victor Marshall

My own work represents another of the small number of attempts to theorize explicitly about aging and dying. I have presented some rather rudimentary theoretical formulations about the social and individual problematics of aging and dying [34, 35] and will extend these here. My theorizing, in the interpretive tradition of sociology and anthropology, explicitly relates the social psychology of aging and dying to a metaphor. This metaphor sees the aging individual as coming to recognize that he or she is entering the last chapters of life's autobiography, and wanting that autobiography to be a story that "makes sense."

People are, in some senses, "dying" all of their lives, given human mortality, but this is not a salient aspect of the lives of most people until later in life [27]. As people see age-peers die, as they attain their parents' age at death, and as their own health declines, recognition of their own mortality increases [34, pp. 97-108]. Munnichs used the term, "awareness of finitude" to refer to age-related recognition of impending death [36, p. 4]. I defined awareness of finitude as "the individual's estimate of the amount of time left to him before he dies" [37]. Not everyone makes such predictions, but making such estimates is associated with planning for the future and more favorable attitudes toward death [38].

Drawing on developmental psychology [39, 40] and also Butler's [41] conceptualization of the life review, my work [34, 35] suggests that heightened awareness of finitude triggers increased self-reflection and reminiscence in preparation for death. Life review is considered by Butler to be a universal process of reminiscing over one's past experiences in an attempt to integrate these events and images of one's self into a whole [41]. This is similar to the personal retrospection that Erikson believes occurs during the eighth identity crisis [39]. People who review and interpret their past are, metaphorically, writing the last chapters of their life story in an attempt to legitimate and find meaning in past events and acts.

Legitimation of biography can be a solitary process, but it is more likely to be successful if done socially. Myerhoff provides a vivid example of the social legitimation of biography in her account of how an elderly Jewish immigrant benefited from a community ritual: the man had the good fortune to die in the middle of his birthday party, surrounded by friends and family who had publicly gathered to celebrate and validate his life [42].

In addition to biography, people facing death confront the task of making sense of death itself—the end of the story. Through similar processes of legitimation, people draw on cultural meanings about the appropriateness of death, developing or adopting linguistic formulations which make the death of others, as well as their own death, appear to be appropriate [34, 35].

The gerontological literature contains other examples of how social relationships enhance the legitimation of biography and its culmination in death. In age-dense or communal settings such as retirement villages or seniors apartment buildings, people are reminded frequently of death. Under some circumstances, this facilitates the development of meanings and social organization for death and dying [37, 43-46] (for a discussion where this does not occur, see McDonald [47]). Hospice services include volunteer roles which explicitly validate the biographies of dying patients. In hospice units, patients are encouraged to bring family objects from home. Life course events, such as birthdays and weddings, are ritually marked, reinforcing legitimation and continuity of biography [48, 49].

The social psychological processes of legitimation in turn lead to socio-cultural changes through the social construction of meanings and behavioral patterns which deal with aging and dying [37, 45]. Processually, aging and dying are viewed as a "terminal status passage" or "career," in symbolic interactionist terms [50]. This career, like any other, has both personal and social dimensions. The career notion theoretically links the social psychological and social structural dimensions.

It should be apparent that my approach is highly derivative of some of the approaches I have cataloged above, as well as of a number of other works. This is, I hope, a strength rather than a weakness of the work. My attempts to contribute to a theory of aging and dying suffer from the "cognitive" basis of my assumptions about human nature. In emphasizing the meaningfulness of aging and dying, I probably understate the pain of it, or other emotional and affective aspects [51, pp. 470-486]. A more general limitation of my theorizing is its explicitly stated failure to attempt a truly cross-cultural analysis which extends to societies and cultures outside the "western" tradition of individualism.

Miriam and Sidney Moss

Miriam and Sidney Moss have published work that is highly resonant with my own, but which also more explicitly includes reference to bereavement, especially in the case of the death of very old people [18, 52]. They are concerned primarily with reaction to the death of persons aged eighty and older, which happens increasingly to be the typical case of death. They write of a "disenfranchisement of a survivor's response to the death of an old person." They observe that there is a general societal devaluation and stigmatization of the aged, and that most old people die following months or years of decline, with increasing prevalence of chronic conditions, episodes of acute illness, and dependency on others. There is a loss of social relationships and a decline in functional role occupancy and involvement.

Older people's attitudes toward their impending death and the death of others among their social relations are complex, the Moss's say, and there is a shifting calculus of life expectancy. Many older people die without family present, or in an age-segregated environment where any death is more or less routine and taken for granted.

For all these reasons, they argue, "the lives and the deaths of older people tend to decrease in social value" [52, p. 217]. Moss and Moss link an understanding of bereavement to an understanding of the experience of dying by noting that the process of bereavement "leads to a shift in one's sense of finitude" [52, p. 218]. Bereavement may lead to renewed or intensified questions about the existential meanings of life and death; the loss may move a person to the head of the queue, with no one ahead of them in a typical or expected sequence of dying [53]. Mourning occasions stimulate discourse about the appropriateness of death, which allows socialization or rehearsal for death.

From a social psychological perspective, Moss and Moss argue that "the central issue of later life is the preservation and maintenance of self-integrity, self-continuity, [and] self-identity." Outliving others may lead to a sense of triumph or accomplishment; it may also lead to a diminished sense of self. Grief work can be important in the maintenence of identity as an older person nears death; yet the ritual assistance in grieving is diminished in the downplaying of ritual in the case of the very old. This is what is meant by disenfranchising grief in very old age.

THEORETICAL QUESTIONS FOR
FUTURE CONSIDERATION

If we are to have a theory of aging and dying, it will have to incorporate components which explain the variability, cross-temporally and cross-culturally, in the meaning of death. Seen at the level of societies, such meanings provide the cultural framework for the social institutions that deal with death and dying situated in later life. Seen at the level of the individual, they provide the stock of knowledge that people have available in order to make sense of their own course of aging and dying.

There is still disagreement on the meaning of death cross-culturally. For example, Lofland [15] has argued that medical technology plays a major part in determining the meaning of death and that the meaning of death is more complex in high medical-technology societies than in non-modernized societies; but Counts and Counts [54] take issue with this. Based on their own research with the Kaliai of West New Britain in Papua-New Guinea, they argue that the meaning of death can be very complex in non-modernized societies as well, and depends on the perceived cause of death and on the status of the dying person.

Death and dying are undoubtedly associated with profound emotions on the part of the dying person and on those in that person's social world, yet the limited theoretical attempts in the aging and dying area have not addressed the emotional or affective component. Here is an excellent opportunity for theoretical development and research to, perhaps, explicitly link the increasingly important "sociology of emotions."

Riley and Riley have noted that the prolonged period of later life sets new challenges for our ability to control the processes and the meanings of aging and dying [55]. Both positive and negative implications of increased control possibilities are raised. While the five-stage "theory" of dying postulated by Kübler-Ross [1] has become widely accepted in clinical circles, Charmaz argues that these stages ". . . may indeed be a *consequence* of how illness and dying are socially handled in this society, rather than a psychological process of adjustment to death" [56, p. 155]. Our theories may come to have social control implications for the dying, regardless of their power to describe reality, if they become the basis of expectations for how people ought to die. While Kübler-Ross' theory has been widely discredited on scientific grounds (see Kastenbaum [57, pp. 209-215]; Marshall [34]; and Marshall and Levy [13]), it has been important in the social construction of the reality of the dying process, with behavioral implications for the dying. The danger of this potentially self-fulfilling prophecy, as applied to aging and dying, is greater because the clinical database on which the Kübler-Ross framework rests includes very few older patients. Learning more about the social construction of aging and dying career stages should be high on the agenda for theorists.

One of the most frequently asserted propositions about aging and dying is that the shift of the typical age of death to late life reduces the impact of death on the society. Yet another is that death in later life, as socially constructed, has a longer duration now than in non-modernized societies. Counts and Counts take issue with this, but theirs is something of a voice in the wilderness on this issue [54, 58]. At the same time, the work of Counts and Counts clearly demonstrates the socially constructed nature of age categories, categories of the dead, and the very process of aging and dying [20]. There is little of such work for modernized societies.

These are only a select list of issues which I find theoretically interesting (see also Marshall and Levy [13] and Riley [26]). They are unsettled issues arising out of the theoretical work mentioned above. As stated, they appear to be isolated or fragmentary. Perhaps if theoretical questions such as these could be framed in relation to a larger theoretical whole, this sense of fragmentation could be overcome.

TOWARD A THEORY OF AGING AND DYING

We do not yet have any highly-developed theory of aging and dying, and certainly not a well-tested theory of any sort. However, a number of propositional statements can be taken from the literature just reviewed, with various degrees of specificity. In some cases it is necessary to boldly go somewhat beyond the literature, and I also do that in the list I present here. While far from complete, this list might provide a launching point for further theory development. The following, therefore, are offered for further consideration.

Some Theoretical Statements/Propositions about Aging and Dying

1. Modernization leads to a shift in the typical age of death to the later years, where it is seen as the normal or typical end of a life course (changing demographics of death and dying).
2. Greater predictability in the temporal location of death has increased the probability that it will be viewed as "natural," thereby decreasing the difficulty in providing legitimating formulae to account for death (death taken for granted).
3. The longer duration of dying, as socially constructed, increases the need for institutionalized organizational arrangements for those who are old and dying, and for those in their immediate social milieu (duration of dying).
4. The longer duration of dying increases the importance of shared meanings for dying as a process, and for death as an outcome or

state. Such processes will be operative at a general socio-cultural level but also at specific institutional levels such as in the social institutions which provide care for the aging and dying (cultural meanings of death).

5. With the increased importance of science in modernized society, there is greater desire to exercise control over the "contingencies" of death and dying, such as its timing, association with pain, social characteristics; this desire for control is despite the increased acceptance of the inevitability of death per se (social control).

6. Rapid social changes in the timing of death and its location in relation to the life course, as well as changes in the relative importance of religion and science as meaning systems for legitimation, will have combined with cohort effects to produce a "cultural lag" in the legitimation potential of culture in highly modernized societies to "explain" death (cultural explanation for death).

7. While the social institution of retirement decreases the impact of death on the economic institutional sphere of society, death continues to affect the organization of family and informal social spheres, leading to succession processes in kinship roles (disruptiveness of death).

8. Awareness of finitude, the recognition that one's time to death is limited and growing nearer, increases in the middle years and even more so: when individuals reach an age which exceeds that of the death of parents and other family members, when age peers die, and when they experience marked health changes (awareness of finitude).

9. Heighted awareness of finitude leads to a shift in time perspective which gives somewhat less importance to the future, extends in duration less far into the future, and gives more attention and attributed importance to the present and the past (time perspective).

10. Heightened awareness of finitude leads to increased individual and social reminiscence processes (the "life review"), as people seek to construct a view of their life as a whole, as that life draws to a close (legitimation of biography).

11. Heightened awareness of finitude leads to increased concerns about the meaning of death itself (legitimation of death).

12. Heightened awareness of finitude leads individuals to increased attempts to secure control over the process of dying (personal control).

13. Social processes of legitimation are superior to individualized processes (social construction of reality).

14. Ritual disenfranchisement in many deaths of very old people decreases the ability for legitimating meanings to be developed and applied to make the death of others and impending death acceptable (ritual and social construction of reality).
15. Successful legitimation of biography and of death is associated with increased satisfaction with life as a whole (social construction of reality).
16. At subcultural and cultural levels, micro-processes of legitimation of death and dying will contribute to the development of changed meanings (culture) and associated behaviour patterns (social institutions, social system) concerning aging and dying.

CONCLUSION

These statements I offer as a contribution to the development of a theory, or theories, of death and dying. Such an important facet of the human condition begs for sustained theoretical attention if anything does. Theory development should take the form of further attempts to 1) phrase the statements/propositions more precisely, 2) set out conditioning and contextual parameters (this is particularly important as most of these statements may refer to socio-culturally specific social processes), and 3) link related statements/hypotheses logically into theories or at least "theorets."

This is an area in which understanding is clouded by the high emotions engendered by mortality and finitude. Our understanding may be further hindered by the disattention to our finitude which accompanies what Heidegger called the "thrownness" into the world of everyday life which characterizes the human condition. We just don't go about deliberately focusing our attention on death and dying, particularly our own, because we are too engrossed in our everyday lives. Those who spend most time with the aging and dying in contemporary society may have their own need for knowledge in order to control their conditions of work; yet this very need for control may lead to an uncritical acceptance of the simple answer (as I think has happened with respect to the Kübler-Ross framework). Explicit theorizing about aging and dying may be particularly helpful under these circumstances.

REFERENCES

1. E. Kübler-Ross, *On Death and Dying*, Macmillan, New York, 1969.
2. B. G. Glaser and A. L. Strauss, *Time for Dying*, Aldine, Chicago, 1968.

3. H. Feifel (ed.), *The Meaning of Death*, McGraw Hill, New York, 1959.
4. R. Fulton (ed.), *Death and Identity*, John Wiley, New York, 1965.
5. B. G. Glaser and A. L. Strauss, *Awareness of Dying*, Aldine, Chicago, 1965.
6. J. H. Turner, *The Structure of Sociological Theory*, Irwin-Dorsey, Georgetown, Ontario, 1982.
7. C. Geertz, *Local Knowledge*, Basic Books, New York, 1983.
8. V. W. Marshall, Social Perspectives on Aging: Theoretical Notes (Ch. 3), in *Aging in Canada: Social Perspectives* (2nd Edition), V. W. Marshall (ed.), Fitzhenry and Whiteside, Toronto, pp. 39-59, 1987.
9. D. Field, *Nursing Dying Patients*, Tavistock/Routledge, London, 1989.
10. A. Kellehear, *Dying of Cancer: The Final Year of Life*, Harwood Academic Publishers, Melbourne, 1990.
11. M. Kelner and I. L. Bourgeault, Patient Control over Dying: Responses of Health Care Professionals, *Social Science and Medicine, 36*:6, pp. 757-765, 1993.
12. D. W. Moller, *On Death Without Dignity: The Human Impact of Technological Dying*, Baywood, Amityville, New York, 1990.
13. V. W. Marshall and J. A. Levy, Aging and Dying, in *Handbook of Aging and the Social Sciences* (3rd Edition), R. Binstock and L. George and Associates (eds.), Academic Press, San Diego, pp. 245-260, 1990.
14. K. H. Wolff (ed. and trans.), *The Sociology of Georg Simmel*, The Free Press of Glencoe, New York, 1950.
15. L. Lofland, *The Craft of Dying: The Modern Face of Death*, Sage, Beverly Hills, 1978.
16. E. Crimmins, Life Expectancy and the Older Population: Demographic Implications of Recent and Prospective Trends in Old Age Mortality, *Research on Aging, 6*, pp. 490-514, 1984.
17. J. A. Brody, Facts, Projections, and Gaps Concerning Data on Aging, *Public Health Reports, 99*, pp. 468-475, 1984.
18. M. S. Moss and S. Z. Moss, The Death of a Parent, in *Midlife Loss: Coping Strategies*, R. Kalish (ed.), Sage, Newbury Park, California, 1989.
19. B. Malinowski, *Magic, Science and Religion, and Other Essays*, The Free Press, Glencoe, Illinois, 1948.
20. D. A. Counts and D. R. Counts, *Aging and its Transformations: Moving toward Death in Pacific Societies*, University Press of America, Lanham, New York, 1985.
21. A.-M. Guillemard, *La retraite: Une mort sociale*, Mouton, La Haye, Paris, 1972.
22. R. Blauner, Death and Social Structure, *Psychiatry, 29*, pp. 378-394, 1966.
23. J. Hockey, *Experiences of Death: An Anthropological Account*, Edinburgh University Press, Edinburgh, 1990.
24. P. Berger and T. Luckmann, *The Social Construction of Reality*, Doubleday Anchor, Garden City, New York, 1967.
25. E. J. Cassell, Dying in a Technological Society, *Hastings Center Studies, 2*, pp. 31-36, 1974.

26. L. V. Pratt, Business Temporal Norms and Bereavement Behavior, *American Sociological Review, 46*, pp. 317-333, 1981.
27. J. W. Riley, Jr., Dying and the Meanings of Death: Sociological Inquiries, *Annual Review of Sociology, 9*, pp. 191-216, 1983.
28. T. Parsons, Death in American Society: A Brief Working Paper, *American Behavioral Scientist, 6*, pp. 61-65, May 1963.
29. T. Parsons and V. M. Lidz, Death in American Society, in *Essays in Self-Destruction*, E. S. Shneidman (ed.), Science House, New York, pp. 133-140, 1967.
30. N. James and D. Field, The Routinization of Hospice: Charisma and Bureaucratization, *Social Science and Medicine, 34*:12, pp. 1363-1375, 1992.
31. R. Hertz, *Death and the Right Hand*, R. Needham (trans.), Cohen and West, Aberdeen, 1960.
32. E. Cumming and W. Henry, *Growing Old: The Process of Disengagement*, Basic Books, New York, 1961.
33. A. R. Hochschild, Disengagement Theory: A Critique and Proposal, *American Sociological Review, 40*, pp. 553-569, 1975.
34. V. W. Marshall, *Last Chapters: The Sociology of Aging and Dying*, Brooks/Cole, Monterey, California, 1980.
35. V. W. Marshall, A Sociological Perspective on Aging and Dying (Ch. 5), in *Later Life: The Social Psychology of Aging*, V. W. Marshall (ed.), Sage, Beverly Hills, London and New Delhi, pp. 125-146, 1986.
36. J. Munnichs, *Old Age and Finitude*, Karger, New York, 1966.
37. V. W. Marshall, Socialization for Impending Death in a Retirement Village: A Case Study, *American Journal of Sociology, 80*, pp. 1124-1144, 1975.
38. J. Keith, *Old People as People: Social and Cultural Influences on Aging and Old Age*, Little Brown and Company, Boston, 1982.
39. E. Erikson, *Identity and the Life Cycle. Psychological Issues 1* (whole issue), 1959.
40. B. L. Neugarten, Dynamics of Transition of Middle Age to Old Age, *Journal of Geriatric Psychiatry, 4*, pp. 71-87, 1970.
41. R. Butler, The Life Review: An Interpretation of Reminiscence in the Aged, *Psychiatry, 26*, pp. 65-76, 1963.
42. B. G. Myerhoff, A Symbol Perfected in Death: Continuity and Ritual in the Life and Death of an Elderly Jew, in *Life's Career: Aging*, B. G. Myerhoff and A. Simic (eds.), Sage, Beverly Hills and London, 1978.
43. A. R. Hochschild, *The Unexpected Community*, Prentice-Hall, Englewood Cliffs, New Jersey, 1973.
44. J. F. Gubrium, Death Worlds in a Nursing Home, *Urban Life, 4*, pp. 317-338, 1975.
45. V. W. Marshall, Organizational Features of Terminal Status Passage in Residential Facilities for the Aged, *Urban Life, 4*, pp. 349-368, 1975.
46. P. M. Keith, Perceptions of Time Remaining and Distance from Death, *Omega, 12*, pp. 307-318, 1982.

47. J. J. McDonald, *Knox Village: Community and Control in an Australian Retirement Village*, doctoral thesis, Dept. of Sociology, La Trobe University, Bundora, Australia, 1990.
48. J. Levy, The Staging of Negotiations between Hospice and Medical Institutions, *Urban Life, 11*, pp. 293-312, 1982.
49. J. Levy, A Life Course Perspective on Hospice and the Family, *Marriage and the Family Review, 11*, pp. 39-64, 1987.
50. E. C. Hughes, Cycles, Turning Points, and Careers, reprinted in *The Sociological Eye: Selected Papers on Institutions and Race*, E. C. Hughes, University of Chicago Press, Chicago, pp. 124-131, 1971.
51. M. C. Kearl, *Endings: A Sociology of Death and Dying*, Oxford University Press, Oxford, 1989.
52. M. S. Moss and S. Z. Moss, Death of the Very Old (Ch. 19), in *Disenfranchised Grief: Recognizing Hidden Sorrow*, K. Doka (ed.), Lexington Books, Lexington, Massachusetts, pp. 213-227, 1989.
53. V. W. Marshall and C. J. Rosenthal, Parental Death: A Life Course Marker, *Generations, 7*, pp. 30-31, 39, 1982.
54. D. A. Counts and D. R. Counts, The Cultural Construction of Aging and Dying in a Melanesian Community, *International Journal of Aging and Human Development, 20*:3, pp. 229-240, 1984-85.
55. M. W. Riley and J. W. Riley, Jr., Longevity and Social Structure: The Potential of the Added Years, in *Our Aging Society: Paradox and Promise*, A. Pifer and L. Bronte (eds.), W. W. Norton, New York, pp. 53-77, 1986.
56. K. Charmaz, *The Social Reality of Death*, Addison-Wesley, Reading, Massachusetts, 1980.
57. R. J. Kastenbaum, *Death, Society, & Human Experience*, The C. V. Mosby Company, St. Louis, 1977.
58. D. A. Counts and D. R. Counts, Introduction: Linking Concepts. Aging and Gender, Aging and Health, in *Aging and its Transformations: Moving toward Death in Pacific Societies*, D. A. Counts and D. R. Counts (eds.), University Press of America, Lanham, New York, pp. 1-24, 1985.

PART II

Patient and Family Issues

In this second section we examine some of the specific issues with which the aged and those who care for them must deal. Dementing disorders affect approximately 5 to 6 percent of the population aged sixty-five years and over in Western societies with the prevalence rising to 20 percent or more in those over eighty-five years of age. If milder forms of the illness are included in these statistics, an additional 10 percent or more of those aged sixty-five years and over may have the illness. Austrom and Hendrie point out that approximately one-half of all nursing home residents have some form of dementia. As the eighty-five years and older population is the fastest growing segment, the problem is likely to become worse in the future.

Austrom and Hendrie point out that little special training is offered to prepare staff adequately to deal with the challenges associated with caring for dementia patients. Staff members lack basic knowledge in terms of general and specific behavioral management skills. For example, patient charts at a large health care facility revealed that staff were noting many behaviors as problematic even when the behaviors were consistent with a diagnosis of Alzheimer's. However, they found that specialized staff training and ongoing support can have a tremendous impact on staff/patient interaction as well as staff morale.

Langer points out that the fastest growing segment of the population is the generation that is parenting those who are in mid-life or over. Although there is gerontological research on the burden of caregiving aged parents, in-depth analyses of the ethical basis of behavior and the interaction between generations are rarely articulated. As children grow to adulthood and parents age, patterns of behavior governed by their values and beliefs must be re-examined in the light of a "generational shift." Easing this transition becomes a mutual task for both generations and it is a challenge to the ethical sensibilities of adult children as they walk the tightrope of being supportive of their parents' selfhood while also caring for themselves.

The tasks of adults who care for parents are finishing business or resolving past conflicts, and responding to loss. Operationalizing these tasks begins by searching for the answers to very powerful moral questions such as how adult children can form equitable and mutually satisfying partnerships with parents in decision-making processes. How can one be the child and still respond without eroding parental autonomy? How can one negotiate closeness while maintaining other social responsibilities? Adult children often ask the question, "What about me?" when overwhelmed by competing obligations.

The Moss's focus is on the adult child's anticipation of the death of an elderly parent. They have two primary goals: first to view bereavement as a multidimensional process that may begin before death, and second to explore a number of themes of anticipation, with particular attention to the dialectic of holding on and letting go.

Dr. Stephen Connor reminds us that patients have rights which may come into conflict with the philosophies of health care professionals, including hospice philosophy. Patients and families have the right to denial in the face of hope and caregivers must respect that right.

Dr. Colin Murray Parkes shows that the dangerous effects of bereavement on physical and mental health can be mitigated in two ways: by anticipatory guidance and by counseling and offering support to the bereaved. He believes that there are two reasons we don't like to plan for the things we dread. We feel as if we could prevent them from happening by not planning for them; and on the other hand when you start to anticipate (or look forward to) something you may begin to "look forward" to it. It is not considered ethical to "look forward" to the death of your loved one.

Parkes argues that since most of us will one day be bereaved we should all receive pre-bereavement counseling or education. In the face of a life event of this magnitude we might expect that every married woman who reaches the age of forty would be advised to sign up for a widowhood course. Yet, there are no schools for widows. Logically such services ought to be provided but they are not because of confidentiality and the tendency of the family to deny their own needs in favor of the patient's; as well as the need of medical and nursing staff to take control of the patient away from the family.

Hill discusses the "avoided spot," the external or internal "place," that is associated with an anguishing episode, a violation or death, becomes entangled and overgrown with a mythology of now distorted memories and imaginings, and as a consequence, within the "victim's" life, it is invested with an enormously negative influence. Often a client's non-acceptance is portrayed in an inability or a refusal to mourn, thus maintaining a fantasy that the deceased person is still alive. When the avoided spot is confronted the person is freed at last to relinquish the lie and make the transition from imploded grief to an open expression of that grief.

Klass indicates that in the resolution of parental grief one finds experience that has spiritual qualities. First, the parent finds, renews, or modifies the bond to that which transcends immediate biological and social reality. Second, the parent discovers or modifies a worldview which answers the questions of how the world functions and what is the parent's place and power in the world. Klass holds that there are a series of mutually interdependent issues with which parents become involved: how the universe works; the place and power of the self; the bond with the child; the bond with the Transcendent; the meaning ascribed to the parent's life; the meaning ascribed to the child's death; and finally, community/family membership.

CHAPTER 6

Preserving the Dignity of the Invisible Person: Educating Long-Term Care Staff about the Care and Treatment of Alzheimer Disease Patients

Mary Guerriero Austrom and Hugh C. Hendrie

Alzheimer disease (AD) patients suffer from cognitive decline and personality deterioration over the course of their illness. As a result of the problematic behaviors associated with AD and ensuing personal limitations, they are usually institutionalized and therefore at risk of being dehumanized. The problem is not an uncaring staff but rather, an ill-equipped one. By learning to define the behaviors and not the patient as the problem, the staff can better treat the AD patient as a person, and thereby help the patient retain their dignity.

ALZHEIMER DISEASE AND DEMENTING DISORDERS

Dementing disorders affect approximately 5 to 6 percent of the population aged sixty-five years and over in Western societies with the prevalence rising to 20 percent or more in those over eighty-five years of age. If milder forms of the illness are included in these statistics, an additional 10 percent or more of those aged sixty-five years and over may have the illness [1, 2]. Approximately one-half of all nursing home residents have some form of dementia and AD accounts for approximately two-thirds of all cases of dementia in North America [3]. This, therefore, poses an enormous public health problem for Western societies. As the eighty-five years and older population is the fastest growing segment, the problem is likely to become worse in the future.

AD is a slowly progressive disorder with an insidious onset. It manifests itself with degrees of short-term memory loss, inability to learn and to adaptively use new information, as well as the deterioration of many aspects of the patient's personality. As the brain further degenerates, the ability to communicate and to perform the activities of daily living become progressively impaired. Psychological responses of the AD patient include depression, suspiciousness, paranoia, agitation, hypochondriasis, anxiety, social withdrawal, inappropriate behavior, belligerence, and emotional lability [4-7]. Finally, in the latter stages AD results in inanition, amentia, and death (frequently from bronchopneumonia).

Stages in the development of AD have been described as a progressive loss of the patient's ability to function independently. However, the disease progression can be unpredictable with plateaus lasting up to several years with no decline of function, followed by a time period characterized by rapid deterioration. The average duration of the disease has been reported to be between five to ten years following diagnosis. However, because of improvements in medical care, there appears to be an increase in the survival rates of patients with AD [8-11].

CARING FOR THE ALZHEIMER DISEASE PATIENT

In most cases, family members care for AD patients for as long as possible, often to the detriment of the caregiver's physical, emotional, and social well-being. Our research with 244 primary family caregivers of AD patients indicated that 55 percent of the caregivers reported physical stress or exhaustion, and over 75 percent reported dissatisfaction with their current state of health [1, 10]. These results are consistent with the general caregiving literature [12-14].

Most families seek long-term care (LTC) for their loved ones at some point. While the decision to institutionalize a loved one is almost always distressing and accompanied by guilt, the demands of providing twenty-four-hour care eventually overwhelm the family caregiver. In our clinical and research work, we have found that the most common reasons for LTC placement are the patient's increasing care and safety needs, which exceed the caregiver's capabilities, and secondly the caregiver's declining health.

Most LTC facilities strive to provide home-like environments and individualized programs. The reality, however, is that these facilities are institutions and many routines and practices tend to de-individualize residents. Residents who are demented and, usually not able to effectively communicate verbally, are at an even greater risk of being de-humanized or becoming *invisible* once institutionalized than non-demented residents. Perhaps the idea of the patient becoming invisible and the family's struggle to help preserve his or her identity is best described by Schreiber in her account of watching her mother die from a terminal illness. Although it was not AD, the impact on the patient and family is similar.

> I took a picture . . . of Mom and me looking eternally young . . . and placed it on her bedside table . . . not for her to see, but for the nurses and aides . . . to see that she had been like them, is still one of them, even now, when she is so nearly invisible [15, p. 266].

Where AD patients are integrated with other residents, the problems become even more acute as AD patients are often disruptive to other residents and their visitors. This behavior is problematic for already stressed staff members. Even when AD patients are segregated in Special Care Units (SCUs), staff members often experience difficulty with their care. The problem, we believe, is not an uncaring or unprofessional staff, but rather an ill-equipped one. Very little special training is offered to prepare staff adequately to deal with the unique challenges associated with caring for AD patients. A common problem we have found is that staff members lack basic knowledge about AD in terms of general and specific behavioral management skills. For example, audits of patient charts at a large health care facility with three SCUs revealed that staff were noting many behaviors as problematic even when the behaviors were consistent with a diagnosis of AD.

As the disease progresses for example, many patients may wander, have emotional outbursts if demands on them exceed their capabilities, experience day-night reversal, and can become suspicious. Often they direct their anger and hostility toward their caregivers. One of our greatest concerns is that once a patient is labeled as a problem, staff are less likely to respond as quickly to his or her needs. However, we have found that specialized staff training and ongoing support can have a tremendous impact on staff/patient interaction as well as staff morale. Defining the patient's behavior as a normal consequence of the disease and providing training to the staff on behavioral management techniques have effectively reduced the frequency of incidents reported by staff members [16].

Through our research, we have been able to demonstrate the effectiveness of training on staff members' ability to cope with the behavioral problems commonly manifested by AD patients. A training intervention program designed to increase staff knowledge about AD and increase positive staff/patient interaction was developed. The program was delivered to the staff members of two of three SCUs in two-hour intervals every other week for eight weeks. Staff members of the third SCU served as a control group. All staff members were administered AD Awareness Questionnaires pre-training and six weeks post-training. In addition, the patient charts were audited prior to and following the training. The frequency and type of incidents reported by the staff, as well as the staff's reactions to the incidents, were noted.

At baseline, a total of 633 incidents were recorded with an appropriate intervention noted in 38.2 percent of the cases. At eight weeks post-training, 498 incidents were reported with a significant increase in appropriate responses (63.1%). Staff performance on the AD Awareness Questionnaires also increased following the training for the two trained SCUs, while performance remained unchanged for the control group staff over time. The results indicate that teaching staff members patient management techniques can have a positive impact on patient/staff interaction. For details about the training program and methods refer to Guerriero Austrom [17] and Guerriero Austrom and Leichty [16].

RESPONDING TO COMMON PROBLEMS ASSOCIATED WITH ALZHEIMER DISEASE

An important key to meeting the challenges of caring for AD patients is understanding some of the common behavioral manifestations of memory loss and then working with the patient rather than trying to modify the patient's behaviors by reasoning and rationalizing. It is essential to remember that the patient is not willfully or purposefully "misbehaving." Therefore, it is up to the caregiver to respond accordingly by adapting their own behavior.

We have found that if the caregiver can attempt to understand and learn to accept the changes and behaviors described, rather than attempt to modify patient behavior, a major hurdle to effective care can be met. Discussing these common problems early in the training program helps to shift the emphasis away from "problem patients" to problems caused by the disease. Once caregivers accept the fact that the patient is not intentionally driving them mad and redefine the problem behaviors as a consequence of the disease, the challenges of care are seen in a different light and they can "forgive" the patient and themselves for some of the difficulties. Below are examples of some common misinterpretations of patient behavior followed by more appropriate ways of interpreting these behaviors.

Patient Denies the Memory Loss

Caregivers are often frustrated when the patient simply will not admit that they are having trouble remembering. It is important for the staff to remember that the patient has suffered memory loss and that they are *unable to remember*. Denial is an appropriate and adaptive emotional response in the short term. It is a way of protecting one's sense of self by believing "This is not happening to me" or "I am not having this trouble." The patient may try to cover up the memory loss, or direct their frustration at the caregiver by becoming angry when confronted with the reality. Protracted denial can be maladaptive because it often interferes with important long-range planning. However, once long-range legal and financial issues are addressed, it is much more humane to allow the patient their own reality rather than forcing him or her to accept the truth. As the disease progresses and short-term memory becomes non-existent, many patients live in the past since their long-term memory remains intact. We believe that it is better for patients to be allowed to live with those things which are most comforting.

Many patients decline to a point where they no longer recognize themselves in a mirror, yet they are able to recognize photos of their wedding day or school graduation. Encourage family members to bring in photos of the patient when they were younger. Working closely with family caregivers to learn a little about the patient's past can help establish a relationship with both the patient and the family. Another way to help preserve the patient's identity for staff members and visitors is to place a photo of the patient and a brief biography of his or her life on the door to their room. This information also provides visitors with ideas for conversation, which can be difficult at times.

Patient Does Not Try to Remember

A major problem associated with AD is lack of attention span. Yet caregivers often feel that the patient is simply being lazy, "If he or she would try harder and pay attention, they could remember." In the earliest stages of the disease, some memory stimulation may be helpful, for example, by keeping a calendar or a list of medications which need to be taken. However, if trying to perform activities designed to stimulate cognitive functioning frustrates the patient even more, it should be stopped.

Do not force the patient to remember or insist that he or she try harder. Rather offer him or her the information or ask questions about what they are trying to accomplish. Compensate for the patient's losses.

Fluctuations in Memory

Just as we have our good days, so does the AD patient. His or her mood and memory may fluctuate due to exercise, nutrition, hydration, side effects of medication, presence or absence of pain, etc., just as ours would. When this happens, it tends to reinforce the misconception that the patient does not try to remember or only remembers what he or she wants to. However, fluctuations in memory and cognitive skills are quite normal. Take advantage of the good days by encouraging walks, participation in activities, and outings. Accept the bad days and help the patient cope with the ups and downs by remaining supportive and noncritical of their remaining abilities.

Patient Asks Repetitive Questions

Caregivers often feel the patient is doing this to annoy them, surely he or she can control that behavior, given that the question has been answered fifteen times in ten minutes. Keep in mind that the patient cannot remember having asked the question fifteen times already. They no longer have the appropriate skills to gain attention and may really be attempting to communicate pain, fear, or some other concern. It is important to pay attention to the patient's nonverbal cues in order to decipher an underlying problem.

If the patient appears calm, not in physical or psychic pain, try distracting them with a walk (outside if the weather permits), a favorite snack, or an activity. If, however, the patient is behaving in an anxious or agitated manner, they may be in some physical or emotional pain. Try to calm the patient and move them to a quiet area, check for obvious sources of pain, and remain calm and comforting.

Accusations

The patient may constantly accuse caregivers or others of stealing his or her possessions which can leave caregivers frustrated or angry. Accusing others, however, is one way for the patient to save face and cope with the insecurity caused by not being able to remember where he or she has put things. Respond to the accusations calmly; suggest that perhaps the item was misplaced and help him or her look for it. If this behavior happens often, you may discover that the patient has a favorite hiding place. If the item cannot be found easily, distract the patient with an activity, snack, or an outing. If the item is critical, suggest to the family that they bring in an extra one while you look for it. Always try to remain calm and reassuring.

Lowered Inhibitions

A previously demure patient may begin behaving in sexually inappropriate ways. These behaviors are not indicative of pre-morbid personality traits but additional symptoms of the disease. Damage to certain areas of the brain, as a result of AD, often leads to a loss of impulse control and the patient simply cannot help it. We have found that defining the problem as a function of the disease helps caregivers (staff and family members alike) cope with the behaviors more effectively.

While patient's rights must be protected, if the inappropriate behavior is upsetting others, calmly distract and remove the patient from the area. If one patient is annoying another, calmly and gently separate them. Do not over react. Patients can sense their caregiver's emotional state from their behavior, even if they no longer comprehend the spoken word. Patients can also feel shame, disgrace, and pain, even if they cannot communicate. It is important, therefore, that these situations be handled with sensitivity.

When a patient suffers from a dementing disorder, it does not mean that they no longer need or desire human contact. On the contrary, a warm hug or soft touch may be what the patient needs but cannot ask for. Having large stuffed animals or pets available may fill a comfort need. Do not overlook the possibility of an underlying physical cause, or medication side effects, as responsible for the inappropriate sexual behavior. Talk to the patient's physician.

Wandering

All behavior has a purpose, even if one does not understand its meaning. For example, an AD patient may wander because they are looking for something. They often search for something comforting such as a childhood home or their mother. Or a patient may begin to wander in the late afternoon because for thirty-five years on the job, that is when he or she went home. The need to leave and go home is extremely strong and the pattern is so ingrained that many non-demented residents also report a similar sense of restlessness in the late afternoon. A patient may wander because he or she is in pain and can no longer communicate that. It is up to the staff member to determine the underlying cause of the behavior. While the problem solving process may be time consuming initially, the benefits to the patient far outweigh the time commitment. Finding adequate solutions to the problem of wandering, for example, is far more humane and preserves the patient's dignity than do chemical or physical restraints.

COMMUNICATION IS ESSENTIAL

A fundamental problem appears to be difficulty in communicating. Once a patient cannot communicate, staff members report greater difficulty in patient management issues. Simply because one can no longer communicate verbally, however, does not mean that they are not trying to tell us something. One of the greatest needs of human beings is to be understood [18]. Imagine therefore, the psychic distress one must feel when this is no longer possible via the usual methods. Patients may use other means to communicate and it is up to the caregiver to decipher that meaning. A key issue for staff members to bear in mind is that the patient can no longer function rationally, hence, they cannot change their behavior. Staff members, however, still have rational control over their environment. They must change and adapt their behavior in order to help the AD patient.

Communication skills deteriorate progressively. Following is a description of the most common communication difficulties experienced by AD patients and how one can help [19]. (Also, refer to Gwyther [20] for additional information and specific guidelines on communicating with the AD patient.)

In the earliest stages of the disease, the patient may have occasional difficulty finding words, trouble remembering names of familiar objects or people, and substitute words that sound similar or have similar meanings. It is usually less frustrating for the patient to be given the correct word. If, however, this is upsetting, ignore it. When the word they are searching for is unclear, ask the patient to show you or describe what they mean.

As the disease progresses, the patient will have greater difficulty communicating thoughts and may be able to say only a few words. The patient may ramble by stringing commonly used phrases together. The sentence may seem to make sense but it actually does not. When these types of communication problems occur, one can try to guess what the patient wants to say. Ask him or her if you are guessing correctly; guessing incorrectly may confuse the patient further. Respond to the patient's feelings and be alert to nonverbal cues. When words no longer make sense, consider the patient's emotional state and feelings. AD patients have the capacity to feel and experience emotions throughout the entire course of their illness.

In latter stages of the disease, the patient may only remember a few key words; they may repeat phrases over and over; cry out intermittently; mumble unintelligible phrases; and eventually may not speak at all. If the patient can still shake his or her head, ask simplified questions about his or her needs. Establish a regular routine of checking his or her comfort. Check that the patient's clothing is comfortable, that their room is warm, that there are no sores or rashes on the skin, and that regular feeding and toileting procedures are established.

COPING WITH FAMILY MEMBERS

Spouses usually seek LTC when their partner can no longer be managed at home, often when the caregiver's health and physical resources fail. Adult-child caregivers often have different motivations for institutionalizing an AD patient. Due to the various demands of families, careers, and civic responsibilities on their time they have been appropriately referred to as the "sandwich generation" [21]. They often see LTC as a solution to one of their problems. Although they may not visit as often as spousal caregivers, or may live or move far away, the displaced anger and guilt is often similar to that experienced by spousal caregivers.

Family caregivers often have a difficult time relinquishing control over their loved one's care and their guilt is often displaced as anger toward the staff and the facility [22]. Too often, however, patients with "difficult family members" suffer the consequences. Staff members spend less time with the patient, set up barriers to effective communication and avoid the family caregivers, in order to protect themselves from further attack. However, if staff members can understand and appreciate the root cause of a family's anger, they can work to diffuse the anger and cultivate a collaborative relationship so that both parties "win" and the patient receives optimal care.

COMMON FAMILY FEARS AND CONCERNS

Family members often express their concerns and fears as hostility toward the staff. By employing some of the suggested strategies to diffuse the anger and concern expressed in the following statements, LTC staff and family members can become partners in the patient's care.

No one can care for my loved one like I can.

This is true. No institution can provide the twenty-four-hour care like the family member, but that does not necessarily mean that the care will be bad. It will simply be different. It is important to acknowledge the family's fears and concerns, empathize with them, and not discount their anxieties. It is important that staff members listen with their hearts. Walk a mile in their shoes. How would you feel if it were your parent, spouse, or sibling that was being institutionalized. The reality is that most of us will have to face a similar decision some day.

I am no longer an important part of my loved one's care.

Acknowledge the tremendous job the family has done so far and stress that their involvement in the patient's care is not over. Ask for their help in giving the patient the best care possible. With direction, encouragement, and appreciation, families can ease the staff's burden. Prepare the family for what to expect. Explain the routine and that the patient may become more disoriented at first. Keep the family involved in the patient's care. Although this may be more time consuming initially, the long-term benefits will be great.

For many caregivers, especially the spouse, caregiving was their primary role. Many caregivers had reduced or given up their jobs to care for their loved one. Thus, once they institutionalize the patient, many family caregivers can become depressed. They are not only losing a loved one, but also a major sense of purpose in their lives. Family members may also feel guilty at having had to seek long-term care. They may be breaking a promise to a loved one who, in the past, may have asked not to be placed in a nursing home. The caregiver may not be able to understand these feelings in themselves. Be patient, supportive, and understanding of their losses. The first parting after the patient has been placed is often unbearable for the family members. One caregiver fondly remembers the staff member who called her at home the first night and told her how much fun the patient was having at a social event. This one small thoughtful gesture was extremely comforting to a distraught daughter.

Lack of privacy; other patients are always wandering in and out of the room.

If their loved one is in an SCU, explain to family members that most patients wander and it doesn't bother most residents. But if their loved one is agitated by this behavior try to respect the wishes for privacy whenever possible. Apologize when necessary.

Staff do not spend enough time helping with meals. It always took me two hours to feed him/her.

Reassure the family that you are doing the best that you can with the patient's feeding routine. Enlist the family's help at meal time. Suggest that they prepare the patient's favorite finger foods. Encourage field trips and outings at meal times. Let patients eat when they are hungry.

Personal belongings are always getting lost.

Encourage family members to remove valuables from the patient's room. Recommend easy loose-fitting clothing. Always respond to family complaints and strive to avoid them the next time. Let all the staff members know about a family's concerns so that the patient's care is consistent.

An "emotional bank account" is a helpful concept in understanding family and patient care. If you make an emotional deposit, you will have a balance from which to draw, if you withdraw too much without ever making a deposit, you are operating in a deficit economy. A very insightful and empathic staff member learned this principle early. She reported how a family member came to her, extremely angry that the patient did not have her dentures and demanded to know where they were, criticizing the staff for letting it happen. Rather than responding defensively with her own frustration and exasperation, the staff member dropped everything and conducted a thorough search of the patient's room, the SCU, and finally the kitchen, until the dentures were found. She was, of course, two hours behind in her charting but she was miles ahead in her relationship with that family. She reported how appreciative and cooperative the family member became, the anger and frustration dissipated, and that family member always had a warm smile for her.

In their pain, families often look for things on which to displace their anger, such as the dentures described above, or misplaced articles of clothing. But if you can find the patience to listen and respond to the request, the rewards can be tremendous.

SUMMARY

Caring for AD patients is challenging. It is not difficult to understand why LTC staff can become frustrated. By first learning about the effects of the disease on the AD patient's personality, staff members can become more sympathetic about the patient's behaviors and will be receptive to employing effective management techniques. More importantly, through education and training, staff members can become partners with family members in helping to preserve the dignity of the AD patient and preventing them from becoming invisible.

ACKNOWLEDGMENTS

This work was supported in part by the Indiana Alzheimer Disease Center and NIA Grant #PHS P30 A610133-01. The authors thank Beth Reeves for her assistance in the preparation of the manuscript.

REFERENCES

1. M. Guerriero Austrom and H.C. Hendrie, Quality of Life: The Family and Alzheimer's Disease, *Journal of Palliative Care, 8*:3, pp. 56-60, 1992.
2. W. A. Rocco, L. A. Amaducci, and B. S. Schoenberg, Epidemiology of Clinically Diagnosed Alzheimer's Disease, *Annals of Neurology, 19*, pp. 415-424, 1986.
3. A. F. Jorm, *The Epidemiology of Alzheimer's Disease and Related Disorders*, Chapman and Hall, New York, 1990.
4. American Psychiatric Association, *Diagnostic and Statistical Manual of Mental Disorders* (3rd Rev. Edition), APA, Washington, D.C., 1987.
5. M. Guerriero Austrom, B. S. Richards, and H. C. Hendrie, Alzheimer's Disease: Providing Care for the Family, *Indiana Medicine, 80*, pp. 648-651, 1987.
6. H. P. Palmer, Alzheimer's Disease and Critical Care, *Journal of Gerontological Nursing, 9*, pp. 86-90, 1983.
7. B. Reisberg, Stages of Cognitive Decline, *American Journal of Nursing, 84*, pp. 225-228, 1984.
8. E. M. Gruenberg, Epidemiology of Senile Dementia, in *Neurological Epidemiology: Principles and Clinical Applications*, B. S. Schoenberg (ed.), Raven Press, New York, pp. 437-455, 1978.
9. H. C. Hendrie, S. Hall, and M. Guerriero Austrom, Some Thoughts on the Cross-Cultural Prevalence of Dementia, in *Mechanisms of Psychological Influence on Physical Health with Special Attention to the Elderly*, L. L. Cartensen and J. M. Neale (eds.), Wiley & Sons, New York, pp. 161-184, 1989.
10. M. Guerriero Austrom, *Alzheimer's Disease Family Caregiver Well-Being: A General Model*, unpublished doctoral dissertation, York University, Toronto, 1989.
11. G. P. Wolf-Klein, F. A. Silverstone, M. S. Brod, A. Levy, C. J. Foley, V. Termotto, and J. Breuer, Are Alzheimer's Patients Healthier?, *Journal of the American Geriatrics Society, 36*, pp. 219-224, 1988.
12. W. E. Haley, E. G. Levine, S. L. Brown, J. W. Berry, and G. H. Hughes, Psychological, Social, and Health Consequences of Caring for a Relative with Senile Dementia, *Journal of the American Geriatric Society, 35*, pp. 405-411, 1987.

13. J. Pearson, S. Verma, and C. Nellett, Elderly Psychiatric Patient Status and Caregiver Perceptions as Predictors of Caregiver Burden, *Gerontologist, 28,* pp. 79-83, 1987.
14. C. C. Pratt, V. L. Schmall, S. Wright, and M. Cleland, Burden and Coping Strategies of Caregivers to Alzheimer's Patients, *Family Relations,* pp. 27-33, January 1985.
15. L. Schreiber, *Midstream,* Viking Penguin, New York, 1990.
16. M. Guerriero Austrom and M. Leichty, *Training Staff of Alzheimer Disease Special Care Units,* paper presented at the 46th Annual Scientific Meeting of The Gerontological Society of America, New Orleans, Louisiana, November 19-23, 1993.
17. M. Guerriero Austrom, *Evaluation of a Training Program for Staff of Specialized Alzheimer's Disease Units,* poster presented at the 45th Annual Scientific Meeting of The Gerontological Society of America, Washington, D.C., November 18-22, 1992.
18. S. R. Covey, *The Seven Habits of Highly Effective People,* Fireside Simon and Schuster, New York, 1989.
19. D. Springer and T. H. Brubaker, *Family Caregivers and Dependent Elderly: Minimizing Stress and Maximizing Independence,* Sage, Beverly Hills, California, 1984.
20. L. P. Gwyther, *Care of Alzheimer's Patients: A Manual for Nursing Home Staff,* American Health Care Association and the Alzheimer's Disease, and Related Disorders Association, Durham, North Carolina, 1985.
21. E. M. Brody, "Women in the Middle" and Family Help to Older People, *Gerontologist, 21,* pp. 471-480, 1981.
22. M. Guerriero Austrom and H. C. Hendrie, Death of the Personality: The Grief Response of the Alzheimer's Disease Family Caregiver, *The American Journal of Alzheimer's Care and Related Disorders & Research,* 5:2, pp. 16-27, 1990.

CHAPTER 7

Inevitable Losses—
Ethical Issues for Adult
Children with Aging Parents

Pearl E. Langer

This chapter evolved from a workshop that I conducted, which was inspired by my work as a family therapist specializing in counseling later-life families. Add to this my experience teaching professionals who work in the field of gerontology and mix with a hefty dollop of "my life as an adult child." The rationale for examining the topic of ethical issues for adult children with aging parents is several-fold.

First, the fastest growing segment of the population is the generation that is parenting those who are in mid-life or over. Definitive research corroborates that family members do engage in mutually supportive behaviors, particularly that which is helpful to older parents [1-3]. Yet, although there is a significant amount of gerontological research on burden, caregiving, solidarity, etc., in-depth analyses of the ethical basis of behavior and the interaction between generations are rarely articulated.

As one researcher notes, "No one has done research on relational morality in families" [4]. The literature on loss and bereavement suffers from a similar deficiency of having little to say about adult children and the ethical dilemmas which result from parents aging [5, 6]. In addition, the field of family therapy has only recently begun to show signs that families are actually peopled by women and men over the age of fifty, and that moral issues do affect relationships [7, 8]. These three disciplines have traditionally exhibited little capacity for the crossover of knowledge that would be enlightening for practitioners in

93

any of these fields and which might promote the development of needed resources for later-life families struggling with ethical dilemmas.

Second, adult children are routinely faced with the need to make decisions with and for parents (when cognitive or physical function is impaired). There are few guidelines for family members, and particularly for the children, who often must re-work what is expected of them in fulfillment of their filial obligations. As children grow to adulthood and parents age, patterns of behavior governed by their values and beliefs must be re-examined in the light of developmental and bio-psychosocial changes. A "generational shift" takes place as power shifts from the first generation and the second generation begins to practice being the first. Easing this transition becomes a mutual task for both generations and it is often a challenge to the ethical sensibilities of adult children as they walk the fine tightrope of being supportive of the maintenance of their parents' selfhood while also caring for self. In my practice, I see this enacted over and over again: adult children trying to be the "good" son or daughter, while carrying on with a life that includes work and other relationships. Where the screw really turns and what often lies under their anxiety is the growing realization that parents are mortal. Supportive care is laced with the grief that bubbles below the surface when mother has another birthday, or when father is no longer able to drive. And what of the tug of roles in caring for a parent with a life shortening illness, the "dancing in quick time" as I call it, that exhausts and leaves little time to grieve? When a parent is there but not there, in the other world of a dementia, how can a child be good and cope with this "ambiguous loss?" [9]

A major developmental task for adult children is to remain connected to their parents while beginning to let them go. We may divide this task into several "mini" tasks which often create moral dilemmas, or "a tension between self and other" [4]. The tasks are caring for and about parents, finishing business or resolving past relational conflicts, and responding to loss. Operationalizing these tasks begins by searching for the answers to very powerful moral questions such as how adult children can form equitable and mutually satisfying partnerships with parents in decision-making processes. How one can be the child and still respond without eroding parental autonomy. How one negotiates the closeness required in times of illness or other crises, while maintaining other social responsibilities. Adult children often ask the question, "What about me?" when overwhelmed by competing obligations. The answer is often shrouded in the ambiguity that heightens stress and anxiety. And finally, how does one do the unthinkable, letting go emotionally and physically of a parent?

The preceding provides a rationale for those who work with later life families and a knowledge base to enable parents and adult children to walk the relational tightrope as safely and as satisfyingly as possible. The goal of this chapter is to bring light to some of these moral dilemmas which are so often a major part of the adult child's life, and to place these within a framework of ethical theory and concepts. Ethical principles that are most relevant to family interaction will be defined, ethical issues for adult children with aging parents will be described using case examples, and the "minefields" or problem areas will be delineated. Suggestions for intervention strategies will be made for dealing with these, as well as some ideas for future research.

The discussion is limited to the unique ethical concerns of the second generation as a complete family systems analysis is beyond the scope of this chapter. As a family therapist, I am most sensitive to the interactional dynamics of family systems and this piece should in no way negate the fact that the ethical perspectives of aging parents must also be taken into account when the generations come together to reach satisfying common goals.

ETHICS AND FAMILIES: SOME DEFINITIONS

I have chosen to describe certain ethical principles which are particularly relevant to the "condition" of aging parent-adult child relations. These principles of thought and behavior often collide with pervasive cultural beliefs and values of Western society—the denial of death, negative stereotyping of the elderly, and the myth that "in the good old days" adult children cared for their parents better than they do now [10]. No generation in the past has had such prolonged parent-caring years, and women, who are usually the primary caregivers to older parents, are recognized as having great difficulty juggling work outside of the family and work inside with few community support services [11]. Cultural expectations of parent-child relations are often demanding and unrealistic. Those who work with later-life families can attest to the difficulties of adult children whose moral sensibilities are being pulled in all directions and who may feel slightly "crazy" and often, immensely guilty.

According to Webster's *Encyclopedia Unabridged Dictionary*, "ethics" is "a system of moral principles" involving "values relating to human conduct, with respect to the rightness and wrongness of certain actions and to the goodness and badness of the motives and ends of such actions" [12]. These moral principles are guides of "how to be," of how to decide what should or ought to happen between people, and in this case, between adult children and their parents.

Ethical issues for adult children and parents are bounded by 1) mutuality, obligation, and responsibility; 2) the consideration of the needs of both parents and children; 3) the historical experiences of the family—ways of relating, value systems and world views, and problem solving; 4) the availability of resources both within and without the family; and 5) the immediate context of decision making that is affected by socio-cultural and political mores and events (see Thompson [4] for an explanation of "contextual morality").

The Concept of Relational Ethics

Relational Ethics arise in the context of family first, and then in other social relations. They may be defined as "a relational demand that persons maintain a fair balance of equity between what they are entitled to take and what they are obligated to give in relationships" [7]. Another definition of relational morality is "the interactional process through which pairs negotiate common expectations and understandings" [4].

Simply put, we are describing the loyalty of family members to each other, the trust which this implies, and the ability to balance the fair or just give and take between generations. Relational ethics are about trust, loyalty, who owes what to whom and when, obligations, and mutuality. For example, a middle-aged daughter knows that in her family women have taken aging parents into their homes rather than "buy" assistance. There is a legacy of trust in family loyalty which will ensure that older members are cared for by family only. And, this woman knows that her children will learn that this is considered a fair way to treat those who have nurtured them. Over time, each generation builds trust in the give and take process [13]. Boszormenyi-Nagy and Krasner are firm in their assertion that adult children cannot repay the nurturing and protection that has been offered by their parents in the past, though many try. They feel that the repayment is contained in the continuing legacy of care for younger generations to come. Selig, Tomlinson, and Hickey review the moral and ethical factors involved in filial duty and caregiver stress with implications for professional intervention [14]. In much the same vein as Boszormenyi-Nagy and Krasner, they call attention to the mutual, but not unqualified, filial obligation based on "pay back."

Adult children draw on their life experience, their values, and beliefs to answer questions of relational morality. It is very important for those who work with the adult child and family to explore and to gain a sense of the parameters of these moral imperatives in order to facilitate problem solving that will fit family and individual values. Moral values originate primarily in the family of origin and they may change with time. Older generations model these values and behavior, and they are transmitted in this manner through generations. The rules of behavior based on these values are often implicit rather than explicit. For example, when an adult child was asked how it was decided that all of her siblings would share the cost of sending their parents on a winter vacation, she replied that reciprocity between family members had always been part of the family value system.

Older generations often inculcate values through story telling [15]. The stories are often of family survival in the face of almost unendurable hardship and loss: "We made it through the Depression because we all pulled together." Or, "During the war, we lived with your grandparents when your father went overseas. That way, I could work while they cared for you." This verbal "legacy" teaches children that the continuity of family is based on loyalty and trust. Trust, as I will discuss later in this chapter, is an important component of the morality in relationships. When trust is lost, the developmental tasks of the adult child become difficult and almost impossible to accomplish. When relational ethics are permeated with mistrust and an imbalance between receiving and giving occurs, a spiraling destructive cycle can develop between parent and child. Distrust begets less giving which begets less receiving which begets less trust and so on. Conflict, physical and emotional cutoff, and destructive behavior attend this way of relating [16]. For example, a son may be contemplating reaching out to his father from whom he has been cut off for many years, after hearing that the seventy-year-old man is having difficulty living alone. Conflict built between the two when the son turned down his father's wish that he enter the family business. Groomed to inherit this role, he decided to become a musician. Trust had been broken and the father disinherited his son, and the conflict spiraled into complete cut-off for many years. Now, when the father's health is failing, the son must decide what is, if anything, owed to his father.

SOME IMPORTANT FORMAL ETHICAL PRINCIPLES FOR THE ADULT CHILD–OLDER PARENT RELATIONSHIP

The most important formal ethical principles for adult children—parent relationships are autonomy, beneficence, and justice.

Autonomy

This may be translated as freedom of choice, self-determination, control of decision making, and other actions of the individual [17]. It also implies the exercising of personal goals within a context which may threaten autonomy [18]. Autonomy has three dimensions: physical (mobility, least restrictive environment, physical independence), psychological (control over environment, choice of options), and spiritual (continued sense of identity over time, decision making, and life lived consistent with the person's long-term values and life meaning). Paternalism is the opposite principle.

Example: The son and daughter of a couple in their seventies who live in a city 500 miles away from them, would like their parents to sell their home and move to a retirement facility in the children's home town where all comforts and conveniences will be provided for them. The children will feel better keeping an eye on father who has a heart condition and on mother whose arthritis is worsening, and so there is now a subtle but consistent attempt to persuade the parents to move from their friends, religious community, and the father's part-time job. The parents are attempting to "hold their ground" while being understanding of their children's worry. The ethical dilemma in this case is how to determine when the desires of adult children infringe upon the autonomy of their parents. Also, when does the desire to do good actually do harm? This involves another principle, that of beneficence.

Beneficence

This is the promotion and protection of the best interest of the individual by seeking the greater balance of good over harm.

Example: A daughter informs the attendant physicians that her mother, who is suffering from a terminal illness and is unable to make her wishes known, does not want any surgical procedures to be carried out on her, and the daughter is determined to do everything in her power to let her mother die in peace. Unfortunately, the daughter's brother disagrees and wants everything possible done to keep his mother alive. Their dilemma reflects their differing values about what is good and what is harmful for their dying mother.

Justice

This is the principal of fairness, particularly in the allocation of resources. Callahan exposes the ethical dilemmas of a society in which dwindling resources do not meet the needs of the growing aging population [19, 20]. Families are being challenged to provide for the needs of its oldest members in a morally acceptable manner and the state is portrayed, with some justification, as not providing a fair share of services to these families. This leaves many of them with heart-wrenching dilemmas of how best to care for their aged members.

> Example: Sam's wife of fifty years has died and he lives alone in a rural area where services such as home-making and meals-on-wheels are hard to come by. His son has a growing family but has managed to keep his father in his own home with the help of his wife. His wife has now found a job and her husband has taken on a second job to meet the financial demands. The moral dilemma for this son and his family is to determine what is fair, what are their limits, how much can they sacrifice for their parent, and what is fair treatment of him. The double bind for them is giving too little or giving too much, and they must contend with the fact that there are few societal supports, particularly in rural areas that could help them keep Sam independent.

The preceding discussion of the ethical context now provides a base for exploring some problematic issues for parents and children.

MINEFIELDS

Introduction

Minefields are related to the special issues for adult children already mentioned—decision making regarding the care of parents, finishing business, and responding to loss. In this section, I want to describe some potential trouble spots under these same headings. There are few families, in my experience, in which the aging process of family members does not cause emotional "shock waves." Curiously, many adult children who I counsel do not know that what they are experiencing is the norm and they often feel, particularly the women, that they are not meeting their obligations effectively enough. This is often accompanied by guilt as they have had little experience in parent care and not much in the way of information or guidance. Paradoxically, in some of the more troubled families, the working out of these problems often does not include the parents, who may then have to resort to coercion and bargaining to maintain a sense of power and control over how decisions are made about their lives. Or, they may just acquiesce to the well-meaning, but misguided ministrations of their children, and suffer feelings of powerlessness and isolation.

This is an appropriate place to mention the effect of gender on the feelings and responses of adult children. Feminist scholarship has provided a new lens through which the giving of care in families can be viewed. In any discussion of problematic ethical issues for adult children, it would be foolhardy to neglect the differing caregiving experiences of men and women, for their responses are affected by how they are socialized and by social policy (or the lack thereof), which must support their caring. Baines, Evans, and Neysmith write that "it is women who learn to take their place in society as informal caregivers to children and elderly relatives, and who transfer this to the public sphere and provide formal caring services" [21]. More than their male counterparts, females are encouraged to identify with others and to develop altruistic patterns of interaction [22, 23]. It is this different socialization of women and men within a patriarchal society which does not value the giving of care, which raises the spectre of guilt for women. In my experience, it is very rare for a man in counseling to tell me about the guilt that he feels because he isn't "doing enough" for his parents. These are the words that I usually hear from women. Thus, when working with ethical issues it is important to remember that there will be differing emotional and practical issues for men and women to which the professional must be sensitive when devising strategies for change. This implies a review and redefinition of gender roles toward a more equitable distribution of responsibility.

For the most part, adult children will respond according to the ethical and moral principals that they have used in the past and while the process is embedded in this continuity, there must also be flexibility and new ways of relating to one's parents within new contexts which are always changing rapidly. Some special and problematic issues are described in the following section.

Caring For and About Parents

The process of supporting parents emotionally and instrumentally contains a number of "hot spots." There will be mutual decision making about activities such as shopping, transportation to appointments, or social activities, finding appropriate accommodation if change is necessary, introduction of community support services, the use of medical services, and planning for the future. Emotional support to help parents deal with changes is important and the adult child must also negotiate reciprocal behaviors such as being able to receive support from parents [24]. The fifty-year-old professor who loves his in-laws tries to disguise his anger as he talks about his father-in-law who refuses to tell his family where he keeps his money or his will. There can be no discussion and no planning of this man's death and therefore there is a lot of uncertainty for the family.

The giving of support can be exhausting and frustrating for adult children. It can also eat away at relationships that must take a back seat to that of the parent-child one. This is explosive ground and can result in conflict.

A loyal daughter is torn between continuing her daily visits with her mother and being at her job or with her new grandchild. Again, we look at the ethical issues implied in whose needs are going to be met. If I need my parent to collaborate and plan with me what do I do when my need is resisted? How can I fulfill my obligation as a dutiful child? What personal limits have to be reached before resentment and perhaps depression set in? Allowing others to help in parent care is fraught with ambiguity, particularly when there must be relocation to a long-term care facility. If I do not help my parent relocate, she will be in danger. If I do, then I will feel guilty about allowing others to do my job and I promised that I would never "put away" my parent. Caring is like a two-sided mask—fulfilling and healthy, but often painful and difficult.

The child who has an abusive parent often has a terrible struggle with the ethical issues of helping the parent while experiencing the pain of what has happened in the past [25]. Between the wish for what might have been and the reality of what was, the present intrudes and forces yet another need to confront what might be. There is a risk of disappointment and great emotional distress.

Old rivalries and resentment between siblings often compound problems which resurface around the care and support of elderly parents [26]. This can take the form of a contest about who is most worthy of a parent's love, money, attention, anger, or gratitude. Conflicting values may breed mistrust and siblings may find it hard to swallow the fact that the favored one is not always the one who does the most. A daughter whose loyalty takes the form of constant worry about her parents may be angry because her siblings refuse to be caught up in her constant pressure for them to worry more. She therefore redoubles her efforts to clean her mother's apartment, take her out on weekends, bring food and monitor her life. This competition costs her a marriage and sibling support. Alliances between siblings will be formed based on previous history, values, gender, and age, and this can be cause for resentment.

It would be unrealistic not to mention inheritance and other financial considerations which often cause the loudest explosion and most damage in families, especially between siblings. Again, there may be differing opinions about who is owed what. There are "horror stories" in most families about the division of spoils and the resulting splits between brothers and sisters which can divide families for generations to come.

Finishing Business

Go to any large family gathering where the generations are represented. Observe who speaks to whom, which relatives are missing, or who is seated in the least-favored seat beside the kitchen. Find out if there are any secrets in this family—a child conceived out of wedlock, an aunt who eloped with a salesman, a grandparent who is an alcoholic. Watch the two brothers, both in their seventies, circle each other warily. Their loyal children and *their* children follow the dictum that brothers (and families) who fight over a family business must never talk to each other again. Watch for the parent who isn't invited to the wedding of his granddaughter because there was an argument when his son married someone unacceptable many years ago.

A clergy person tells a story of officiating at the funeral of an elderly man. One of the sons had been cut off from the father for many years. As the father lay dying, the clergy person contacted the son to see if he could bring them together before the death. When the son refused, he then asked what terrible event could have transpired to keep him from his father's death bed. The son answered, "You know, quite truthfully, it has been so long that I don't really remember what the quarrel was really about." So much time wasted and so little time to reconnect!

Finishing business is about mutual forgiveness and connecting differently to accomplish this. A caveat—there are situations in which understanding is attainable, but not forgiveness, and this is also a form of finishing business. Two films, "Dad" and "I Never Sang For My Father," are realistic and poignant portrayals of the finishing of business in which the adult children strive to be true to themselves while attempting to learn about and support their aging parents. The legacy of unfinished business is couched in the language of regret and conflict and as most family therapists know from their work with families, these conflicts and cut-offs will usually surface again in later generations in other contexts.

Responding to Loss

Minefields in loss situations often present themselves when decisions must be made when a parent is ill or dying. Rando writes about the anticipatory grief and mourning that accompany a prolonged illness [27]. The "roller coaster" of crisis and remission, and the continuing slide toward death can cause premature detachment of the family from the ill person. This is isolating for the parent who is ill and will prevent supportive exchanges between parent and child. Similarly, adult children whose parents are cognitively impaired must face the loss of the person they knew because the only resemblance to the old self is physical. This "ambiguous loss" [9] has a "here but not here" quality which presents the moral dilemma of how to treat the impaired parent. Guilt often accompanies the feelings of wishing for the parent's death in order to release them from this horrible state. Scharlach and Fredriksen discuss the difficulties for adult children of coping with the death of a parent and the process of letting go [6].

Increasing parental frailty also reminds adult children of their own mortality and the decisions that they and their children will have to make. Caring children may exhibit hovering behavior in an attempt to cope with their fears of loss. Some of this is to be expected and can be positively supportive and meaningful to parent and child. If taken too far, the autonomy of the parent can be threatened and the whole family system can be disrupted, i.e., a daughter cared for her acutely ill mother over a period of several years and as the mother's health deteriorated, she asked for a priest to make her confession. The daughter refused time after time because she could not face the loss of her mother. Her brothers and sisters had great difficulty advocating for their mother and the conflict that ensued became the "unfinished business" of that generation.

The institutionalization of a parent is one of the most poignant and difficult crises for a family. Decisions about relocation are usually made reluctantly when all resources, and this includes the primary caregiver, have been exhausted. The stress of this move reverberates on the entire family and requires a huge adjustment.[1] Institutionalization is a moral dilemma for adult children that flies in the face of cultural teaching about honoring one's parents. This cultural ethic is vague when guilty and confused children seek guidance on how to accomplish this with the least amount of pain for all.

[1] See Forbes, Jackson, and Kraus [28] for a bibliography.

Decision making about advance directives, living wills, and other legal issues with and for a dying parent, may break the family code of not talking openly about death and yet research has shown that families cope better with this life cycle transition if openness can be maintained within the family system [29]. When parents and children need to talk openly and honestly, how moral is the silence that surrounds them? Secrets are "toxic" and destructive, causing misunderstandings and conflict in families.

The surviving parent/adult child relationship is rarely mentioned in the literature on grief. The adult child may have a problem knowing how to support the parent and often, at least for a time, must fill a social role that was maintained by the deceased spouse. Nadine Gordimer, the Nobel prize winning author, illustrates this difficult stage in her short story "L, U, C, I, E." The daughter of the title explains: ". . . it was one of those journeys taken after the death of a wife when the male who survived sees the daughter as the clone woman who, . . . will protect him from the proximity of death and restore him to the domain of life" [30]. Death-bed promises to care for a surviving parent are often laden with unrealistic expectations and can deteriorate into loyalty traps that are morally difficult to extricate oneself from.

INTERVENTIONS: GOALS AND METHODS

It is impossible to define all the "minefields" and how families will respond to them, for each family will attract its own kind of trouble and will respond as only that particular family and the individuals within it know how. The primary goal of intervention with adult children and their parents is to facilitate and support adjustment to the issues previously discussed, in order that the individuals can get on with their lives. This section will define some ways to intervene in the complex ethical issues that face families without going into great detail, which is beyond the scope of this chapter.

Thompson suggests that scholars have emphasized filial responsibility rather than the mutual intergenerational responsibility that needs to be the underpinning of a "moral dialogue" between parents and adult children [4]. This "dialogue," she states, has four essential processes, which can be viewed as desired outcomes of intervention. They are: 1) attribution, which makes sense of responsibility; 2) disclosure, which emphasizes the sharing of claims and needs; 3) empathy, which appreciates the viewpoint of the other; and 4) cooperation, which denotes shared understanding and common solutions. Each process, she says, builds from the one before. In my experience, families often engage in this dialogue as part of the process of problem solving and this "give and take" between generations is both helpful and healing.

Counseling

Some families do just fine on their own, but for those who have become "stuck" in a minefield, a guide can help. This could be a family therapist, chaplaincy staff, a hospital ethicist, a social worker, nursing staff, a physician, or anyone who is trained in counseling families. Counseling later-life families in the "moral dialogue" is a specialized task, given the special issues that face them, and the fact that many older persons are fearful of any kind of counseling. Also, the time spent with families on their problems may be shortened by the mandate of the agency or institution in which they are seen, and professionals will need to develop brief creative ways of counseling. Counseling requires motivation on the part of family members, and a context that is both "safe" and helpful. Having worked with many families in a number of settings, I have found that if the context is one in which there is trust and where there is access to a "mediator/facilitator," families are often more eager to resolve outstanding problems.

Interventions must be tailored to fit family values, world views, and beliefs. Guidance about what options are available is very important for easing ethical impasses and family members need education about the aging process of not only the oldest generation but also of the middle generation and how this affects interaction between them. They also need to know about relationships between adult siblings and what affects these relationships in the course of decision making for older parents. Education about resources such as support groups, respite care, financial and legal counseling services, and medical supports is crucial. Information about living wills and other legal directives is also very important. Family meetings should be encouraged as planning time both with or without a facilitator. I often give reading material to families (see Bibliography) and names of relevant films because these can be useful ways to teach family members about how to resolve dilemmas and to "normalize" their situation.

If the problems are very serious and adult children and their parents are unable to forge a meaningful resolution to ethical issues, then family therapy can be most useful. Several models address the problems of later-life families, particularly that of finishing business and caregiving. These transgenerational therapies [31], which include contextual therapy [32] and Bowenian therapy [33], are helpful. I find that in my own work with adult children and their parents I use an eclectic mix of structural family therapy [34], feminist family therapy

[35], grief therapy or counseling [36, 37], and case-management techniques. What is most important is the opening up of the family system to allow a "dialogue" to take place to resolve problems. Assessment is done through questioning the family about their history, their values and beliefs particularly about aging and loss, their coping skills and strengths, stressors, and desired outcomes. Family members may present with anger, emotional and physical fatigue, and feelings of helplessness which must be addressed so that communication can move the family from problem to solution. Tasks may be given and outcomes assessed in subsequent meetings. Problems must be defined from the perspective of *all* the family members, with attention to individual needs and dynamics.

For the Professional

Not all families or their individual members want or need counseling. Be aware of the different limitations of families to tolerate intervention. Also, be aware of your own limits as a helper. Remember, each family is unique and the values, world views, and beliefs of the individuals in them must be respected. As a professional, one needs to model openness, flexibility, and to be aware that one's own values will affect the family. There is no "value-free" counseling or therapy.

CONCLUSION

This chapter is meant to be an introduction to the understanding of ethical issues between adult children and their parents. The field of ethics has provided a structure for viewing this interaction and as the adult child walks the path of staying connected but letting go of the parent, he or she meets ethical dilemmas for which there are no quick or easy answers. It is hoped that this chapter will be just one of the many that will guide that walk. Given the paucity of research on this issue, it is self-evident that much more work will need to be done by investigators. My one wish would be that the investigation be carried out using cross-disciplinary collaboration. The fields of gerontology, family studies, and bereavement have much to offer each other. These include ways in which to look at generations within families and how they interact with one another, how gender and culture affect ethical decision making, and familial coping with grief and the experience of loss.

REFERENCES

1. B. J. Bowers, Family Perceptions of Care in a Nursing Home, *The Gerontologist, 28*, pp. 361-368, 1988.
2. E. M. Brody, Parent Care as a Normative Family Stress, *The Gerontologist, 25*, pp. 19-29, 1985.
3. E. Shanas, Social Myth as Hypothesis: The Case of Family Relations of Old People, *The Gerontologist, 19*, pp. 3-9, 1979.
4. L. Thompson, Contextual and Relational Morality: Intergenerational Responsibility in Later Life, in *Aging Parents and Adult Children*, J. A. Mancini (ed.), Lexington Books/D. C. Heath, Lexington, Massachusetts, 1989.
5. M. S. Moss and S. Z. Moss, The Death of a Parent, in *Midlife Loss: Coping Strategies*, Sage, Newbury Park, California, 1989.
6. A. E. Scharlach and K. L. Fredriksen, Reactions to the Death of a Parent during Midlife, *Omega, 27*:4, pp. 307-319, 1993.
7. T. D. Hargrave and W. T. Anderson, *Finishing Well: Aging and Reparation in the Intergenerational Family,* Brunner/Mazel, New York, 1992.
8. G. A. Hughston, V. A. Christopherson, and M. J. Bonjean (eds.), *Aging and Family Therapy: Practitioner Perspectives on Golden Pond*, Haworth Press, New York, 1989.
9. P. Boss, W. Caron, and J. Horbal, Alzheimer's Disease and Ambiguous Loss, in *Chronic Illness and Disability*, C. S. Chilman, E. W. Nunally, and F. M. Cox (eds.), Sage, Newbury Park, California, 1988.
10. C. N. Nydegger, Family Ties of the Aged in Cross Cultural Perspective, *The Gerontologist, 23*, pp. 26-32, 1983.
11. E. M. Brody, *Women in the Middle: Their Parent Care Years*, Springer, New York, 1990.
12. *Webster's Encyclopedic Unabridged Dictionary of the English Language,* Portland House, New York, 1989.
13. I. Boszormenyi-Nagy and B. Krasner, *Between Give and Take: A Clinical Guide to Contextual Therapy*, Brunner/Mazel, New York, 1986.
14. S. Selig, T. Tomlinson, and T. Hickey, Ethical Dimensions of Intergenerational Reciprocity: Implications for Practice, *The Gerontologist, 31*, pp. 624-630, 1991.
15. E. Stone, *Black Sheep and Kissing Cousins: How our Family Stories Shape Us*, Penguin Books, Markham, Ontario, 1988.
16. I. Boszormenyi-Nagy, The Context of Consequences and the Limits of Therapeutic Responsibility, in *Familiar Realities: The Heidelberg Conference (41-51)*, H. Stierlin, F. B. Simon and G. Schmidt (eds.), Brunner/Mazel, New York, 1987.
17. B. J. Collopy, Autonomy in Long Term Care: Some Crucial Distinctions, *The Gerontologist, 28* (supp.), pp. 10-17, 1988.
18. A. Horowitz, B. M. Silverstone, and P. Reinhardt, A Conceptual and Empirical Exploration of Personal Autonomy Issues within Family Caregiving Relationships, *The Gerontologist, 31*, pp. 23-31, 1991.

19. D. Callahan, What Do Children Owe Elderly Parents, *The Hastings Centre Report*, Briarcliff Manor, New York, pp. 32-37, April 1985.
20. D. Callahan, *Setting Limits: Medical Goals In an Aging Society*, Simon and Schuster, New York, 1987.
21. C. Baines, P. Evans, and S. Neysmith, *Women's Caring: Feminist Perspectives on Social Welfare*, McClelland and Stewart, Toronto, 1991.
22. C. Gilligan, *In a Different Voice: Psychological Theory and Women's Development*, Harvard University Press, Cambridge, 1982.
23. N. Nodding, *Caring: A Feminine Approach to Ethics*, University of California Press, Berkeley, 1984.
24. R. Blieszner and J. Mancini, Enduring Ties: Older Adults' Parental Role and Responsibilities, *Family Relations, 36*, pp. 176-180, 1987.
25. W. J. Jarrett, Caregiving within Kinship Systems: Is Affection Really Necessary?, *The Gerontologist, 25*, pp. 5-10, 1985.
26. S. H. Matthews and T. T. Rosner, Shared Filial Responsibility: The Family as the Primary Caregiver, *Journal of Marriage and the Family, 50*, pp. 185-195, 1988.
27. T. A. Rando, *Grief, Dying, and Death: Clinical Interventions for Caregivers*, Research Press, Champaign, Illinois, 1984.
28. W. F. Forbes, J. A. Jackson, and A. S. Kraus, *Institutionalization of the Elderly in Canada*, Butterworths, Toronto, 1987.
29. F. Herz Brown, The Impact of Death and Serious Illness on the Family Life Cycle, in *The Changing Family Life Cycle*, B. Carter and M. McGoldrick (eds.), Gardner Press, New York, 1988.
30. N. Gordimer, L, U, C, I, E, *Granta, 44*, Penguin Books, Markham, Summer 1993.
31. L. Giat Roberto, *Transgenerational Family Therapies*, Guilford Press, New York, 1992.
32. I. Boszormenyi-Nagy and G. Spark, *Invisible Loyalties*, Brunner/Mazel, New York, 1984.
33. M. Bowen, *Family Therapy in Clinical Practice*, Jason Aronson, New York, 1978.
34. S. Minuchin, *Families and Family Therapy*, Harvard University Press, Cambridge, 1974.
35. L. Braverman (ed.), *A Guide to Feminist Family Therapy*, Harrington Park Press, New York, 1988.
36. E. J. Rosen, *Families Facing Death*, Lexington Books/D. C. Heath, Lexington, Massachusetts, 1990.
37. W. Worden, *Grief Counseling and Grief Therapy*, Springer, New York, 1982.

BIBLIOGRAPHY

Greenberg, V. E., *Your Best Is Good Enough*, Lexington Books/D. C. Heath, Lexington, Massachusetts, 1989.

Hooyman, N. R. and Lustbader, W., *Taking Care of Your Aging Family Members*, The Free Press, New York, 1986.

Silverstone, B. and Hyman, H. K., *You and Your Aging Parents: A Family Guide to Emotional, Physical, and Financial Problems*, Pantheon Books, New York, 1989.

CHAPTER 8

Anticipating the Death of an Elderly Parent

*Miriam S. Moss and Sidney Z. Moss**

Death of an elderly parent is not a common area of interest for bereavement counselors or death educators. Yet it is a death experienced by most of us as we go through middle age. Parents rarely die violently from disasters, suicides, or accidents. Rather, they generally die as a result of chronic health conditions. Their deaths are ordinary, but they are not ordinary people, they are our parents.

Our focus in this chapter is on the adult child's anticipation of the death of an elderly parent. We have two primary goals: first to view bereavement as a multidimensional process that may begin before death, and second to explore a number of themes of anticipation, with particular attention to the over-arching dialectic of holding on and letting go.

Victor Marshall (Chapter 5 in this volume) has highlighted some of the major themes in the interface between gerontology and thanatology. The question remains, however, why is there so little clinical and theoretical research focusing on the death of older persons when 72 percent of all persons who die in the United States are age sixty-five and over [1]? Why have there been so few behavioral scientists who have examined the interface between gerontology and thanatology (exceptions include [1-6])?

There are no clear social and cultural rules about how to respond to the death of an old person. We suggest that in large part bereavement

*This chapter was supported by National Institute on Aging grant # ROIAG08481.

for an old person's death is disenfranchised [6]. Doka has defined disenfranchised grief as grief in response to "a loss that is not or cannot be openly, publicly mourned , or socially supported" [7, p. 4]. Deaths of old persons are often thought to be fair and timely and less socially disruptive than other deaths. In general, they may be seen as the least tragic of deaths [8, 9]. There is a "pecking order of death" [3], suggesting that it is the normal order of things when the oldest die first. Several researchers have reported that parent death evokes less intense emotional responses than death of a spouse or a child [10-12], and that the process of bereavement for an old person may be devalued with fewer funeral rituals [11]. This does not, however, deny the significance of the impact of parental death. The death of older persons is more likely anticipated than the death of younger persons [11]. Most old people who die have surviving children and we focus here on the meaning for these children of parental death, particularly as it is anticipated. Anticipation of death should not be equated with the duration of an illness, or forewarning of the loss, or learning of a terminal diagnosis [13, 14]. Even when death occurs after a long illness, family members often see it as sudden or unexpected. Bass and his colleagues found that one-third to one-half of persons whose older relative had died after a long-term illness perceived the death as sudden and/or unexpected [15].

A clear operational definition of suddenness has not been agreed upon by clinicians or researchers. Some measure of duration of forewarning has been most commonly used [16, 17]. In spite of terminal diagnoses, increasing frailty, repeated crises and remissions, when death arrives it is often perceived as unexpected. There is an almost universal sense of shock at the moment that death occurs. The impact of finality, irreversibility, and the ending itself combine to make the experience, as one fifty-eight-year-old daughter said of her eighty-nine-year-old mother's death, "an expected surprise." In light of the frequency of death of old persons from long-term health problems, it may be that sudden death may have different connotations and meanings across the life course. Anticipation includes the daughter's response both to the actual loss evoked by the mother's increasing impairment and to potential future losses in the mother's functioning [18]. In addition, there is the future loss resulting from the death itself.

For the past three years we have been listening to women as they describe their bereavement for their elderly mothers who have recently died. Throughout their bereavement they have emphasized interrelated processes of holding on and letting go. Rando has suggested that anticipatory grief involves three "contradictory" demands of "simultaneously holding on to, letting go of, and drawing closer to the dying patient" [14, p. 14]. In our study, daughters make significant efforts to hold on and thus to maintain continued strong ties with their mother. They do this through their feelings, attitudes, and behaviors as they affirm the parent-child bond. Often they give increasing attention to her during her final stage of life. At the same time, daughters increasingly think about letting go of the tie as they recognize the likelihood of their mother's death and see themselves as living in the world after their mother has died. Anticipating and preparing for a mother's death involves a process of letting go. Central to anticipation are hope (a wish to hold on to mother) and threat (a fear of the need to let go) [9]. Neither hope nor threat are involved in the same way after the reality of the death.

These two seemingly contradictory processes of holding on and letting go are reflected in each of the four themes which have been central for many daughters as they explored with us the meaning of their mother's death. The focus here is on the themes as they are played out in anticipation. First, the death of a parent is seen as a normative experience; second, bereavement involves both an affective and cognitive component; third, it is a transitional experience; and fourth, it is an active process. As we review the four themes it will become clear that they are not discrete but rather they are interwoven. Further, they tend to occur regardless of the specific context of the mother's death. We will examine ways in which each theme may be expressed by the daughter before the end of her mother's life. The daughter's anticipation of mother's death may be heightened if a mother becomes frail or confused, if a serious medical condition is diagnosed or becomes life threatening, or when a mother moves to a nursing home. Although there is considerable uncertainty in anticipation of the death, these themes recur with sufficient saliency to warrant our exploration.

METHOD

The study which forms the basis of our discussion focuses on the process of bereavement of 103 middle-aged daughters for their recently deceased widowed mothers. Volunteer participants responded to a range of media and other outreach (e.g., to clergy and health care professionals, as well as staff of hospices, nursing homes, and funeral homes). By design all of the daughters were married, their ages ranging from forty to sixty-eight (average 52). The mothers were all widowed, over age sixty-five (average age 81). Thus, the daughters were dealing with the death of their last parent. All but two of the respondents were white. Although there was a considerable range in

Table 1. Anticipation of Mother's Death ($n = 103$)

1. Were there times before she died when she was distant or withdrawn from you?
     YES: 40%
     NO: 60%

2. Toward the end of her life, did you sometimes feel you were distant or withdrawn from her?
     YES: 32%
     NO: 68%

3. Before she died did you have thoughts about the possibility of her death?
     A lot: 51%
     Somewhat: 26%
     A little: 15%
     Not at all: 8%

4. Did you and she talk together about her dying?
     A lot: 14%
     Somewhat: 22%
     A little: 31%
     Not at all: 33%

5. Before she died, did your mother ask you to do any particular things after she died?
     YES: 44%
     NO: 56%

6. Did you say goodbye to her in any way before she died?
     YES: 59%
     NO: 41%

7. Did she say goodbye to you in any way before she died?
     YES: 29%
     NO: 71%

8. Before she died did you worry about how she would handle her future decline or the process of dying?
     A lot: 31%
     Sometimes: 36%
     Seldom: 15%
     Never: 18%

Table 1. (Cont'd.)

9. Before she died did you think about how you would adjust and manage
   after she died?
   A lot: 17%
   Sometimes: 38%
   Seldom: 27%
   Never: 18%

10. Some people say they began to grieve *before* their mother died. Was that
    true for you?
    A lot: 43%
    Somewhat: 19%
    A little: 17%
    Not at all: 21%

11. Before she died were there times when you were so overcome with grief
    that you couldn't say or do some of the things you would have liked?
    YES: 33%
    NO: 67%

---

education and income, the average socio-economic status was middle
and upper middle class (mean education 14.9 years; mean family
income $56,000). Qualitative interviews, lasting an average of 3.5
hours were held three to six months after the death, and then again one
year later. In addition, after each interview daughters completed a
structured self-administered questionnaire. The items in the self-
administered questionnaire that focused on anticipation are presented
in Table 1.

One of the major limitations of this research is that all of the data
were collected after the parent's death. Thus, our understanding of
anticipation is based solely on retrospective information. Prospective
data from an entirely different study that included forty-nine
daughters and daughters-in-law who were family caregivers for their
elder will be mentioned briefly because the data indicate some con-
gruence with our retrospective material.

The study sample was selected to include four groups representing
discrete contexts of the mother's death: heavy caregiving daughters
who lived with their mother and gave intensive hands-on care for at
least six months prior to death; distant daughters who had lived at
least one and a half hour's drive away for more than a year prior to the

death; local light caregivers, daughters whose mothers were relatively independent, or were being cared for by another adult child; and nursing home daughters whose mothers had resided in a local nursing home for at least six months.

MAJOR THEMES IN ANTICIPATION

Bereavement is a Normative Experience

Parental loss may be thought of as the most normative and on-time loss for middle-age children. Looking back over the twentieth century there is evidence that parent death is now taking place at a later age [19]. Winsborough predicted that mother's death is increasingly occurring over a smaller segment of the life span, and thus becoming more of a normative middle-age transition [20]. He estimated that half of the women born in 1970 will experience their mothers' deaths in the fifteen-year period between the ages of forty-nine and sixty-four; while for the 1920 cohort one-half experienced mother's death over a period of twenty-four years from ages thirty-five to fifty-nine.

The daughters describe bereavement for their mother as part of the natural order of life and death. As a child grows up, she may have a sense of anticipatory orphanhood [21], thinking that in some future time she will live beyond the death of her parents. The basic expectation is that parents die before their children.

Middle-aged persons commonly are confronted by the deaths of older persons in their network: other family members, as well as friends of their parents and parents of their friends. In this study, each of the daughters was selected because she had already experienced the death of her father—an average of seventeen years earlier.

At the same time that the daughter begins to let go as she anticipates the death of her mother, she also holds on to her lifelong connection with her mother. We question Weiss' assumption that most people relinquish parents as attachment figures in adolescence, and subsequently see the parent as part of their past selves, not their current selves [22]. We suggest that although most adult children live in separate households and have created families of their own, their bonds with a parent last a lifetime and are maintained as highly significant reciprocal attachments through the life course [23-25]. The tie is non-substitutable and continues regardless of the quality of the relationship. A living parent is often seen as offering security and protection, continuity, affirmation of self and family to his or her adult children. The meaningful associations across the decades continue in spite of intermittent separations and conflict. Daughters tend to expect continuity of the tie. They wish to maintain a sense of family closeness which can provide comfort and support. They can further legitimize holding on to mother by using a complex calculus for her life expectancy based on the age of other family members who had lived considerably longer.

Bereavement has Strong Affective and Cognitive Components

Bereavement, as defined here, involves more than the emotional responses of grief, such as sadness, crying, anger, and yearning. There are also aspects of anticipation in which daughters experience shifts in their cognitive view of mother, their relationship with her, with their family, and with their world. Wortman and Silver [26] and Janoff-Bulman [27] stress evaluative components of bereavement and the importance of shifts in world view when basic assumptions such as the continuity of life are challenged. Themes of holding on and letting go are intertwined in the emotional and cognitive aspects of bereavement. Next we explore three aspects of bereavement which have both cognitive and affective components: partial grief, adaptation anxiety, and the illusion of invincibility. Each has a strong emotional component, as well as a process of cognitive reframing in which the perceptions of the mother and her situation are modified to create a new reality.

Partial Grief

Daughters are alert to and often monitor their mothers' physical and mental decline. Both daughter and mother tend to see these declines as deficits and losses. Little is known about whether and how they communicate their perceptions or their feelings. Daughter's emotional response to the decline is termed partial grief [18, 28]; it reflects the daughters' deep sadness and helplessness in witnessing their mothers' decline. Many daughters reported that they had been more upset about their mothers' increasing frailty than about the prospect of the death.

In the self-administered questionnaire, four-fifths of the daughters indicated that they began to grieve before their mother died, and more than half of these reported that they did it "a lot." This grief may have been largely partial grief. It was significantly correlated with the mother's poor functioning in activities of daily living ($r = .28, p < .01$) and with her poor cognitive capacity ($r = .34, p < .001$). The intensity of her emotional response was measured by the question, "Before she died were there times when you were so overcome with grief that you couldn't say or do some things you would have liked?" One-third said "yes." This uncontrolled grief beforehand was not correlated with the level of the mother's physical or cognitive functioning beforehand; rather it was associated with adaptation anxiety (see the following).

Mrs. Schmidt's experience exemplifies partial grief. Her seventy-six-year-old mother died after more than three years in a nursing home. She had suffered from multiple sclerosis for fifteen years, and was diagnosed with cancer just two months before she died. She had much pain and suffering throughout her adult life.

> Mrs. Schmidt: I'd been living with, you know, just this gradual deterioration, you never knew when all of a sudden things were just different—now she couldn't walk anymore. Just two years ago she was still using a wheelchair, and now she couldn't use a wheelchair. Now she can't move her feet. Now she can't lift her legs. Now she can't get out of bed. Now she has liver cancer . . . It's just the whole pattern over the years had been this gradual deterioration, so in the last year it was just another piece of it. And it was just sort of this inevitable progression that you knew you were going to have to face. . . . I couldn't stand to see her suffering the way she was. It was because I couldn't stand to watch what she was going through and to think that she really had to go through that.

> Interviewer: Would you say you did any kind of grieving before she died?

> Mrs. Schmidt: I think I was grieving for her a long time . . . like watching the living dead.

Mrs. Schmidt exemplifies many daughters who sought to preserve the image of a maximally functioning mother. They were repeatedly confronted with the reality of decline and the need to reframe their perceptions.

Adaptation Anxiety

Adaptation anxiety includes both the daughter's anxiety about how her mother will handle her dying and anxiety about how she, the daughter, will adjust to the mother's dying and death. These multiple anxieties involve a complex combination of holding on and letting go. Over two-thirds of the daughters indicated they worried "sometimes" or "a lot" about how their mother would handle her future decline or the process of dying. Daughters tended to describe their mother as wanting to maintain her habitual daily functioning, holding on to life as she knew it. If the mother had evidenced serious decline, the daughter was sometimes anxious about whether later she would be able to reclaim her preferred image of the more competent vital mother.

Some daughters, such as Mrs. Schmidt previously, expressed empathy with their mothers' feelings about their decline and suffering. Daughters, however, generally emphasized their own feelings before their mother died, and few daughters spontaneously spoke at length about how they thought their mother felt about dying and death. The daughters' emphasis on the self, rather than the other, might be a manifestation of the process of letting go and distancing oneself from the dying mother.

While their mother was still alive, many daughters had begun to project themselves into the uncertain future, and to think of the ways in which they would respond to her dying and her death. Lebow has stressed the role of uncertainty in anticipating the death of a close family member [29]. Several daughters told us that they anticipated being devastated and possibly falling apart when their mother died. The work of worrying is analogous to wives' anticipation and rehearsal for widowhood [30, 31]. One daughter whose mother had declined precipitously, was caring for her at home. She became increasingly anxious about how she would handle the stress of having her mother die at home. She was relieved that her mother was hospitalized for the last few days of her life.

As daughters draw on their own strength and resourcefulness in meeting the challenges and crises which occur during the parent's decline, daughters can feel more competent and less anxious about their mother's dying and death. Thus, over time a daughter can change her view of her own coping capacity. In spite of their anxiety, the daughters generally perceived their mother as strong and able to handle her decline. This could have tempered the daughter's anxiety.

Illusion of Invincibility

Daughters often see each remission by their mother as confirmation of their mother's strength and her ability to survive subsequent life crises. This illusion of the mother's invincibility is a way in which the daughter holds on to the bond. When a mother expresses a wish to let go and die, the daughter not infrequently encourages her to live longer, stressing her mother's past strengths and reinforcing mother's wish to participate in some future family event.

Medical diagnoses play a major role in determining the holding on and letting go process. If a mother lived longer than the doctor had predicted, the daughter often attributed this to the mother's inner strength and determination to live. The mother's invincibility is further fostered when daughters who were heavy caregivers felt that their mothers' longevity resulted in part from the daughter's support of her strengths. Mothers with advanced dementia may fit Boss et al.'s [32] model of ambiguous loss, that is, as being physically present but psychologically absent. To reduce the ambiguity, daughters tend to affirm every shred of mother's competence and mental clarity. They may rely on more positive perceptions by others, and hold on to hope for improvement. Holding on and letting go is an interactive process between the mother and daughter. It occurs in partial grief when the daughter as well as the mother holds on to the signs of the mothers' competency; each reluctantly letting go as the mother declines. In adaptation anxiety, each may simultaneously worry about her own and the other's ability to handle the stresses of holding on and letting go that occur toward the end of life. Both mother and daughter tend to protect each other as they hold on to the illusion of invincibility in the face of decline and increasing closeness to death. The interactive process goes beyond the dyad to include other family members and caregiving professionals.

Bereavement is Perceived as a Transition

The daughter's bereavement is a process, not an event. It may begin with the anticipatory orphanhood of earlier years, and continue to be fueled by multiple changes in the life of the parent, the life of the child, and shifts in the family. Bereavement continues through the period of dying and after the death. Rather than describing their experiences as going through stages of grief until they finally recovered, daughters tended to describe themselves as moving from the reality of having a living mother to the reality of having a dead mother. Anticipating the mother's death involves a synthesis of stability and change. It is a process of integrating the past with the present, and "constructing a future in the light of the past and the present as it is being defined" [33, p. 165]. In this process the daughter manages both to hold on and to let go of her mother.

Uncertainty generally occurs whether or not the onset of an illness or condition was sudden or gradual, whether or not there had been a clear diagnosis of terminal illness or a prediction of life expectancy [34]. There is much uncertainty about how, where, when and with whom a mother will die. There may be a sense of being in limbo, of not having control [35]. Each daughter wants to avoid feeling overwhelmed and helpless in the face of the mother's decline and death. Remissions and relapses only serve to complicate the processes of both holding on and letting go for both daughter and mother. Anticipation of the last part of life and of the death itself is set in the context of this uncertainty.

Albert and Kessler have suggested that an ending involves continuity, positive affect, review of the past, and evaluation of the timing of the ending [36]. As the daughter approaches the ending of her mother's life these same processes are part of the transition: there is a wish to maintain the tie with the living parent, a desire to hold on to the positive aspects of the relationship, a strong urge to share reminiscences, and a recurrent consideration of the rightness and fairness of the pending death as the daughter experiences partial grief and anticipates a future after her mother has died.

Daughters reported a process of continuing to integrate the meaning of their mother's potential death into many aspects of their lives. Central to the process of transition are shifts in perception of the mother, of the relationship, of the likelihood of the death, and of the future after the death. These shifts, in effect, create a different sense of reality. This seems to be largely what daughters spoke of when they described having been prepared for the loss. Within this cognitive process themes of holding on and letting go are inseparable. Daughters simultaneously see their mother as a person who will continue to live and as a person who is dying.

One-third (32%) of the daughters said that toward the end of their mother's life they sometimes felt distant and withdrawn from her, and somewhat more (41%) said there were times when the mother was distant or withdrawn from the daughter. In a Philadelphia Geriatric Center study of family caregiving the same anticipatory grief questions were asked of forty-nine women who were currently caring for their parent or parent-in-law living in a nursing home, and roughly similar responses were found (36% and 52% respectively). In our parent death study the mother was seen as more distant and withdrawn when she had lower physical ($r = .27, p < .01$) and cognitive functioning ($r = .27, p < .01$). Mothers were also seen as more distant when the daughters reported that there was a poorer quality of the mother-daughter relationship ($r = .44, p < .001$). Although two-thirds of the daughters (68%) did not feel they were distant or withdrawn from the mother toward the end of her life, most (92%) had recurrent thoughts of the mother's death. This is congruent with attachment theory which stresses that fear of loss is associated with holding on. It does not fit with Freudian theory, which suggests that anticipation of death is characterized by decathexis and withdrawal [37].

At the same time that the daughter may recognize that her mother has little time to live, she continues to anticipate future interactions and family occasions with the mother, and tries to maximize the quality of the end of the mother's life. Daughters often increase their time spent with their mother and try to be available to her.

Some daughters viewed death as a means to reunite family members. They suggested that death is a way in which the mother could rejoin not only the father and other deceased relatives, but could offer her a promise of future reunion with the daughter. After the death, most (81%) of the sample agreed with the statement "I think I will be with my mother again some day."

In addition to holding on to their mother, daughters were also letting go. Daughters often anticipated the loss of protection, support, companionship, affirmation of self, loss of a family home, and saw the future as threatening the continuity of their sense of self and of family. If long term future plans were made, they increasingly tended to exclude the mother. Combined with the daughter's feelings of sadness, helplessness, and guilt, as well as anxiety about possible family conflicts over inheritance, can be anticipation of relief from constant concerns and caregiving burdens. Additional expressions of letting go are evidenced by the mother's wish to die, as well as the daughter's wish that death would end her mother's suffering.

Mrs. Ibsen illustrates a number of aspects of transitions which can occur toward the end of a mother's life. Her mother, with a history of cancer and heart problems, had lived in an assisted-care facility for three years. Mrs. Ibsen described changes in the way she saw her mother, herself, and their relationship.

Interviewer: In the last year or so were you aware of your mother aging?

Mrs. Ibsen: Yeah. She was eighty-four, she had turned eighty-four in March and had the congestive heart failure the summer before, and we didn't think she was going to pull through that. I was very aware of her aging. . . . I was conscious of her going to die over these last couple of years . . . Before the congestive heart failure she had kind of bouts of heart, cancer, these last few years. . . Mother's aging process made me feel like I feel old. . . Then you see your own mortality.

As she saw the shortening of her mother's remaining life, she made efforts to understand her mother better and to draw closer to her. This was a transitional process that emphasized strengthening of the bond.

> Mrs. Ibsen: We really worked out stuff so that we had a really wonderful relationship by the time she died. . . . And [my kids] also experienced that [improved relationship] because they remembered her when they were little, how really critical and rigid she was; and by the time she died they were much closer. . . . I think I was very much aware of what was going on, so I think there was a lot of preparation for her death. A lot of talking about it on her part too. I mean just [her] planning of the funeral, and knowing what the significance of death was for her. . . . I don't think her death came as such a tragic shocking event. We were pretty well prepared for it on one level. As much as you can be in talk.

Bereavement is an Active Process

Attig has highlighted the significance of the survivor's active role in the bereavement process [38]. Daughters in our study emphasized their active roles in anticipation of the death. They thought about the goals of terminal care for their mother, and frequently made specific decisions about treatment. Often daughters encouraged other family members, particularly siblings, to join in decision making. Some daughters whose mothers had intractable pain or who had lost all quality of life wished for their mothers' death, primarily for their mother's relief but also for their own.

Daughters often report that they had begun to plan the funeral and to think about the distribution of the mother's property (particularly her house) and special keepsakes they would treasure. Becker suggests that this anticipatory behavior can be adaptive for adult children who face the likely death of their parent [39].

A daughter also has the opportunity to decide in what ways she will communicate her concerns and feelings with her mother. Two-thirds of the daughters (64%) talked with their mother about her dying. Conversely, over one-third indicated that they never talked with her about it. Some daughters were not willing to think about the likelihood of their mother's death. Twenty-three percent of the daughters said they rarely or never thought about their mother's pending death. Fourteen percent of the forty-nine women in the Philadelphia Geriatric Study whose parent was currently living in a nursing home replied similarly.

Mrs. MacIntire told us that as her mother became more frail, her mother periodically brought up her pending death. Her mother offered to show Mrs. M how to cook some of Mrs. M's favorite foods; but Mrs. M refused. Her mother also wanted to talk about her funeral plans and things she wished to have done after her death, but Mrs. M suggested instead that her mother talk with another daughter about these topics, which she did. Although 60 percent of the daughters in our study did say goodbye to their mother in some way before her death, only half that proportion (29%) said that their mother had in some way said goodbye to them.

Mrs. Ibsen, whom we discussed above, spoke about this:

Interviewer: Before she died were you able to say things to her which made the ending seem right for you?

Mrs. Ibsen: Yeah, I was able to say that I loved her, and that I was glad I was there. What I didn't say was that I, we didn't talk about her dying right then . . . Partly I think it was because . . . the moments that she was awake were so precious and she was so grateful for us to be there, it was more of just being there for her in the present. And there wasn't really the opportunity or the time to talk about this [because it] may be the last moment. I mean we shared our love and she was grateful that we were there, but we didn't have time really to say goodbye.

Daughters often told us that they had hoped their mother's death would be an easy one, with minimal pain or discomfort, and with family present. When the death occurred after extended intense suffering with no family present the daughters spoke of feeling deprived of a rightful ending, and were guilty that they had not acted in some way to help their mother have a better death. Thus, some daughters felt that their behavior was important to their dying mother's well-being.

Very often daughters make active choices as they balance personal and cultural forces. Daughters often control their expression of feelings in response to the cultural disenfranchisement of grief for the death of an old person.

In addition, a daughter controls her expression of sadness and upset in order to protect her mother, as well as other family members from feeling her pain in addition to their own. It can be difficult for a daughter to express her sadness when her mother tells her not to cry for her, particularly when her mother says that she wants to die. Additionally, daughters often want to look strong for themselves and their family to demonstrate that they can cope with the impending loss. Expressions of grief and talk about adaptation anxiety are often considered signs of weakness, and the daughter may feel she is threatened with loss of control. Alternately, the display of grief is felt as an active affirmation of love, and siblings are particularly sensitive to the frequency and depth of each others' responses to the anticipated death of the parent. There are subtle ways in which each judges the adequacy of the other's reactions to bereavement, e.g., as expression of guilt, deep affection, or shallow concern.

Thus, a daughter repeatedly makes decisions explicitly or implicitly as to how she will behave while anticipating the death: how and with whom she will express her feelings, thoughts, and behaviors over time. As a daughter anticipates the death of her mother she often actively takes on family roles which her mother is no longer able or willing to carry. Daughters may become the family matriarch, the central family kin-keeper [40], or take on the role of mentor or source of emotional support.

DISCUSSION

It is important to understand the meaning and the impact of the death of elderly persons. If educators and researchers focus on relatively rare, often sudden deaths and largely ignore the normative experiences of death in old age, we may be saying to ourselves, to the lay public, and to the academic community that death in old age is not worthy of our attention. We suggest that although deaths of old persons are commonplace, they are no less important than deaths of young persons, untimely deaths, or deaths due to disasters. Educators and researchers have an obligation to increase their understanding of and sensitivity toward ordinary normative deaths.

Much clinical and behavioral research has been done to examine the interface of anticipatory grief and grief after the death (see for example [4, 13, 26, 41]), and there have been a plethora of conflicting findings. The focus of this chapter has been to explore multiple interrelated themes of anticipation of the death of an elderly mother. We would expect that each of these themes in anticipation could be differentially associated with a range of bereavement reactions after the death. Elsewhere, we have delineated seven interrelated aspects of bereavement after a mother's death: grief or emotional upset, somatic response, acceptance, sense of personal finitude, guilt, and ties with the deceased mother including a sense of comfort in thoughts of the deceased, and an expectation of future reunion [42]. Each of these aspects has elements of both holding on and letting go.

Some research has found an association between a higher level of stress prior to death and more intense emotional reaction after death (for example [4, 15]). In line with this, we might expect that greater adaptation anxiety and more intense grief in anticipation of the death would be associated with more intense expression of grief after the death. If there is a continuity in holding on to the mother over the period of bereavement, we may expect that more holding on prior to the death as reflected in feeling less distance may be followed by greater comfort in thoughts of the parent after the death. Thinking about the mother's potential death can be an inner rehearsal laying the groundwork for later acceptance. If there is continuity in letting go, then we would expect that more anticipatory thoughts about the death beforehand would be associated with greater acceptance of the death after it occurs. Our preliminary quantitative analyses support each of these expectations. In later qualitative analyses we will further explore the association between the processes of bereavement before and after death.

We suggest that the characteristics of the process of bereavement for parental death in old age are applicable to the process of bereavement for other family members over the life course. Anticipation of parental death may offer an alternative model for our thinking about the anticipation of the death of other family members, particularly of spouses or persons with chronic conditions or life threatening illnesses. We have described how death in old age tends to be anticipated. Even with younger persons there is often a progression of illness which leads to the anticipation of death. Holding on and letting go are integral to the entire process of anticipation. The four themes we have discussed: bereavement as a normative experience; bereavement involving both affective and cognitive components; bereavement as a transition; and bereavement as an active process, may be relevant to anticipation of deaths across the life course.

REFERENCES

1. United States Bureau of Census, *1990 Census of Population and Housing: Summary Population and Housing Characteristics*, U.S. Government Printing Office, Washington, D.C., 1990.
2. R. A. Kalish, The Social Context of Death and Dying, in *Handbook of Aging and the Social Sciences* (2nd Edition), R. H. Binstock and E. Shanas (eds.), Van Nostrand Reinhold, New York, pp. 35-61, 1985.
3. R. Kastenbaum, Death and Bereavement in Later Life, in *Death and Bereavement in Later Life*, A. H. Kutscher (ed.), Charles C. Thomas, Springfield, pp. 27-54, 1969.

4. D. A. Lund, Conclusions about Bereavement in Later Life and Implications for Interventions and Future Research, in *Older Bereaved Spouses*, D. A. Lund (ed.), Hemisphere Press, New York, pp. 217-231, 1989.
5. V. W. Marshall and J. A. Levy, Aging and Dying, in *Handbook of Aging and the Social Sciences* (3rd Edition), R. H. Binstock and L. K. George (eds.), Academic Press, New York, pp. 245-260, 1990.
6. M. S. Moss and S. Z. Moss, Death of the Very Old, in *Disenfranchised Grief: Recognizing Hidden Sorrow*, K. Doka (ed.), Lexington Books, Lexington, Massachusetts, pp. 213-227, 1989.
7. K. J. Doka, Disenfranchised Grief, in *Disenfranchised Grief: Recognizing Hidden Sorrow*, K. Doka (ed.), Lexington Books, Lexington, Massachusetts, pp. 3-11, 1989.
8. R. A. Kalish and D. K. Reynolds, *Death and Ethnicity: A Psychocultural Study*, University of Southern California Press, Los Angeles, 1976.
9. P. C. Rosenblatt, *Bitter, Bitter Tears*, University of Minnesota Press, Minneapolis, 1983.
10. J. M. Leahy, A Comparison of Depression in Women Bereaved of a Spouse, Child, or a Parent, *Omega, 26*, pp. 207-217, 1992-93.
11. G. Owen, R. Fulton, and E. Markusen, Death at a Distance: A Study of Family Survivors, *Omega, 13*, pp. 191-225, 1982-83.
12. C. M. Sanders, A Comparison of Adult Bereavement in the Death of a Spouse, Child and Parent, *Omega, 10*, pp. 303-322, 1979-80.
13. R. Fulton and D. J. Gottesman, Anticipatory Grief: A Psychosocial Concept Reconsidered, *British Journal of Psychiatry, 137*, pp. 45-54, 1980.
14. T. A. Rando, Anticipatory Grief, in *Encyclopedia of Death*, R. Kastenbaum and B. Kastenbaum (eds.), Oryx Press, Phoenix, pp. 12-17, 1989.
15. D. M. Bass and K. Bowman, The Impact of an Aged Relative's Death on the Family, in *Gerontology: Perspectives and Issues*, K. F. Ferraro (ed.), Springer, New York, pp. 333-356, 1990.
16. C. M. Parkes and R. S. Weiss, *Recovery from Bereavement*, Basic Books, New York, 1983.
17. M. S. Stroebe, W. Stroebe, and R. O. Hansson, *Handbook of Bereavement: Theory, Research, and Intervention*, Cambridge, New York, 1993.
18. N. C. Kowalski, Anticipating the Death of an Elderly Parent, in *Loss and Anticipatory Grief*, T. A. Rando (ed.), Lexington Books, Lexington, Massachusetts, pp. 187-199, 1986.
19. P. Uhlenberg, Death and the Family, *Journal of Family History, 5*, pp. 313-320, 1980.
20. H. H. Winsborough, A Demographic Approach to the Life Cycle, in *Life Course: Integrative Theories and Exemplary Populations*, K. W. Back (ed.), Westview Press, Boulder, pp. 65-77, 1980.
21. M. S. Moss and S. Z. Moss, The Death of a Parent, in *Midlife Loss*, R. A. Kalish (ed.), Sage Publications, Newbury Park, California, pp. 89-114, 1989.
22. R. S. Weiss, Loss and Recovery, *Journal of Social Issues, 44*, pp. 37-52, 1988.

23. G. O. Hagestad and B. L. Neugarten, Age and the Life Course, in *Handbook of Aging and the Social Sciences* (2nd Edition), R. H. Binstock and E. Shanas (eds.), Van Nostrand Reinhold, New York, pp. 35-61, 1985.
24. A. S. Rossi and P. H. Rossi, *Of Human Bonding*, Aldine de Gruyter, New York, 1990.
25. L. E. Troll, *Family Issues in Current Gerontology*, Springer, New York, 1986.
26. C. Wortman and R. C. Silver, Reconsidering Assumptions about Coping with Loss: An Overview of Current Research, in *Life Crises and Experiences of Loss in Adulthood*, L. Montado, S. H. Filipp, and M. J. Lerner (eds.), Lawrence Erlbaum, Hillsdale, New Jersey, pp. 341-365, 1992.
27. R. Janoff-Bulman, *Shattered Assumptions: Toward a New Psychology of Trauma*, Free Press, New York, 1992.
28. M. Berezin, Partial Grief for the Aged and Their Families, in *The Experience of Dying*, E. M. Pattison (ed.), Prentice Hall, Englewood Cliffs, New Jersey, pp. 279-286, 1977.
29. G. H. Lebow, Facilitating Adaptation in Anticipatory Mourning, *Social Casework, 57*, pp. 458- 465, 1976.
30. R. O. Hansson, J. H. Remondet, and M. Galusha, Old Age and Widowhood, in *Handbook of Bereavement*, M. S. Stroebe, W. Stroebe, and R. O. Hansson (eds.), Cambridge University Press, New York, pp. 367-380, 1993.
31. J. H. Remondet and R. O. Hansson, Rehearsal for Widowhood, *Journal of Social and Clinical Psychology, 5*, pp. 285-297, 1987.
32. P. Boss, W. Caron, S. Joral, and J. Mortimer, Predictors of Depression in Caregivers of Dementia Patients: Boundary Ambiguity and Mastery, *Family Process, 29*, pp. 245-254, 1990.
33. J. S. Tyhurst, The Role of Transition States—Including Disasters—in Mental Illness, in *Symposium on Preventive and Social Psychiatry*, Walter Reed Army Institute of Research, U.S. Government Printing Office, Washington, D.C., pp. 149-172, 1957.
34. B. Raphael, *The Anatomy of Bereavement*, Basic Books, New York, 1983.
35. J. Rolland, Chronic Illness and the Family Life Cycle, in *The Changing Family Life Cycle*, B. Carter and M. McGoldrick (eds.), Gardner Press, New York, pp. 433-456, 1990.
36. S. Albert and S. Kessler, Processes for Ending Social Encounters: The Conceptual Archaeology of Temporal Place, *Journal for the Theory of Social Behavior, 6*, pp. 147-170, 1976.
37. S. Freud, Mourning and Melancholia, in *Complete Psychological Works*, Standard Edition, Vol. 14, J. Strachey (ed.), Hogarth Press, London, pp. 243-258, 1957.
38. T. Attig, The Importance of Conceiving of Grief as an Active Process, *Death Studies, 15*, pp. 385-393, 1991.
39. M. R. Becker, *Last Touch: Preparing for a Parent's Death*, New Harbinger Publications, Oakland, California, 1992.
40. C. J. Rosenthal, Kinkeeping in the Familial Division of Labor, *Journal of Marriage and the Family, 47*, pp. 965-974, 1985.

41. T. A. Rando, A Comprehensive Analysis of Anticipatory Grief: Perspective, Processes, Promises, and Problems, in *Loss and Anticipatory Grief*, T. A. Rando (ed.), D. C. Heath, Lexington, Massachusetts, pp. 3-37, 1986.

42. M. S. Moss, S. Z. Moss, R. Rubinstein, and N. Resch, Impact of Elderly Mother's Death on Middle Aged Daughters, *International Journal of Aging and Human Development, 37*, pp. 1-22, 1992-93.

CHAPTER 9

The Ethics of Hope and Denial

Stephen R. Connor

> Death then, being the way and condition of life, we cannot love to
> live if we cannot bear to die.
>
> —*William Penn*

This chapter derives from experiences, both successful and unsuc-
cessful, while working with hospice patients facing impending death. I
am a pragmatic researcher—I examine the phenomena of what we do
with patients that seems to work well. I then try to explain it in ways
that help us to understand how to help them more effectively.

ETHICS OF TRUTH TELLING

The following principles were adapted from the psychosocial work
group of the International Work Group on Death, Dying and Bereavement, in *Statement of Assumptions and Principles Concerning
Psychological Care of Dying Persons and their Families*, which I
chaired [1].

1. Right to choose whether or not to be told you are dying.

This can be a controversial statement because many people feel that
patients must be informed of their condition, particularly if it is a
diagnosis such as AIDS where lack of knowledge can have important
consequences for the rights of others. However, the ethical arena we
are concerned with in this chapter is bedside ethics. Individuals may
request that they not be told of news that they may not be able to face.
Good communication techniques suggest that caregivers ascertain

whether the patient wants to be told bad news at any particular time [2].

2. Right to be told you are dying.

If one asks for the truth then it should be given. When giving bad news it is necessary that accurate information be provided. Nowadays there is a general belief that patients have a right to be told their diagnosis. However sometimes there is no disclosure of prognosis in the belief that it will somehow harm the patient—this should be avoided.

3. Right to acknowledge or not acknowledge that one is dying.

After a patient is told that he/she is dying it is their business to do with that information whatever they must. To expect that we all would or could face reality the same way shows a lack of respect for the complexity of the human experience.

DENIAL THEORIES

Sigmund Freud was the first to identify the psychological mechanism of denial [3]. He referred to it as "disavowal of reality" [3, p. 184]. He elaborated on this in his analysis of fetishism where an inanimate object is transformed into a sexualized object through a process of substitution [4, pp.152-157]. Later he expanded the concept of denial from a necessarily psychotic process to that which could be neurotic, affecting only one current in the mental life [5, pp. 144-207]. His daughter Anna saw denial as the necessary component to all defenses [6].

Psychoanalytic thinkers generally view denial as a defense mechanism in a fixed intrapsychic structure that is relatively unchanging; a primitive defense reverted to when reality becomes too painful or harsh.

In contrast Haan compared both defenses and coping processes [7]. She viewed defenses as rigid, compelled, reality distorting, and undifferentiated. Coping processes were flexible, purposive, reality-oriented, and differentiated. The coping corollary to denial was concentration [7, pp. 372-378]. Kübler Ross was the first to discuss how denial is used by the terminally ill [8]. In her view denial was an adaptive coping mechanism. A first stage reaction of the dying person, a kind of shock absorber replaced later by other stages.

Lazarus and Golden has written about both the positive and negative functions of denial [9]. Denial like processes have both beneficial and harmful consequences. His emphasis on cognitive appraisal helps us understand how reactions to serious illness vary from individual to individual. Reactions depend on how the person evaluates the significance of what is happening to their well-being.

Weisman wrote extensively about denial [10]. He saw denial as a process that changed with time. To understand this he proposed three degrees of denial: *First order denial,* denial of the primary facts of the illness; *second order denial,* denial of the significance or implications of the illness; and *third order denial,* the inability to believe that the illness will result in death.

DENIAL RESEARCH

I recently conducted a research project which examined the effects of psychosocial intervention on denial in terminally ill patients [11]. During the research, subjects who used denial-related coping techniques were assessed before and after a psychosocial intervention to measure its' effects on denial and defensiveness. A control group (not receiving the intervention) was also assessed.

It was proposed that people using denial are on an intrapsychic/ interpersonal continuum. Intrapsychic deniers deny in order to preserve a weak ego. They are who we think of when we think of someone as "being in denial." Those who cannot handle and deny obvious reality. Though most patients doubt the accuracy of their diagnosis and prognosis or refuse to believe it at first, the person who steadfastly ignores reality, refuses to cooperate in treatment, and cannot be reasoned with is probably manifesting intrapsychic denial [12, p. 164]. It is suggested that psychosocial intervention with this group is not therapeutic.

Interpersonal deniers, in contrast, are often open with you about their prognosis but when family members or physician are around act optimistic (for example, by discussing future plans). They may feel guilty about the burden they believe they are placing on others, are fearful of rejection, or of harming others by being open. Unfortunately not being open is what leads to abandonment and prolonged emotional distress. All this at a time when the presence of loved ones is needed most. Psychosocial intervention with these people is helpful especially if aimed at opening communication with important people in the patient's life.

Obviously people don't fit neatly into these categories. Patients may be at different points on this continuum at different times. Psychosocial intervention should always be aimed at meeting people where they are. Often people cannot benefit from psychosocial intervention until they've had some time to gain emotional distance and develop more adaptive coping abilities. The kind and amount of intervention should be guided by their responses.

Hope

The presence of hope in a dying patient is thought by some to be an expression of denial. This is not the case. Of course there are different kinds of hope besides hope for cure. There is hope for absence of pain and suffering, absence of conflict, and hope for caregivers you can trust. Some patients need to believe that there is even a small possibility that life will continue. To insist that all of a dying person's hope is unrealistic seems cruel. We cannot predict the future and have all known patients who have gotten better in spite of a very grave prognosis.

Probably the most common reaction seen in dying patients is ambivalence. This is characterized by a fear of dying and at the same time a desire for release from all the indignities surrounding the death. This may seem contradictory but the coexistence of opposing feelings is a particularly human trait.

When responding to dying patients who maintain hope it is helpful to support them by continuing to be hopeful while at the same time trying to help them face the reality of impending death. A common problem patients experience is the belief that they must maintain a positive attitude and not allow any "negative" thoughts to enter their minds (by negative is meant any thought that might acknowledge the possibility of dying). Many around the dying person exhort the patient not to think negatively when they bring up their fears and feelings. This is a way of avoiding the dying person's painful feelings and isolates the patient. Acknowledging the reality of death does nothing to hasten death. While being hopeful doesn't necessarily lengthen life, it can often help make the dying process more bearable.

Case Examples

The following case examples illustrate the concepts that I have addressed, the corresponding psychosocial intervention that was used, and its effect.

Case #1 — The first case involved a sixty-eight-year-old female with widespread metastatic breast cancer diagnosed in 1988. At hospice intake she and her supportive husband were unable to discuss the progression of her illness. It was notable that in both of their family histories their fathers had died before their mothers. The husband had recently suffered a minor heart attack and the patient was fearful of aggravating his condition by talking openly about her own medical prognosis. She protected him from emotional distress and felt guilty about the possibility of dying before him.

Intervention

Who would it be most effective to intervene with? Since the denial involves the communication between husband and patient, it would be best to work with the couple. During an interview I was able to get them to talk openly with each other about her worsening condition. There was no more need for a conspiracy of silence. Their fears and self blame were openly expressed. They were able to drop their defensiveness and stop using denial. This was a case where denial was clearly an interpersonal phenomena and even a single intervention was quite effective.

Case #2 — The second case involved a forty-six-year-old male patient with metastatic melanoma. He had a supportive wife and three young daughters. A few years earlier, he led a very active life and had just returned from a one-year trip with his family on a boat in the Caribbean. He was an engineer who was working on a very important engineering breakthrough. Since diagnosis he had been part of a wellness group and believed that keeping a positive attitude would help him get well.

At hospice intake he was too weak to get out of bed but was unable to confront the possibility of dying. His wife understood that he was dying and recognized the need to support him and help with his care. She was concerned that his daughters would have a very hard time if they were unable to say goodbye to him before he died. His mother-in-law had come to help but her husband had recently died.

Intervention

This family needed more time to come to grips with the severity of the situation. Psychosocial intervention with the wife first and then the patient was most effective. The wife was receptive to intervention and was then able to help the patient to confront the reality of his impending death. During the first meeting with the patient it was clear that he did not want to acknowledge the reality of his condition even though he could not get out of bed. He was encouraged not to rush but to take his time. His need for hope was acknowledged. I worked with his wife for two days to help her prepare her husband to accept help. We focused on how he could acknowledge the possibility of death while simultaneously maintaining his hope for recovery.

In the final two weeks of his life he was able to finally express some sadness and some acknowledgment that he had been blaming himself for his illness. He was able to talk openly with his daughters and to say goodbye. This had to be done rather rapidly as he only lived another three weeks. In this case the intervention had to be paced to his readiness, though there was definitely an interpersonal basis to the continued avoidance.

Case #3 — The third case involved a sixty-four-year-old female patient diagnosed with lung cancer two and a half years earlier. Her family was dysfunctional and in conflict. Her husband and her two middle children (in their 30s) were still living at home. There was a lot of anger and a complete unwillingness to acknowledge her prognosis. The death of one of their female children at two years old had never been addressed or resolved. Their main motivation for hospice admission was because of a financial need for medication coverage. The patient's husband was an alcoholic who was openly hostile and frequently in conflict with his only surviving daughter.

Intervention

This family was generally resistant to psychosocial intervention. Our plan was to support their defenses and not to intervene with the apparent denial. We needed to set clear limits but not to confront. We expected to have to tolerate some displaced anger. In this case denial served a more intrapsychic function. While the patient was hospitalized a social worker who was not part of the team attempted to work with the patient in an attempt to help her face her prognosis. Her husband misinterpreted this communication and became very angry. He physically threatened the social worker and we had to intervene with the police. This episode brings to light the importance of developing a psychosocial treatment plan that all caregivers are aware of and follow. In this case it was best not to intervene psychosocially. The family never acknowledged that the patient was dying.

CONCLUSION

My experience leads me to believe that patients often test us to see how fearful or anxious we are about death. If we are too quick to reassure or comfort them and cannot tolerate their distress they avoid burdening us with their true feelings. When we become models for them, showing them that it is possible to talk openly about death without being overwhelmed, it increases the possibility that they will be able to face their own mortality.

The following points are important to remember:

- People have a right to decide how much information they want to hear and acknowledge.
- Denial functions as a protective mechanism and can be adaptive or maladaptive.
- Hope is essential for the emotional survival of some patients.
- Most people face death with ambivalence.
- We must accept patients where they are—in terms of their ability to face reality.
- Psychosocial intervention can be done if paced to the patient's reality.
- To be effective we must be able to tolerate patient's emotional pain and our own anxiety about death.
- When working with dying patients, we need to remember that it is their death, not ours and we must not impose our own needs on their experience!

REFERENCES

1. Psychosocial Work Group of The International Work Group on Death, Dying & Bereavement, A Statement of Assumptions and Principles Concerning Psychological Care of Dying Persons and their Families, *Journal of Palliative Care*, 9:3, pp. 29-32, 1993.
2. R. Buckman, *How to Break Bad News: A Guide for Health Care Professionals*, University of Toronto Press, Toronto, 1992.
3. S. Freud, *The Loss of Reality in Psychosis and Neurosis*, Standard Edition XIX, 1924.
4. S. Freud, *Fetishism*, Standard Edition XXI, 1927.
5. S. Freud, *An Outline of Psycho-analysis*, Standard Edition XXIII, 1940.
6. A. Freud, *The Ego and Mechanisms of Defense*, Hogarth Press and the Institute of Psychoanalysis, London, 1948.
7. N. Haan, Coping and Defense Mechanisms Related to Personality Inventories, *Journal of Consulting and Clinical Psychology*, 29:4, pp. 373-378, 1965.
8. E. Kübler-Ross, *On Death and Dying*, Macmillan, New York, 1969.
9. R. S. Lazarus and G. Golden, The Function of Denial in Stress, Coping and Aging, in *Biology, Behavior, and Aging*, E. McGarraugh and S. Kiesler (eds.), Academic Press, New York, 1984.
10. A. D. Weisman, *On Dying and Denying: A Psychiatric Study of Terminality*, Behavioral Publications, New York, 1972.
11. S. Connor, Denial in Terminal Illness: To Intervene or Not to Intervene, *The Hospice Journal*, 8:4, pp. 1-15, 1992.

12. S. Connor, Denial, Acceptance and Other Myths, in *Dying, Death, and Bereavement: Theoretical Perspectives and Other Ways of Knowing*, I. Corless, B. Germino, and M. Pittman (eds.), Jones & Bartlett Publishers, Boston, 1994.

CHAPTER 10

Ethical Service to the Family Before and After Bereavement

Colin Murray Parkes

It is generally assumed that members of a society should act together to prevent suffering. When we know something is harmful we have a duty to prevent or minimize that harm. It is unethical to ignore child abuse, to do nothing to prevent the spread of infection, or to permit an industry to poison our water supply.

Bereavement has been shown to have dangerous effects on physical and mental health. We cannot prevent bereavement but research shows two ways to mitigate its damaging effects:

1. By *anticipatory guidance*. There is good reason to believe that unexpected and untimely deaths are more damaging than deaths that have been anticipated [1].
2. By *counselling and offering support to the bereaved* [2, pp. 1450-1454; 3, pp. 179-188].

If this is the case we might agree that it is unethical to withhold such services yet, there are several reasons why it is still only a minority of people who receive help either before or after bereavement. Are there ethical objections to the universal provision of pre- and post-bereavement help?

ETHICAL SERVICE TO FAMILIES BEFORE BEREAVEMENT

One can argue that since most of us will one day be bereaved we should all receive pre-bereavement counseling or education. Most married women will one day be widows. In the face of a life event of this magnitude we might expect that every married woman who reaches the age of forty would be advised to sign up for a widowhood course. Yet, there are no schools for widows. Why not?

I suspect that there are two reasons, on the one hand we don't like to plan for the things we dread. We feel as if we could prevent them from happening by not planning for them; and on the other hand when you start to anticipate (or look forward to) something you may begin to "look forward" to it. It is definitely *not* considered ethical to "look forward" to the death of your husband. Freud pointed out the danger of death wishes. When you wish someone dead and they die you become a psychological killer. It is as if the thought was father to the act. For the same reason we do not buy coffins until after people are dead. If it is unethical to preplan for the demise of one's spouse is there anything than *can be done* as death approaches?

The dying patient's troubles will soon be over, those of the family may just be beginning. It follows that *the unit of care when someone is dying should be the family, which includes the patient*, rather than just the patient with the family as an optional extra which we take on if we have time. I would state this as a *first principle of terminal care*. But there are five powerful reasons why it is seldom followed because of:

1. Conflicts with the principle of *confidentiality*.
2. The tendency of the *family* to *deny their own needs* in favor of the patient's.
3. The need of medical and nursing staff to take *control* of the patient away from the family.
4. The lack of an established financial or operational *contract* to provide care for anyone but the patient.
5. The recognition of the *magnitude or complexity of the problems faced by the family*.

1. Confidentiality

Much has been written about the patient's "right to know" but what of the family? Legally the family has no *right* to know anything unless the patient chooses to tell them or gives permission for them to be told. This code of confidentiality bars doctors from revealing information about a patient and this can cause serious problems, as doctors who treat patients with AIDS are only too aware. This is not the place to discuss ethical issues surrounding the risk of cross-infection with AIDS, but there is a separate set of issues that concern the communication of a bad prognosis particularly when a patient is afraid that the family will then guess at the diagnosis. In such cases, clearly we should attempt to persuade the patient to allow disclosure. Since the family is bound to find out eventually, it is better to face the issue now, while there is still time to help them to come to terms with its implications, than to wait until it is too late to clear-up the psychological mess.

I recently found myself trying to deal with the consequences of non-disclosure in a family in which a woman who had recently divorced her husband failed to warn her three teenage children that she was dying of cancer. The anger and confusion that this caused in the children led to enormous complications for her family who were then faced with the problem of providing proper care *after* her death. Here it was the patient who thought she was protecting her children by keeping things secret.

In other cases it is the caring staff who excuse their silence on the grounds that any communication with the family would involve a breach of confidentiality. Psychiatrists are often guilty of this. Those whose preferred way of working is on a one-to-one basis may seal themselves off in a little world with the patient and pass on nothing to the family or the other members of the medical/nursing team.

2. Family Denial of Need

As long as the patient is alive his or her needs will tend to take preference over those of the family. "Don't you worry about me, doctor," they say, "He's the one who comes first." To care for the patient, family members often make great sacrifices: giving up jobs, neglecting their friends and children, and ignoring their own needs for medical or psychological care. This self-sacrifice is an important way of making restitution for any previous lack of care. Soon it will be too late to say "I'm sorry." By showing such devotion they ensure that, in the future, they can say "We did everything possible."

Doctors and nurses sometimes fail to understand the importance of this caring. "You go home," we say, "There's nothing more you can do." If the family takes our advice and the patient dies during the night they may never forgive themselves. Similarly we often take away the opportunity to care from the family. "Don't you worry," we say, "We'll look after him." Again, we deprive the family of their last opportunity to make restitution for any previous lack of care.

So part of the caring for the family is allowing them to care for the patient. But there is a limit. Perhaps the patient still has a long time to go, the family members are exhausted, and at the limit of their resources and strength. They may need permission to take a day off, acknowledgment that they too have needs. If we are working closely with the family, plenty of opportunities will arise when we can meet their needs *as well as* those of the patient. The two do not *have* to compete.

3. Medical and Nursing Control

Often families are made to feel like intruders in a foreign territory. We decide when they should be allowed to visit, as if visiting were an inconvenience and an interruption to the important work of curing the patient. Family members who ask questions may be treated with suspicion, Are they questioning *our* judgment?" If the family ask to see a doctor, they may become a nuisance, sometimes they seem to be competing, they may even imply that they know better than we do how to treat the patient as if he were *their* patient not *ours*.

One might expect this to become less of a problem when it is clear that a cure is no longer possible and the doctors have failed in their primary function. Yet, it is precisely because the doctor has failed that he is put on the defensive. Far from recognizing the special importance of the family at this time and relinquishing his or her claims, the doctor may become distant and attempt to regain control by an excessive and inappropriate use of power. The only ethically defensible position for the professional to take when someone is dying is to admit that we are powerless to prevent death and to use what little power we have left to support the family and to relieve distressing symptoms in the patient.

When the family feels that they can cope, we should encourage the patient to go home and when they can't cope at home we should help them to cope in the hospice or hospital. In either setting our position is in support of them. In a sense we become part of this family.

4. Contracts

All of this is very different from the traditional contract by which a patient buys a service from a doctor. It is time that planners faced the implications of a system in which the family are both carers and cared for. A health care system that is concerned with prevention and care rather than cure requires a contract which offers this type of service. Anything else is misleading and may be a confidence trick and ethically undefensible. Support implies very much more than the provision of accurate information to the family. It requires a thorough sophisticated assessment of family needs and a plan for family support, which is followed up and monitored as required.

5. Magnitude of the Problems

Staff whose work brings them close to people who are dying are often in awe of the enormous trauma that is being inflicted on the patient and their families. We have only an inkling of the implications of the death and of the intensity of the emotions to which it gives rise. Death undermines the habits of thought and behaviors that have been built up over many years. It calls in question the meaning of much that people have taken for granted and raises existential and spiritual questions to which we have few answers. It may even cause us to look with apprehension at our own existence. Small wonder that carers back away and that family members feel lost and unprotected.

It follows that, if we are to expect staff to involve themselves in these awesome situations, they should have the training, the support, and the time to enable them to do it properly. We may not be able to prevent death but we can stand by the family at this time and help them, little by little, to confront the issues that arise.

These issues may be psychological, social, or spiritual and we need to be prepared to pay attention and to have faith that given time and support the family will transcend the most devastating of losses. This faith comes in part from proper training, which teaches us how people can come through the transitions in their lives and in part from whatever source of spiritual or existential meaning we have found in our own lives. Those who lack what used to be called "bottom" (a central core of purpose or direction in their lives), will find that they have no way to respond to the anguish of those whose life has lost all meaning.

Of course nobody can deal with more than one problem at a time and the proper response to an overwhelming wave of problems is not to try to solve them all simultaneously, but to recognize the impossibility of this and to break them down into "bite sized chunks." In this way we help to make the extraordinary ordinary and to re-establish a degree of control.

AN EXAMPLE OF AN ETHICAL FAMILY-ORIENTED SERVICE AT ST. CHRISTOPHER'S HOSPICE, SYDENHAM

St. Christopher's was opened twenty-seven years ago and was the first of the new-style hospices that have spread across the world. Because it has attracted students from many countries it has not remained static and is still, in my view, one of the best examples for organizing and structuring care for the dying and bereaved. Initial contact with hospice staff is usually made while the patient is still at home and the help is provided by the Home Care Team (nurses, doctors, and social workers who visit the home and provide support to patients and families). The nurses are expected to draw a genogram of the family and to inquire in a systematic way into their needs. The nurses' conclusions are recorded in a special section of the case notes—the "pink sheets." These include a family risk assessment which makes use of previous research to identify family members who are at special risk.

The social worker has prime responsibility for families and meets regularly with the rest of the team to discuss family problems. Most, but not all, patients are admitted to the in-patient unit of the hospice at some time. Often this is for pain control and many patients subsequently return home, but there are also many cases where the patient's presence at home is creating too much anxiety in the family who may fear that they will not be able to cope if the patient should die at home. Also, patients may have attended the Day Hospital where they had the opportunity to get to know and trust the staff of the hospice, consequently, they often prefer to be admitted as their condition deteriorates.

On the wards, patients receive close attention from the medical and nursing staff who also involve the family in the care at the bedside. In one research project, I found that 53 percent of patients had a family member at the bedside for six or more hours per day at St. Christopher's compared with only 9 percent of cancer patients who died in other hospitals in the vicinity. Relatives also spent more time talking to each other and were more likely to know the doctor's name [4, p. 517; 5, p. 120].

Family members are not intruders, neither are they "honored guests." They belong in the hospice which is, in a sense, an extension of the family. The statement which best distinguished St. Christopher's from other hospitals in the view of surviving family members was, "The hospital is like a family," which was agreed to by 90 percent of relatives of St. Christopher's patients as compared with less than 10 percent of relatives of patients dying in other hospitals.

In these circumstances it is hardly surprising that the general level of anxiety at St. Christopher's was very much lower than that of the relatives of patients who died elsewhere. The hospice provides a special room and coffee bar where relatives can relax when not on the ward. The wards are well equipped with space for relatives, both at the bedside and in separate sitting rooms, where they can meet the medical and nursing staff for private conversations. Most deaths are very peaceful with the family at the bedside.

When a death occurs the pink sheets are separated from the case notes and passed to the social worker. The risk assessment, which will already have been initiated, is completed in the light of all the information gleaned from the staff. On this basis bereavement follow-up is offered to about one-third of families. The counselors are all volunteers who have been carefully selected and trained for this purpose. They visit bereaved people in their homes about six to eight weeks after bereavement and provide whatever counseling is thought necessary. Most clients are seen four to six times. In addition, all bereaved families are invited to return to the hospice for a combined non-denominational religious service and social event where they meet again with the ward staff about nine months after bereavement. All are sent a remembrance card on the anniversary of the death. A minority are seen by a social worker or are invited to attend a special group. We have run groups for adult bereaved children, parents with young children, and for several other purposes. The benefits of the service have been established by systematic research [3].

There are, of course, many other types of services for the bereaved. Some of these are self-help or mutual support groups without any expert help. Unfortunately, I have come across several of these groups that have run into difficulties because of their lack of professional support. My preference is for a service in which bereaved people can work alongside professionals and trained volunteers. This model is the one adopted by Cruse, the foremost national organization for the bereaved in the United Kingdom. Cruse now has 180 branches and over 3,000 trained volunteer counselors, many of whom have themselves been bereaved. They not only provide counseling, but over the years, they have developed so much expertise in this area that they are now training doctors, nurses, and social workers.

Many of those who come for help and take advantage of the service end up as volunteers. And so the wheel comes full circle. Instead of dividing the world into doctors and patients, social workers and clients, we find people who have come through the fire of grief committing themselves to acquire the knowledge that will enable them to help others to do the same. In the end we are all in the same boat, it is in all our interests to create and support ethical service to the dying and bereaved.

APPENDIX I
CHECK LIST OF ETHICAL SERVICE TO THE FAMILY

I. Before Bereavement

Those who care for the families of patients with late stage terminal illness should ensure that:

1.1 A sophisticated assessment of family needs is made in every case in which a family exists and provided that the principal family members have no objection.

1.2 All nursing, medical, and social work staff are trained to draw a genogram (family tree), assessing family risk and provide support to families.

1.3 Details of family assessment and care are recorded in a special part of the notes.

1.4 All principal family members are informed in writing of the help that is available to them and of the fact that information may be recorded for the purposes of follow-up. Also, of their right of access to that information.

1.5 In all settings in which people are cared for as they come close to death, a pleasant room is provided in which communication between staff, patients, and families can be conducted in complete privacy.

1.6 Family care is part of the total package of care that is included in all contracts for payment of services to those with terminal illness. It should be described accurately in written or oral information given to them.

1.7 While strict confidentiality is maintained *within* the team, every effort is made to ensure that relevant information is shared with those members of the team who meet and support the family.

1.8 Recognize that family members have a right and, often, a need to provide as much care to the patient as is safe and appropriate. When the patient is in residential care (e.g., in a hospice/hospital) there is no restriction on visiting although family members may be encouraged to take a "day off" from time to time. The professionals see their primary role as being in support of the family and only take over when it is clear that the family cannot cope or is likely to do harm.

1.9 Attention is paid in the selection of staff to their own vulnerability and social supports. They need basic trust in themselves, others and ultimate meaning; these are reflected in a reasonable degree of self-confidence, respect for others, and a sense of purpose.

1.10 These attributes are maintained by means of a network of staff support from senior staff with appropriate training in psychology, social relations, and spiritual issues.

II. After Bereavement

Those who care for bereaved families should ensure that:

2.1 All meetings with newly bereaved people take place in a peaceful, quiet, and private environment where they will be free from interruption.

2.2 Persons requesting autopsy, transplant, or other special permissions from family members are properly trained for this and provide sensitive and appropriate information about the purpose of the intervention and feed-back about its consequences.

2.3 All persons likely to be traumatized by bereavement are given the opportunity to have their need for support assessed in a systematic and tactful way.

2.4 When possible this takes place before bereavement. In other cases it takes place as soon afterward as practicable given the sensibilities of the newly bereaved person.

2.5 All of those who ask for help or are deemed to be at risk are offered the help of an accredited counselor.

2.6 Counselors, who may be volunteers, are only accredited when properly selected, trained, and approved. Full accreditation follows satisfactory completion of a period of service under supervision.

2.7 Full information about reliable sources of help to the bereaved is given to all those likely to need them.

2.8 Counseling is offered to all those who are thought to need it whatever their ability to pay, race, color, sex, religious preference, or type of bereavement.

2.9 Training programs make trainees able to understand and respond with confidence to most of the needs of bereaved clients which result from bereavement. Programs also make counselors aware of the limits to their own competence and the need to consult others and to refer on those clients whose special needs require other types of expertise. Teaching should be conducted by properly qualified persons and should include a balance of didactic and experiential learning.

2.10 Whenever people are referred to other agencies for care a routine check is made to ensure that the care is given.

2.11 Services for the bereaved have the consultant backing of a psychiatrist, a social worker, and a chaplain or priest from each major denomination in the community served. Where appropriate some of the roles of the psychiatrist can be conducted by a psychologist.

2.12 Supervision by a properly trained and approved supervisor is provided regularly to all counselors.

2.13 Systematic records are kept of all meetings between clients and counselors, these are kept securely and are accessible only to staff directly involved.

2.14 All communication between clients and counselors is privileged and confidential within the caring team. Only in case of threatened suicide, murder or similar danger to others or if action is needed to obtain care for a mentally ill person is it justifiable to break confidentiality.

2.15 People are *not* selected as counselors if they have suffered a major bereavement within the last two years and those counselors who become bereaved cease to provide counseling to other bereaved people until they have been re-approved. Apart from this, experience of bereavement is not a reason for barring people from counseling unless it has given rise to unresolved problems, neither is it, on the other hand, an essential qualification.

2.16 A range of types of counseling (individual and group) are provided to meet the range of needs that exists in the population served. This takes into account the ethnicity and other demographic characteristics of that population.

REFERENCES

1. C. M. Parkes and R. S. Weiss, *Recovery From Bereavement*, Basic Books, New York, 1983.

2. B. Raphael, Preventive Intervention with the Recently Bereaved, *Archives of General Psychiatry, 34*, pp. 1450-1454, 1977.

3. C. M. Parkes, Evaluation of a Bereavement Service, *Journal of Preventive Psychiatry, 1*, pp. 179-188, 1981.

4. C. M. Parkes, Terminal Care: Evaluation of In-patient Service at St. Christopher's Hospice. II. Self Assessment of Effects of the Service on Surviving Spouses, *Postgraduate Medical Journal, 55*, p. 517, 1979.

5. C. M. Parkes and J. L. N. Parkes, "Hospice" versus "Hospital" Care—Re-evaluation After 10 Years as Seen by Surviving Spouses, *Postgraduate Medical Journal, 60*, p. 120, 1984.

CHAPTER 11

Confronting the Avoided Spot

Reverend Peter Hill

She had enjoyed the thrill of diving from the high tower on many occasions, but this time the dive went painfully wrong. Treading water in the old Manly harbourside enclosure, her body burning from the impact of a "belly-buster," my mother then in her late teens was acutely aware of the nature of the challenge: she could swim back to the promenade ladder, climb the tower and confront her fears, or retreat to the beach and possibly never dive again. She chose to dive.

CONFRONTING THE PAINFUL SPOT

Following a distressing and sometimes devastating event, there are those who instinctively know they must return to the "painful spot" and do so. Ten days after their daughter's death in the hospital's Intensive Care Unit—she had choked on a piece of meat—Ray and Janine[1] appeared at the entrance of the unit carrying a large basket of fruit for the staff. That took courage.

Barbara's twenty-year-old son had chosen Sydney's North Head to leap to his death. His body was recovered in the sea a week later. Prior to her eventual visit to the headland, Barbara had mentally constructed a "Wuthering Heights" fantasy of black jagged rocks and a restless boiling sea. However, on the day of her visit, accompanied by a friend, conditions were calm, sunny and benign; the whole episode proved to be immensely healing. So too for Graham, when he visited the impact spot where his son had died in a car crash. The torn bark

---

[1] Names have been changed to protect confidentiality.

149

and burnt grass were re-growing. Somehow nature's healing prompted the beginning of his own.

Yet many fail to return and find it increasingly difficult, almost impossible to do so, developing a very entrenched pattern of avoidance. For those who do eventually return, the occasion can become one of significant healing.

CONFRONTING THE AVOIDED SPOT

Over the past fifteen months, Dan, a policeman, had gone to extraordinary lengths to detour around the site, where he had been in attendance, following one of Australia's worst bus crashes. Over twenty people had died. Since that day when he had covered many mangled bodies, Dan's life had begun to disintegrate; particularly his marriage, health, and work—especially his relationship with colleagues. Not surprisingly Dan's eventual return triggered a massively cathartic reaction, but perhaps more surprisingly it evoked a memory long suppressed, enabling him to acknowledge the person with whom he was really angry. No longer did he need to alienate those who were closest to him. The change was immediate.

For Denise it was a maternity ward, avoided for twenty years— there is something about a geographic spot that "earths" all the internal confusion, fears, and distorted memories enabling the person to begin to deal with the crippling legacy that has followed the initial event. This was graphically true for Jan and Darryl who were orthopedic patients following the overturning of their truck. Jan in particular, was regularly terrorized by a nightmare wherein she found herself pinned beneath the truck, uncertain of the fate of her baby and fearing incineration before help could arrive. With the help of an ambulance officer we were able to locate the exact spot and on discharge from hospital, the visit unearthed lost items such as a can of hair spray and a child's toy. Part of the spontaneous ritual that followed included stones hurled at the offending wall that had arrested the progress of the truck: "You no longer have any power to terrorize me, for I have been back . . ."

Of course, it is not always possible or even appropriate to return to a specific location. Jenny, a minister's wife and formerly a nurse in London, was prepared to travel back to England to find the flat where some years before, she had stood by helplessly, while two intruders raped her flatmate. Jenny found another way to successfully confront her fears without the necessity of taking the trip. In the film "Prince of Tides," Savannah, a patient in a New York psychiatric ward, is in an acute state of psychosis. Barbara Streisand who plays the part of the psychiatrist, persuades Savannah's brother Tom to "be his sister's memory." For years the family had shared and guarded a terrible secret by a refusal to remember, and now in the telling of the story, Tom on his sister's and his own behalf, confronts the avoided spot.

However, so often it is the re-visiting of the avoided location that facilitates a new movement in the person's life. What is it that is so efficacious for providing a new momentum and healing? The present chapter is an attempt to understand better the dynamics of this process.

THE CLOSED LOOP
OF AVOIDANCE AND FEAR

We have noted that fear is more manageable when confronted early. The more protracted the avoidance however, the more exaggerated and entrenched is the fear. The "spot," both external and internal, that is associated with an anguishing episode, a violation or death, becomes entangled and overgrown with a mythology of now distorted memories and imaginings, and as a consequence, within the "victim's" life, it is invested with an enormously negative influence.

Christie had survived the wild sea three years before, but the off-duty policeman who attempted to rescue her had not. Christie, however, had not survived the bitter and condemning outburst of a spectator on the beach that day, who vomited over her the accusation, "You have no right to be alive. That man died because of you!" Is it any wonder that three years later, the unavoidable impression on meeting Christie was a face that exemplified frozen sadness. In many ways her life had stopped on the beach called "Tallows." So many like Christie have become emotionally petrified, calling to mind those citizens of ancient Pompeii whose bodies were forever fixed in the expression of that last moment as the volcanic ash engulfed them.

The post-resurrection account found in the Gospels seems to rather aptly express the loss of spontaneity and freedom experienced by many living victims: "The doors were locked because of fear." It is into this very situation that Jesus appears, confronting the cowed disciples with the "avoided spot" located in his hands and side. We might well wonder how many there are around us, living significantly crippled and tortured lives behind locked doors—people like George, a trained teacher, who could no longer teach because of the paralysis of anxiety, a legacy of the "family shadow" rarely ever mentioned. George's parents were Czech Jews who had "survived" Auschwitz.

It seems to be evident that there are numerous dysfunctions that accompany this closed loop of avoidance and fear. Among them are absorption with a past event and the detachment that is part of it: depression and even despair, entrenched grief, chronic and global anger, and a range of physical symptoms. The person has become truly "victimized."

THE COUNSELOR BECOMES AWARE OF AVOIDANCE

As the client unfolds her story the counselor may become aware of the long-term avoidance of a crash site (she has never been back), a hospital ward, beach, cliff top, photograph, name, cemetery, or any discussion within the family of a tragic event or deceased family member. And yet the very process that has commenced in counseling, may suggest a readiness, even if it be a hesitant and anxious readiness, to "return" to the avoided spot; a readiness to confront what has become "the monster."

It is this very terminology that John Marsden uses so graphically in his story of the child Alzire and the monster: "Alzire realised how much power the thing had drawn from her fear; how much fear had magnified its size. When she confronted it, she was surprised to see how small it really was" [1, p. 177].

THERAPEUTIC FACTORS

The impetus for healing that accompanies such confrontation involves a number of therapeutic factors. For example, upon realizing the impasse can be broken, hope begins to emerge and perhaps hope more than anything else, provides the needed momentum for change. Like a spring thaw, the pack ice begins to break up. While despair has a tendency to paralyze, hope energizes. It is this very juxtaposition that is so evident in one of the major transitions in the life of ancient Israel recorded in Isaiah 40. Addressing these exiled people who felt forgotten and abandoned by their God [2] and who had lost their "song" [3], the prophet arrests their attention: "Those who hope in the Lord will renew their strength. They will soar on wings as eagles; they will run and not grow weary, they will walk and not grow faint" [4].

Frequently where a death has occurred, the client's non-acceptance is portrayed in an inability (or better, a "refusal") to mourn, thus maintaining a fantasy that the deceased person is still alive. When the avoided spot is confronted (be it guilt, anger, a regret, or "disembodied" grief), the person is freed at last to relinquish the lie and make the transition from imploded grief to an open expression of that grief.

SEPTIC ANGER

It would seem that the more we counsel persons who have sustained major and crippling losses and bereavements, violations and injustices, the more we find ourselves working with their anger. The flip side of immobilizing fear that has rendered the person a perpetual victim, is anger. Anger that is covertly or overtly directed toward the driver of the other car, the rapist, parent, spouse, doctor, and of course, the person's God.

Herein lies a particular problem, at least within the Church, but not exclusively so: Christians often have difficulty acknowledging and dealing with anger and tend to resort to a range of euphemisms which in themselves are a form of avoidance. Presumably it is acceptable to be "annoyed" or "sad" but not angry. Cartoon character Hagar the Horrible and companion Lucky Eddy seem to exemplify a somewhat similar dilemma, when on one occasion finding themselves up to their waistlines in water, Hagar gives vent to the terrifying realization, "It's quicksand! Don't Panic!" In the following frame having descended to their armpits Hagar continues, "And don't struggle," whereupon Lucky Eddy now riveted with terror and up to his chin in water asks, "Is it okay to worry?"

Is it okay to be angry? Frequently the counselor will find himself or herself facilitating and validating the open and honest acknowledgment of anger and even rage. As the story is told, the arousal of the counselor's own anger can be very permission-giving; the problem sometimes being that many victimized persons (for example a molested child) had no ability at the time to recognize their own anger, let alone express it and as a consequence in many instances, have turned it on themselves and thus travel, or limp through life perceiving themselves to be unlovable and even "trash." Their acknowledgment and appropriate expression of anger can be an enormously empowering experience. It can be one of the therapeutic milestones toward liberation from the past event. The counselor recognizing this may find herself in a celebratory mood at this breakthrough, as the long-time victim begins to emerge from his defensive world [5]. However, there is another issue we wish to address: what we ultimately do with our anger seems in large measure to determine our quality of life, health, relationships, and overall spirituality.

The loss of two young children had soured Rebecca's life and left her angry toward a God who was not to be trusted. Following a good deal of working through these issues, the happy day arrived when she announced that she had forgiven God. Rebecca's subsequent life change and service toward other bereaved parents, have overwhelmingly indicated the healing reality of those words. There is then, clearly a difference between "getting angry" and "being angry" as a chronic stance toward life; a sort of "over-against" attitude.

The apostle Paul seems to draw this distinction and yet implies the possibility of a choice being available when he says, "If you are angry, be sure that it is not a sinful anger. Never go to bed angry—don't give the devil that sort of a foothold" [6]. Anger over some past event, now granted a permanent resident status within our life, undergoes a nasty metamorphosis. It becomes septic, putrefied and fly-blown, and is more accurately identified as resentment, hostility, hatred, and bitterness [7, p. 14f]. The person becomes victim twice over: victim of the original hurt she sustained and now also victim of her own choice. She has perhaps unwittingly "entertained not an angel," but a devouring beast.

Yet it is this very choice that is implied by the apostle's words concerning anger, that offers hope. There does remain a choice. In giving the person responsibility for the now putrefied state of an old anger, the implication is that it can be transcended. To put it another way, "It is not so much what happens to us, but what we do with what happens to us," that finally determines the way we make our passage through life. Could this be what the apostle means elsewhere when he says that we can be "more than conquerors through Christ who loved us" [8]? One need not be the perpetual victim permanently saddled with the stinking corpse of old hurts. *No Longer a Victim* was the title of Cathy Ann Matthews' first book, herself a victim of childhood sexual abuse.

But is this not to beg one of life's big questions? How does a person transcend deep and grievous wounds, violations, and betrayals? How does one transcend the septic anger that entrenches the original event in heart and mind? How??

There can only be one word when all is said and done—"forgiveness!" But what a loaded word, especially in the present context. Certainly forgiveness is so much more than "a word," for when this choice is made, it so often is the end result of a long and sometimes bitter struggle. Cathy Ann Matthews again, powerfully puts words to that struggle in her later book, *Breaking Through*.

Revenge is mine: I've earned it,
through all the years of suffering
from the evil abuse in my childhood.
But it is not sweet.
To contemplate it gives me no pleasure.
It eats at my very being.
Anger and hatred fill my heart with pain,
my eyes with coldness.

I have cause for them all,
even self-destroying bitterness.
They are justified, right and proper.
I was terribly wronged.

Yet where is the joy?
Where the longed for release?
Why am I still enslaved
by the pain from my childhood?
There is no freedom in hating
It does not affect the offender.
It eats up the one who is hating,
and heaps more sorrow on sorrow.

In what then lies my release?
Anger, revenge have failed
to ease my endless aching
and stop it stifling my soul.
The answer, "You need to forgive them,"
seems futile, weak, ineffective.
The apparent foolishness of forgiveness
led to Christ's death on a cross.
How can the act of forgiving
defuse my anger and suffering?
Overcome my ceaseless strivings,
give me an inner peace?
I don't know how forgiving
washes away the dirt of hating,
leaving me clean and peaceful,
freed from desire for revenge.
A miracle lies in forgiving.
What wonder it works in my soul!
Such pain it removes, then by giving,
God fills my being with love [9, p. 224f].

Elizabeth O'Connor similarly has no doubts concerning the central necessity of forgiveness in the healing of hurts:

Forgiveness is integral to letting go. We are bound to the people we cannot forgive. Holding even a small grudge takes up space in the soul and captures the energy needed for moving on. To bless the people who are our oppressors, is the only way to heal the wounds they have inflicted and to break the chains that bind us [10, p. 52].

Forgiveness is too big and grand to be encapsulated in any one definition. Some things however, that could be said about it are these:

- It is unnatural: our sense of fairness tells us that people should pay for their wrongs.
- It is totally realistic about a wrong-doing.
- It does not assume the high moral ground.
- It is an initiative, while hate and vengeance are reactions.
- It is love's antidote to hate.
- It stops the endless round of vengeance and hurting; it is a choice to live with an "uneven score."
- It is "love's toughest work and love's biggest risk. If you twist it into something it was never meant to be it can make you a doormat or an insufferable manipulator."

Forgiveness lies at the center of the Christian Gospel and herein we grasp its breadth and depth, as well as its cost. If then, forgiveness is the means of transcending septic anger, human forgiveness is itself an experience of transcendence for it arises out of the liberating discovery that we ourselves have been forgiven by God. Law and grace (the requirement and the empowerment) are juxtaposed in the words "Forgive one another as in **Christ God forgave you**" [11].

Far from the pale and distorted caricature that forgiveness is sometimes dismissed as—a weak and soft option where supposedly the victim is being asked to excuse the perpetrator, a contemptible notion—forgiveness has a grandeur about it that commands our respect.

It is not difficult to understand the hesitancy and even resistance toward the notion of forgiveness, held by some therapists working in an area such as that of sexual abuse. The person may well have found her way into this area of work because of an experience of victimization she herself has sustained. However it ought to be said, that if her own still septic anger is one of the driving factors in the therapists work, then this will likely compromise her effectiveness when it comes to dealing with, and the healing of anger in the life of a client. In fact the question may not be raised, for to do so could be seen as a betrayal; a blurring of the inviolable boundary between perpetrator and victim.

We need to be reminded of O'Connor's words: "We are bound to the people we cannot forgive." Forgiveness properly understood does not negate the validity of anger and rage as a response to violation and injustice; it transcends them and frees the person to move on.

Joanne had been sexually abused by two older brothers over a period of eight years. She had learned effectively the lesson of self-hatred. Following the breakdown of a disastrous marriage, she found faith and then learned that "Christians must forgive!" Joanne had lived for three years with the supposition that she had forgiven, and yet the "must" of forgiveness for a self-hating and sometimes suicidal victim, was yet another burden imposed on her, another form of oppression. It was only as Joanne was enabled to acknowledge and direct her hatred toward her offending brothers, that she realized her "forgiveness" was but an external conformity. It was not real, for at that point she had no choice. Paradoxically, it was the owning of her hatred toward her brothers that provided Joanne with a real choice. She could now continue to hate or she could forgive. In time she made the momentous shift toward the latter.

ACCEPTANCE

One final question: In confronting the avoided spot we have observed the significant impetus this so often occasions for healing: "What is it, in essence, that has taken place within the life of the person?"

The word that seems to fit best is "acceptance." For a decision to face the avoided reality, is a decision at least in embryo, to come to terms with or to make peace with the wounding event. For months, years and even a lifetime "It" has lodged as an undigested mass within, frequently accompanied by some somatic expression such as a lump or a pain that never goes away.

At last the process has begun, to digest the mass, passing the waste products that have attached themselves to the initial injurious experience, while integrating the good. A process of expulsion and integration which after all is true of any good digestive system.

Acceptance is a facing of our shadow side and acknowledging that it has been and is part of our life. It is granting the alien citizenship:

> A man who took great pride in his lawn
> found himself with a large crop of dandelions.
> He tried every method he knew
> To get rid of them. Still they plagued him.
> Finally he wrote the Department of Agriculture.
> He enumerated all the things he had tried
> and closed his letter with the question:
> "What shall I do now?"
>
> In due course the reply came: "We suggest
> you learn to love them."

The conclusion that followed: "My lawn, of course, was ruined. But how attractive my garden became" [12, p. 65ff].

Author Henri Nouwen employs the word "hospitality" when we "make space for events in our lives, rather than fearfully shutting them out" [13]. Richard Foster writes,

> We must not deny or ignore the depth of our evil, for, paradoxically, our sinfulness becomes our bread. When in honesty we accept the evil that is in us as part of the truth about ourselves and offer that truth up to God, we are in a mysterious way nourished. Even the truth about our shadow side sets us free (John 8:32) [14].

Acceptance acknowledges that while we cannot change the circumstances, we can change our attitude toward those circumstances. Such acceptance is not a passive resignation, "Oh well I'll have to accept it won't I," which is tantamount to capitulation to external pressures. It is, rather, an active and internal choice and can only be real when the person is ready. Any attempt to push a client into "acceptance" which amounts to a facade of change (for example, "I learned that Christians must forgive, therefore I forgave them"—see Joanne previously) is therapeutic imperialism which is manipulative, pointless and worse, it is dangerous because it overlays hostility with hypocrisy and therefore leaves the person self-deceived.

Acceptance on the other hand should be a decision to close a chapter and a commitment to rejoin the present. It is a squaring up with a reality and the integration of head and heart—a pre-requisite to health, wholeness, and peace.

The person who has lived for so long as "victim" blaming others for who they are, is released to grow and take responsibility for his own life becoming increasingly outward bound. It comes as a great joy to hear such a person one day say, "I now want to use my experience to help others." These are not the "crusaders" energized and driven by a still festering septic anger; these are the "wounded healers" in our communities. The "wounded healer" rather than inflicting her wound on others, accepts that her "now-healing-wound" becomes the means of another's healing. These are among the truly beautiful people in our world. They have found new life beyond (and even within) their pain and because of their enhanced sensitivity and compassion they become bearers of hope who are not fearful of becoming incarnational. They stand in the noblest tradition of all reflecting the Suffering Servant of whom the prophet spoke centuries before His crucifixion.

By his wounds we are healed [15].

REFERENCES

1. J. Marsden, *The Journey,* Pan, Sydney, London, 1988.
2. Isaiah 40:27
3. Psalm 137:1-4
4. Isaiah 40:31 (N.I.V.)
5. A. Campbell, *The Gospel of Anger,* SPCK, London, 1986.
6. Ephesians 4:26,27, J.B. Phillips.
7. A. V. Campbell, Anger and Hostility, in *A Dictionary of Pastoral Care,* SPCK, London, 1987.
8. Romans 8:37
9. C. A. Matthews, *Breaking Through,* Albatross, Sydney, 1990.
10. E. O'Connor, *Cry Pain, Cry Hope,* Word, Texas, 1987.
11. Ephesians 4:32 cf. Jesus' words: Matthew 6:12 and 18:21-35.
12. A. de Mello, Dandelions, in *The Song of the Bird,* Image, New York, 1984.
13. H. Nouwen, *The Wounded Healer,* Doubleday, New York, 1972.
14. R. Foster, *Prayer,* Hodder and Stoughton, London, 1992.
15. Isaiah 53:5

CHAPTER 12

Spiritual/Religious Issues in Grief: Consolation and Meaning

Dennis Klass

It has become common of late to differentiate "spiritual" from "religious." In a pluralistic and individualistic world, the distinction probably represents a protest against the particularity of most religions, and it represents the modern split between personal experience and social forms. But religion and spirituality cannot be fully separated in the individual's experience or in the study of spirituality because the reality known in spiritual moments is maintained over time by symbols, rituals, and affiliations that have a religious character; and the reality known in spiritual moments is often perceived using symbols handed down through religious traditions. As we look at the spiritual, some ideas from religious traditions and from the comparative study of religions will be helpful.

For experience to qualify as spiritual, two characteristics would be implied. First, in a way that seems vitally important, or as Tillich said, as an "ultimate concern," we encounter or merge with that which was formerly understood as not-self or other [1]. In psychological terms, we can think of times when the ego boundaries become permeable so the individual feels at one with another, with the divine, or with the environment. In such moments the distinction between inner and outer reality blurs. In most religious traditions, it is the extreme (or supreme) of such moments which are described. In Sufi Islam it is *Identity*; in Buber's Judaism it is the *I-Thou*; in Bhakti Hinduism it is *Dar'san*.

Second, in a way that seems vitally important, we become aware of a higher intelligence, purpose, or order that we do not control, but in which we can participate, and to which we can conform our life. When we participate or conform to the higher intelligence, purpose, or order, we live more authentically, more meaningfully, than when we live by other norms and standards. Because such order can be codified in precept and example, it is the center of religious teaching; *Dharma* in Hinduism, *Doctrine* in Christianity, *Tao* in Chinese religion.

These two characteristics are in constant interplay. Turner finds both elements in religious rituals of passage [2]. He calls encounter and merger liminality.[1] In liminal situations, the usual boundaries are not in effect, so the individual is in touch with the transcendent. His term for order is *communitas*. He says that in *communitas* individual and social boundaries are discovered, altered, or maintained. In religious ritual, he finds an alternation between these two ways of being.

SPIRITUALITY AND THE BOND
WITH THE DECEASED

The process of resolving parental bereavement is something like Turner's ritual passages, for it is a transitional state. When a child dies, the parent experiences an irreparable loss, for the child is an extension of the parent's self [3, pp. 389-417; 4, pp. 154-165]. When a child dies, a part of the self is cut off. Many parents find the metaphor of amputation useful. Like amputation, parental bereavement is a permanent condition. Bereaved parents do adjust in the sense that they learn to invest themselves in other tasks and other relationships, but somewhere inside themselves, they report there is a sense of loss that cannot be healed. Ideas in this chapter are from a chapter of the Compassionate Friends, a self-help group [5].

In the resolution of parental grief we find experience that has spiritual qualities. First, the parent finds, renews, or modifies the bond to that which transcends immediate biological and social reality. This liminal connection provides solace, or comfort, in a world that is forever diminished. Second, the parent discovers or modifies a worldview which answers the questions of how the world functions and what is the parent's place and power in the world.

A recurring pattern in Compassionate Friends is that both finding solace and establishing or maintaining a worldview are intimately intertwined with the parent's continuing interaction with the inner

---

[1] From the latin *limen,* which means door, or wall. Thus the word signifies both the limits of human existence and also openings between the world of living humans and other worlds.

representation of their dead child. Inner representation can be defined following Fairbairn [6], as: 1) those aspects of the self that are actualized in interaction with the deceased person; 2) characteristics or thematic memories of the deceased; and 3) emotional states connected with those parts of the self and with those characterizations and memories.

Phenomena that indicate interaction with the inner representation of a deceased person are a sense of presence, hallucination in any of the senses, belief in the person's continuing active influence on thoughts or events, or incorporation of the characteristics or virtues of the dead into the self. These phenomena have a sense of awe and mystery about them, for it feels to the parent that the child is still active in the parent's world [7, pp. 283-311].

Inner representations of the dead are not simply individual phenomena, but they are maintained and reinforced within families and other social systems. In the Compassionate Friends, the sense of unity with other bereaved parents within the bonds to their dead children can be seen in the "TCF Credo":

> We reach out to each other with love, with understanding and with hope. Our children have died at all ages and from many different causes, but our love for our children unites us . . . Whatever pain we bring to this gathering of The Compassionate Friends, it is pain we will share just as we share with each other our love for our children.

INTERDEPENDENT CONSTRUCTS OF THE SPIRITUAL

As we begin to understand the spiritual experience of solace and worldview, we find ourselves dealing with a series of mutually interdependent constructs:

- How the universe works
- Place and power of the self
- Bond with the child
- Bond with the Transcendent
- Meaning of the parent's life
- Meaning of the child's death
- Community/family membership

If any one of these constructs change, there is a corresponding change in each of the other constructs. For example, the meaning of the child's death must be congruent with the understanding of how the universe works or else one or the other must be modified. The place and power of the self in the universe and the meaning of the parent's life are often defined in terms of a long-standing sense of connectedness in the bond with the Transcendent and in terms of community and family membership. The bond with the child is often felt as continuous with the parent's bond with the Transcendent. If the parent feels cut off from God, the meaning of the parent's life, the quality of community bonds, the bond with the child, and the place and power of the self must be recast.

In the two elements of the spiritual, encountering or merging with the other and finding order, we will see a constant interplay of these seven constructs. We will first look at solace and the bond with the immortal child and then at the process of maintaining or modifying worldviews.²

INNER REPRESENTATIONS AS SOLACE

Horton finds that the majority of people have a history of solace that they nurture [8]. The defining characteristic of solace is the sense of soothing. To console means to alleviate sorrow or distress. Solace is that which brings pleasure, enjoyment, or delight in the face

---

² Scholars in different disciplines have looked at some of these constructs, though none seem to have looked at their interaction, which is the focus of this chapter. Researchers have investigated meaning of the parent's life and meaning of the child's death in terms of meaning of life, coping styles, and religiosity (Craig, 1977; Cook and Wimberley, 1983; Hare-Mustin, 1979; Miles and Crandall, 1983; Videka-Sherman, 1982; Wilson, 1988; Freely and Gottlieb, 1988; Peterson and Greil, 1990; Smith, Range, and Ulmer, 1991, 1992; Florian, 1989; Bohannon, 1991; Sherkat and Reed, 1992; Schwab, 1990; Hoekstra-Weebers, Littlewood, Boon, Postma, and Humphrey, 1991; Edmonds and Hooker, 1992). Community and family membership appears in the literature as social support (for general bereavement see: Arling, 1976; Bowling and Cartwright, 1982; Lopata, 1973; Maddison and Walker, 1967; Parkes and Weiss, 1983; Silverman, 1986; Vachon et al., 1982; Rosenblatt, Spoentgen, Karis, Dahl, Kaiser, and Elde, 1991; on bereaved parents see: Bourne, 1968; Carr and Knupp, 1985; Kowalski, 1984; Schreiner, Gresham, and Green, 1979.) While the continuing bond with the child is cited as evidence for pathology in some contemporary grief theory, there is a long tradition of research that finds maintaining the bond with the deceased is a healthy part of the resolution of bereavement (Kalish and Reynolds, 1981; Yamamoto, Okonogi, Iwasaki, and Yoshimura, 1969; Rees, 1975; Glick, Weiss, and Parkes, 1974; Silverman, 1986, 1987; Lopata, 1973, 1979; Moss and Moss, 1980; Goin, Burgoyne, and Goin, 1979; Tessman, 1978; Bushbaum, 1987, Cath and Herzog, 1982; Lehman, Wortman, and Williams, 1987; Rubin, 1985; Hogan and DeSantis, 1992; Stroebe, Gergen, Gergen, and Stroebe, 1992; Stroebe, 1992). The bond with the transcendent, how the world works and the place and power of the self is largely found in studies of comparative belief systems, philosophies, and artistic expressions (Chidester, 1990; Sullivan, 1989; Doka and Morgan, 1993; Bertman, 1991; Carse, 1980; Amato, 1985; Huntington and Metcalf, 1979; Holck, 1974) and is similar to ideas found in personal construct theory (Woodfield and Viney, 1984; Nerken, 1993).

of hopelessness, despair, sadness, and devastation. Most adults can easily identify a solace filled object to which they repair when they need soothing: a memory of a special place or person, a piece of music or art, an imagined more perfect world, a sense of divine presence. The earliest form of solace is the child's transitional object [9, pp. 84, 89-97; 10] such as a security blanket. The security these objects provide helps children explore new situations and adjust to unfamiliar environments [11, pp. 468-469; 12, pp. 170-177]. Winnicott finds our ability to participate in cultural, artistic, and religious symbols and myths is an extension of our early transitional objects [10].[3]

INNER REPRESENTATIONS AS SOLACE

What forms of relationships to their dead children do parents maintain as solace in their lives? The following are four common ways among members of the Compassionate Friends: A) linking objects, B) religious ideas and devotion, C) memory, and D) identification.

A. Linking Objects

Linking objects are objects connected with the child's life that link the bereaved to the dead; in so doing, they evoke the presence of the dead [13]. One parent had many memories of being at the beach with her child. Her memory of those times also include natural mystical experiences [14, pp. 155-163] in which her bond with nature and with the child are intertwined. In a newsletter article she wrote that the child "was especially awed by the setting sun and as we walked to beaches, always he would stop and watch the sun go down—I did too! I was so happy with him."

> In February I went to Padre Island and one lonely evening I walked the beach alone . . . It was there I begged Him to show me a sign that E. lives—to "please send me a sand dollar," . . . But I only wanted just one sand dollar—just one! Watching the fading sunset and listening to the roar of the waves, darkness began to fall, so I turned to go back when there by me feet, the waves pushed up one lone sand dollar—a small but perfect sand dollar! My prayer had been answered.

The answer to her prayer for a sign that the child still lives is the linking object of the sand dollar. Now that she has had the intense

---

[3] Also see Grolnick, Barkin, and Muensterberger, 1978.

experience of finding the sand dollar, the memory of this experience can be evoked to serve as a linking object.

B. Prayer, Ritual, and Religious Ideation

Linking objects can have a numinous sense [15] about them, for they function like relics of the saints in which "any personal possession or part of a person's body . . . can carry the power or saintliness of the person with whom they were once associated and make him or her 'present' once again" [16, p. 51]. The numinous feeling is clearer in the many people who sense the presence of the child in their religious experience of prayer, ritual, and religious ideation. The inner representation of the child is merged with something bigger, but something of which the parent feels a part. One mother wrote to her dead children of her sense of presence at Catholic Mass:

> Every time I attend the sacrifice of the Mass, at the part where our Blessed Lord comes into our hearts, I feel so close to your angelic presence. What a divine experience! The only problem is that it doesn't last long enough. If only the others could share these feelings.

Ideas and devotion can also be part of spirituality that is not confined to church doctrines. On her child's birthday, one mother wrote as if from her child:

> I would have been twenty today, bound by earthly constraints. Do not cry Mom. I am forever, I am eternal, I am ageless. I am in the blowing wind, the first blades of grass in the spring, the haunting cry of the owl, the shriek of the hawk, the silent soaring of the turkey vulture . . . I am the weightless, floating feeling when you close your eyes at night; I am the heaviness of a broken heart . . . Like an invisible cocoon I surround you. I am in the moonlight, the sunbeams, the dew at dawn . . . For I was, I am, and I will always be. Once T., now nameless and free.

Almost all parents in the study feel that the child is in heaven. Several people in the study felt the child to be with another significant person who had died.

> It was hard after my father died because I always had this sense that I didn't know where he was. But I was busy with L. because she was so sick all the time. After L. died I was really bothered that I didn't know where she was and that somehow that meant that I didn't know she was safe. That lasted two years. One day I started

crying and I realized I wasn't just crying for L. I was missing my father. And suddenly I just thought, "Daddy is taking care of L. She is OK because she is with him and that's where he is. It is like they are together." That sounds so simple-minded. I don't believe in heaven or afterlife. I think we just live on in memory. But it just feels like I don't have that to worry about either of them any more. I know that they are together.

C. Memories

Bereaved parents can find solace in memory. Unconflicted and peaceful memory is often at the end of a difficult process of separating self-representation from the inner representation of the child. This use of memory as solace seems similar to what Tahka calls "remembrance formations." He says once the remembrance formation

> has been established, its later calling back to mind, reminiscing about it and dismissing it again from the mind are invariably experienced as activities of the self taking place exclusively on the subject's own conditions. Although it is experienced as a fully differentiated object representation, no illusions of its separate and autonomous existence are involved. In contrast to fantasy objects possessing various wish-fulfilling functions, it includes the awareness that nothing more can be expected from it and therefore, in its fully established forms it has chances for becoming the most realistic of all existing object representations [17, p. 18].

In a newsletter article reflecting on her life five years after her daughter died, a mother wrote:

> I still feel the warmth of love when I think of A. I still laugh when I think of some of the witty and wacky things she said or did. I still cry when the loneliness of her absence pierces my heart and I miss her as much as I did at the beginning of this journey.
>
> I have a new relationship with A. It is internal, redefined, relevant, valued. Our relationship and memory are captured within me always to draw upon.

D. Identification

In identification, the inner representation of the child is integrated into the self-representation in such a way that it is difficult to distinguish the two. Solace is found in a sense of reinvigorated life, in renewed feelings of competence.

Identification has a social aspect. With adequate social support, pain is shared and in that sharing the relationship with the child is shared within the supportive relationship. As the Compassionate Friends song says, "Our children live on in the love that we share."

Often identification is found in a decision to live fully in spite of the death. One parent wrote:

> I came to the decision that I was to try to use my gift of life to the utmost as my son had used his . . . there is a joy in my life now . . . We have sought positive ways to remember (him). Members of our family continue to give books to a memorial shelf of books (at the library) . . . started by (his) friends . . . Members of our family periodically give blood to the Red Cross, hoping to help others who may need that gift in their struggle for life . . . Life will never be the same. I will always be disappointed that (he) did not have a longer life, but I will always be proud of him and love him. I continue to search for ways to being (be? bring?) love, home and meaning in my life as I try to make use of my one gift of life.

SOLACE AND IMMORTALITY

In these solace-giving experiences, the child remains immortal, in the sense that the inner representation of the child remains a real, living presence in the parent's inner and social world. Lifton finds the sense of immortality is "man's symbolization of his ties with both his biological fellows and his history, past and future" [18, p. 685]. The parents' bond with the child already symbolizes the parents' ties to their biological, personal, and cultural history. The immortal inner representation of the child maintains those bonds.

Winnicott notes that the relationship to culture, including art and religion, is the same blend of inner and outer reality first seen in the child's transitional object [9, 10].[4]

In many of his sonnets Shakespeare asks how a dead friend or lover can live on. He seems finally to settle upon the immortality of his own art, for if he can join the reality of the deceased to the "eternal lines" of the poem, the dead person is made immortal.[5] Thus Shakespeare locates the immortality of the dead in his art much the way bereaved parents locate their dead children in their experience of solace:

---

[4] Also see Grolnick, Barkin, and Muensterberger, 1978.

[5] Also see Hubler, 1952.

And every fair from fair sometime declines,
By chance or nature's changing course untrimm'd;
But thy eternal summer shall not fade
Nor lose possession of that fair thou owest;
Nor shall Death brag thou wander'st in his shade,
When in eternal lines to time thou growest:
        So long as men can breath or eyes can see,
        So long lives this and this gives life to thee. (Sonnet 18)

For their parents, dead children do not lose possession of that fairness they embodied, nor do they wander only in Death's shade. They have lived just the summer, but their summer does not fade; it remains eternal in a part of the parent's psyche and in the social system where the parent feels most at home.

INNER REPRESENTATION
AND WORLDVIEWS

The death of their child forces parents to re-examine their worldview, that is, to either reaffirm or modify their basic understanding about themselves and about the justness and orderliness of their world. The parents' experience of their immortal child is intertwined with their discovery of underlying order, purpose, or intelligence to which they align their lives.

Worldview, a concept taken from the comparative study of religion [19, 20], can be defined as sets of beliefs, myths, rituals, affiliations, altered states of consciousness, and ethical standards by which individuals and communities know how the universe functions and know what station or power the individual holds within the universe. Worldviews are maps of both visible and invisible reality on which individuals locate external and internal events, from which individuals discover or choose religious, political, or ideological affiliations, and upon which individuals base moral judgments and actions.

Worldviews are not held as abstractions, but as a collection of symbols, myths, beliefs, personal experience, altered states of consciousness, and ritual behaviors that can have varying degrees of internal coherence or intellectual consistence.

Erikson says that worldviews rest within the most elementary feelings and earliest human experience, the basic trust developed in the preverbal interactions between mother and child [21]. Fowler [22] and Wilber [23, 24] have shown that worldviews can be maintained at any developmental level and changing worldviews is central in the individual's movement into higher developmental levels. While worldviews through the history of humankind show amazing diversity, the range available to an individual in a particular time and place is limited.

EFFECT OF TRAUMA ON WORLDVIEWS

Traumatic events challenge worldviews. Janoff-Bulman suggests that,

> [t]he coping task facing victims is largely a difficult cognitive dilemma. They must integrate the data of their dramatic negative experience and their prior assumptions, which cannot readily assimilate the new information. Victims must rework the new data so as to make it fit and thereby maintain their old assumptions, or they must revise their old assumptions in a way that precludes the breakdown of the entire system and allows them to perceive the world as not wholly threatening [25, p. 121].

After a traumatic event, the worldview is like a Piagetian schema in the face of new information. The schema must assimilate the new experience and as the experience can no longer be fitted into the structure of the schema, the schema must accommodate.

As a way of introducing the connection between solace in the bond to the now-immortal child and worldview, we can look at a Compassionate Friends newsletter article written by a clergyman about how the key to his finding a renewed, though changed, faith was a dream of his dead son.

> There he was! Walking toward me as if coming out of a mist. There he was—that lanky 17-year-old whose life I loved better than my own. He looked deeply into my eyes and with a grin on his face, the way he used to do when he was "buttering me up." Not a word was spoken, but everything was said that needed to be said for my turning point to come.
>
> It was time to resume life. I would not be bitter, but in loving memory I would be better. I would live again because I knew that my boy lived again. My own Christian faith was to be retrofitted. It offered meaning and purpose within the shadow of my loss. It asserted that though God does not intend my sufferings, He involves Himself in them. My pain and loss were not to be the end of life. Rather, it was to be a beginning—a beginning to a more compassionate life of quality and caring.

We notice that the boy is not alive in heaven in this account; he is in a dream. The grin on the boy's face renews the bond between father and son, allows the father to renew the bond with the Heavenly Father who is involved in the father's pain, and helps the father re-establish his place in the community as the authoritative interpreter of life's meaning. The clergyman finds his faith in a sense of the boy's presence, not in the sacred texts. Indeed, the son's wordless presence marks the occasion for the sacred texts to speak to the father.

In the Compassionate Friends we consistently find a strong connection between the solace-filled bond with the dead child and the parent's maintaining or remolding a worldview.

THE INNER REPRESENTATION IN THE RESTORATION OF MEANING

We will examine five of the ways we found parents holding worldviews. A) We encountered some parents who found a new and compelling worldview during the illness and death of the child and all their experience fit into that worldview. B) We found parents who interpreted symbols within their worldview in a new and more profound way. C) We encountered parents who reinterpreted the death of the child in a way that allowed them to maintain their former worldview. D) When the symbols or affiliation of the parent's worldview were not useful, we found that some parents lived in a divided world. They maintained a bond with the Transcendent that was linked to the child, but in other parts of their life, they felt cut off from the God in whom they still believed. E) We found some parents who changed their worldview.

A. Increased Religiosity through Affiliation

We found parents in our study for whom the world had become an authentic and meaningful place during and after the death of their child. In these cases, the parents had found a religious faith prior to the death and that faith had been nurtured in an intense network of interpersonal relationships. The experience of their child's illness and impending death had occasioned a major accommodation in the parent's worldview as they changed their understanding of how the universe works and of the place and power of both them and their child in that universe. Now all experience could be assimilated into the worldview.

These parents felt a direct bond with the Transcendent which seemed, to them, indistinguishable from the bond with the dead child.

The inner representation of the child was part of the religious symbols by which they lived, and part of the supportive community in which the symbols were maintained.

One woman reported that in the process of his dying, her teen-age son provided the model for her and her husband's present worldview.

> I think about the times when B. was so worried about me. His concern was for me. He was strong, a wonderful example for me. He just loved us and we could feel it. B. brought us the example of showing love and now we continue that with our other children. The kids all recognize it too. It is a beautiful experience. We believe in heaven, that B. is where he should be. We feel that his purpose has been fulfilled; and for us, we are still working on it.

B. Reinterpreting Symbols

Many parents did not find the strength they needed from religious symbols as they held them before their child died. Some parents reinterpret symbols from their religious tradition in the light of the new reality. There is some accommodation, but no change in the developmental level of the schema. In Wilber's terms, they translate, but do not transform [24]. That is, there is a change in the surface structure of the worldview, but no change in the deep structure.

The parent/child bond is at the core of the central Christian symbol. Usually believers see themselves as the child of the father God. But a few parents in our study changed to see God in terms of their own parental role. Their present reality can be assimilated into this paradigmatic symbol. One mother wrote:

> Last year, in preparing a Christmas memorial service for our Compassionate Friends group, I had another "faith experience." I always believed God sent his only son to die for us. Last year it hit me that if this is true, this makes God a bereaved parent too! I felt even closer to him, because I realized He knew how I felt (at least sometimes). Whenever I can see human qualities in God, it makes Him more real to me.

C. Reinterpreting the Event

If a bad event can be reinterpreted in a way that makes some good come out of it, religious symbols and affiliations can be maintained. The perception of the event is modified so that it can be assimilated into the worldview with little accommodation. Virtually all the parents in our study forcefully rejected a simple reinterpretation—that their child's death was God's will or that any good that comes from the death made the death acceptable. At the same time they accepted that good may come from a bad thing. A mother struggling with the question "Why?" said:

> I just cannot accept that there is no reason for this. There has got to be some purpose. R. was a beautiful girl. She didn't deserve to die. I am a good mother. I cannot accept that God just lets things happen. I feel these changes in me. I see good things happening, like the way the kids at the school responded and the pages in the year book. There is a reason for this and good will come out of it.

In this account, we can see the use of the inner representation of the child. The good that came from the death is the expression of shared love for her child. The bond she still feels with her daughter is validated in the bond others still feel. She feels changes in herself that are the growth in identification as she feels that in her relationships with others, she is beginning to exemplify some of the admirable traits of her daughter.

D. Divided World

Some parents cannot grow in or maintain the symbols that support their world, but neither can they abandon their old worldview and move to a new one. That is, they seem neither able fully to assimilate nor to accommodate. In those cases, the parents divide the world of their lostness from the parts of the self that still maintain a trustworthy world. For most of these parents in our study, it is the internalized inner representation of their child that connects them with a benevolent world even as they feel cut off in other parts of their psyche. In a meeting a father talked of the months of praying during his daughter's illness:

> Some of the children would get better and some would not. One night as she was going to sleep N. asked me, "Daddy, how does God decide who gets the miracles?" I didn't know what to answer her. I still don't. I guess I still believe in miracles. How else do you account for the kids I saw get better with no explanation. But we didn't get one. So where am I now?

E. Developing New Meaning

Worldviews are remarkably resilient even in the face of overwhelming pain, but for some parents, the symbols of their old life do not serve well in the new world of parental bereavement. One woman had a miscarriage sixteen years before we interviewed her and then thirteen years before the interview her two year old daughter died in an accident that she thought she should have been able to prevent. She described herself as very religious after a Protestant conversion experience when she was seventeen years old. She was in this "religious phase" when she miscarried. Then she got cancer and while she was recovering, the toddler died. After the death and cancer she asked "what else can happen? Well, I felt like God was saying, 'This is what else can happen and I can do a lot more'. " In her feeling of being a failure and being punished, she would "wonder if in the back of my religious beliefs, if she (the dead child) can see all that we do. If she is ashamed of me as her mother. Would she want me to be her mother again." So, the inner representation of the child played a role in her strong sense of inadequacy.

About five years before the interview, she began slowly to change her worldview. She developed a mentor relationship with a superior at work who encouraged her to take on new responsibilities and showed that he thought she had admirable qualities. She went back to school for her undergraduate degree and was finishing a masters when we interviewed her. In this new self she began to feel that she was worthwhile. In that new sense she said of her hopes for her living daughters:

> I've grown to accept maybe it will be and maybe it won't be. But I've tried and I've finally come to the realization that I've done and tried as much as I can. I'm not going to blame myself any more for the mistakes they make . . .
>
> Interviewer: In answer to the question that you asked R., "Would you still want me for a mother?" you're saying?
>
> I think I'm not saying "would you want." I'm saying, "Well, regardless, I am. I was and I am." I have to answer for whatever I am.

CONCLUSION

The defining characteristics of spirituality are, first, in a way that feels vitally important, the individual encounters or merges with that which formerly felt like not-self or other; and, second, in that encounter or merger, the individual becomes aware of an underlying order in the world to which the individual may harmonize his/her life. In our study of bereaved parents in the Compassionate Friends, we have seen these characteristics first, as they find solace in connection with that which transcends the physical and biological and, second, as they affirm or modify their worldview, that is their understanding of how the universe functions and of what is their place and power in the universe. We have seen that the bond with the child who has died is bound up with their solace in the presence of other unseen realities and with their perception of an underlying order in the world. These spiritual aspects of the resolution of the grief are central elements as parents rebuild their lives for living in a changed world.

REFERENCES

1. P. Tillich, *Systematic Theology*, Volumes I-III, University of Chicago Press, Chicago, 1951, 1957, 1963.
2. V. Turner, *The Ritual Process: Structure and Anti-Structure*, Cornell University Press, Ithaca, 1969.
3. T. Benedek, Parenthood as a Developmental Phase, *Psychoanalytic Association Journal*, 7, pp. 389-417, 1959.
4. T. Benedek, Discussion of Parenthood as a Developmental Phase, *Journal of the American Psychoanalytic Association*, *23*, pp. 154-165, 1975.
5. D. Klass, *Parental Grief: Resolution and Solace*, Springer, New York, 1988.
6. W. D. Fairbairn, *An Object-Relations Theory of the Personality*, Basic Books, New York, 1952.
7. L. Dawson, Otto and Freud on the Uncanny and Beyond, *Journal of the American Academy of Religion*, *58*:2, pp. 283-311, 1989.
8. P. C. Horton, Solace, in *The Missing Dimension in Psychiatry*, University of Chicago Press, Chicago, 1981.
9. D. W. Winnicott, Transitional Objects and Transitional Phenomena, *International Journal of Psychoanalysis*, *34*, pp. 89-97, 1953.
10. D. W. Winnicott, *Playing and Reality*, Basic Books, New York, 1971.
11. R. H. Passman, Arousal Reducing Properties of Attachment Objects: Testing the Functional Limits of the Security Blanket Relative to the Mother, *Developmental Psychology*, *12*, pp. 468-469, 1976.
12. R. H. Passman and P. Weisberg, Mothers and Blankets as Agents for Promoting Play and Exploration by Young Children in a Novel Environment: The Effects of Social and Nonsocial Attachment Objects, *Developmental Psychology*, *11*, pp. 170-177, 1975.
13. V. D. Volkan, *Linking Objects and Linking Phenomena*, International Universities Press, New York, 1981.
14. R. Hood, Eliciting Mystical States of Consciousness in Semistructured Nature Experiences, *Journal for the Scientific Study of Religion*, *16*:2, pp. 155-163, 1977.
15. R. Otto, *The Idea of the Holy*, J. W. Harvey (trans.), Oxford University Press, New York, 1923.
16. L. E. Sullivan (ed.), *Death, Afterlife, and the Soul: Selections from the Encyclopedia of Religion*, M. Eliade (editor-in-Chief), Macmillan, New York, 1989.
17. V. Tahka, Dealing with Object Loss, *Scandinavian Psychoanalytic Review*, 7, pp. 13-33, 1984.

18. R. J. Lifton, On Death and the Continuity of Life: A 'New' Paradigm, *History of Childhood Quarterly, 1*:4, pp. 681-696, 1974.
19. N. Smart, *Worldviews: Crosscultural Exploration of Human Beliefs,* Charles Schribner's Sons, New York, 1983.
20. N. Smart, *The World's Religions,* Prentice-Hall, Englewood Cliffs, New Jersey, 1989.
21. E. K. Erikson, *Childhood and Society* (2nd Edition), W. W. Norton and Company, New York, 1963.
22. J. W. Fowler, *Stages of Faith,* Harper and Row, San Francisco, 1981.
23. K. Wilber, *The Atman Project,* Theosophical Publishing House, Wheaton, Illinois, 1980.
24. K. Wilber, *Up From Eden,* Shambhala, Boulder, Colorado, 1981.
25. R. Janoff-Bulman, Assumptive Worlds and the Stress of Traumatic Events: Applications of the Schema Construct, *Social Cognition, 7*:2, pp. 113-136, 1989.

BIBLIOGRAPHY

Amato, J. A., *Death Book: Terrors, Consolations, Contradictions, and Paradoxes,* Ventl Amati, Marshall, Minnesota, 1985.
Arling, G., The Elderly Widow and Her Family, Neighbors and Friends, *Journal of Marriage and the Family, 38*:4, pp. 757-767, 1976.
Bertman, S. L., *Facing Deaths: Images, Insights, and Interventions,* Hemisphere Publishing Corporation, New York, 1991.
Bohannon, J. R., Religiosity Related to Grief Levels of Bereaved Mothers and Fathers, *Omega, Journal of Death and Dying, 23*:2, pp. 151-159, 1991.
Bourne, S., The Psychological Effects of Stillbirth on Women and Their Doctors, *Journal of the Royal College of General Practice, 16,* pp. 103-112, 1968.
Bowling, A. and A. Cartwright, *Life After Death: A Study of the Elderly Widowed,* Tavistock, London, 1982.
Bushbaum, B. C., Remembering a Parent who has Died: A Developmental Perspective, in *The Annual of Psychoanalysis,* Volume XV, International Universities Press, Madison, pp. 99-112, 1987.
Cath, S. H. and J. M. Herzog, The Dying and Death of a Father, in *Father and Child,* S. H. Cath, A. R. Gurwitt, and J. M. Ross (eds.), Little Brown, Boston, pp. 339-353, 1982.
Carr, D. and S. F. Knupp, Grief and Perinatal Loss, *Journal of Obstetric, Gynecologic, and Neonatal Nursing, 14*:2, pp. 130-139, 1985.
Carse, J. P., *Death and Existence: A Conceptual History of Human Mortality,* John Wiley and Sons, New York, 1980.
Chidester, D., *Patterns of Transcendence: Religion, Death, and Dying,* Wadsworth, Belmont, California, 1990.
Cook, J. A. and D. W. Wimberley, If I Should Die Before I Wake: Religious Commitment and Adjustment to the Death of a Child, *Journal for the Scientific Study of Religion, 22*:3, pp. 222-238, 1983.

Craig, Y., The Bereavement of Parents and Their Search for Meaning, *British Journal of Social Work*, 7:1, pp. 41-54, 1977.

Doka, K. J. and J. D. Morgan (eds.), *Death and Spirituality*, Baywood Publishing Company, Amityville, New York, 1993.

Edmonds, S. and K. Hooker, Perceived Changes in Life Meaning Following Bereavement, *Omega, Journal of Death and Dying*, 25:4, pp. 307-318, 1992.

Feeley, N. and L. N. Gottlieb, Parents' Coping and Communication Following Their Infant's Death, *Omega, Journal of Death and Dying*, 19:1, pp. 51-67, 1988.

Florian, V., Meaning and Purpose in Life of Bereaved Parents Whose Son Fell During Active Military Service, *Omega, Journal of Death and Dying*, 20:2, pp. 91-102, 1989.

Glick, I. O., R. S. Weiss, and C. M. Parkes, *The First Year of Bereavement*, John Wiley and Sons, New York, 1974.

Goin, M. K., R. W. Burgoyne, and J. M. Goin, Timeless Attachment to a Dead Relative, *American Journal of Psychiatry*, 136:7, pp. 988-989, 1979.

Grolnick, S. A., L. Barkin, and W. Muensterberger (eds.), *Between Reality and Fantasy, Transitional Objects and Phenomena*, Jason Aronson, New York, 1978.

Hare-Mustin, R. T. Family Therapy Following the Death of a Child, *Journal of Marriage and Family Therapy*, 5, pp. 51-59, 1979.

Hoekstra-Weebers, J. E. H. M., J. L. Littlewood, C. M. J. Boon, A. Postma, and G. B. Humphrey, A Comparison of Parental Coping Styles Following the Death of Adolescent and Preadolescent Children, *Death Studies*, 15:6, pp. 565-575, 1991.

Hogan, N. and L. DeSantis, Adolescent Sibling Bereavement: An Ongoing Attachment, *Qualitative Health Research*, 2:2, pp. 159-177, 1992.

Holck, F. H. (ed.), *Death and Eastern Thought*, Abingdon Press, New York, 1974.

Hubler, E., *The Sense of Shakespeare's Sonnets*, Princeton University Press, Princeton, New Jersey, 1952.

Huntington, R. and P. Metcalf, *Celebrations of Death, The Anthropology of Mortuary Ritual*, Cambridge University Press, New York, 1979.

Kalish, R. A. and D. K. Reynolds, *Death and Ethnicity, A Psychocultural Study*, Baywood Publishing Company, Amityville, New York, 1981.

Kowalski, K. E. M., *Perinatal Death, An Ethnomethodological Study of Factors Influencing Parental Bereavement*, unpublished doctoral dissertation, University of Colorado at Boulder, 1984.

Lehman, D. R., C. B. Wortman, and A. F. Williams, Long-Term Effects of Losing a Spouse or Child in a Motor Vehicle Crash, *Journal of Personality and Social Psychology*, 52:2, pp. 218-231, 1987.

Lopata, H. Z., *Widowhood in an American City*, Schenkman, Cambridge, Massachusetts, 1973.

Lopata, H. Z., *Women as Widows, Support Systems*, Elsevier, New York, 1979.

Maddison, D. and W. L. Walker, Factors Affecting the Outcome of Conjugal Bereavement, *British Journal of Psychiatry, 113,* pp. 1057-1067, 1967.

Miles, M. S. and E. K. B. Crandall, The Search for Meaning and its Potential for Affecting Growth in Bereaved Parents, *Health Values: Achieving High Level Wellness,* 7:1, pp. 19-23, 1983.

Moss, M. S. and S. Z. Moss, The Image of the Deceased Spouse in Remarriage of Elderly Widow(er)s, *Journal of Gerontological Social Work,* 3:2, pp. 59-70, 1980.

Nerken, I. R., Grief and the Reflective Self, Toward a Clearer Model of Loss Resolution and Growth, *Death Studies, 17,* pp. 1-26, 1993.

Parkes, C. M. and R. S. Weiss, *Recovery from Bereavement,* Basic Books, New York, 1983.

Peterson, S. A. and A. L. Greil, Death Experience and Religion, *Omega, Journal of Death and Dying, 21*:1, pp. 75-82, 1990.

Rees, W. D., The Bereaved and Their Hallucinations, in *Bereavement, Its Psychosocial Aspect*s, B. Schoenberg et. al. (eds.), Columbia University Press, New York, pp. 66-71, 1975.

Rosenblatt, P. C., P. Spoentgen, T. A. Karis, D. Dahl, T. Kaiser, and C. Elde, Difficulties in Supporting the Bereaved, *Omega, Journal of Death and Dying, 23*:2, pp. 119-128, 1991.

Rubin, S. S., The Resolution of Bereavement, A Clinical Focus on the Relationship to the Deceased, *Psychotherapy, 22*:2, pp. 231-235, 1985.

Schreiner, R. L., E. L. Gresham, and M. Green, Physician's Responsibility to Parents After the Death of an Infant, Beneficial Outcome of a Telephone Call, *American Journal of Diseases in Children, 133*:7, pp. 723-726, 1979.

Schwab, R., Paternal and Maternal Coping with the Death of a Child, *Death Studies, 14*:5, pp. 407-422, 1990.

Sherkat, D. E. and M. D. Reed, The Effects of Religion and Social Support on Self-Esteem and Depression among the Suddenly Bereaved, *Social Indicators Research, 26*:3, pp. 259-275, 1992.

Silverman, P. R., *Widow-to-Widow,* Springer Publishing Company, New York, 1986.

Silverman, P. R., The Impact of Parental Death on College-Age Women, *Psychiatric Clinics of North America, 10*:3, pp. 387-404, 1987.

Smith, P. C., L. M. Range, and A. Ulmer, Purpose in Life, A Moderator of Recovery from Bereavement, *Omega, Journal of Death and Dying, 23*:4, pp. 279-289, 1991.

Smith, P. C., L. M. Range, and A. Ulmer, Belief in Afterlife as a Buffer in Suicidal and Other Bereavement, *Omega, Journal of Death and Dying, 23*:3, pp. 217-225, 1992.

Stroebe, M., Coping With Bereavement, A Review of the Grief Work Hypothesis, *Omega, Journal of Death and Dying, 26*:1, 19-42. 1992.

Stroebe, M., M. M. Gergen, K. J. Gergen, and W. Stroebe, Broken Hearts or Broken Bonds, Love and Death in Historical Perspective, *American Psychologist, 47*:10, pp. 1205-1212, 1992.

Sullivan, L. E. (ed.), *Death, After Life, and the Soul: Selections from the Encyclopedia of Religions,* Macmillan, New York, 1989.

Tessman, L. H. *Children of Parting Parents,* Jason Aronson, New York, 1978.

Vachon, M. L. S., A. R. Sheldon, W. J. Lance, W. A. L. Lyall, J. Rogers, and S. J. J. Freeman, Correlates of Enduring Distress Patterns Following Bereavement, Social Network, Life Situation and Personality, *Psychological Medicine, 12,* pp. 783-788, 1982.

Videka-Sherman, L., Coping with the Death of a Child, A Study Over Time, *American Journal of Orthopsychiatry, 52*:4, pp. 688-698, 1982.

Wilson, D. C., The Ultimate Loss, The Dying Child, *Loss, Grief, and Care, 2*:3-4, pp. 125-130, 1988.

Woodfield, R. L. and L. L. Viney, A Personal Construct Approach to the Conjugally Bereaved Woman, *Omega, Journal of Death and Dying, 15*:4, pp. 1-13, 1984.

Yamamoto, J., K. Okonogi, T. Iwasaki, and S. Yoshimura, Mourning in Japan, *American Journal of Psychiatry, 125,* pp. 1661-1665, 1969.

Note: A very painful conflict on the Compassionate Friends national board has lead to the organization of a new national self-help group of bereaved parents. The new group is named Bereaved Parents of the USA. The local chapter in which the research for this chapter was conducted has voted to affiliate with the new organization. So, although the text refers to the Compassionate Friends, it should now be referred to as a local chapter of Bereaved Parents.

PART III

Moral Dilemmas

As indicated before, our problems seem to grow more rapidly than
our ability to understand them or to subsume them under our ethical
principles. It is only in the last thirty years that life expectancy, and
the possibility of keeping dying persons alive for long periods has
brought into renewed focus the problems of euthanasia, elder abuse,
and the problems of the developing world.

Abuse of elderly people is not a new phenomenon, but recognition of
this problem certainly is. Esther Gjertsen points out that in the United
States it was not until the 1970s that the first studies about elderly
abuse appeared in the literature. Definitions and descriptions of
elderly abuse, defined as physical abuse, psychological abuse, financial
abuse, and violation of rights, came as late as 1979. In the United
States and Canada between 2 and 5 percent of the elderly population
are victims of abuse. Although definitions of elder abuse vary in the
literature, there have been four major categories of abuse identified by
the majority of researchers. These are physical abuse, psychological
abuse, financial or material abuse, and neglect.

The Honourable Flora MacDonald, former member of the Parliament of Canada, and one-time Canadian Ambassador to the United
Nations, points out that by the year 2000, 80 percent of all humanity
will live in countries of the developing world. There will exist the
greatest human potential, the greatest market, and the greatest suffering. Meanwhile the remaining 20 percent of the world's population
consumes 80 percent of the world's production. It costs more to keep a
cat as a family pet for a year in Canada than a struggling individual is
able to earn in that year in one of the poorer countries of Africa.

Hunger, starvation, lack of health and education facilities,
brutality, and death await the forty million women and children who
are refugees. Efforts to help these people are often needlessly bungled

181

by the rules and regulations of United Nations conventions that govern refugee policy globally, thereby encouraging a double standard for refugee situations in the countries of the South and those of the North. In Canada most of our attention, energy, and resources are concentrated on the few thousand people who reach shores to claim refugee status, while very little is done about the forty million others who remain in perilous circumstances, and for whom survival is a daily quest.

In order to explore some of the complex dilemmas and interactions that confront us in dealing with euthanasia, Margaret Somerville examines the ways in which language is employed in the debate. This examination includes exploration of how language is used to label or characterize situations in order to deal with these situations in certain pre-determined ways. With the above in mind, Somerville defines euthanasia as "an intervention or a non-intervention by one person, to end the life of another person, who is terminally ill, for the purpose of relieving suffering, with the intent of causing the death of the other person, except where the primary intent is either to provide treatment necessary for the relief of pain or other symptoms of serious physical distress, or non-provision or withdrawal of treatment is justified, in particular, because there is a valid refusal of treatment or the treatment is futile."

Somerville does not believe that the anti-euthanasia side is necessarily pro-pain. She says that "failure to take all reasonable steps to relieve pain and thereby leaving people in pain is not only a human tragedy and contrary to the most fundamental concepts of human rights, it should be treated as at least legally actionable medical malpractice and, arguably, even as a crime."

Somerville asks if our "euthanasia talk" is covering-up some other reality. There is much discussion of euthanasia, but less of death—talking about death is difficult. Could it be that euthanasia is the conscious mechanism that we use to suppress the larger awareness of death? Is it less fearful to talk of euthanasia than death, and consequently, our discussion of death is being carried out in the context of euthanasia? We used to talk about death "in religion," but the major decline in adherence to organized religion means that many no longer talk about death in that context.

Somerville believes that advocacy of euthanasia is connected with a desire for control. Control is related to relief of suffering. Suffering is present when one has a sense of one's own disintegration and a loss of control over what happens to one. To move from chance, which the occurrence of death has largely been, to choice, which is the promise of euthanasia, can reduce suffering. Persons may see euthanasia as avoiding present suffering either at the present time, or in the future. Euthanasia may, also, fulfill a need or desire for certainty, which is related to a need or desire for control. Stated in another way, euthanasia can be viewed as reducing uncertainty which reduces anxiety, and, consequently, it provides reassurance. Euthanasia is a "do something" response.

These dilemmas are not easily solved. Abuse of the elderly, ignoring the needs of the developing world, and the desire for euthanasia are all rooted in the achievement orientation of our culture. Essentially, we view a person as one who contributes to [our] society and if distance, age, or illness prohibits such achievement, then we view their lives as less valuable. Coming to terms with these issues would demand a restructuring of our basic thinking and our basic values.

CHAPTER 13

The Abuse of the Elderly

Esther Magrethe Gjertsen and Cand Polit

In the well known "Frognerpark" in Oslo, capital city of Norway, the artist, Gustav Vigeland has, through his monumental sculptures, described man's journey of life from birth to death. All phases of life are depicted there: childhood, adolescence, manhood, and old age. Life's beginning and the end of life are expressed in sculptures and friezes. The struggle for survival is expressed in the famous "Monolitten," where one finds the elderly and weak at the bottom of the monument, while the young and strong ones are fighting their way to the top.

Life's bright and dark aspects are also expressed here: happy and safe childhood; the family as the safe and close social network; falling in love; jealousy; pregnancy; birth and death; tenderness and care; as well as sorrow, loneliness, and despair.

Major attention is given to old age, including sculptures expressing respect for the aged, where the aged represent wisdom, continuity, family history, and the continuance of culture and traditions.

There are also sculptures revealing love and caring between old people who have shared a long life together, and where death is waiting at the next crossroad. You will find sculptures expressing care and love for the old ones by the young and strong, but many sculptures also express anxiety on the part of the aged. Fear, lack of hope, and confusion dominate their facial expressions, and some scenes reveal direct physical abuse by the young ones, directed against the weak and the aged.

ELDER ABUSE AND SOCIETY

Abuse is the key word in this chapter, abuse of the elderly, the way it is expressed in present society and in the culture of the Western world. I will focus primarily on private abuse, as found in families (behind closed doors), protected by traditions governing people's right of privacy, which causes abuse to remain a hidden problem. Our apathy is clouded behind the popular slogan "Live and let live." In its ultimate consequence, this means that we do not care at all. We remain passive in regard to what happens to our neighbors, and avoid taking action, even where it is quite clear that we have a moral obligation to do so.

Before addressing private abuse of the elderly I would like to discuss some aspects concerning abuse of the elderly in society generally. Indeed in our society today, public abuse against the elderly and weak who do not possess the strength and ability to fight for their rights, does exist.

WHAT IS ABUSE?

It is *abuse* when old people are made to share their room in a nursing home with other people, strange to them, when they become so old and weak that they are not able to take care of themselves in their own homes.

It is *abuse* when old people in nursing homes will have to go to bed at 3 P.M. because there is not adequate nursing staff on duty to help them to go to bed later in the evening.

It is *abuse* when old people in nursing homes must remain in bed all through the weekend, because, for financial reasons, there are not enough staff available to assist the old ones with their self-care.

It is *abuse* of the elderly when they become undernourished and feeble because the nursing staff do not have enough time to help the elderly eat. Research reports have indicated that in nursing homes and hospitals, there is a high percentage of elderly who are suffering from malnutrition, not because food is not available or of poor quality, but because of inadequate staffing. Old people with few or no relatives are particularly vulnerable to this type of abuse.

It is *abuse* of the elderly when a couple who have shared a long life together must part because one of them has become so feeble that he or she needs institutional care, and the community does not create opportunities for the spouse to share a room with the partner, if this is what the couple desires.

It is *abuse* of the elderly when technology is replacing human care. Recently in Norway, a nursing institution caring for demented elderly, has started electronic surveillance of confused patients. This was less expensive than using manpower and the institution was saving a considerable amount of money. More than twenty nursing homes in Norway have introduced this method. An electrode is attached to the patient which transmits signals. For example, if the patient is approaching the exit door, a signal will be alerted and the door will be locked automatically or a frightening sound will be unleashed, thus stopping the patient who attempts to leave the room.

It is *abuse* of the elderly when they are released from hospitals and sent home to empty apartments, without a private network to care for them. Newspapers are filled with tragic stories of elderly people who have died in solitude and whose bodies have remained in the home for days and weeks without having been noticed by others.

It is *abuse* of the elderly when they are subjected to street violence, robbed of their purses, social security money, and personal belongings, because society has not budgeted enough funds to give protection to the elderly against street criminals.

It is *abuse* of the elderly when we take away from them the right to make their own daily life decisions.

I could make this list much longer. However, I have tried to emphasize that abuse of the elderly does not only appear on the private level. It happens perhaps even more on the public or institutional level, and you might say that the more feeble and demented the elderly, the greater the danger for abuse, and the more difficult it is to prove that abuse has really occurred.

Abuse of the Elderly, A Serious and Prevalent Problem

Abuse of elderly people is not a new phenomenon, but recognition of this problem certainly is. In the United States it was not until the 1970s that the first studies about elderly abuse appeared in the literature. Definitions and descriptions of elderly abuse, defined as physical abuse, psychological abuse, financial abuse, and violation of rights, came as late as 1979 [1].

A number of other studies [2-5] have added knowledge to these early reports of elder abuse.

Occurrence

Studies in the United States and Canada have suggested that between 2 and 5 percent of the elderly population are victims of abuse [6, 7]. Pillemer and Finkelhor in one study suggest that 3.2 percent of the elderly admitted that they were abused: 2 percent had been physically abused, 1.1 percent psychologically abused, and 0.4 percent neglected [7]. Podnieks reported similar results from an investigation in Canada [8].

In Scandinavia, research concerning abuse of the elderly is limited, but one presumes that the problems concerning abuse of the elderly are the same as in the United States and Canada [9-13].

Elderly abuse has gone largely unrecognized in Scandinavia, as it is one of the last forms of family violence to come to public attention. This is due to a number of factors, including: lack of awareness of the issues on the part of the medical profession and other health care workers; the inability of victims to report abuse because of isolation and illness; and the unwillingness of victims to report abuse because of shame, fear of retaliation on the part of the abuser, and/or fear of institutionalization.

Although definitions of elder abuse vary in the literature, there have been four major categories of abuse identified by the majority of researchers. These are physical abuse, psychological abuse, financial or material abuse, and neglect.

Definition of Elder Abuse

"Elder abuse is the abuse and neglect of people sixty-five years old and more in private residential settings in any of the following four categories. The abuser may be a family member, friend, neighbor, paid carer, or other persons in close contact with the elderly person."

Physical Abuse

The infliction of physical pain or injury, or physical coercion. Examples include hitting, slapping, pushing, burning, physical restraint, and sexual assault.

Psychological Abuse

The infliction of mental anguish involving actions that cause fear of violence, isolation, or deprivation and/or feelings of shame, indignity, and powerlessness. Examples include treating the elder person as a child, humiliation, emotional blackmail, blaming, swearing, intimidation, name calling, and isolation from friends and relatives.

Material/Financial Abuse

The illegal or improper use of the old person's property or finances. Examples include misappropriation of money, valuables, or property; forced changes to a will or other legal documents; and denial of the right of access to or control over personal funds.

Neglect

The failure to provide adequate food, shelter, clothing, medical care, or dental care. This may involve the refusal to permit other people to provide appropriate care. Examples include abandonment; failure to provide food, clothing or shelter; inappropriate use of medication; and poor hygiene or personal care.

Causes of Elder Abuse

The following are theories which seek to explain causes of elder abuse. The older person who is dependent on others for care because of physical and/or cognitive impairment is vulnerable to abuse. The abuser may have a psychopathology causing him or her to become abusive. Also, a history of family or domestic violence, or stress on the part of the caregiving person may be the cause.

While initially carer stress and the dependency of the older person were considered major causative factors in elder abuse [14, 15], more recently attention has turned to the personality traits or psycho-pathology of the abuser. A growing body of evidence suggests that alcoholism, drug abuse, psychiatric illness, or cognitive impairment in the abuser may be more significant as causes of abuse than the dependency of the victim [7, 16].

Most abusers are family members: a spouse, adult child, or another close relative. They usually live with the victim. They may be financially dependent on the person they are abusing. Although poverty, poor financial circumstances, and lack of resources may play a part in the occurrence of abuse, it is seen in all social groups, in urban and rural settings, and in all religious and racial groups [17].

Groups in Risk Areas

Approximately 20 percent of the elderly people in Scandinavia are expected to need help from other family members in order to perform their daily activities, or assistance in their self-care. This group is particularly vulnerable to abuse.

The abused elderly person is in most cases a woman (75% in Scandinavia) and the abuser a member of the family: son, wife, husband, or daughter. Abuse of the elderly occurs in families with serious personality problems, in families where the breadwinner has overspent his or her resources over a long period of time, and where such persons have their own complex personal problems. Families facing severe financial problems, or families having extreme living and housing conditions are also commonly found to be abusive. However, abuse is more prevalent in families with psychiatric, alcohol, and/or drug problems. The more risk variables, the greater the risk for abuse.

The reasons are complicated, and both socially as well as individually orientated. The usual factors that trigger the abuse are mental illness, misuse of stimulants, deep-seated family conflicts, and social isolation. The most common causes are extreme pressure on family members which can lead to burn out and general exhaustion. The old person may be difficult to handle, threatening, restless, complaining, emotionally immature, and may need extensive nursing care.

If the children of the elderly have themselves been exposed to abuse, for example in childhood, there may be an element of revenge involved. Other sociological factors that may increase the problems are:

- Families with fewer children to share problems
- Families living far away from their relatives
- Houses/apartments not suitable for more than one generation
- More women working outside the home
- Stagnation of national economy leading to a slower rate of developing caring facilities for the elderly
- An increase of the elderly in the population, especially elderly more than eighty years of age

Signs of Abuse

As with child abuse, which has a longer history of recognition, the presence of an individual sign, or numbers of signs, may not be conclusive proof that abuse has occurred. However there are signs, or rather clusters of signs that indicate elder abuse or mistreatment (see Table 1 and Figure 1).

Table 1. Common Indicators of
Elder Treatment

Abrasions	Decubiti
Lacerations	Dehydration
Contusions	Malnutrition
Burns	Inappropriate clothing
Freezing	Poor hygiene
Depressions	Over sedation
Fractures	Over/under medicated
Sprains	Untreated medical problems
Dislocations	Behavior that endangers health

Abuse: Unexplained bruises, repeated falls, lab values inconsistent with history, fractures or bruises in various stages of healing. (Any report by patient of having been physically abused should be followed up immediately.)

Neglect: Listlessness, poor hygiene, evidence of malnourishment, inappropriate dress, decubiti, urine burns, reports on being left in an unsafe situation, report on inability to get needed medications.

Exploitation: Unexplained loss of social security or pension checks, any evidence that material goods are being taken in exchange for care, any evidence that personal belongings of elder (house, jewelry, car) are being taken without consent or approval of elder.

Abandonment: Evidence that the elder has been "dropped off" by someone at the emergency room or family unit who has no intention of coming back for the elder.

Other risk situations: Drug or alcohol addiction in the family, isolation of elder, history of untreated psychiatric problems, evidence of unusual family stress, excessive dependence of elder or caretaker.

Figure 1. Examples of high-risk signs and symptoms.

Intervention

As the number of dependent elderly in the community increases, we can expect more cases of abuse, especially neglect and financial abuse, which appear to be closely related to the dependency of the victim. Policymakers need to take this increase in the dependent elderly population into account when planning future services for the elderly.

Funding for community services for older people should be increased according to demographic change and documented growth in demand. Availability of respite care both in the home and in institutions needs to increase; and crisis care and emergency short-term institutional care should be made available.

Homecare-nurses, social workers, and home service assistants are important witnesses when abuse of elderly people occurs. Through their way of working they gain insight into the families' way of living and they often visit them during a long period of time. Costa reported that home care corporation staff and visiting nurses are the professionals who report cases of elder abuse most often [18].

General practitioners are also important witnesses because they are the major source of health care for the elderly, and should be aware of the possibility of abuse occurring in situations where an old person is disabled and dependent, or where there is a history of psychopathology or violence within the family.

Medical officers in accident and emergency departments need to have a high degree of watchfulness when dealing with an injured elderly patient with a past history of unexplained trauma or untreated injuries, or an older person presenting a combination of poor nutrition, poor hygiene, and inadequately treated medical problems.

Prevention of neglect or abuse can be challenging. An important step would be to develop a therapeutic alliance with caregivers as opposed to an adversarial relationship. It is necessary to keep a family focus rather than attempting to "rescue" the ill elder. Intervention is more likely to be effective if help is offered to all family members [15].

Hospitalization can provide the opportunity to develop a therapeutic alliance with the family. Helping the abused or neglected elder is often best approached by first addressing the needs of the stressed caretaker. Quinn and Tomita write that most elders choose to remain with their caregiver, despite abuse or substandard care. Therefore, helping professionals must learn to care for the stressed family as a whole [19].

Feelings of shame and guilt may drive the caregiver away from accepting a helping relationship. If the health professional values caregivers as individuals of value, their self-esteem may gradually increase. It is imperative to convey to the family that their efforts are recognized. Many professionals experience a great deal of anger, in regard to abusive and neglectful caregivers and hence find it difficult to communicate empathy.

One approach to stopping the problematic behavior is to increase contact with the family following discharge. Periodic contact decreases isolation and increases their awareness that concerned healthcare providers are monitoring their progress. This ongoing contact can be a powerful influence in decreasing the likelihood of abuse or neglect. Furthermore, any deterioration of the situation can be detected early [20].

CONCLUSION

Abuse and neglect of older adults is largely an invisible problem. Those who are vulnerable are often hidden from the public eye. Troubled families characteristically maintain an isolated social existence and, therefore, the mistreatment of elders can occur without the knowledge of neighbors or concerned community members.

Factors that operate to keep the problem hidden include society's emphasis on family privacy, the victim's unwillingness or inability to report the problem, stereotypes about the aged, and denial. Although the problem of abuse and neglect of elders is not as prevalent as child maltreatment, it is a significant social problem in need of increased public awareness.

The population of elderly and old people will grow in years to come. Even today, Europe has the highest proportion of older people in the world. In Europe, there are more than thirty million people above seventy-five years of age. By the year 2010, more than 20 percent of the

Table 2. Clusters of Signs Indicating that Abuse has Occurred

- Frequent visits to the GP and/or accident and emergency department
- Frequent and unexplained falls
- Injuries which are inconsistent with the explanations given: fresh or healed fractures, bruises, welts, sores, lacerations, bite marks, burns or scalds (especially to the mouth), puncture wounds
- Evidence of neglect: malnutrition, dehydration, hypothermia, withheld medication
- Evidence of over medication: poisoning, stupor
- Evidence of undue physical restraint (marks from tying)
- Deprivation of warmth: clothing, footwear
- Deprivation of aid to mobility and perception: walking aids, sticks, frames, glasses, hearing aids, dentures (absent or ill-fitting)
- Deprivation of personal effects: money, possessions
- Deprivation of social contacts: isolation

Table 3. Some Theories about Elder Abuse [9]

- The elder person's dependency physically and/or psychologically on another member of the family
- Extraordinary amount of stress on behalf of the caregiver
- Learned abusive behavior, hereditary
- Caregiver psychopathological personality
- Family pattern of social exchange/family structure
- Alderism

Table 4. The Oslo Project:
Four Most Important Factors for Triggering of Elder Abuse [9]

• The old person is socially isolated
• The caregiver (abuser) has an alcohol/drug problem
• The caregiver (abuser) has a mental illness/psychopathological personality
• Family conflicts

Table 5. The Oslo Project: Case-Story [9]

• Woman, seventy-eight years old
• Lives with son, approximately fifty-three years old
• Isolated, few or no family/neighbor contacts
• The abused has poor health, physical and/or mental impairments
• The perpetrator has low income, unmarried/divorced, suffers from emotional distress and/or alcoholism
• The relationship to mother ambivalent, often hostile, and financially dependent on the older parent
• Type of abuse: slaps, kicks, burns, threats, pushing, physical neglect, financial exploitation

Table 6. The Oslo Project—Reporting Cases of Abuse of
Forty-Two Elderly over a Four-Month Period of Time

Type of Abuse Reported Cases		Type of Abuse Reported Cases	
Scolding	34	Refusing food	14
Humiliation	31	Stealing valuables	11
Physical neglect	28	Kicking	10
Financial exploitation	25	Locking up	9
Beating	19	Withholding medication	5
Deprivation	18	Sexual exploitation	5
Threats about institutionalization	15		
		SUM	254

total population will consist of elder people. Plans to meet the needs on behalf of the elderly, and policies to prevent abuse and neglect of the elderly must start today. (The European Community as begun to do this as evidenced in 1993, when the European Community promoted all kinds of activities to improve elderly peoples health and quality of life, with the European Year For Older People.)

REFERENCES

1. E. E. Lau and J. I. Kosberg, Abuse of the Elderly by Informal Care Providers, *Aging, 299*, pp. 11-15, 1979.
2. M. Block and J. Sinnott (eds.), *The Battered Elder Syndrome; An Exploratory Study*, University of Maryland, College Park, Maryland, 1979.
3. T. Hickey and R. Douglass, Mistreatment of the Elderly in the Domestic Setting. An Exploratory Study, *American Journal of Public Health, 71*, pp. 500-507, 1981.
4. J. Steuer and E. Austin, Family Abuse of the Elderly, *Journal of the American Geriatric Society, 28*, pp. 372-376, 1980.
5. T. A. O'Malley et al., Identifying and Preventing Family Mediated Abuse and Neglect of Elderly Persons, *Annals of Internal Medicine, 98*, pp. 998-1005, 1983.
6. C. McCreadie, *Elder Abuse, An Exploratory Study*, Age Concern Institute of Gerontology, London, 1991.
7. K. A. Pillemer and D. Finkelhor, The Prevalence of Elder Abuse: A Random Sample Survey, *Gerontologist, 28*, pp. 51-57, 1988.
8. E. Podnieks, *National Survey on Abuse of the Elderly in Canada*, Ryerson Polytechnical Institute, Toronto, 1990.
9. G. Stang and A. R. Evensen, Eldremishandling frem i lyset, *Tidsskr Nor Loegeforen., 105*, pp. 2475-2478, 1985.
10. I. Hydle and G. Stang, Kan kunnskap forhindre vold i familien? *Nordisk Medicin, 99*, p. 2, 1984.
11. L. Tornstam, Abuse of Elderly in Denmark and Sweden. Result from a Population Study, *Journal of Elder Abuse & Neglect, 1*, pp. 35-44, 1989.
12. S. Johns, I. Hydle, and O. Aschjem, The Act of Abuse: A Two-Headed Monster of Injury and Offence, *Journal of Elder Abuse & Neglect, 3*, pp. 53-64, 1991.
13. S. Linderot and A. L. Nasstrom, To Cooperate. Cooperation and Network between Professionals within the Care of the Elderly. Report Series: Ide'utvickling, *Hogskolan i Ostersund, 10*, 1985.
14. R. S. Wolf, Elder Abuse Ten Years Later, *Journal of the American Geriatric Society, 36*, pp. 758-762, 1988.
15. T. Fulmer, Mistreatment of Elders; Assessment, Diagnosis, and Intervention, *Nursing Clinics of North America, 24*, pp. 707-716, 1989.
16. E. Bristowe and J. B. Collins, Family Mediated Abuse of Noninstitionalized Frail Elderly Men and Women Living in British Columbia, *Journal of Elder Abuse Neglect, 1*, pp. 45-64, 1989.

17. M. Godkin, R. Wolf, and K. Pillemer, A Case Comparison Analysis of Elder Abuse and Neglect, *International Journal of Aging and Human Development*, *28*, pp. 207-225, 1989.
18. J. J. Costa, *Abuse of the Elderly. A Guide to Resources and Services*, D. C. Heath and Company, Lexington, Massachusetts, 1984.
19. M. J. Quinn and S. K. Tomita, *Elder Abuse and Neglect: Causes, Diagnosis, and Intervention Strategies*, Springer, New York, 1986.
21. K. A. Pillemer, Risk Factors in Elder Abuse: Results from a Case-Control Study, in *Elder Abuse. Conflict in the Family,* K. A. Pillemer and R. S. Wolf (eds.), Auburn House Company, Dover, pp. 239-264, 1986.

CHAPTER 14

International Responsibilities
to Aged and Dying

Honourable Flora MacDonald

The activities I engage in bring me into close contact with thousands of people for whom survival is measured one day at a time—indeed, many will not live to see the next morning. My work in filming the weekly series, "North-South," for VISION T.V., in chairing the International Development Research Centre which has 1650 current research projects in over seventy developing countries, and in lending my support on the ground to organizations such as OXFAM and CARE Canada, affords me the opportunity to see at firsthand the enormous differences between the lifestyles and concerns of peoples in countries of the North and those of the South. The inequities are so immense as to be almost impossible to describe or to grasp.

By the year 2000, 80 percent of all humanity will live in countries of the developing world. Here we will find the greatest human potential, the greatest market, and the greatest suffering. Meanwhile the remaining 20 percent of the world's population consumes 80 percent of the world's production.

The contrast was highlighted for me just the other day in these stark terms: it costs more to keep a cat as a family pet for a year in Canada than a struggling individual is able to earn in that year in one of the poorer countries of Africa.

For me, the disparity between peoples of the North and those of the South is an ethical issue, the effects of which are not unrelated to the theme of ethical aspects of care for the aged. We should ask the question: "Who or what is morally and ethically responsible for this disparity, this grave injustice which continues to deepen in its intensity, and which results in the deaths of hundreds of thousands of people every year?"

Let us consider one aspect of this disparity between the North and South—to the plight of the more than forty million refugees and internally displaced persons in the world. Let me flag for you, at the outset, the very real difference between these two terms—refugees and internally displaced persons. The first refers to those who have made it across an international border to seek refuge elsewhere. The second denotes those who have been uprooted within their own county, but who have been unable or unwilling to find sanctuary beyond their borders. In dealing with the refugee crisis, I would first like to situate it in the post-Cold War era, and then look at the situations in Somalia and Mozambique.

In 1993 I was in Sri Lanka as Canada's representative at the funeral of the late President Premadasa. His assassination was only the most recent in a series of brutal killings—killings that have robbed that beautiful island of its long-held and justifiable reputation as a bulwark of democracy, peace, and stability. But for ten long years, ethnic conflict and its repercussions have been the major news story emanating from Sri Lanka. Thousands of deaths and hundreds of thousands of refugees are the ongoing legacy of that conflict. The president's assassination is but the most devastating episode in the Sri Lanka horror story. As I watched the funeral proceedings I was reminded of another gathering and another Asian leader.

Some years ago at a Commonwealth Heads of Government meeting in Lusaka, Zambia, Prime Minister Lee Quan Yew of Singapore was asked to give a global overview of the current world situation. The year was 1979, a time of severe east-west tensions, shortly to be exacerbated by the Soviet invasion of Afghanistan. Prime Minister Lee likened the world situation to one in which the two super-powers formed a giant overriding arch, primarily to keep one another in check—while at the base of that arch, a plethora of regional squabbles, many fomented by, but also disciplined by the superpowers, raged on.

I wonder how the former Prime Minister of Singapore would describe the world situation today. With the discipline of the Cold War era gone, and with the disappearance of half of that overriding arch, regional wars have taken on a new and vicious dimension, often with unanticipated and unpleasant consequences. The world of today is very different from the one we knew ten years, even five years, ago.

In autumn 1992 a headline in the *Montreal Gazette* highlighted that difference. It read: "Ethnic violence: the curse of the 21st century." And it went on to say:

Communal violence of the kind sweeping the Balkans and Somalia is likely to be an enduring feature of the post-Cold War world, threatening to widen conflicts, and mocking schemes of collective security based on national boundaries that ignore newly liberated passions. Ethnic conflict is the most likely problem of the politics of the 21st century. The doctrine of national self-determination, which has been a standard of the 20th century, is going to become the curse of the 21st. According to the Royal Institute of International Affairs, there are an estimated 125 ethnic or minority disputes in the former Soviet Union alone, about 25 of them are classified as armed. Similar ethnic conflicts smoulder amid the chaos of Somalia, in the townships of South Africa, in India, in Sri Lanka, in the Middle East, in Central and South East Asia. There are anywhere from 500 to 3,500 groups of people in the world that describe themselves in some manner as a nation, but only 180 or so recognized nation-states, making the potential for future ethnic conflict virtually unlimited.

I draw the readers attention to this article because it pretty succinctly sums up the kind of world in which we increasingly find ourselves. The question is, do we have the instruments and the mechanisms to be able to function in this kind of world?

Our global organization, the United Nations, has merited praise for a number of its activities in the past. It has also, and increasingly, been the target of much criticism. Whether the locale is Cambodia or Bosnia, Somalia or Angola, the United Nations is seen as not being able to handle difficult situations. Much of the criticism may be unfair. After all, the United Nations was set up fifty years ago to deal with a world emerging from the Second World War. Its framework was fashioned to respond to ideological, not ethnic conflicts. And for most of its history, the dominance of ideology as determined by the superpowers dictated the role of the United Nations. More recently, however, the end of the Cold War and the emergence of ethnic and regional conflicts in many parts of the world, have catapulted the United Nations headlong into a very different and much more active role—one for which, many think, it is ill prepared.

If the *Gazette* article is correct in its prophecy, the number of ethnic and regional conflicts is slated to escalate dramatically. If that were to occur, what hope is there that the United Nations will be able to perform even the flawed role that it does today? And it is important to note that almost without exception, the special missions of the United Nations in the past couple of years have been triggered by the needs of refugees.

The *Gazette* article was headlined, "Ethnic Conflict: The Curse of the 21st Century." We know from experience that where ethnic conflicts occur, large numbers of refugees and internally displaced are an immediate result. According to the United Nations High Commission for Refugees, the numbers of the two groups—refugees and internally displaced—are increasing by an estimated ten thousand every day. Another four million by the end of this year.

One of the most striking things about this refugee population is that of 80 percent of those more than forty million are women and children. Think of it: some thirty-two million—the young, the elderly, the pregnant, the mothers, the most vulnerable groups—are women and children. Do they claim our attention and concern only when the eye of the television camera focuses on them and brings them into our homes? And when the camera moves on, does our concern do likewise?

In the past several years I've had the opportunity to visit a number of refugee communities in various parts of the world—to see for myself the terrible human toll that is taken when people are forced to flee not knowing where they will find safety, when their homes and crops are destroyed, when their families are dispersed, when their very lives are threatened.

I'm distressed, appalled, by what I see—hunger, starvation, lack of health and education facilities, brutality, death. But I'm also angry—angry because so often efforts to help these people are needlessly bungled. Angry at the rules and regulations of the U.N. conventions that govern refugee policy globally—rules that encourage a double standard for refugee situations in the countries of the South and those of the North. Angry because here in Canada we concentrate most of our attention, energy, and resources on the few thousand people who reach our shores to claim refugee status, while we do very little about the forty million others who remain in perilous circumstances, and for whom survival is a daily quest.

The existing refugee system developed largely in the context of superpower tensions and ideological disputes. The principal international accords defining responsibilities for victims of humanitarian crises—the U.N. Convention on the status of refugees and the Geneva Protocols—were adopted as the Cold War was taking shape. The office of the U.N. High Commissioner for Refugees (UNHCR) provided assistance and protection for people displaced by Cold War conflicts. People leaving communist regimes were routinely granted refugee status.

However, an increasing proportion of individuals displaced by events that in the colloquial sense would make them refugees do not conform to current laws and mandates. They don't fall within the U.N. Convention on refugees.

Consider, for a moment, that original refugee convention of 1951. It defined a refugee to be any person who: "owing to well-founded fear of being persecuted for reasons of race, religion, nationality, membership, of a particular social group or political opinion, is outside the country of his nationality and is unable, or owing to fear, is unwilling to avail himself of the protection of that country—or return to it."

That refugee definition, still generally accepted as the standard on which Western governments base their asylum decisions, is explicit limited in its legal force to refugees affected by events occurring prior to 1951 in Europe, thus excluding the rest of the world's refugees from its protection mandate. Although the geographic limit and cut-off date were subsequently dropped in the 1967 protocol, the implicit bias remained untouched. Refugees were those who had escaped the brutality of fascist regimes during the Second World War, or those who were fleeing persecution from communist regimes in the Cold War.

The notion of a well-founded fear of persecution based on deprivation of civil and political rights accorded easily with the Western view of soviet-style communist repression of dissidents and minorities. It accommodated the bona fide needs of those people. At the same time, it enabled the West to score points in the Cold War's ideological battle by encouraging disaffected elements within the East bloc to "vote with their feet." The five enumerated grounds of the convention and protocol definition encompass many of the truly serious grounds for human rights violations. So also does its use of the term "persecution" to refer to the horrors, arbitrary arrests, and the like that have befallen untold numbers in our lifetimes. But the convention definition excludes many other grounds which quite legitimately could be included.

For example, internally displaced persons who would have been considered refugees had they crossed an international border, are not included. Neither are massive movements of people due to armed conflicts. As well, there is no mention in the five enumerated grounds of the convention, of people fleeing persecution based on gender— women who are victims of sexual abuse and discriminatory traditions.

The incompleteness of the convention mandate has been obvious in the Third World, where it has been superseded in Africa and Latin America by a more inclusive definition that reflects more accurately the reality of forced migration in those parts of the world.

Both the Organization of African Unity (OAU) and the Organization of American States (OAS) have adopted conventions which not only include as refugees persons falling within the definition of the refugee convention and protocol, but, in addition, they extend protection to persons compelled to flee their country due to foreign aggression, foreign domination, internal conflicts, massive violations of human rights, or other circumstances that have seriously disturbed public order.

The result of these two quite different definitions of a refugee is leading to the creation of two quite different bodies of refugee law and judgments globally—one for the North and one for the South.

That difference is most acutely apparent when a Third World refugee seeks asylum in the West. That's because most Western states have made the 1951 Refugee Convention part of their national legal codes. Here in Canada, for instance, our refugee admissions policy is based on the U.N. Convention.

The result is that the narrow "persecution" standard of the refugee convention is insufficient grounds for granting asylum when the applicant's life or freedom is endangered by one of the broader causes of flight recognized by the OAU and OAS. This has led to innumerable protests by member countries of these two organizations who put their case bluntly stating:

> Being a war refugee is as legitimate a reason for fleeing one's homeland and seeking the protection of another state as is the prospect of political persecution.

When we think of refugees, we in the West (or North) normally think in terms of the U.N. Convention definition of a refugee—people who have fled their own countries to seek sanctuary elsewhere. We seldom stop to consider the internally displaced.

But the numbers of internally displaced persons—the people who haven't been able to make it across an international border—are increasing at a much faster pace than that of convention refugees.

Civil wars, internal strife, and ethnic tensions have caused an estimated twenty to thirty million people to become displaced in their own countries. Many internally displaced persons are subject to gross and persistent human rights violations. Because they have not crossed a border, the internally displaced often fall beyond the mandates of refugee and relief organizations, and may have little access to international assistance and protection. Their own governments may deny them food and other material assistance. Frequently they find themselves even more vulnerable after they have sought refuge in other parts of their own country—they become victims of physical assaults, deliberate starvation, mass expulsion, and forced labor.

To the approximately twenty million people who qualify as external or convention refugees, the U.N. High Commission for Refugees provides food, shelter, medicine, rehabilitation, and training. The UNHCR also acts to protect these refugees from physical assaults or other violations of the security of the person, and facilitates their resettlement, or voluntary return when conditions warrant.

The second group, the twenty to thirty million internally displaced persons, have no comparable agency to turn to when they are forced from their homes. The international community's response to such situations, when there is one, has been ad hoc. Such efforts fall under the rubric of Humanitarian Assistance which generally lacks a coordinated approach. In some situations, assistance has been provided but with little protection.

Some of the largest and most severe occurrences of internal displacement occur in Africa. The number of internally displaced in that continent increased threefold from approximately five million in 1980 to over fifteen million in 1992. That means that 65 percent of the world's internally displaced persons are in Africa, the great majority of them women and children.

Refugee women face enormous hardship at all stages in their flight. Under normal, that is peaceful, conditions their lives are far from easy. They are responsible for feeding of the family, including planting and harvesting the agricultural products, for selling some of their produce, managing the household, and being primary caregivers. As refugees or displaced persons, they must of course assume these traditional responsibilities, but they must do so in new and unfamiliar surroundings and without the traditional support systems that were part of village life.

Fleeing one's village is trauma enough, but when you are forced to do so in the midst of civil and ethnic conflict, aggravated by famine, lacking adequate food and water resources, it's a wonder that as many women and children survive as do so. We have no idea, of course, how many hundreds of thousand perish en route to a safe haven.

Most of those I've talked with want nothing more that to be able to return to their homes and villages—to a political climate that is peaceful, stable, and secure.

Given the grim situation, at a time when we are supposed to be advancing toward a new world order, what directions should we be taking to improve the global refugee situation? If the solutions do not spring easily to mind, at least we can be posing some of the obvious questions that desperately need answering.

Without the political edge that the Cold War sometimes provided humanitarian initiatives in refugee crises, will the political will, resources and patience be there for the North to initiate appropriate humanitarian action and sustain it through long periods of difficulty? Or will situations requiring humanitarian action and resolve be either ignored or handled in a precipitous manner to achieve quick but perhaps not long-lasting solutions?

Is it possible to provide humanitarian assistance on a more equitable, non-ideological, non-partisan basis than has been the case in the past?

Should the United Nations become increasingly involved in efforts to ensure the security of humanitarian operations and/or gaining access to people to provide them with humanitarian assistance?

Is military intervention an acceptable humanitarian act if it is done to relieve human suffering? What reforms should the United Nations take regarding assistance and protection for internally displaced persons—in particular, for women? What action is justifiable should a government refuse entry of international aid agencies on the grounds of interference with its sovereignty? What mechanism can the United Nations establish to provide early warning of massive population displacements?

In the light of these questions, I would not willingly choose Somalia, or indeed Mozambique, as ideal places on which to focus. But I do so because certainly the situation in Somalia did not have to deteriorate to the tragedy with which we are all too familiar. And perhaps we can learn from the mistakes that have been made in this instance.

For more than two years Somalia has been engulfed in humanitarian crisis of tremendous magnitude. Hundreds of thousands—an estimated half a million people, died during this period. The health of millions of others has been jeopardized as a result of months of near starvation. The origins of the crisis are to be found in a devastating combination of conflict, drought, and political anarchy. A prolonged civil war left the country with no government and few viable indigenous institutions through which help could be provided.

At the same time, and directly related to the governmental vacuum in Somalia, the international response was slow and inadequate to the task of feeding and caring for the Somali population. Despite the often heroic efforts of many individual aid agencies and their staff who worked under significant security restraints, the international humanitarian system was ill-able to handle the Somali crisis.

When the government of Somalia was overthrown, the U.N. representatives on the scene left with the government. So too did most of the non-governmental agencies. But within days, the *International Red Cross* resumed its activities in Somalia as did *Medicins Sans Frontieres* and *Save the Children U.K.* The U.N. agencies, however, did not return for another year and a half. Unfortunately their reappearance was characterized by the frequent turf wars that erupted between agencies.

Procrastination and delay were the order of the day. Meanwhile the death toll mounted.

In autumn, before the launching of Operation Restore Hope, I spent ten days inside Somalia and in the refugee camps along the Somali-Kenyan border. The memory of those camps will stay with me for the rest of my life. Located for the most part in arid sun-baked desert, with temperatures exceeding forty degrees celsius, with stinging dust-devils hurled about by the searing winds, with water at a premium everywhere, it seemed impossible that people should be able to survive in such conditions. Many didn't. There were few infants and very young children in the camps. They hadn't made it to the feeding centers. One exhausted woman told me how she had walked for fifteen days to get to the border with her children. Another, pointing to two pitifully thin youngsters clinging to her skirts, recounted how she had to throw her baby away when it became ill. Had she stopped to give it the care it needed, the bandits would have killed the other two children, she said.

I noticed other things as well. For example, people were still dying of hunger even after having reached the feeding stations, while nearby bags of beans, rice, and grains remained untouched. Those in charge, while anxious to provide food, hadn't taken into consideration the cultural and traditional customs of the refugees regarding food. Nomads, for instance, who had been forced to seek refuge in the camps, found the food itself, rather than its scarcity, a problem. Their customary diet came from their animals—meat and milk. They had little experience in preparing meals of rice and beans—some had tried to eat them uncooked.

Latrines and sanitation systems are not a part of the normal lifestyle of nomads, and in some centers very little action had been taken to put even minimal systems in place. The stench of excrement was everywhere. Outbreaks of cholera and measles were frequent. In some camps the threat of death from disease surpassed the fear of death from starvation.

In one camp the accommodation was particularly noticeable. And with reason. There, the United Nations High Commission for Refugees (UNHCR) had ordered the construction of accommodation for some fifty thousand recently-arrived refugees. But instead of constructing huts of reeds and skins which would have allowed the air to circulate, the contractors threw up row upon row of small rectangular adobe dwellings with corrugated tin roofs. In the forty-degree plus heat, the shelters became like ovens and many refugees refused to use them.

By contrast, the contributions that many non-governmental organizations have made and continue to make is remarkable. You come away from the horrors of Somalia with a deep appreciation and admiration for their work. CARE Canada, twinned with CARE Kenya, was assigned the responsibility for the operation of the refugee camps along the Somali-Kenyan border. That meant overseeing the distribution of food and water, and putting into place sanitation and hygiene systems in ten camps, each housing 50,000 refugees.

I trailed around after a young Canadian woman in charge of one of these border camps as she gave instructions for the distribution of ration cards, the installation of latrines and the supervision of burial sites, of which there are many. A year ago she had been an accountant in an office in Vancouver; today she supervises one of CARE Canada's refugee camps, carrying out her many duties in the forty-degree heat, knowing she would be at it day-in-day-out for several months without a break.

Through it all she maintained a cheerful determination which I'm sure carried her through a lot of mental anguish. I was so proud of this young Canadian and others like her; the unsung heroes and heroines who don't get enough credit back here at home for the work they are doing, often correcting the mistakes made earlier by U.N. officials.

I may say that the U.N. officers on site did their best to cope with the almost impossible numbers of refugees, but their work was hampered by the lack of a clear mandate and the resources necessary to meet the ever-increasing demands. All too frequently, however, stupid and costly mistakes, and lack of coordination in the operations of its specialized agencies, characterized the U.N.'s efforts at relief in the horn of Africa.

But criticism was not welcome, as the U.N.'s special ambassador to Somalia, Mohamed Sahnoun, found out. His pointed and public comments about the U.N.'s procrastination in dealing with Somalia—that it was too preoccupied with crises elsewhere—and his criticism of the wrangling among the specialized agencies, earned their wrath and with it Sahnoun's early departure from his post. Later when asked about the U.N.'s efforts in Somalia he said: "I do feel that the United Nations has not yet seen the full extent of the disaster in Somalia. I think historians will realize that, and I'm afraid will say that hundreds of thousands of people died and we just watched, powerless."

He added, "The U.N. is going through a very serious crisis because of the post-Cold War situation. We are going to have more countries in crisis which are political and humanitarian, and we have to seriously examine our approaches to these. Somalia is really a test."

It's a test that in many ways the United Nations and its member countries have failed. When President Siad Barre was overthrown in 1991, a mood of euphoria swept Somalia. In the hiatus that ensued, outside assistance and expertise were badly needed and would have been welcomed. But that's when the United Nations' presence in Somalia upped anchor and moved out. And within two months the civil conflict, waged with the deadly weaponry left from the days when Somalia was first a client state of the USSR and then of the USA, was in full swing under the direction of brutal warlords.

Let us turn briefly to another refugee situation in Africa that receives a minimum of attention. Mozambique has been the scene of a devastating civil war for the past fifteen years. In that period, half a million Mozambicans have been killed, 250,000 children have been orphaned, four million people have been uprooted and forced to flee from their homes and villages. Two million of that number have crossed borders into neighboring countries. Little Malawi, one of the poorest countries in Africa, with a population of only eight million, opened its doors to one million Mozambicans. Because that incredible mass migration is little known to the outside world, only minimal external assistance has been provided—$20 million from the UNHCR annually to cover the needs of the one million refugees in Malawi.

There is a unique and particularly vicious aspect to the war in Mozambique. The Renamo Bandits—the surrogate troops for right-wing South Africans and former Rhodesians—established the practice of kidnapping young boys from the villages they overran. This children's brigade, numbering in the thousands, was brainwashed into believing that killing was not only a normal, but a desirable part of everyday life. They were trained to carry out acts of brutality and violence, beginning with the murder of their parents and siblings.

These young men now have to be reintegrated into society. But as one departmental health official said to me, "How will we be able to do this? We have few psychiatrists and psychoanalysts. We're going to need a great deal of outside professional help."

Now that the war in Mozambique is supposedly over, the refugees want desperately to return to their home country. But as yet only a vanguard of the U.N.'s promised peacekeeping force of thousands has arrived. Even more critical, the hundreds of thousands of land mines that line every footpath and bush-track leading from Malawi to Mozambique, remain dangerously in place. The large numbers of disabled in the refugee camps, especially among the children, are mute testimony to the lethal power of the hidden land mines.

When will the United Nations apply the same urgency to the critical need in Mozambique that it does to other parts of the world? Or will we see a deterioration of the fragile peace in this southern African country, until another Angola, replete with a resumption of civil war, confronts us?

Which brings me back to the larger global crisis where I began—the development of massive refugee movements and the humanitarian efforts needed to deal with them. A document issued recently by the Refugee Policy Group in Washington included this statement:

> Throughout the cold war years, the international refugee regime developed with the recognition that little could be done by the international community, in the short term, to reverse the repressive policies of totalitarian states. The framework that emerged to address this situation espoused the fundamental right of people to leave their countries, promoted the principle that refugees should not be returned to places where they would face persecution, and encouraged states to provide asylum to refugees until durable solutions could be found to their plight.

> With the end of the cold war, a new orientation is emerging aimed at addressing humanitarian problems inside countries of origin in order to prevent massive movements of people across international borders. This new orientation needs to be supported to the extent that it addresses the root causes of displacement by working at economic development, human rights, democratization, and the early warning of humanitarian crises [1, p. 1].

Is this the new orientation taking hold? Or are we seeing a hardening of the difference in legal standards for refugees in the industrialized West and those in the Third World?

That difference was apparent in the speed with which the Western powers and the U.N. bureaucracy approached the plight of refugees and internally displaced in Yugoslavia, and the lack of speed in Somalia. Equally apparent today is the lack of speed and effort with which the desperate situations in southern Sudan, Angola, and Rwanda are being addressed, while thousands perish. In April 1993 I was in northern Namibia, along the border with Angola. While I was there the battle for Huamba was raging only a few hundred miles away. Ten thousand people were reportedly killed in that bitter confrontation in Angola, but in the rest of the world the tragedy in Huamba went largely unnoticed. And at the end of April the United Nations discontinued its presence in Angola.

It is events like this that cry out for a much greater measure of accountability on the part of the United Nations and its specialized agencies than presently exists. And I don't mean being accountable in a balance-sheet bottom-line manner, but accountable in a moral sense for its actions or lack thereof—either one of which may leave thousands of people dead. We can now congratulate those responsible for Operation Restore Hope in Somalia. But to whom do we turn for an explanation and an accounting for the months of procrastination on the part of the United Nations which led the former U.N. special envoy to Somalia to comment, "Hundreds of thousands of people died while we just watched, powerless"?

The Refugee Policy Group statement which I quoted from earlier went on to say:

> There can be little doubt that we are at a watershed point in terms of the principles, mandates, structures, mechanisms, capacities, resources, and commitments that define and support humanitarian action.
>
> The astounding configuration of world events has presented the international community with an "open moment" to shape the future of humanitarian action. To these questions the humanitarian community must develop realistic answers that balance political, economic, and humanitarian rationales for engagement. Failure to do so risks, at best, the inappropriate distribution of scarce resources and, at worst, a state of immobilization which watches helplessly as humanitarian crises rage on [1, p. 1].

Yes, we are at a watershed. And the opportunity to correct some of the inequities of the past is at hand. A year ago this seemed to be the trend. When Boutros Boutros-Ghali took over as secretary-general of the United Nations he attempted to inject a new urgency into global humanitarian concerns, to move them higher up the U.N.'s agenda.

Boutros-Ghali created the new post of Deputy Secretary-General for Humanitarian Affairs, appointed Jan Eliasson to the position, and gave him a far-reaching mandate to effect change. Unfortunately, he didn't provide him with much in the way of financial or human resources to carry out his task. Eliasson's mandate includes certain humanitarian issues which up until now have been relegated to the periphery of responsibilities of other U.N. agencies.

For example, the responsibility for internally displaced people has been assumed jointly, when and where it could be, by the United Nations High Commission for Refugees and the United Nations Development Fund. And even though these two agencies have been handicapped, because of lack of funds, in their ability to look after a rapidly growing vulnerable group—the internally displaced—nevertheless they have been reluctant to relinquish any of their authority to the newly-created Humanitarian Affairs Division. The turf war which ensued marginalized Eliasson's responsibility for coordination of humanitarian relief operations in both Somalia and Yugoslavia.

The failure to date of this promising initiative is just one of many reasons why the world's major political institution, the United Nations, is itself due for major over-hauling.

I mentioned earlier that I am angry at the imbalance in the attention we pay to issues concerning refugees. Asylum seekers who arrive in this country unannounced—at the uppermost, fifty thousand a year—get a great deal of media and public attention. The other forty million refugees and internally displaced persons go practically unnoticed.

That attitude is reflected not only in the media, but as well, in the annual outlay of public funds for refugee purposes. These funds are allocated in two ways—the amount we spend to process refugee applicants who arrive in Canada, and the amount we contribute to international agencies responsible for refugee matters. The case of each refugee applicant who arrives at our airports is reviewed by the Immigration Refugee Board. The cost to maintain that system for the fifty thousand applicants is approximately $300 million annually. The amount Canada contributes to the UNHCR to go toward the maintenance of the other forty million refugees is less than $20 million a year.

But we are by no means the most introverted and niggardly country in this regard. The estimated cost of maintaining all the refugee determination systems in the developed world, which jointly process about one million people annually, is between $30 and $50 billion a year. The total budget contributed to the UNHCR for all other refugees is less than one billion dollars.

I'm appalled by this allocation of resources—I think the allotments should be reversed. The thirty to fifty billion dollars surely should be directed to correcting the root causes of mass migrations—to the long-term development of human resources in Third World countries. Because unless the root causes—poverty, lack of education, lack of land, environmental degradation—are addressed, the numbers of those involved in mass migrations will grow.

For too long, U.N. and indeed, non-governmental agencies' efforts to provide humanitarian assistance in crisis situations have concentrated on the immediate need. Little attention has been paid to linking these efforts to long-term development. Such limited action is understandable given the pressures of the moment, but until humanitarian and refugee assistance is firmly integrated into long-term development polices, we will continue to apply bandaids to a badly festering wound.

In addition to linking humanitarian assistance with long-term development, it is critical that some international instrument be devised to address the needs of the internally displaced in a consistent and coherent manner. The U.N., and indeed all its member nations, have shied away from tackling this thorny issue because to do so would intrude both directly and indirectly on the long-sanctified concept of national sovereignty. But the Kurdish crisis in Iraq and the ongoing operations in Somalia and the former Yugoslavia have shown that new thinking is desperately needed. The internally displaced, one of the most vulnerable groups in the world today, must not be allowed to languish in what can justifiably be called a "no man's land" indefinitely.

The question of a more realistic U.N. definition of what constitutes a refugee in the 1990s must be addressed. The dichotomy between the description of refugees in countries of the North and those in the South is quite possibly in contravention of the principles of the U.N. charter. A new definition, in itself, will not and cannot be a solution to the escalating global figures for refugees—the numbers that such a change would accommodate would be a mere drop in the bucket compared to the overall total—but it would rectify a grave injustice.

There are not that many aged among the world's refugees and internally displaced—they, along with the very young, are the first victims of ethnic conflict and uprootedness. And the bereaved can permit themselves only the solace of mourning internally. They must face the never-ending challenge of trying to save yet another individual whose hold on life is precarious at best.

But I hope my remarks have conveyed my feeling that we as nations and as individuals must do more to ensure that our lack of attention and awareness does not further endanger the vulnerable peoples of the world. We must hold our global institutions accountable for their actions and for their failure to act. We have a moral and ethical responsibility both to ourselves and to those far less fortunate than we are, to do so.

REFERENCE

1. Refugee Policy Group, *RPG Review*, Policy Group in Washington, July 1992.

CHAPTER 15

Euthanasia:
Seeking Insights From the Edge*

Margaret A. Somerville

INTRODUCTION

This chapter began its existence as one of a series of lectures on medical decisions at the end of life.[1] In preparing and delivering these lectures, two common, but powerful and important insights were strongly reinforced. First, our debate about euthanasia concerns much more than that matter, itself, for both individuals and society; and, second, the role of language is immensely important in forming the

*This chapter is an abbreviated and edited version of a longer article, "The Song of Death: The Lyrics of Euthanasia," which appeared in the *Journal of Contemporary Health Law and Policy, 9,* pp. 1-76, 1993. It appears here under the title used for the corresponding presentation at the 11th International King's College Conference on Death, Dying and Bereavement.

[1] Brendan F. Brown Lecture, The Catholic University of America, Washington, D.C., November 1990. Other lectures included, "Reasonably Well or Dead: Squaring the Curve," the Walter Zuckerman Memorial Lecture on Medical Ethics, Mount Auburn Hospital, Cambridge, Massachusetts, November 1990; "The Polemics of Euthanasia," speech delivered at the Joint Assembly of the Catholic Health Association of Canada and the United States, Montreal, Quebec, June 1991; "Euthanasia as a Mirror: Visions of Self and Society" speech delivered at the Seventh International Hospice Institute Symposium, "Management of Terminal Illness: An Update," Washington, D.C., July 1991; "'This Way to the Egress': Legal and Illegal Exits—The Euthanasia Debate," speech delivered at the XV Conference on the Law of the World, World Jurist Association, Barcelona, Spain, October 1991; "Legalizing Euthanasia: Which Way The Tide?" speech delivered at the 9th International Conference on Care of the Terminally Ill, presented by Palliative Care Medicine, McGill University, Montreal, Quebec, November 1992; and "Euthanasia: The Death(ly) Debate," Lowther Lecture, York University, Toronto, Ontario, January 1993.

issues in this debate and responses to those issues. This is true, because consideration of euthanasia requires both thinking and feeling, and language forms and affects how we both think and feel, and whether these functions are integrated or separated.

In order, therefore, to explore some of the complex dilemmas and interactions that confront us in dealing with euthanasia, we need to examine the ways in which language is employed in this context, including in, but not limited to, the law. Language is used in describing and formulating the issues raised by euthanasia, in handling these, and in eliciting responses to the approaches taken. This examination also needs to include exploration of how language is used to label or characterize situations in order to deal with these situations in certain, pre-determined ways. Moreover, we also need to recognize that language is relevant both to "talking about" euthanasia and to "doing" (carrying out) euthanasia.[2] Perhaps, the most striking recent example of this is the book, *Final Exit* [2]. This book "talks" about euthanasia in order to advocate euthanasia, but it can also be directly involved in "doing" euthanasia, for example, in those cases where people have been found dead with the book beside them, open at the pages containing the detailed instructions which they have followed to kill themselves.

DEFINITION

Nowhere is the use of language more important and, sometimes, more confused and confusing, than when it is employed for the purposes of definition. This is especially true with respect to the definition of euthanasia. Even when one has an overriding aim of neutrality and precision, it is difficult to define accurately and clearly, which interventions or noninterventions should and which should not be regarded as constituting euthanasia. Such a definition is, however, essential and the range of possibilities with respect to it are explored in this section.

The etymological origins of the word euthanasia—"good death"—are today common knowledge, as a result of the publicity that has surrounded the topic. The use of this terminology, quite apart from its definitional content (that is, what does and does not constitute euthanasia), merits consideration. For everyone, at some level, death is "bad" in the sense of sad and unhappy, but some ways of dying are "less bad" and "less unhappy" than other ways and these are "good deaths." We all hope, and hope to be assisted, to be in the latter category with

<hr/>

[2] For a discussion of the difference between the use of language to "talk about" an activity (e.g., law or psychiatry) and "to do" that same activity, see [1].

respect to our own deaths. The issue on which we disagree, is what should be the limits, if any, placed on such assistance.

With the above in mind, it is proposed that euthanasia be defined as "an intervention or a non-intervention by one person, to end the life of another person, who is terminally ill, for the purpose of relieving suffering, with the intent[3] of causing the death[4] of the other person, except where the primary intent is either to provide treatment necessary for the relief of pain or other symptoms of serious physical distress, or non-provision or withdrawal of treatment is justified, in particular, because there is a valid refusal of treatment or the treatment is futile."[5] This definition excludes the provision of reasonably necessary

---

[3] Normally, in law one is responsible for acts which one intends. Intention to kill another person, in a legal sense, is present when either there is a desire to kill the other person, or death is the certain or almost certain result of the act or omission (in a situation in which there is a duty to act) in question. The difficulty, in the context of the present discussion, is to establish legal immunity for (i) giving adequate treatment for the relief of pain or other symptoms of serious physical distress, even when this could shorten life, if this is reasonably necessary to relieve pain or other symptoms of serious physical distress (which would be given with an intention to kill, in the technical legal sense, if the treatment was certain or almost certain to shorten life); and (ii) respecting valid refusals of treatment; and (iii) withholding or withdrawing futile treatment, when this will or could result in death; while prohibiting other interventions undertaken with an intention to cause death. There are two possible approaches. Either to define euthanasia as including all interventions in which there is an intention to cause death, except the provision of reasonably necessary treatment for the relief of pain or other symptoms of serious physical distress, or respect for a valid refusal of treatment, or withholding or withdrawing futile treatment. Or, alternatively, one can require a motive to kill (which is not present in giving treatment necessary to relieve pain or other symptoms of serious physical distress, or in respecting a valid refusal of treatment, or withholding or withdrawing futile treatment) as part of the definition of euthanasia. The former approach is adopted here. It should be noted that in this text, the terms *primary intent, primary purpose,* and *motive* are used synonymously. The term *direct intent* is not used, but also, means the same.

[4] In general, I have chosen to use the term "to cause death," rather than "to kill," but these terms can be synonymous. It is interesting to consider the difference in nuance between the two terms, and to compare them with the term "to allow to die." The words "to kill" most often are used to describe interventions or non-interventions causing death, that are regarded as unjustifiable. In contrast, "allowing to die" tends to be used to describe non-interventions that are regarded as justifiable. The provision of reasonably necessary pain relief treatment that could or would shorten life is an intervention often referred to as causing death, but not in general as killing, probably because it is regarded as justified, indeed, required.

[5] The term futile is used to include both medically useless treatment and that in which benefits, if any, of the treatment are minimal and are clearly outweighed by its harms, that is, the treatment would be clearly "disproportional." It is recognized that such determinations unavoidably involve value judgments, which is often a source of criticism of approaches depending on these concepts. The solution is not to avoid such approaches when these are otherwise the best ones (as it is proposed is true with respect to determinations regarding when treatment is futile), but to surround them with sufficient safeguards. What would constitute these cannot be explored in this text.

treatment for the relief of pain or other symptoms of serious physical distress, which could or would shorten life, provided that, although there could be an intent to cause death in giving such treatment, the primary intent is to relieve pain or other symptoms of serious physical distress, and is not to cause death. The definition also excludes justified withholding or withdrawal of treatment, in particular, in order to respect valid refusals of treatment,[6] on the basis that, in such cases, first, there is no intention to cause death, although there is an intention to allow the person to die; second, the primary intent is either to respect the person's right to refuse treatment or not to impose futile treatment; and, third, death is not caused, from the perspective of the law, by the failure to provide or by the withdrawal of treatment, rather it is caused by the person's underlying condition.

In short, one can have euthanasia, in the sense of this term as defined, by omission as well as by act, but not all omissions of treatment that result in death, constitute euthanasia. What is important, therefore, is to distinguish omissions of treatment that constitute euthanasia from omissions of treatment which do not constitute euthanasia.

There is sometimes a fine line between allowing a person to die and causing the death of another person. This is especially true in relation to withdrawing or not providing treatment other than pursuant to a competent patient's informed refusal of treatment or "advance directive" to this effect. But the important point is that there is a line and, it is proposed, the nature of interventions on one side of this line is different in kind from that of interventions on the other side. In another context, I have described the situations which define such lines as "marker events" [3]. These function to allow that which occurs on one side of the line to be seen as different in kind, in particular regarding precedent setting effect, from that which occurs on the other side of the line. In relation to differentiating conduct that constitutes euthanasia from that which does not, the "marker event" is comprised of a "mens rea" (state of mind) of an intention to cause death *and* an "actus reus" (conduct) of an act or omission that causes, in the legal sense of this term, the death of the other person, except where the situation involves the provision of necessary treatment for the relief of pain or other symptoms of serious physical distress.

---

[6] A valid refusal of treatment is an informed refusal of treatment given by either a competent adult person or a factually competent minor; or a refusal pursuant to a valid "advance directive," whether in the form of a "living will" or a durable power of attorney for health care, or given by some other legally recognized substitute decision maker, when such a refusal is within the scope of the authority of this decision maker.

Because pain relief treatment, which could or even would shorten life but which is reasonably necessary to relieve pain, involves an intention, in a legal sense, to cause death, it raises difficulties with respect to potential criminal liability. Such treatment must be able to be given with legal immunity. Consequently, where the motive is to relieve pain and *not to kill*, the intervention must be justified, despite the possible presence in a technical legal sense of an intention that death will result.[7] In other words, motive can be regarded as an excuse or a justification—a defense—protecting against or negating, respectively, criminal or other liability in such circumstances, which is the analysis most consistent with traditional theory in criminal law [4]. We need also to keep in mind that providing adequate pain relief treatment could extend life, as the person is less physically and psychologically distressed, in which case failure to provide it shortens life.

The subject of pain relief treatment is a critical one in the context of a discussion of euthanasia. Fears of being left in unbearable pain, or even more horrific, the reality of this occurring, which still far too often happens, is probably a strong impetus for many persons to argue that euthanasia should be made available. We need to be acutely aware that the attitudes of some individuals and the structure of some systems contribute to failure to provide adequate pain relief treatment. For instance, I recently learned of a case in which a man, dying of disseminated carcinoma, was being given Tylenol™ for severe pain. A physician on night rotation changed the order to morphine. The next night, she was again called to see the man, because he was in very severe pain. She found that during the intervening day, the man's attending physician had canceled the order for morphine and written another order for Tylenol™. When questioned, the attending physician said that he thought the man was "a complainer" and, in any case, he did not want to have "addicted patients," two responses that one would hope not to hear from any physician practicing medicine in the 1990s. In another case, I was told that a young resident considered giving a dose of potassium chloride to a dying patient in severe pain, because the hospital ward supply of morphine had run out that night and no more could be obtained until the hospital pharmacy opened the next morning. We must ensure that not only health care practitioners are humane, but also that we have humane systems in our health care

---

[7] There is increasing evidence, however, that medically advanced pain relief regimes do not shorten life, in which case concerns that they do, may become obsolete (personal communication with Professor Norelle Lickiss, Director, Palliative Care Services, Royal Prince Alfred Hospital, Sydney, Australia, December 1992).

institutions.[8] The most effective and important means of achieving this in the area of medical interventions at the end of life is to promote the teaching and provision of high standards of palliative care. *All* physicians need some familiarity with the concepts and practice of this area of medicine, as well as there being a need for specialization in it.

Failure to take all reasonable steps to relieve pain and thereby leaving people in pain is not only a human tragedy and contrary to the most fundamental concepts of human rights, it should be treated as at least legally actionable medical malpractice and, arguably, even as a crime. Certainly, to provide necessary pain relief treatment, even that which could shorten life, must not be seen as criminal. This has been explored in much greater depth elsewhere [6], the point here is that those who oppose euthanasia, but fail to take steps to ensure that adequate pain relief treatment is provided (or even worse, oppose this, if it could shorten life) do much to promote the case for euthanasia.

In summary, no matter whether one promotes the view that euthanasia should be available to those who request it or believes that euthanasia should be prohibited, it is important to deal with the various situations which require decision-making concerning interventions at the end of life, separately from each other. In particular, situations which involve an intention to cause death should be dealt with separately from other situations in which there is no such intention, and within the former group further distinctions are necessary. In order to undertake such a discussion, the terminology must be very clear. Consequently, in the remainder of the text, to repeat, the term "euthanasia" is used in the strict sense of meaning an intervention (other than the provision of reasonably necessary treatment for the relief of pain or other symptoms of serious physical distress) or a non-intervention including withdrawal of treatment (other than pursuant to a valid refusal of treatment or where the treatment is futile) undertaken for the purpose of relieving suffering in circumstances of terminal illness, with the intention of causing the death of the person who is subject to the intervention or non-intervention. A narrow definition is needed because euthanasia, as defined, is *different in kind not just degree* from other measures, which can also mean that life is not prolonged or even that death is "caused" in the sense that it occurs sooner than it would otherwise do. In particular, it is argued that the "analogy between foregoing treatment and active euthanasia is simply

[8] It also merits considering whether establishing a system, such as that described, could be regarded as "systems negligence" and, therefore, could give rise to a possible action in negligence directly against the hospital for damages by persons who are harmed as a result [6].

false" [7]. Most persons who are in favor of euthanasia would disagree with this statement. They argue that the outcome is the same—namely death—and that once allowing death to occur is justified, how this is brought about is morally, and ought to be legally, irrelevant [8]. Recognizing for the sake of argument that this could be true, does not justify making it true by treating all interventions at the end of life as the same, in particular, regardless of whether or not they involve an intention or a primary intention to cause death. Rather, each category of intervention needs separate justification, if it is to be justified.

If one imagines a continuum with a very liberal pro-euthanasia position at one end and a very stringent pro-life position at the other, the position which is being advocated in this text is somewhere in the middle. This position is much more difficult to articulate, define, and defend than either of the poles, and moreover one can be and is attacked from both sides. In part this may explain why some persons choose one or the other pole. I have suggested elsewhere that living in "the purple-pink middle" may represent what we see, at least initially, as an "impossible combination" of attitudes, values, and beliefs [9]. But while it is usually the most difficult position, it may also be the most honest one, in that it best accommodates and even reconciles what we say and what we do. It is proposed that the most acceptable position with respect to interventions or non-interventions at the end of life, is to recognize rights to adequate treatment for the relief of pain and other symptoms of serious physical distress, and rights to refuse treatment, even when any of these approaches could or will shorten life, and to prohibit all other interventions or non-interventions undertaken with an intent of causing the death of the person to whom they relate.

WHY ARE WE TALKING OF EUTHANASIA NOW?

(A) Is it an Indirect Way of Talking About Death?

We need to ask whether our "euthanasia talk" is covering-up some other reality. There is much discussion of euthanasia, but, I suggest, less of death—talking about death is difficult. Indeed, we have been described as a society that is unusually fearful of death—a death-denying society [10]. This term is interesting because denial requires some minimal level of consciousness of the "thing" feared in order to suppress the larger consciousness of that "thing." Could it be that euthanasia is the conscious mechanism that we use to suppress our larger awareness of death? Is it less fearful to talk of euthanasia than death, and consequently, our discussion of death is being carried out in the context of euthanasia? We used to talk about death "in religion," but the major decline in adherence to organized religion means that many of us no longer talk about death in that context. In recent times, we have not talked about death in any context, except possibly in symbolic and ritualized form in literature and the arts. Could it also be that talk of euthanasia de-conditions us to the fear of death, especially, because at the same time as we speak of the feared "event," we simultaneously speak of controlling it through the use of euthanasia? As Winslade has said, "[t]he need to control death whether by postponing it or hastening it—seems to rest on a deep fear and denial" [7]. Could it even be that our "euthanasia talk" is a terror management device, for both individuals and society? Greenberg and his colleagues propose that the thought of death raises the deepest terror, which we then need to manage [11]. We do this by seeking to achieve a consensus that affirms our most important values, which, in turn, provides reassurance. Could this explain the strong polarization and conflict on euthanasia, in that each "side" wants consensus in order to have the reassurance that results from having its values affirmed? Could it also be that this terror is so great that we would rather be dead, than living in fear of death, particularly, imminent death, and euthanasia is seen as allowing us to achieve this outcome?

It seems that advocacy of euthanasia is connected with a desire for control. Control is related to relief of suffering. Suffering is present when one has a sense of one's own disintegration and a loss of control over what happens to one [12]. To move from chance, which the occurrence of death has largely been, to choice, which is the promise of euthanasia, can be to reduce suffering. Persons may see euthanasia as avoiding present suffering (either because they seek euthanasia at the time, or because it allays present fears—which are a form of suffering—that they can avoid suffering at some time in the future) or future suffering. Euthanasia may also fulfill a need or desire for certainty, which is related to a need or desire for control. Stated in another way, euthanasia can be viewed as reducing uncertainty which reduces anxiety, and consequently, it provides reassurance. Euthanasia could also be a "do something" response. When faced with fearful situations our anxiety tends to be increased by inactivity and decreased by activity, because in the latter case we feel that we can and are "doing something" to remedy the situation. This also provides a feeling of greater control which likewise reduces anxiety. Further, it is interesting to note in this context, that an attitude on the part of some physicians that is manifested in their telling patients that they can do nothing more for them, may be a precipitating cause of some patients seeking euthanasia [3, p. 111].

The availability of euthanasia could also inflict suffering. There could be a fear that it would be practiced in ways that would mean that the individual loses rather than gains control. Similarly, there could be present fear about future use of euthanasia—not simply fear at a future time about its use at that time. It has been alleged that some old persons in The Netherlands fear physicians and hospitals because they fear they may be subjected to euthanasia [14, p. 26]. In other words, instead of giving more control to the individual, euthanasia may, overall, result in less control. Even such situations as seeing oneself as a burden on society when one is old and ill, and as needing to do the "right thing" by requesting euthanasia is a loss of individual control and freedom of spirit. Both the anticipation and experience of these are suffering inflicting. It has also been suggested that allowing euthanasia means that persons must face a choice whether or not to use it and could have to justify their choice to continue living, because "the existence of the option becomes a subtle pressure to request it" [15, p. 17]. Situations that raise such issues are very likely to be a source of suffering.

Euthanasia may also be a vehicle for addressing much wider and deeper realities that operate at conscious, unconscious, and symbolic levels.[9] In a study of the stance on euthanasia taken by major world religions over approximately a millennium, Young et al. propose

> that "reason alone" has never been the sole guiding principle by which individuals have killed themselves or others when ill or old. Rather, reason has often been used either to affirm or to cover the operation of deeper values that are not expressly identified. These have included the heroic ideal of the self-willed death among warriors threatened with defeat or the derivative ideal among ascetics or philosophers of self-willed death to demonstrate their version of courage. Unlike the ancient world's desire for a heroic form of death and Nazi Germany's legitimation of euthanasia to create a "super race," today's societies are entertaining the idea of self-willed or assisted death to avoid suffering or ensure "dignity." Since the pain of dying can be effectively treated in most cases, what accounts for the current movement to legalize euthanasia [16]?

As well as seeking consensus on values for the sake of consensus because we need the reassurance that such consensus provides [16, p. 17], what deeper values could we be seeking to affirm or to cover, in arguing for, or likewise against, euthanasia?

---

[9] See also the discussion under (iii) *Sanctity of Life and Quality of Life* (p. 224).

The analysis of the French psychoanalyst, de Hennezel, is of great interest in this respect, because it shows some of the enormous complexities we are dealing with in our discussion of euthanasia. In particular, it shows that two emotions, fear and love, and the relationship between them, are central to the euthanasia debate. De Hennezel argues "that a fine death is an illusion, a myth . . . which people tell themselves to appease their anguish," and that our society is "governed by th[e] myth of a good death." She proposes that there are two versions of this myth. One view sees a "good death [as] . . . a discreet and rapid death, unconscious, and, particularly, of no bother to anyone else." This corresponds to a view of the world in which death is denied; medicine is all powerful; caregivers see death of their patients as a failure; and death is "experienced in great solitude and with no guideposts or values." This is "[a] world of affectivity, efficiency, performance, with priority given to cost-effectiveness [and] consumption . . . [a] world of objects not of subjects, in short, a world stripped of souls and spirit, a world without love" (see also [18]). The other view of a good death comes from "a new humanism . . . try[ing] to bring life and death together as one. An accompanied death, a socialized death, one experienced in lucidity up to the end becomes the desired good death" [17, p. 33]. The view of the world behind this vision is a much less certain one. In fact, its essence is recognition: of the uncertainty of many of us about the meaning of life and death; of the need for sensitivity to others and the humility to allow others to experience in their own, not our, way; and that there are possibilities of extremes of either "nothingness or . . . mystery of the beyond." It is "an appeal to change our way of loving." This "new concept of 'dying well' . . . is no longer an illusion or a myth, but a permission to experience one's death as one wishes, to experience it fully, with the assurance of being loved and accepted no matter what. This of course requires that someone else be capable of that degree of true love" [17, p. 34].

If we accept the propositions set out previously, it could lead to the conclusion that we should reject euthanasia, because it is too "easy," in the sense of simplistic, rational, cold, and unloving, as an approach or response in dealing with death, at least at the societal level, even if not in some exceptional cases at the individual level. And yet, those in favor of euthanasia argue exactly the contrary, namely, that euthanasia is among the great humanitarian causes [13, p. 112]. The important point to note here is that our arguments are of this nature. This means that in dealing with euthanasia, we are dealing with some of the most fundamental and critical issues of our humanness, as both individuals and a society. In short, whether we are "pro" or "anti" euthanasia, we agree that euthanasia is a central focus in our discussion of these fundamental issues; where we disagree, is whether allowing or prohibiting euthanasia best promotes our human spirit and our humanness and humanity.

(B) Is There a Newly Perceived Need for Euthanasia?

(i) Modern Medical Technology

Some people attribute the augmented perceived need for euthanasia as being yet one more effect of modern medical technology. It is possible that our sense of "playing God" to keep alive persons, who in past times would certainly have been dead, may have given us a sense of power not only over death, but perhaps over life. In short, once we use technology to prolong life, perhaps there is some correlative sense in which we feel we may use it to shorten life. Certainly we do not need new technology to kill; this possibility is as old as the human species itself.

It may be, however, that a fear of the overuse of medical technology has contributed to calls for euthanasia. This fear is summed up in statements such as that persons would rather be dead than left "to the mercy of doctors 'and their machines' " [14, p. 24]. The development of rights to refuse treatment has been one response to these fears. Rights are a major currency of the law. In contrast, medicine tends to give priority to fulfilling needs. Trying both to fulfill the needs of persons and respect their rights can sometimes give rise to a situation of conflict, in particular, in relation to refusals of treatment with modern medical technology. Some such situations in which rights have predominated to allow persons to refuse treatment at the expense of fulfilling major and serious needs (which they have or are perceived to have) have been described as "rotting with your rights on" [19]. Whatever we may view as the "correct" approach in such cases, it may be very important to ensure that "people die with their rights on," if we are to prevent the abuse of overuse of medical technology and, equally as important, the fear of this. Such fear is harmful in itself and is likely to promote advocacy of euthanasia.

(ii) Individual Rights

Emphasis on rights of individuals has been a phenomenon of major importance in many of our Western societies, but it may now have peaked, which one hopes does not mean that it will decline from that peak, although other concerns also need to be incorporated into our analysis and practice. In particular, emphasis on the rights of individuals has been and is essential to ensure respect for each person, which is crucial in the context of health care, if that context is to be humane.

Calls for the legalization of euthanasia have frequently been phrased in terms of respect for individual rights. Most of us recognize a claim to a death that is respectful of the person—sometimes called a dignified death, although this term can be misleading—but disagree on what are the limits for achieving this. In particular, we disagree whether there is a right to this, because such a right may require actions which we find unacceptable and a right of one person necessarily connotes a duty of another, even if only to refrain from doing anything that would infringe on that right. It is important to recognize points of consensus when they exist, and then where our disagreement begins. Differences of opinion, especially regarding such strongly held beliefs as those concerning euthanasia, can have a very different tone when a discussion starts from a point of agreement rather than disagreement.

(iii) Sanctity of Life and Quality of Life

There has been a move in our society from relying exclusively on a sanctity of life or vitality principle, to relying as well or sometimes alternatively, on a quality of life principle, which includes concepts of a life not worth living and even "wrongful life." Initially, "wrongful life" was a claim for damages in tort, usually on the part of handicapped children arguing that in their cases, life itself, that is, being born, constituted a damage for which compensation should be available through the courts. Although in most of these cases the plaintiffs were not successful, some were (see, for example [20]). There has been a relatively recent case in which the precedent set in these cases has been used at the other end of life. The plaintiff had refused cardio-pulmonary resuscitation, but was given it after a cardiac arrest and, when resuscitated, was hemiplegic. He has sued for damages for "wrongful life" [21].

Recognition of a quality of life principle is often linked to euthanasia, in particular, by the two opposing groups who argue for a broad definition of euthanasia—that is, some groups in the pro-life movement who argue that any intervention that would shorten life should be prohibited, and persons who are pro-choice on euthanasia. The former oppose use of the principle, the latter would give it priority over a sanctity of life principle. But one is not necessarily a proponent of euthanasia or an adversary of a sanctity of life principle, if one agrees that quality of life is a valid consideration in making decisions concerning treatment at the end of life. Consideration of quality of life is not unjustified, indeed, it may be ethically required in some circumstances, for example, in making decisions concerning the allocation of medical resources at a governmental (macro) or institutional (meso) level. The need to consider quality of life arises in part from the possibilities made available by modern medical technology. It has been well said that once we were "reasonably well or dead" [22]—today we can be very sick for a very long time at the end of our lives, because life can be prolonged by the use of modern medical technology. Such circumstances can sometimes raise valid concerns about the quality of life of the persons whose lives are prolonged.

WHY DO WE WANT TO MEDICALIZE EUTHANASIA?

Does euthanasia seem kinder, gentler, and in a "safer forum" if it is carried out in a clinical context [23]? Does this show both "approval, acceptance and care of the patient" [18] and of his or her decision for euthanasia? In speaking of physician-assisted suicide, it has been said that

> [s]eeking a physician's assistance, or what can almost seem a physician's blessing, may be a way of trying to remove . . . stigma and show others that the decision for suicide was made with due seriousness and was justified under the circumstances. The physician's involvement provides a kind of social approval, or more accurately helps counter what would otherwise be unwarranted social disapproval [15, p. 21].

Could euthanasia provide a precedent for some other interventions that would also be carried out "in the medical context," which would have important, potentially dangerous, societal impact? For example, in the United States, physicians' involvement in carrying out capital punishment is a case in point. Such interventions can in a sense be given trial runs or attempts made to make them acceptable through their utilization in a clinical or purportedly clinical context, before their much more controversial application outside such a context. These questions may seem alarmist, but they are ones which we need to ask and with a certain degree of equanimity.

In summary, we must enquire whether we may at least in part be dealing with euthanasia in a medical context in order to eliminate or reduce reactions that we would otherwise have to one person killing another. Moreover, to the extent that we expect modern medicine to be our source of miracles, could it be that when no miracles are possible, death is a miracle substitute or even a different kind of "miracle," but one still provided by medicine if it occurs through euthanasia carried out by a physician?

WHY DO WE TECHNOLOGIZE EUTHANASIA?

We need to ask, for example, in the much publicized case of Dr. Kevorkian assisting Mrs. Janet Adkins' death, why did Dr. Kevorkian and Mrs. Adkins resort to a suicide machine which was even given a special, trademarked name, the Thanatron™ [24]. One obvious reason is in order to try to avoid prosecution for murder by eliminating the possibility that Dr. Kevorkian could be held, in law, to have caused Mrs. Adkin's death. Through use of the machine, Mrs. Adkins could be regarded, in law, as causing her own death, in which case the situation was one of suicide—and if anything, assistance in suicide on the part of Dr. Kevorkian, which was not at that time a crime in Michigan[10]—not murder. It is worth noting, however, that even in the case of Mrs. Adkins, where Dr. Kevorkian did not intervene after the initial intravenous lines had been inserted and Mrs. Adkins herself activated administration of the lethal drugs, a charge of murder was considered. In two subsequent cases Dr. Kevorkian did intervene, in one instance to remedy a defect in the machine after it had been started. With respect to these cases, charges of murder were laid against him [25] but were found to be without foundation [26, 27].

There may, however, be a less obvious reason why we technologize euthanasia. We often speak of the technological imperative in medicine, that is, that we have technology, and, therefore, think or feel that we must use it. The presence of technology elicits a response to use it and much discussion in bioethics has been concerned with attempting to work out principles and guidelines for when we ought (there is a duty), not ought (there is no duty), or ought not (there is a duty not) to use technology. Could the case of euthanasia be a variation on this technological imperative response? Could it be that in euthanasia cases, such as those involving Dr. Kevorkian, that rather than the technology preceding and eliciting a certain response, a certain response—namely, euthanasia—is desired and recognition of this precedes and elicits the technology which will generate the desired response?

---

[10]Since these events, legislation has been passed in Michigan making it a crime to assist a person to commit suicide. Act 84, *Public Acts of 1992*, 1992 Mi. ALS 84; 1992 Mi. P.A. 84; 1992 Mi. HB5501.

Does the use of technology somehow come between us and the person to whom we apply the technology[11] such that we do not feel that it is our act that creates the result—in the case of euthanasia, death of the person—but rather that this is caused by the technology? Does the use of technology allow us to distance ourselves, to dis-identify in some degree, from the fact that we are killing another person in the act of euthanasia?

Why Would Euthanasia be Allowed or Not Prosecuted but Not Legalized?

The criminal law of all countries prohibits culpable homicide—murder and manslaughter. Euthanasia is prohibited pursuant to such laws. A majority of countries also prohibit assisting suicide, although in modern criminal law suicide itself is often not a crime. There are also examples, of which The Netherlands is the main one, of countries which allow euthanasia under certain conditions, but have not legalized it at least in a strict legal sense.[12]

In short, the current approach in The Netherlands may maintain a certain symbolism of upholding the principle of sanctity of life, while allowing practices that are inconsistent with this. This same mechanism can be seen operating in the French legal and medical systems. A report entitled "French Health Ministry Supports Doctor Over Euthanasia" reads as follows:

> Leon Schwartzenberg, an eminent French Cancer Specialist, has been suspended for one year by the Paris board of the French Medical Association. The suspension follows Schwartzenberg's admission that he had helped an incurable patient to die. Claude Evin, the French Health Minister, has now joined Schwartzenberg in filing an appeal, and in calling for a broad public debate on euthanasia. Evin said: "The main thing is to relieve suffering, even if that means the end of life." Neither Evin nor Schwartzenberg favour a change in legislation, however. Schwartzenberg has said: *"for the French, anything that is law is normal, and euthanasia can never be normal"* (emphasis added) [28, p. 22].

---

[11]It is of interest that the way in which I wrote this sentence, initially, was "Does the use of technology somehow come between us and the person to whom the technology is applied . . ." as though there was not necessarily a human agent involved in applying the technology. This, in itself, would seem to demonstrate the point I am making here, that the use of technology (or even just contemplation of its use) causes or at least allows us to depersonalize situations in which it is employed.

[12]It seems that this situation will be maintained even after legislative approval of the "Netherlands Reporting Procedure for Euthanasia."

A similar approach of *de facto*, but not *de jure*, legalization of euthanasia has recently been advocated for Canada. The proposal of Sneiderman, a law professor, who does not oppose euthanasia, is summarized in the headline accompanying an article written by him: "Don't make it murder, but don't make it legal." Sneiderman writes that

> [i]n the rare situation in which the physician is driven to desperate measures (as [occurred recently] in a Montreal case [in which a physician gave a lethal injection of potassium chloride to a terminally ill person with AIDS who was suffering greatly]), the law has the capacity to stay its hand as a merciful response to a merciful act. But that is a far cry from granting physicians the legal authority to practice euthanasia. As philosopher John Rawls says, "It is one thing to justify an act; it is another to justify a general practice." Given the current crisis over a health-care system unable to meet the reasonable needs of all our ailing people, we cannot guarantee that euthanasia would be practiced solely as the medical measure of last resort. In short, one cannot say that the time for euthanasia has come to Canada [29, p. A19].

In summary, even those who do or would allow euthanasia at an individual level, recognize the danger of this at the societal level. An important issue, therefore, is whether it is possible to prevent approved micro level practices from establishing macro level precedent. Almost certainly, it is not. Consequently, quite apart from moral arguments, it is proposed that euthanasia should not be allowed at the micro level because of the macro level effect of this.

HIDDEN DECISION-MAKING AND EUTHANASIA

It is often alleged that much euthanasia takes place in society, but that it is performed secretly and the fact that it occurs is hidden. It is further alleged that this situation is the result of euthanasia being illegal. Recent studies, however, show much hidden (at least in the sense of unreported) euthanasia in The Netherlands [30, p. 40; 31[13]], where euthanasia is *de facto* legal. Consequently, the cause of euthanasia being hidden may not only (or even not at all, because even if legal it may still be hidden) be the result of its being illegal. We usually react strongly in post-modern Western societies against hidden

---

[13]See J. Keown [31], citing G. F. Gomez, who states that in less than 2 percent of cases of euthanasia was the prosecutor notified.

decision-making and actions, but should we always do so? To respond
to this question requires that some distinctions be made. Do we believe
that hidden decision-making itself is wrong and in all or just some
circumstances, or do we rather believe that most cases of such decision-
making involve unethical or illegal decisions, that these need to be
prevented, and this can best be achieved by eschewing hidden decision-
making? We need to be open-minded enough to ask whether there is a
place for hidden decision-making and actions by individuals, although
not by institutions or society, in some very unusual situations. We need
also to ask whether, beyond taking certain steps, trying to eliminate all
hidden decision-making regarding euthanasia would do more harm
than good. In particular, we need to ask whether legalizing euthanasia,
in order to try to avoid hidden decision-making, would do more harm
than good even if we were to achieve the aim of eliminating hidden
decision-making concerning euthanasia.

We can compare euthanasia with abortion regarding the possible
effects of hidden decision-making. Whether or not one agrees that
abortion is morally acceptable, abortion is an example where creating
circumstances which give rise to this being carried out in a hidden
manner, causes a major increase in serious risk for women who have
abortions, and may not deter women from having abortions. This is one
argument against using law to prohibit abortion in the early stages of
pregnancy. Another argument is that the law is ineffective to prevent
early abortion, especially in light of the availability of new methods of
abortion, in particular, the "abortion pill," which do not require the use
of sophisticated medical techniques or facilities.

Even if it were true that hidden instances of euthanasia occur, we
must recognize that in considering legalizing and institutionalizing
euthanasia, we are considering altering the fundamental presumption
against killing each other on which the morality and law of a civilized
society are based. Why are we so widely and actively considering a
change in this? Could there be some socio-biological, genetic, or
environmental factor that is causing the current rise in interest in and
promotion of euthanasia? One would need to examine other historical
periods and other cultures[14] and probably other species to even begin to
have some idea whether this could be the case. It is, however, important to be aware that what we perceive or feel as our primary motives
in carrying out certain acts may be covering other very complex
realities in this regard. For instance, empathy, compassion, and mercy,
while dominant motives on the part of most persons in situations in

---

[14]As for example, Young has done in her work, see [16].

which they advocate euthanasia, may not be the only motivations present. It is just possible that factors such as an increasingly crowded world or even overwhelming fear about one's own death, especially in the context of the ethos of a secular, pluralistic, post-modern society, could be playing a part in persons' advocating euthanasia.

SEEKING INSIGHTS: THE DIFFERENCE BETWEEN BEING ANTI-EUTHANASIA AND BEING "PRO-LIFE"

There are two senses in which there is a difference between being anti-euthanasia and being pro-life. The first is that not all or even, possibly, most persons who are anti-euthanasia would regard themselves as members of the pro-life movement, nor are their objections to euthanasia religiously based, as can be true (or at least is often assumed to be true) for members of the pro-life movement. Moreover, non-pro-life anti-euthanasia persons, unlike some pro-life persons, advocate provision of necessary treatment for the relief of pain and other symptoms of serious physical distress, respect for valid refusals of treatment, and withdrawal of futile or "disproportional" treatment, even when any of these could or will shorten life. The second difference is that some anti-euthanasia persons including some in the pro-life movement, would allow capital punishment, that is, they do not oppose all killing of other humans and in this sense, while they are anti-euthanasia, they are not uniformly pro-life.

What could one learn by comparing euthanasia and capital punishment, sadly, a form of killing legalized in some jurisdictions? There are four possible positions that persons could take: 1) that they are against capital punishment and against euthanasia; 2) that they agree with capital punishment, but are against euthanasia; 3) that they agree with capital punishment and euthanasia; or 4) that they are against capital punishment, but agree with euthanasia. What underlying philosophy would each of these positions represent? The first is a true pro-life position in that it demonstrates a moral belief that all killing (except, usually, as a last resort in self-defense) is wrong. The second position represents the view of some fundamentalists, namely, that to uphold the sanctity of life value requires prohibition of euthanasia, but capital punishment is justified on the grounds that this punishment is deserved and just according to God's law. The third position is that of some conservatives who see capital punishment as a fit penalty on the basis that one can forfeit one's life through a very serious crime, but that one can also consent to the taking of one's own life in the form of euthanasia. The fourth view is that of some libertarians, that one can consent to the taking of one's own life but cannot take that of others.

Through such analyses, one can see where the various groups agree with each other and disagree. For example, the true pro-life persons and the fundamentalists agree with each other in being against euthanasia, and some conservatives and civil libertarians agree with each other in arguing for the availability of euthanasia. On the other hand, the true pro-life and civil libertarians join in their views in being against capital punishment, whereas the fundamentalists and some conservatives agree that this is acceptable. In short, with respect to the issue involved here, the taking of one person's life by another, various groups can coalesce and agree in certain instances in which this issue arises, while they may be radically divergent in others. We need to be aware of these possibilities of a mixture of consensus and divergence as between different groups, in assessing the political realities, public policy stances, and analysis relevant to euthanasia.

SEEKING FURTHER INSIGHTS: ANTI ANTI-EUTHANASIA AND ANTI "PRO-EUTHANASIA" ARGUMENTS

Although the aim is the same, and there is necessarily overlap between various arguments in both cases, there can be a difference in the content of the propositions used when arguing for allowing euthanasia, as compared with arguing against the anti-euthanasia position. The same is true with respect to arguing against the "pro-euthanasia" position, as compared with arguing for the anti-euthanasia one.

Arguments Against the Anti-Euthanasia Position

1. Suffering and Mercy

Euthanasia is advocated as being suffering reducing by those in favor of its being allowed and, therefore, persons who are anti-euthanasia can be perceived as being pro-suffering. No humane person advocates suffering, but unavoidable suffering is not seen as entirely negative by everyone. Some cultures or religions attribute value to suffering. This is to propose that suffering is not always the greatest evil, such that actions, including euthanasia, aimed at relieving suffering are always a lesser evil and are, therefore, acceptable. Not ending life is characterized by some pro-choice on euthanasia advocates as an act of infliction of suffering, rather that being seen as an example of our inability sometimes to relieve suffering. We need to ask whether this is, yet, another example of the "do something" syndrome. Not being able to act to try to improve a very distressing situation makes us highly anxious, and we do not readily accept that there are some situations in which we cannot or ought not to "do something." We assume that "doing something" is better than "doing nothing" and that "doing something" will improve the situation either in moral or practical (including not infrequently political) terms.

Physicians may experience and display an especially powerful versions of "do something" phenomenon. Physicians can be very uncomfortable, even highly anxious, if they feel unable to intervene to improve a patient's situation, especially if the patient is seriously ill, as all terminally ill patients are. One response to such patients can be to more-or-less abandon them—to visit these patients less often and to spend little time with them. Another response is "[t]he great temptation of modern medicine, not always resisted, . . . to move beyond the promotion and preservation of health into the boundless realm of general human happiness and well-being" [32, p. 55]. While physicians may do much good in trying to achieve such objectives, not all ways of doing so are acceptable or do more good than harm. In particular, "[i]t would be terrible for physicians to think that in a swift, lethal injection, medicine had found its own answer to the riddle of life. It would be a false answer; given by the wrong people" [32, p. 55].

Being anti-euthanasia is also regarded by some persons as a non-merciful stance. It is difficult to argue against persons who see themselves as merciful. Proponents of euthanasia argue that it is unethical not to provide euthanasia, because this is unmerciful, that is, prohibiting euthanasia is not only non-beneficent, but also even maleficent. There is a stronger moral obligation not to do harm that to do good, although distinguishing whether a given situation should be characterized as one or the other can sometimes be difficult. Consequently, to argue that failure to provide euthanasia is unmerciful and that this is maleficent, is a stronger argument in favor of euthanasia than simply arguing that to provide it is to confer a benefit. It is, however, also argued that euthanasia is compassionate and beneficent, in particular, that it benefits the patient, the family, the health care professionals who are involved, and society.

2. "Reasonably Well or Dead"

It is argued as well, that not to allow euthanasia contravenes the aim that persons be either "reasonably well or dead." It is true that, largely as a result of modern medical technology, we can now be very sick and live for a considerable time and that the "wellness curve," rather than gradually declining over a period of time, can be "squared" with euthanasia. In other words, euthanasia allows one to go directly from being reasonably well to dead. It is possible, however, also to "square" the morbidity curve by good palliative care and pain relief treatment, rather than euthanasia; that is, wellness or at least a sense of well-being, is not necessarily dependent upon the absence of disease.[15] Stated another way, in the vast majority of cases, euthanasia should be unnecessary in the sense of its being the only option for avoiding serious suffering if good palliative care, including adequate pain relief treatment, is provided.

3. Liberty

It is also argued that euthanasia should be available to those who want to die, as a matter of respect for personal liberty and, therefore, that those who oppose euthanasia fail to respect important liberty rights. We need to be careful, however, with equating "wanting to die," in the sense that a person feels that he or she is ready for and even would welcome death and "wanting to be killed." Many, and probably most, people at the end of their lives are "ready to die," but this does not mean that they "want to be killed."

Further, as noted already, the availability of euthanasia is not one-sided in the impact it would have on liberty. While it can be regarded as extending a persons' range of choice concerning how and when they die, its availability can also act as a pressure to request or agree to euthanasia, which is to restrict a persons' liberty [15, pp. 17-18 (referring to Velleman)]. There is also a more subtle way in which the availability of euthanasia could interfere with liberty. At a recent conference, Denise Ross from the Dana Farber Cancer Institute, described a conversation she had with a young terminally ill patient about pain management. He raised the issues of assisted suicide and euthanasia. She discussed these with him, but told him she felt obliged to inform him that she would not assist him in these ways. He replied: "Of course not. I wouldn't feel comfortable talking to you about this, if you would" [33]. It is possible that we need to have a trusted and trustworthy institutional forum in which to explore such matters, without fear of being subjected to the kinds of intervention that we discuss. The forum used to be organized religion, but for many persons now, medicine has replaced this. A liberty interest would be breached

---

[15]Moreover, in one sense, with rapidly emerging, highly sophisticated, medical diagnostic techniques, the well among us, are only the undiagnosed sick. I am indebted to Dr. Ken Flegel, M.D., MRCP(C), of the Royal Victoria Hospital, Montreal, for this insight.

by not retaining such a forum. This is one argument why, even, if euthanasia were to be legalized, it should not become a part of medical practice.

Arguments Against the "Pro-Euthanasia" Position

1. Precedent

It is accepted that, at an individual or micro level, persons of "good conscience" can believe that euthanasia is morally acceptable in certain circumstances, in particular, circumstances of intense, unrelievable suffering. It is argued, however, that even if one accepts this, euthanasia is unacceptable because of the precedent that allowing it would set at the societal level. In this respect, can it be argued that it is even more important in a secularized world than in a religiously-based one, not to allow euthanasia, because our worldly acts are the only sources of our values? Further, what would happen in a secularized world with a shortage of health care resources if we allowed euthanasia? Would persons be graded on a scale of "useless" to "highly useful" and resources allocated or, alternatively, euthanasia provided according to the relative degrees of perceived utility of the persons concerned? Would this give rise to a euthanasia line or continuum ranging from unethical or less ethically acceptable acts of euthanasia to more ethically acceptable ones? This ethical continuum can be compared with the law's "digital" approach to dealing with such a range of conduct. Unless all acts of euthanasia would be allowed, the law would require that a line be drawn across the range of acts dividing them into two groups. One group of these acts would be legally acceptable and the other group legally unacceptable, although the acts that make up each group would not be equally acceptable or unacceptable, respectively, from other perspectives, including most importantly, from an ethical perspective. Where would the law draw a line on the euthanasia continuum? Would some instances of euthanasia that most persons would regard as doubtfully ethical, or even unethical, be characterized as legal?

2. Other Arguments

Further arguments against the pro-euthanasia position that have been explored by others, in particular, Singer and Siegler [34, pp. 1881-1883], Wolf [35, pp. 13-15], Callahan [36, pp. 4-5] and Capron [37, p. 31], will be simply summarized here. They include perversion of the proper aims of medicine, if physicians are the persons who carry out euthanasia. This would be to turn medicine from an aim of healing and caring to one of eliminating the person who needs care. Euthanasia will extend into *all* physician-patient interactions, not just those directly involving euthanasia [37, p. 31]. In particular, euthanasia can desensitize and brutalize those who carry it out. This is a particularly disturbing possibility, when those same persons are our healers and caregivers—physicians and other health care professionals. Moreover, the major separation of the two roles of the witch doctor (the modern physician's ancient predecessor), that of healer and death inflictor, the most influential and important articulation of which is to be found in the 2,000-year-old Hippocratic Oath, would be reversed. As Kass so powerfully states, "the deepest ethical principle restraining the physician's power is not the autonomy or freedom of the patient; neither is it his own compassion or good intention. Rather, it is the dignity and mysterious power of human life itself" [15, p. 17]. Euthanasia puts the "very soul of medicine" on trial [15, p. 16].

As has been discussed at various points throughout this text, the symbolism of euthanasia is unacceptable, even if it is carried out for the most humane reasons, as it constitutes the most serious derogation from the sanctity of life value. It has been well said, that sanctity of life has been unduly identified with and confined to the religious commandment. There are also secular reasons—moral, rational, and medical—for respecting sanctity of life and rejecting euthanasia and these need to be explored [14, p. 24].

To allow euthanasia would inflict suffering and have potentially dangerous effects on certain already vulnerable groups, for example, handicapped persons or chronically ill persons. The same grounds on which euthanasia would be carried out on others would often be true of these persons and, even if they are not at risk of being subject to euthanasia, the fact that others in a similar position are subject to it, devalues their lives.[16]

There is also, it is proposed, a greater danger of abuse if euthanasia were legalized than if it is not. Even if this cannot be established, those advocating euthanasia should at least have the burden of proving the contrary. Possible abuses include that euthanasia could be involuntary, that is, carried out without consent or against the wishes of the person; or carried out secretly despite its being, indeed, because it is, legalized; or persons would be encouraged to seek euthanasia; or it could be so-called "surrogate euthanasia," that is, a person other than

---

[16]It has also been noted (see, for example [38]) that up to March 1993, *all* of the recent highly publicized cases of physician-assisted suicide in North America had involved the death of women—historically a vulnerable group.

the one being euthanized, authorizes euthanasia; or euthanasia could be applied in a discriminatory manner in terms of the persons who are subject to it [34, p. 1882]. As Singer and Siegler state, these risks are especially serious in an era of "cost containment, social injustice and ethical relativism" [34, p. 1883].

The availability of euthanasia may also detract from developing better care for dying persons, as the quick and easy answer is to use euthanasia, rather than to carry out research in order to develop and improve such care. Indeed, it can be asked whether, if euthanasia had been available, we would have developed the often sophisticated palliative care techniques that we have today [35, pp. 13-15]. It would be interesting to examine the situation in The Netherlands in this respect, to determine the availability of palliative care resources and hospices and to see whether or not the euthanasia response was, or is, related to the unavailability of or inaccessibility to such care. The availability of euthanasia could also create pressure to accept or to request it to relieve burdens on one's family and society.

Euthanasia would also be likely to interfere with current legal approaches to refusal of treatment. As Wolf points out, the courts would be reluctant to stay out of decisions at the end of life, if euthanasia were one option [35, pp. 13-15]. Moreover, we might not have developed mechanisms such as "advance directives," if euthanasia had been an option.

Most contentiously, perhaps, one can argue that euthanasia interferes with the final stage of our human development—dealing with death. Euthanasia is a short-term, simple, easy in some senses, appealing to some, solution. But we need long-term perspectives on euthanasia, which may be more complex and difficult in many respects. Through these, we are more likely to work out the mystery and complexity of our dying and with this our living, because the latter is necessarily related to the former.

Finally, euthanasia would set a precedent of universal application, because, at some point each of us must face death. This universality can be regarded as beneficial from the point of view that there will be strong personal identification with the possibility that, if euthanasia were legalized, it could be applied to us, which should make people think very seriously about whether or not they agree with the precedent that legalizing euthanasia would set. At some stage, each of us would be the person on the other side of "the veil of ignorance" to whom the euthanasia decision could apply—the veil behind which Rawls suggests we should make difficult decisions, on the basis that we do not know at the time of the decision, which actor we will be when the decision is implemented [39, pp. 12, 137]. The universality of the application of a euthanasia precedent is also immensely frightening in the potential extent of its use.

There are some fine lines which we should never cross and, it is proposed, one of these is that separating euthanasia, as defined, from other interventions or non-interventions at the end of life.

CONCLUSION

We are not only logical rational beings, we are also emotional, intuitive, spiritual (which is not the same as religious) ones. Our "ways of knowing" are complex, diverse, and vast.

Much of the argument for euthanasia is logical and rational (for example, that there is no difference between actively killing and allowing to die), but it can also be emotional (for instance, that we have obligations to be merciful and relieve suffering). The arguments against euthanasia are also logical (for example, the "slippery slope" argument) and emotional (for instance, the sanctity of human life). For some persons, the arguments are also religious or possibly just spiritual.

Euthanasia (as defined) should be seen as different in kind not just degree from other acts or omissions that could or do shorten life. It is argued that one crosses a great divide in undertaking intentional killing; that while pain and other symptoms of serious physical distress should be relieved, it must always be the pain or other symptoms that one seeks to eliminate and not the person with the pain or symptoms. Moreover, even if euthanasia were to be justified in an individual case, the societal level effect that legitimizing this would set, especially legitimation through authorizing legislation, is unacceptable.

When we disagree, it is important to delve below the level of our disagreement and to try to find a deeper consensus. To start from consensus and move to disagreement, has a different effect than starting from disagreement. The two poles of the euthanasia debate are clear: pro-choice on euthanasia—no interventions, including infliction of death, aimed at reducing or eliminating suffering should be prohibited; pro-life—all interventions that could or would shorten life should be prohibited. It is much more difficult to belong to the middle of this debate and to draw a line somewhere in the grey (or purple-pink) [9] zone between the poles, and to argue that some actions that shorten or fail to prolong life are prohibited and others, even those with the same outcome as a prohibited action, are allowed. Where we should agree is that none of us is pro-suffering and none of us is anti-death when "its time has come." Where we disagree is the means that may be used to reduce suffering or to cause or to allow death to occur.

The euthanasia debate is an immensely important one, which is likely, more than the debate on any other current issue, to set legal and ethical tones of our societies as they become societies of the twenty-first century. We will learn and need to learn much along the way, because this is a complex debate, with micro and macro impact; unconscious origins; conscious realizations and insights; major effects on symbolic and value factors; and links to many other societal issues outside the context of euthanasia, including balancing rights or claims of individuals with rights or claims of the community when these conflict. Is prohibition of euthanasia an example of sacrificing the individual who desires euthanasia, for the good of the community which would be harmed by the precedent set in allowing euthanasia? Is euthanasia the final act of love of caring individuals and a caring society? Or is euthanasia an isolation ritual whereby the individual is expelled from the collective, the members of which bond to each other through shared guilt? [40, pp. 75-76] To decide such questions will take wisdom, compassion, courage, and hope—the antithesis of despair, which so often is (but often need not be) present in situations which give rise to calls for euthanasia. How we deal with euthanasia is likely to be one of the most important mirrors of ourselves, our society, and our relationships—both as intimates and strangers. We need, therefore, to take great care in fashioning the lyrics of the songs that we sing about it, because these lyrics will play a crucial role in determining the reality regarding euthanasia that gives rise to these reflections. Moreover, our decisions and actions in relation to euthanasia will create not only immediate reflections, but also themes and echoes of enormous importance for those who come after us to live in the world of the future. We need to sing "the song of life: the lyrics of love." This includes the song of death as an inevitable part of life, but not the lyrics of euthanasia.

REFERENCES

1. M. A. Somerville, Labels vs. Contents: Variance between Psychiatry, Philosophy and Law Concepts Governing Decision-Making, *McGill Law Journal* (forthcoming).
2. D. Humphry, *Final Exit*, The Hemlock Society, Oregon, 1991.
3. M. A. Somerville, Birth and Life: Establishing a Framework of Concepts, *Connecticut Law Review, 21*, p. 667, 1989.
4. M. A. Somerville, Medical Interventions and the Criminal Law: Lawful or Excusable Wounding?, *McGill Law Journal, 26*, p. 82, 1980.
5. *Yepremian v. Scarborough General Hospital,* (1980) 110 D.L.R. (3rd) 513 (Ont. Court of Appeal).
6. M. A. Somerville, Pain and Suffering at Interfaces of Medicine and Law, *University of Toronto Law Journal, 36,* p. 286, 1986.

7. M. A. M. de Wachter, Euthanasia in The Netherlands, *Hastings Center Report, 22*:2, p. 23, 1992.

8. Notes, Physician Assisted Suicide: The Right to Die with Assistance, *Harvard Law Review, 105*, p. 2021, 1992.

9. M. A. Somerville, New Perceptions, Old Values From Inner and Outer Spaces, *Canadian Speeches, 65*, pp. 65-68, 1992. (Convocation Address, Spacing-in and Spacing-out: Searching for the Purple-Pink Middle, University of Windsor, Windsor, Ontario, June 1992.)

10. H. Becker, *The Denial of Death*, Free Press, New York, 1973.

11. J. Greenberg, *At Different Times, in Different Ways, We All Board the Same Train: The Management of Terror in Everyday Life,* Plenary Address, 9th International Congress on Care of the Terminally Ill, Montreal, November 3, 1992.

12. E. Cassel, The Nature of Suffering and the Goals of Medicine, *New England Journal of Medicine, 306*:11, pp. 639-644, 1982.

13. L. Israel in interview with Jacques Nerson, Pr. Lucien Israel: L'Euthanasia est un meurtre, Le Figaro, 6 mars, pp. 111-112, 1993.

14. R. Fenigsen, A Case Against Dutch Euthanasia, *Hastings Center Report, 19*:1 Special Supplement, pp. 22, 24, 1989.

15. D. W. Brock, Voluntary Active Euthanasia, *Hastings Center Report, 22*:2, pp. 10-19, 1992.

16. K. K. Young et al., unpublished abstract, 1992.

17. M. de Hennezel, *The Myth of the Perfect Death: The New Meaning of Death in the Context of AIDS,* Plenary Address, Caring Together/Entraide: Conference Proceedings, Ottawa, p. 33, 1991.

18. B. Campion, Love and the Quality of Life, [Toronto] *The Globe and Mail,* p. A4, August 1990.

19. T. G. Gutheil, In Search of True Freedom: Drug Refusal, Involuntary Medication, and 'Rotting With Your Rights On,' *American Journal of Psychiatry, 133*, p. 340, 1980.

20. *Curlender v. Biosciences Laboratories,* Cal. App. 3d, 811; 165 Cal. Rpt. 477 (1986), (Ct. App.).

21. D. Margolick, Patient's Lawsuit Says Saving Life Ruined It, *New York Times,* p. A24, March 18, 1990.

22. J. F. Fries, Aging, Natural Death, and the Compression of Morbidity, *New England Journal of Medicine, 303*:3, p. 130, 1980.

23. M. A. Somerville, Human Rights and Medicine: The Relief of Suffering, in *International Human Rights Law: Theory and Practice,* I. Cotler and F. P. Eliadis (eds.), The Canadian Human Rights Foundation, Montréal, p. 505, 1992.

24. A. Hister, Kevorkian Offers Cold Comfort on Euthanasia Debate, [Toronto] *The Globe and Mail,* p. C8, September 14, 1991.

25. Reuters News Agency, Doctor Charged with Murder in Assisted Suicide, [Toronto] *The Globe and Mail,* p. A9, February 6, 1992.

26. M. Betzold, Cleared 'Suicide Doctor' Urges Other Physicians to Join Him, [Montreal] *The Gazette,* p. B5, July 22, 1992.

27. Editorial, Who Has the Final Choice? [Montreal] *The Gazette,* p. B2, July 28, 1992.
28. French Health Ministry Supports Doctor over Euthanasia, *New Scientist, 28,* p. 22, July 1990.
29. B. Sneiderman, [Toronto] *The Globe and Mail*, p. A19, August 17, 1992.
30. J. Keown, On Regulating Death, *Hastings Center Report , 22*:2, p. 39, 1992.
31. J. Keown (citing G. F. Gomez), *Regulating Death: Euthanasia and the Case of The Netherlands,* Free Press, New York, 1991.
32. D. Callahan, When Self-Determination Runs Amok, *Hastings Center Report, 22*:2, p. 52, 1992.
33. D. Ross, *Conflicts in Managing Intractable Pain and Suffering,* American Society of Law and Medicine Conference, 1992 Annual Meeting, October 30-31, 1992, Cambridge, Massachusetts (unpublished.)
34. P. A. Singer and M. Siegler, Euthanasia—A Critique, *New England Journal of Medicine*; *322*:26, p. 1881, 1990.
35. S. Wolf, Holding the Line on Euthanasia, *Hastings Center Report 1989*; *19*:1 Special Supplement, 1989.
36. D. Callahan, Can We Return Death to Disease? *Hastings Center Report 1989*; *19*:1 Special Supplement, 1989.
37. A. M. Capron, Euthanasia in The Netherlands: American Observations, *Hastings Center Report*, *22*:2, 1992.
38. A. Trafford, Wishing to Die: Are Women Really More Open to Assisted Suicide? *Washington Post,* reprinted in *The Gazette,* Montreal, p. D5, March 15, 1993.
39. J. Rawls, *A Theory of Justice,* Belknap Press, Cambridge, 1971.
40. D. Schulman, Remembering Who We Are: AIDS and Law in a Time of Madness, *AIDS and Public Policy, 3,* 1988.

PART IV

Issues For
Health Care Providers

In this section we examine the issues specific to the health care provider. Dr. Phyllis Palgi reminds us that every career develops out of one's personal needs, holding oneself up to a mirror to one's life. She quotes Margaret Mead who wrote: "The advances in the application of scientific knowledge to the understanding of man has been dependent on two developments, methods of observing other human beings and methods of observing ourselves, as observers."

Why do men and women become physicians and thrive in that calling? In Israel, where Dr. Palgi teaches, many of the doctors are immigrants which gives them a common experience and often emotional ties with immigrant patients. A number of the older generation of physicians in Israel lived through the Holocaust experience, which they share with patients; to this day, a controlling image that permeates Israeli life. The fact that the majority of doctors are employees in public organizations means that they do not have the luxury of choosing their clients, and willy nilly, they are kept in contact with all sectors of the population. A contact, which, in itself, is a social leveler.

Probably the strongest source of strength for the doctors is the empowerment given to the healer by society to promote survival. He or she is the one who is legally and often morally entitled by society to draw the line between life and death. The doctor's task is to maintain life, but we humans are mere mortals, the phenomenon of death is omnipresent. Doctors are not only to be viewed to be omnipotent but, in these modern times, also to be omniscient. The first source of strength, however, is that the natural outcome of the bio-medical model traced as far back as ancient Greece in the fifth century B.C.E. Doctors, in a very

241

conscious way, see themselves as a link in this great historical chain of scientific yet humanistic healers. The second source of strength of the Israeli professional self is the time-honored image of the healer in the Jewish tradition. The earliest definition of a doctor in Judaic terms is as a messenger and instrument of God. While the fount of the healing power is considered sacred, the actual practice of medicine is more like cleanliness, namely, next to godliness.

Patrice O'Connor investigates how well equipped hospitals are in handling the death and dying processes; what are the obligations of the medical personnel to patients, families, and themselves in meeting needs of the dying in these institutions; and has education for the professional addressed these critical issues of caring for the dying patient and family. Society is being challenged to make changes in order to meet the needs of a population in which the elderly are the fastest growing segment and in which medical technology has made it more difficult for patients to die. With the increase in the number of people with AIDS, and increases in the elderly population, the questions of how much can be spent on health care, let alone on care of the dying, is making North Americans confront their own mortality in uncomfortable ways. She examines the stresses in dealing with the dying process manifested in: role ambiguity, role conflict, and role overload.

The cumulative effect of multiple patient deaths upon staff may lead to eventual depletion and spiritual exhaustion. O'Connor discusses the attitudinal, behavioral, and social factors that manifest themselves by expressions of unresolved grief, the need to be perfect, projection of one's own needs, over-seriousness, lack of sharing, inappropriate sharing at home, norms of solemnity, lack of structured opportunities for sharing, and administrative non-responsiveness. She believes workshops on death awareness can reduce death anxiety.

Connie Holden, a hospice director, proposes that it is not only unnecessary to involve patients and families in life and death decisions, but that it is inhumane and insensitive to do so. The burden of participating in a decision simply outweighs the benefits of being involved in the process. She believes that health care professionals must be prepared to enter into meaningful and helpful discussions related to end-of-life care.

Ben-Joshua Jaffee reminds us of the four tasks to the grieving/mourning process: recognizing and accepting the reality of the loss and understanding how it came about; experiencing and going through the pain of the grief caused by the loss; discovering what is left: adapting to a new life devoid of the lost person; and discovering what is possible:

reinvesting emotional energy in a new and different life. He believes that the second task is the most difficult and, therefore, the most resisted of the four tasks. That task is experiencing and working through, i.e., cathexis, the very painful emotions of sadness, anger, and fear caused by the loss. Jaffee believes that by introducing humor into the clinical situation, the health care professional will overcome the blocks to catharsis.

Elizabeth Latimer believes that good palliative care treatment can be taught. Palliative care is the active and compassionate care of the sick person at a time when the goals of cure and prolongation of life are no longer most important to the patient and indeed, may not be physically possible due to the presence of advanced illness. The focus of palliative care is the provision of physical comfort (symptom control), psychological and spiritual care of the patient and family, and some provision for follow-up bereavement care for family after death has occurred. While specialty services will be available to care for some patients, it is likely that the majority of people who die will be cared for by primary care teams like family physicians, community nurses, and general hospital staff in acute or chronic care settings.

Palliative care encompasses the following focus of intervention: assessing and meeting the emotional support needs of the patient; assessing the needs of families and working to support them; addressing the physical status and symptom control needs of the patient; ethical decision making and setting goals of care with the patient and family; accompaniment of patient and family on the journey of illness toward death, providing support and attentive care all along the way; bereavement support to patient in ongoing losses and to the family during the illness and after the death has occurred. The skills and knowledge base fundamental to caring for the dying should be known by all practitioners and can be taught.

This knowledge includes: familiarity and comfort with the issues of serious illness, loss and death; familiarity and comfort in the presence of the expression of strong emotions; knowledge about interdisciplinary team work and an ability to work with team members of other disciplines; knowledge of symptom control, the depth of detail in knowledge being dictated by the professional discipline; values, beliefs, and attitudes that support the philosophy and ethics of palliative care; knowledge about the psychological, social, and emotional issues which confront seriously ill persons and their families; knowledge about the physical problems which can confront the individual or patient population under care and how to manage them. Because much of the teaching/learning involves subtle shifts in values and attitudes, the process is truly a lifelong event. While ideally teaching/learning will be planned for times when it is of high relevance for students, teachers and course planners can best be seen as those who "sow seeds" of awareness in their students or audience . . . seeds which may not come to fruition for some years after the actual teaching event or opportunity for heightened awareness has actually occurred.

CHAPTER 16

Death, Healing, Heroism and the Chiron Syndrome

Phyllis Palgi with Joshua Dorban

I feel I have been afforded a unique experience in having the opportunity to prepare this chapter. People who focus on subjects which inherently touch on the fundamental aspects of the humanness of our species must have certain special common bonds. I think they share the capacity and readiness to ponder and to exchange insights, and also seek further exposure to a variety of contexts in which people, as a group, relate to death directly or indirectly.

In this spirit, I will present some relevant findings from our larger research on physicians in Israel.[1] In keeping with the vernacular of my profession, anthropology, I have named the ongoing study "The tribe in white coats, which are sometimes green." The themes which I have chosen to address in this chapter emerge as the most salient ones emerging from that study. The research data are based on extensive personal interviews and observations with over 150 doctors in a variety of settings in Israel. This study is not focused on the individual personality of the Israeli doctor, but rather on the individual experience and perception of each member of this professional group, each of whom are involved directly in the healing process.

The material will be presented as Clifford Geertz says "from the point of view of the native." You will be hearing the many voices of the doctors and will be viewing the process of healing through their eyes, and their failure to heal, from their standpoint. The doctors dictated

---

[1] The research data for this chapter was drawn from an interdisciplinary study being conducted with psychologist Joshua Dorban, which is currently in progress.

the text and we interpreted. The beauty and the excitement of psycho-anthropological research is that the hypotheses are only latent and are immersed in ambiguity. One may ask specific questions but the tribes-men are free to hold the reins, for they are the local experts to lead one into the idiom of the culture. The interviews were open-ended and often wide-ranging. The doctors complained about their day-to-day mundane problems, they recalled indelible memories reflecting both personal triumphs and disasters. They tried to assess what really motivated them to study medicine and whether or not they dream of their children following in their footsteps. We also asked all of them in what way they think their careers would have been different if they had been of the other sex. (Incidentally, the males were taken aback by this question. Many had difficulty in envisaging themselves as the other sex, let alone as female doctors. The women doctors who represent about one-third of the research population, thought it was a very relevant question.)

Above all, they discussed what it means to them and their families when they are constantly confronting illness and suffering, a subject to which I shall return again and again. At an early stage of the research, a pediatrician who had come from a poor family in a small Romanian village, said that he believed that the medical profession demanded the highest form of devotion and self-sacrifice from the practitioner and, in fact, that is how he personally behaves. He then added that he is aware that his extreme behavior had deformed his personality and brought anguish and anxiety into his life. But, he said, he knew no other way. Soon afterwards, he took ill, was diagnosed as suffering from severe leukaemia, and ironically had to keep away from children because of his impaired immunity. He died recently in sadness and bitterness. It was then that the image of Chiron, the mythic wounded healer, first came to my mind.

The reality of death is always of social as well as individual concern and is thus expressed symbolically in a myriad of ways. Probably the closest to a universal tendency is the spontaneous creation and con-tinuous cherishing of a mythical past which symbolizes the continuum of life in death and death in life. The grandeur and drama of Greek archetypes such as Chiron have been a source of conscious and uncon-scious inspiration, particularly for societies within or influenced by Western culture.

I singled out the mythic figure of Chiron as the most apt to personify the ubiquitous wounded healer. I hope that through this repre-sentation, I shall be able to entice you to follow the arduous path we took to discover how the Israeli doctor struggles with his own vul-nerability while trying to heal others. Chiron, the most celebrated of the centaurs, was noted for his wisdom, gentleness, and powers of healing. He imparted his art to heroic figures including Achilles, Heracles and, notably, Asklepios, the healer. It was tragic and ironic that this primordial physician, Chiron, was wounded by his own pupil Heracles, who accidentally shot him in the knee with his poisoned arrow. Heracles, shocked, ran up to Chiron, drew out the arrow and applied a remedy to the open wound prescribed by Chiron himself. However, it was in vain, the wounded physician could not heal himself. The pain was excruciating and he longed to die but being the immortal son of a god was unable to do so. When Prometheus was suffering severe pain imposed by Zeus, Chiron freed him by handing over to him his quality of immortality. Chiron, now mortal, descended into Hades, relieved of his incurable wound. Prometheus then won honor as the founder of human civilization. But let me pause now. I am running ahead of myself. I shall first tell you more about the background of the doctors and how we got to our results.

In Israel over 80 percent of practicing physicians are employed by national or quasi-national organizations, so we drew all of our interviewees from these public institutions. Apart from this fact, we sought after diversity in specialty, age, status, and type and place of work. The wide range of ages, from twenty-nine to ninety-one years of age, reflected professional and generational continuity. To divert for a moment, a woman doctor aged ninety-one said that it had been three years since she felt that she had to resign from all medical committees but was sad that she was not working anymore. We found that practically all pensioners are working if their health permits it. An elderly physician commented that if he didn't lay hands on one patient a day then, "I haven't lived that day." Searching after a dynamic picture, we did not place the emphasis on "great men" in the profession nor on those in controlling positions, but rather on those doctors who day after day were in direct contact with the patients, working quietly in the hospital ward or in the neighborhood clinic.

As wisdom is not the monopoly of any one discipline, we used an interdisciplinary approach for the purpose of our interpretations. To quote the philosopher Ben-Ami Scharfstein "If we keep seeing people from a single perspective, we become largely blind to them." Thus, we drew from many sources but mainly from culture theory, psycho-history, and psycho-dynamics. Lifton's concept of the sense of symbolic immortality emerged as a key one for understanding much of the strivings of the Israeli doctors. (Indeed, this is the moment at which I would like to pay tribute to Robert Lifton for the many illuminating hours during which he so generously listened and reacted to my encounters with the doctors.)

Within the scientific community there is awareness that life itself is always richer than any theoretical model. Researchers are thus constantly looking for the missing subtleties so as to be able to explain more. It is now recognized that the researcher him or herself, the approach, the personal history and motivations, are all factors which have an influence. Most doctors know this intuitively from the clinical point of view. They know the power of the placebo stems from the fact that it is the doctor who orders or gives the pill. A Jewish prison doctor who survived Auschwitz told how reassuring words together with a mere aspirin helped desperately ill inmates because the assurance came from the doctor, even though he himself was an inmate.

From my perspective as an anthropologist and medical educator, I would like to explain what my motives were in initiating this study which will be presented on two levels. The first level is the cognitive one, the intellectual pursuit, and the second is a more personal and emotional one. However, in life these lines crisscross. Early 1974, some months after the Yom Kippur War, I was teaching a course on anthropology in a medical school. In the class was a group of students who had come straight from the army camp or from the hospital in which they had been recovering from their wounds. One was an amputee, another had burn scars on his face, and a number were clearly spaced out. Desperate to reach them, I changed the subject of the course to "Thanatos" and then added the term "Eros" to lighten the atmosphere somewhat. Slowly but surely, I got a response.

It was during discussions in this class that I realized the urgent need to introduce a required course on death and dying for our future physicians, the basic necessity having been sharpened by the war. I fully realized how important this was only when faced with fierce opposition by the powers-to-be, opposition culminating when a prominent physician said to me "You and your Department of Behavioral Sciences cannot be responsible for such a course because you are a Ph.D. and only a M.D. knows what death is." Incidentally, I made a special visit from Israel to Montreal to see the Palliative Care Unit of the Royal Victoria Hospital so as to gain knowledge, and more important, confidence. Fortunately, an open-minded Dean came to my aid and this course is now fully entrenched in the curriculum. Through this academic struggle, I gained a further understanding of the disturbing complexity of the physician's confrontation with death. The next step followed: to learn more, in depth, about the reality of the world into which we were plunging our students immediately after their graduation. Our knowledge had to be "experience near" as opposed to "experience distant." We wanted to hear from the doctors, how they felt when they got home and took off their white coats, what was going on in their heads when they couldn't sleep at night because of the events of that long day.

Lou Langness, the anthropologist, pointed out that when Jean-Paul Sartre wanted to understand, intrinsically, the lives of leading writers in France, he sought to discover their fundamental project: what the organizing principle or nexus of meanings and values are that guide a person's way of life. As I see it, literature is to France what medicine is to Israel. I wanted to learn more about the world of the Israeli doctors through the prism of their fundamental project, namely medicine. What gives medicine its aura and its power of attraction as a profession, especially in the Israeli context where in addition to other factors, there are forces which work strongly against Israeli doctors developing an exaggerated sense of elitism that is often found in other countries.

Every researcher who examines the fundamental project of others is holding up his or her own to the mirror. Many years before it was trendy for anthropologists to speak about reflexivity and self-disclosure, Margaret Mead wrote: "The advances in the application of scientific knowledge to the understanding of man has been dependent on two developments, methods of observing other human beings and methods of observing ourselves, as observers" 1933. The medical world is very familiar to me. I grew up with ten doctors in my immediate family. As Robert Murphy says, I had the need to organize systematically what I already knew.

My deep involvement in this study clarified my own fundamental project: the wish to be intrinsically connected to these healers; the wish to understand them; and, hopefully, to contribute to them, yet not be one of them. I need to be an anthropologist so that I can step back, bridge cultures, and seek after some of the elusive universalities as they are expressed within different contexts. One particular uncle and my older brother, both of whom are pediatricians, evoke in me the idealized figures of the past after whom we all hanker. Their image is a far cry from that reflected in the growing genre of medical literature, which address doctor burn-out, impairment, and cynicism, as idealism turns into disillusionment. To date, there is little or nothing written on the subject of the impairment of doctors in Israel. There seems to be no obvious evidence of drug taking or achoholism, elevated suicide rates among them. But Israel is not an island unto itself; Israeli medicine hitches its star to the best of American medicine. We posed the question: how do the Israeli physicians perceive their own functioning in the current turbulent medical ambience? The Hippocratic teachings caution physicians to at least do no harm" to their patients. But the primary question we began to raise was how a physician can protect himself against being harmed when trying to heal others. The apostle Luke, in the New Testament, admonished "Physician heal thyself."

Our first task was to delineate special features of the Israeli context and ascertain whether or not the Israeli physician has distinguishing characteristics. Let us start with the cultural background of the Israeli doctors and certain structural features of the practice of medicine in Israel. As characteristic of the Israeli general population the doctors in our study came from all major world areas. The young graduates tended to be Israeli-born, a substantial block came from Eastern Europe, and a number from Central and Western Europe. The English speaking countries were relatively well represented. When I went over the names of the birthplaces which doctors left to immigrate to Israel, I had a sudden memory of that wonderful poem which had fascinated me as a child, written by William Turner, a Victorian poet. I shall indulge in four lines of it:

> When I was but thirteen or so, I went into a golden land, Chimbarzo, Cotapaxi took me by the hand. I walked in a great golden dream to and fro from school-shining Popocatepetl the dusty streets did rule.

The list of birthplaces of the doctors includes places like Baghdad, Bombay, Cairo, Capetown, Istanbul, Melbourne, New York, St. Petersburg, Rio de Janeiro, Tashkent, and Zagreb. We were surprised when we discerned that at the level of actual functioning and in terms of basic values, beliefs and identities, this heterogenous group emerged as an Israeli variant of what I call Homo Hippocratus." Drawing from physical anthropology, I coined the term "Homo Hippocratus" because of the extraordinary enduring power of the professional self of the physician, a point which emerged clearly in our study. The term "Israeli variant" is to account for the subtle, and sometimes not so subtle, cultural and contextual influences. So as to avoid possible overstatements, let me add, that within the country there are certain culturally different styles of overt behavior in speech; etiquette; and, with regard to some groups, different standards of knowledge. However, on analyzing their responses relating to their medical careers and visions, detached from their life stories, it was difficult if not impossible to know from where they came.

Following Kohut, we present the concept "self" as "What I feel and what I do and the need to be related to others from whom I draw and incorporate so as to satisfy my own individual needs." The professional self is constituted by what "I know both theoretically and practically." We shall argue that the relationship between knowing, doing, and feeling is the crux of the struggle for the doctor who is seeking an optimal position for himself within the matrix of his subselves, particularly finding the balance between the professional and personal self. I would like at this stage to trace the source and implications of the extraordinary power of the professional self of the doctor, which is socio-cultural and psycho-historical.

I shall describe three postulates that make up a single paradigm, which together with the field data, will guide the analysis.

The first postulate is that the core of the professional self, is viewed as a natural outcome of the dominant bio-medical model which can be traced as far back as ancient Greece in the fifth century B.C., when the Hippocratic school of thought on the Isle of Cos rejected supernatural explanations for disease. The Israeli doctors, in a very conscious way, see themselves as a link in this great historical chain of scientific yet humanistic healers. To this day in Israel, as in most medical schools throughout the world, the graduating student takes the Hippocratic Oath in some modified form. An elderly Czechoslovakian born doctor had grown up in a wealthy family that wanted him to become a banker. But he was adamant about studying medicine. He survived the horrors of the Holocaust only to be thrown into jail for Zionist activities. Finally he reached Israel and took up a post as a pediatrician in a community clinic where he was loved and respected. For him, he said, it was a transcendental moment in his life when he was capped and gowned as a M.D.

The second source of strength of the Israeli professional self is the time-honored image of the healer in the Jewish tradition. The earliest definition of a doctor in Judaic terms is as a messenger and instrument of God. While the fount of the healing power is considered sacred, the actual practice of medicine is more like cleanliness, namely, next to godliness. Medicine having been sanctioned by Biblical and Talmudical law has been regarded for centuries as a spiritually endowed vocation and has had an important bearing upon the professional self of the physician in Jewish life. An Israeli doctor in our study, secular in his beliefs, yet highly respected by the ultra-orthodox, was told when called in for a consultation, "First comes God and then you" and "Behind every small doctor there is a large angel."

Numerous doctors in our study reported that they came to medicine not because of their parents' direct pressure, but because of their parents' esteem and respect for the medical profession. They themselves began to feel as if it was almost a mystic inevitability that they be doctors. A young Israeli anaesthetist commented "Doctors are born—not made."

As I mentioned before, there are powerful factors in Israel which moderate a sense of elitism among the doctors and, concurrently, promote a strong sense of identity with the larger society. Here I am touching on a basic tenet within the psycho-history of Israel but, because of time constraints, I shall be brief in my analysis and let the words of the doctors illustrate the following five points:

1. Many of the doctors are immigrants themselves, which gives them a common experience and often emotional ties with immigrant patients.

2. A number of the older generation of physicians in Israel lived through the Holocaust experience, which they share with patients; to this day, it is a controlling image that permeates Israeli life. A doctor tells a story of returning to his hospital in Poland where he had started to work before being incarcerated in Auschwitz. Another ex-inmate was hospitalized with terrible stomach pains, and he, then a young doctor, believed this patient should be operated upon. The head of the department disagreed and the next day the patient was dead. Even now, almost fifty years later in Israel, this doctor feels terrible anguish that someone who had survived the concentration camp should have died from a medical mistake. He feels, perhaps, that he had not stood up strongly enough against authority.

3. The fact that the majority of doctors are employees in public organizations means that they do not have the luxury of choosing their clients, and willy nilly, they are kept in contact with all sectors of the population, which, in itself, is a social leveler.

4. The Israeli army is a citizen army and thus doctors have to serve like all others, three years plus annual reserve duty. In the army there is recognition of the specialness of the healing role. Doctors always serve in their profession and not in a regular military function. This rule does not apply to other professions.

Let me give you three vignettes, each one illustrating one or more of these points which I have outlined.

One of our prominent doctors immigrated to Israel at the age of twelve with his widowed mother and studied under difficult economic circumstances. In addition, he had gone through a life-threatening illness. I asked him if he had ever had a transcendental experience in his life, to which he replied with the following story: "On the day of the formal declaration of the State I was aged eighteen and in the army. I was standing as a guard at the entrance of the room where the ceremony was taking place. At the critical moment of declaration, Ben Gurion called me in so that I could be part of the historic moment. 'That was a transcendental experience for me,' he said."

Many moving stories have been told by young doctors who had dramatic and traumatic experiences at the front. These are the kind of experiences which exposed their different vulnerabilities and showed how they may or may not become wounded healers. An Israeli born orthopedist was flown out to the war zone where sixty Israeli soldiers had been blown up in a major explosion. This young doctor related that he was surprised at his own cool behavior while working around the clock facing gruesome scenes of violent death and injury. "I ate my meals," he said "and slept without problems whenever I could grab the chance." On the first day of his return to his normal hospital job, a little boy, badly injured in a car accident, was brought to him in the emergency room. He looked at the child and collapsed.

A rural family physician was called in urgently to assist when a school bus on the northern Israeli border was attacked by terrorists. He told me that among the victims there was one little girl who died because he did not have the necessary emergency equipment. "She should not have died," he said. "How do you cope with this knowledge?" I asked him. "Well," he answered "a number of lives have been saved since then as a result of this terrible encounter." He explained that he designed a special emergency kit and persuaded his medical organization to make it available for all the rural doctors in the area.

The final postulate, which deals with what is probably the strongest source of power of the professional self for all doctors is the empowerment given to the healer by society to promote survival. He or she is the one who is legally and often morally entitled by society to draw the line between life and death. Ideally, the doctor's task is to maintain life, but as we humans are mere mortals, the phenomenon of death is omnipresent. We yearn for our doctors to be not only omnipotent but, in these modern times, also to be endowed with omniscience. However, in the course of the work, the physician is presented again and again with harsh realities. There is a growing gap between the acceleration of medical knowledge and the doctors' ability to translate this knowledge into cure. A young woman internist felt the more that she learned, the more frustrated she became. She suggested bitterly "I am becoming a brilliant diagnostician but we haven't discovered what to do with all our knowledge." A very experienced South African born gynaecologist commented: "When we are successful, we are considered as gods and when we fail to help we are bitterly torn to pieces. We are made larger than life."

Freud claims that the task of all living human beings is to find the delicate and always imperfect inner balance between life and death forces; between, construction, destruction and reconstruction; between what is feared and thus repressed, and what the person is capable of keeping alive in the memory. We asked the doctors to talk about memories from any period in their medical career. Most responded with eagerness as if they had been waiting for the opportunity to reflect on past experiences.

The content of over 300 memories expressed by the doctors focused on the patient-doctor dyad. Although all doctors in the study are employees of public institutions, it was as if they wanted to draw a magic circle around "I the doctor and my patient who is my responsibility," blotting out any outer reality like the team, the ward, or the clinic. They were trying to relive those wonderful moments when the doctor allows himself to be fully empathetic with the patient, so as to get to the core of the problem. However, they know that they cannot stay within that state too long for it might immobilize decision making and action. For a number of reasons this contrast, the switch from intimacy to distance, is very marked in Israeli hospitals. This is upsetting and incomprehensible to many patients. The doctor belongs totally to his patient during the laying of the hands. I have seen doctors close their eyes to be in full concentration, particularly when listening to the heart beat. It is as if they are communing with the patient and then, suddenly, become strangers once the clinical encounter is over. The general attitude is that the fewer words spoken, the better. A partial explanation of this pattern of behavior may be the shared responsibility for patients in the wards which is characteristic of public medicine. The memories brought us closer to both the inner and outer world of the Israeli doctors, but for further understanding we needed to know more about the cultural influences which mold their actual behavior.

A cultural and historical analysis of Israeli society and its ethos reveals the centrality of the enduring themes of idealized sacrifice and heroism, particularly in troubled times, considered essential for the survival of the Jewish people. The event of the Holocaust imprinted these beliefs onto the cultural map. From the memories, we learned that the most salient feature of the ideal image of the Israeli doctor is that of a hero fighting for the survival of the other. The dominant belief in Israel is that this is the responsibility of the doctor even under circumstances when the patient is reluctant to fight for his or her own life. The memories that doctors shared related to experiences of high drama, passion, and elation. However, they also related their struggles, resistances, heartaches, and feelings of loss. Most of them had their unforgettable story which they regarded as a critical experience in their lives.

From the point of view of the content of the memories, the doctors may be divided into three main groups. The first recalled only successes, the second only failures, and the third group, the largest, made valiant efforts to balance success with failure. Failure was invariably a synonym for the death of a patient. Clearly there was no objective factor determining which memories they chose to relate to us. One doctor added sadly—"Every doctor has his own cemetery." Through the process of evoking significant memories, unwittingly, they too were brought to evaluate their own individual fundamental project and allowed the personal self to come to the fore.

Irrespective of how they represented themselves, all perforce (through external constraints or personal conscience) wrestle with two fundamental dilemmas. The first is when they have a "failure"—does their behavior in any way, medically or personally, fall below the line of the irreducible responsibility expected of a physician? Second, there is the dilemma of how they must protect themselves against feeling too much or feeling too little.

Both extremes are painful for the doctor and not helpful for the patient. On the one hand, feeling too much clouds judgment and on the other hand, the damming back of emotion can lead to blunting of affect in other spheres of life. The idea has been put forward that practicing medicine is one way of handling the anxiety felt about the inevitability of one's own death. Kasper, a psychiatrist, describes the process by which the doctor takes his own fears of death and translates them into intellectual questions and then tries to answer them for others. Part of the power of the professional self is that it immediately ties in with something immortalizing (with a life outside its own); a life that reverberates and may outlive that of the healer. By breathing life into others, the doctor can achieve, in Lifton's terms, a sense of symbolic immortality.

In this age of scientific and technological proliferation, there is an inchoate illusion that death is on the verge of being conquered, hence its connotation of failure. The weakness of the professional self, powerful as it may be, is that it has not created sufficient mechanisms to deal with these so-called failures. At this point, the doctor is on his or her own. Mary Vachon, in her work in Canada, showed that the long-standing professional traditions do not help if the doctor does not develop a personal individual philosophy. Many doctors in Israel expressed their appreciation for being able to work in a team and having a medical hierarchy to support them against the outside world. However, this support is not enough to quiet inner misgivings. We found a range of extraordinarily complex mechanisms used to handle the death of a patient whom a doctor thought, for whatever reason, should not have died. They all found the death of a young person particularly difficult to accept. Mechanisms such as distancing, overidentification, and technical professionalism were aimed at shutting out the reality of death.

Those who reacted with a sense of defeat were like well-trained fighters who were in the battle for the win only, and when they lost, they felt vanquished and impoverished. Some could cushion the blow because they had allowed room for certain aspects of their personal self to develop. A very anxious young cardiologist burst out with the statement that he would never get used to losing a patient, "I hate it, I hate it everytime one of them dies." When I asked him how he managed to continue working, he thought for a moment, and then answered, "It's the medical challenge and also I have a wonderful wife and a bunch of decent kids, but I don't want them to be doctors." We see as "the heroes," as opposed to "the fighters," those who could use their professional self as life-enhancing. A hero derives his strength from integrating his personal fundamental project with the dominant cultural values, within the historical context. Those doctors who followed this heroic image in medicine could develop a personal philosophy of life which made a place for both physical death and their own symbolic immortality.

After much despair an oncologist came to accept the death of his young patients as an existential experience. Out of identification with the human suffering of his patients, and even his love for some, he gained a new perspective on life. He reminisced:

> Four or five years ago there was this beautiful young woman, age forty-five. Her name was Lilian. She died from cancer. She became very attached to me and I have kept her picture to this day. But still I remember what happened to her extraordinary beauty during her last days. It brought me to a crisis so I went to speak to our psychologist. I feel this kind of pain especially when a young patient becomes terminal. The identification is so deep. Deaths continue to be upsetting for us. When one sees life so close to death, one understands more about life. I began to appreciate the little pleasures in life. It is not that I am constantly thinking of death, but rather I value life itself. It adds to our humanization.

Roger Money-Kyrle, the British psychoanalyst, describes how the perception of death is the motivating force behind so much of human development and achievement. He writes:

> Why . . . are nearly all religions so concerned with immortality? Why, in our ambitions, are we so passionately anxious for something of ourselves, a work of art, a scientific contribution, or just our good name, to be accepted and to survive? Why, not only for our

pleasure but for our peace of mind, do we need children who should create grandchildren, and so on? [p. 288]

Why, in short, do we strive for immortality—or at least immortality by proxy? Money-Kyrle answers his own question, "In other words all the striving that fills life is the expression of a ceaseless battle against death." Lifton answers this question from a life-enhancing perspective. He speaks about a

> sense of immortality as, in itself, neither compensatory not pathological but as humanity's symbolization of ties with other biological fellows and with history, past and future. Lack of such ties can lead to a loss of faith dangerous for the individual, for the group and in fact ultimately for our species [p. 277].

In Israel, physicians draw additional strength from forces external to their profession, which has helped prevent them, until now, from showing signs of impairment. Their therapeutic role, which gives them the possibility of a sense of symbolic immortality is therefore strengthened by the Israeli ethos characterized by strong loyalties through familial, societal, and historical ties. However, these are historically turbulent times and the doctor's professional self is not invulnerable. Thus, there is an essential need for more medical introspection alongside the outstanding medical advancements. The message embedded in the Chiron myth is that even the wisest of healers have to acknowledge their intrinsic human frailty so as to be able to heal others who will carry their immortality, albeit symbolically.

REFERENCES

Geertz, C., On the Nature of Anthropology Understanding, in *Culture Theory*, R. A. Shweder and R. A. Levine (eds.), Cambridge Press, 1984.

Lifton, R., A Sense of Symbolic Immortality, in *New Meanings of Death*, H. Feifel (ed.), p. 299, 1977.

Langness L. and G. Frank, *Lives*, Chandler and Sharp, Novato, California, 1981.

Mead, M., More Comprehensive Field Methods, *American Anthropology, 35*:1, pp. 1-15, 1933.

Money-Kyrle, R., An Inconclusive Contribution to the Theory of the Death Instinct, in *Collected Works of R. Money-Kyrle*, D. Meltzer (ed.), Clunie Press, Perthshire, pp. 288-289, 1955.

CHAPTER 17

Living Through Death and Dying: Strategies for the Health Care Professional*

Patrice O'Connor

> There is a season for everything, a time for every occupation under heaven
>
> — *A Time for Dying* [1]

> It's not that I'm afraid to die, I just don't want to be there when it happens.
>
> — *W. Allen* [2]

It is a reality that we will all die. This is a fact of life. *How, when,* and *where* this event will happen are more uncertain although it is clear that the most predictable is *where*. According to the Office of Technology Assessment Task Force Report of 1988, 80 percent of the two million Americans who die each year do so in hospitals [3]. The shift of place of death from home to medical setting is due to the advances in medical care and the philosophy of doing all that is medically possible to forestall death. Denial of death has been facilitated by scientific developments and a sense of death as failure. Death is no longer a family event even though most people express the desire to die at home [3].

The questions then arise: How equipped are hospitals in handling the death and dying processes?; What are the obligations of the medical

---

*Based on a two-year research project on death and its impact on caregivers.

personnel to patients, families, and themselves in meeting needs of the dying in these institutions; and Has education for the professional addressed these critical issues of caring for the dying patient and family?

These questions, along with the shrinking health care dollar, evoke more concerns in the ethical, legal and, moral arenas about such issues as Do Not Resuscitate orders, Living Wills, and the right to die. Humanistic responses have not kept pace with the rapid technological developments creating some very difficult death related issues. With medical technology we can keep the body alive but what about the quality of life? How many times can a body "die" and then be restored to be maintained by machines? Who defines life? Do the wishes of the patient, family, or hospital prevail? Where there is conflict in life and death decisions, medical decisions become legal events and are now settled in the courts. The meeting of all these forces have made this a challenging time for health care and health care professionals.

REVIEW OF LITERATURE

With the increase in the proportion of deaths which occur in hospitals, there has been an increasing debate about appropriateness of the place of death. Death in the opinion of many should be a family affair and occurring at home. However, it is increasingly institutionalized and hidden from public view. As people become less familiar with the process of death they may increasingly assume that terminally ill patients are better cared for in the hospital. However, this need not be the case. Most people want to die at home, but do not do so, for social rather than medical reasons [4, 5].

Society is being challenged to make changes in order to meet the needs of a population in which the elderly are the fastest growing segment and in which medical technology has made it more difficult for patients to die. With the increase in the number of people with AIDS, increases in the elderly population, and with a Gross National Product (at 12%), the questions of just how much can be spent on health care, let alone on care of the dying, is making Americans confront their own mortality in uncomfortable ways [6-8].

Callahan has raised difficult questions concerning the medical goals in our aging society [9]. In particular, he examines the issue of resources being spent on the elderly and, therefore, being unavailable for future generations. As an example he cites the expenses of high technology for an elderly terminal patient and the limited resources being allocated for pre-natal care. Callahan continues his argument by offering an alternative which makes care rather than cure our societal priority [10].

"A good death is one a person would choose for himself" [11]. Since most people would choose to die at home, pain free, surrounded by loved ones, this statement implies a conflict with what is considered the ideal versus reality [4]. McCorkle has applied this notion to the role of the health care professional and notes that the caregiver must also be respectful of the dying person's right to choose and have deep respect for the person's choices especially when they differ from his or her own values and goals [12].

Increasingly, death takes place in a hospital in which the dying person is surrounded by sophisticated technological equipment and professionals whose task structures center on curing diseases and routinizing emergencies. Within this organizational context, dying carries with it the "curse" of failure [13]. What is the role of the health care professional in this situation?

Recent medical literature describes how difficult it is for new, young medical students, interns, and residents to deal with dying patients [14]. Their experiences indicate they must respond to a wide range of situations in dealing with dying patients and families. The difficulty arises when they know the patient and feel they have been a failure if death occurs or if they come "in cold" to pronounce a patient dead and must communicate this knowledge to the family. In addressing these situations, physicians do not want to deny their humanity but need assistance in maintaining perspective [15-17].

Issues of dealing with dying patients are not sufficiently addressed in medical schools and residency programs. The interest of patients and physicians alike are best served when life and death decisions are made jointly. Medical students and residents need help, therefore educators have recommended that these topics be specifically included as curricula [18].

The process of dying can trigger overwhelming emotions not only in the person and family, but also in their professional caregivers. Perhaps, as a result of their education and socialization, physicians often feel helpless in the face of devastating illness and are afraid of projecting helplessness to their patients [19]. Professional caregivers need assistance in expressing their feelings when the disease does not respond to the treatment. They need to be realistic in their expectations and communicate this to the patient and family and at the same time not abandon the patient in the dying process. Patients need to be related to as human beings and not as a disease entity that has failed treatment [20].

Nursing publications contain many articles asking questions similar to those in medical journals: "Can a Patient Die with Dignity in an Acute Care Hospital?"; "What is the Role of the Nurse?"; and "Has the Nurse's Education Equipped Her for this Task?" [21-25]. Degner and Gow have shown that nurses who have had classroom and clinical exposure to death-related issues, and have a required course that included clinical practice, have significantly better attitudes toward caring for the dying [26, 27]. They and others recommend that such experiences be required for all nurses as there would be a benefit for both caregivers and patients.

Acute care hospitals in the United States are generally oriented toward providing aggressive treatment aimed at curing or controlling disease. The reality of dying in the hospital setting may not be addressed with respect to patient or family, let alone the professional caregiver. Stresses in dealing with the dying process may be manifested in many ways including:

1. *Role ambiguity*: role expectations are not clearly communicated
2. *Role conflict*: expectation of various professions are incompatible or are in conflict
3. *Role overload*: extent to which any person is incapable of meeting multiple expectations [28].

Administrators can reduce these stresses by being aware of the strengths and weaknesses of caregivers during the selection process (such as identifying coping mechanisms, exploring unresolved grief, and questioning the presence of social support systems). Through proper staff training and orientation (adopting a role model/buddy system, and offering continuing education programs) and including social support systems (as part of the hospital program such as support groups at work and continuing peer support using formal and informal methods) [29].

Another area of stress for caregivers and families is in delivering the news that a death has occurred. Caregivers, no matter what profession, seem to show a strong dislike in the task of delivering such news, referring to the problematic and uncertain nature of each situation. Along with the "death telling" may come the responsibility of asking for an autopsy or a request for organs for transplantation. Although rare, this is also an uncomfortable part of delivering the bad news because it has to be done immediately after death. The issue of training for death telling would appear to be an important dimension of medical and nursing education [30].

The cumulative effect of multiple patient deaths upon staff may lead to eventual depletion and spiritual exhaustion. Attitudinal, behavioral, and social factors may manifest themselves in expressions of unresolved grief, the need to be perfect, projection of one's own needs, over-seriousness, lack of sharing, inappropriate sharing at home, norms of solemnity, lack of structured opportunities for sharing, and administrative non-responsiveness [31]. Workshops on death awareness can reduce death anxiety. Interestingly, it was observed that older nurses or those who have some clinical experience benefitted more from these programs [32].

Eddy has indicated that health care professionals seeking to cope with the personal and social problems involved in the care of the dying will be more effective if they are able to reduce their own anxiety in the face of death [33]. Murphy's study of 150 nurses who had experienced a death awareness workshop (conducted by comparing them with a control group who had not) measured the effect of the death awareness workshop on their death-related anxiety. The results indicated that the workshop decreased the death anxiety level [32].

The Joint Commission on Accreditation of Healthcare has mandated standards addressing the care of the dying patient and family. These standards have become a part of the overall accrediting survey program in January 1992 [34]. These standards are:

r1.1.1.2.1 The care of the patient includes consideration of the psychosocial, spiritual, and cultural variables that influence the perceptions of illness.

r1.1.1.2.2 The care of the dying patient optimizes the comfort and dignity of the patient through

r1.1.1.2.2.1 Treating primary and secondary symptoms that respond to treatment as desired by the patient or surrogate decision maker;

r1.1.1.2.2.2 Effectively managing pain; and

r1.1.1.2.2.3 Acknowledging the psychosocial and spiritual concerns of the patient and family regarding dying and the expression of grief by the patient and family.

One of the most important challenges facing administrators today is finding ways to motivate and adequately support front-line staff in dealing with the issues of care of the dying patients and their families while meeting their own needs.

STUDY OBJECTIVES

In the St Luke's/Roosevelt Hospital Center in 1991 there were 1,865 deaths. A study was conducted to evaluate the care of these dying patients and family specifically to:

1. Evaluate if an Educational Intervention would result in a decrease in death anxiety in caregivers and result in a change in documentation on the dying patient in the Medical Record.
2. Establish a Templer Death Anxiety Norm for an academic medical center across all departments in dealing with death in the institution in response to the Joint Commission Standards on the care of the dying and their families.
3. Review Medical Records of all deaths for a two-month period using the Latimer Medical Record tool to assess documented terminal care.

DESIGN

The design of the Study was to perform:

1. Medical Record Audits; and
2. Educational Interventions.

PATIENTS

The Medical Records for all deaths that occurred at the St Luke's site for the months of July 1991 (59 deaths and 53 medical records available) and May 1992 (50 deaths and 49 medical records) were available for the audit.

STAFF

All departments and units with direct patient contact in the inpatient setting participated in the Death Awareness Sessions. There were thirty-seven units or departments and 592 staff attended the sessions.

PROCEDURE

A) The July 1991 medical records of the fifty-three deaths at the St Luke's site were audited using the Latimer Hospital Medical Record Audit Tool [35] to establish:
1. type of death
2. location of death
3. demographic of Patients
4. time of deaths
5. documentation on the dying patient in the area of:
   a. Patient Comfort
   b. Patient Counselling
   c. Family Counselling
   d. Interdisciplinary Care
   e. Follow-up Care (family]

B) Two Death Awareness Sessions were held with twenty-five units or departments. Each participant was asked to complete the Templer Death Anxiety Scale [36] before the first session and after the second session. There was a four-week period between the Sessions.

One Death Awareness Session was held with eleven units or departments. Each participant was asked to complete the Templer Death Anxiety Scale before the session.[1]

The major reason for using the Templer Death Anxiety Scale was to establish a norm for an acute care hospital across all departments in dealing with death in the institutions in response to the Joint Commission on Accreditation of Healthcare Organization Standards on the care of the dying and their family.

Session	Time	Content
1	**1st Week**	**Personal Death Awareness** Exercises in Word Association Life Line Time Line Cases Examples Writing their Obituary
2	**4th Week**	**Professional Death Experiences** 1st Professional Death Meaningful Death Experiences Sharing how these deaths affected them personally and professionally What were their expectations for support from other staff and how would they give support

The important factor in both sessions was that the staff had the opportunity to express and listen to one another.

---

[1] The Templer Death Anxiety Scale [38] is an instrument utilizing fifteen True/False statements, measuring death anxiety. This test has been demonstrated to be reliable and valid in repeated trials with health professional groups to assess capacity for dealing with death [32, 37-44].

C) The May 1992 medical records of the forty-nine deaths at the St Luke's site were audited using the Latimer Hospital Medical Record Audit Tool and were compared to the July 1991 audit.

The Latimer Hospital Medical Record Audit is designed to establish whether the essential components of good terminal care are being provided to patients dying in institutions. By identifying gaps in medical records, the audit assists in pointing out actual gaps in patient and family care, thereby assisting in planning for total patient care.

D) Types of Deaths: During the Medical Record audit, it was evident that there were different types of deaths that occur in the Hospital:
   1. Emergency Room Deaths
   2. Long-Term Deaths: Cancer, AIDS
   3. Sudden Deaths
   4. Technical Deaths
   5. Perinatal or Neonatal Deaths.

Each of these is a death but the circumstances and events leading to the death are very different.

RESULTS

Educational Sessions

The median score for the Templer Death Anxiety Scale for the Hospital Center was 6.5. A department or unit with a score over 7.0 was reviewed as having a moderate death anxiety rating.

In order to assess if there was any correlation in the level of anxiety indicated by the Templer Death Anxiety Scale, six programs dealing exclusively with terminal patients (4 Medicare Certified Hospice Programs, 1 Community Outreach department of an acute care hospital, and 1 supportive care program) responded to the Templer Anxiety Scale. The two non-certified programs scored the lowest ratings with 7.0 to 7.6. The certified programs ranged from 7.8 to 8.5. The median score for the total was 8.0 with eighty-five staff responding across all disciplines.

Therefore, it can be assumed that a moderate score over 7.0 does not indicate an inability to care for patients who may be dying or dealing with death in the hospital. There were thirteen departments or units with a median score of 7.0 (Templer Death Anxiety Score—TDAS) or above.

Chaplains–8.15 TDAS

The chaplains were the highest group in the single session. The number of participants was five, chaplain interns were included since they staff the hospital center alone on a twenty-four-hour on-call basis. This does not seem unreasonable as the Hospital Policy is to call the chaplain for each death. During the sessions with the individual units, when asked where they received their support and support for the patients and families during the death and dying process, the usual response was the chaplain. It appears then that the chaplain deals with death and dying across all settings in the hospital. There is an average number of seventy-five to eighty deaths per month at the St Luke's site.

Patient Relations–7.7 TDAS

The next department was Patient Relations who are also available to patients and families during this stressful time. They are called upon during the bereavement period to deal with questions about personal possessions and hospital bills.

Volunteers in AIDS Programs–7.7 TDAS

The next group were the volunteers in the AIDS Programs. One group worked with adults and the other group worked with children. Eighty percent had experienced at least one death during their time as a volunteer. The Hospital Center has the designation of an AIDS Center with an average daily in-patient census of sixty to seventy patients at the St Luke's site. The volunteers stated that they do receive support from the staff in the Volunteers Office, on the units, and in the clinic.

Interns–7.1 TDAS

The Intern score of 7.1 is not surprising because for many of them, it may be their first experience with death. It may be the first time they had to inform a patient and/or family of a terminal diagnosis. As part of the responsibility, they may also have to inform a family about a death of a patient they may or may not have known. These were the tasks they were not prepared for in medical school and had no role modeling at the hospital. The interns suggested that an in-service session separate from the residents should be held so they could openly express themselves and the interns suggested that some role playing exercises be done for the next year's group of interns.

Cardiac Services–9.0-7.25 TDAS

The cardiac services had high scores. Open Heart Recovery Room (OHR) had the highest score of all units—9.0, the Cardiac Care Unit (CCU) scored 7.25. This may reflect the number of deaths in the unit and the delicate balance of the procedures that are performed. One session was held in the OHR with the staff at one end of the ward. When the instructor requested that they move out of the unit, they stated it was easier to be held there and the patients would not know what we were talking about during the session. The staff faced the instructor and she was looking at the patients. After the session on Professional Death Experience, the instructor spoke with two of the patients who were alert and had observed the session. They clearly understood what was being discussed and stated that they were glad to know that someone besides themselves realized that death was on their mind (having just had open heart surgery).

The Cardiac Care Unit expressed stress when they felt that the doctor had not discussed the serious condition of the patient with the patient, family, or staff. The stress came from not being able to be honest in the situation when all realized the patient's condition was terminal.

Medical Service–Three Units: 8.5, 7.1, 8.0 TDAS

There are many factors that may account for these scores. The staff were experiencing stress due to the closing of the unit and the transfer of staff to different units in a new building. The majority of the staff had worked together for a long period of time. The separation was being discussed as stressful. Death anxiety cannot only be related to the patient's condition but to staff situation of loss as well.

This unit had only one session as it was closed the following week. The staff expressed concern since they were being transferred to other units in the hospital and had not had to deal with death in their present unit.

Another unit had just experienced a death of a patient who had no family and the staff had become the surrogate family. Fulton states that this can be very stressful for the staff as they assume the role of family [45].

Surgical Service–8.0 TDAS

This unit had experienced three deaths in one month of patients who had multi-admissions.

CRITICAL CARE UNITS

Emergency Room–7.6 TDAS

The Emergency Room has been described as working in a critical care area where one is confronted with inescapable loss. Despite all the variety of means by which one "distances" or defends against emotional depletion, giving care to those who are losing their health, their body integrity and in many cases their lives is very stressful according to studies by Price and Murphy [31]. In reviewing the deaths in the Emergency Room for the two-month period—there were thirty-nine deaths—twelve patients were dead on arrival and sixteen patients died within thirty minutes after arrival in Emergency Room. Staff stated that the pediatric deaths are the most difficult. They also stated that the Chaplains are a source of support for families and themselves.

Labor and Delivery–8.1 TDAS (Evenings)

The stress-related factors in Labor and Delivery were discussed after the second session of Professional Death Experiences. The issues were related to the stillbirths when the baby remains in the Labor and Delivery area until the family has viewed the baby and then transporting the body to the morgue. This whole process may take a few hours. The staff were reluctant to accept the intervention and asked the instructor who she was, and whether the hospital knew what she was doing. They suggested that because death does not occur in their department, there was no need for the intervention. Vachon has suggested in her studies on stressful areas in the hospital setting that the Labor and Delivery department is second only to the Emergency Room in terms of stress, because of the complications that may occur [29].

DISCUSSION OF EDUCATIONAL SESSIONS

Comments and Observations During the Educational Sessions

- Most staff could recall their first death in a professional setting and these usually occurred when they were students. Their experiences ranged from being supported by professional staff to being left alone and feeling frightened and traumatized.
- The staff shared their memories with one another and their stories about certain patients and circumstances were retold. Some of the

staff were surprised at how some deaths affected other staff members.

- The differences in what was considered to be a difficult death was evident. The Emergency Room staff stated that the pediatric deaths are the most difficult while the NICU staffers stated that adult deaths are the most difficult for them.
- With the opening of the new building and the closing of some units, staff stress was evident. The loss of the old and familiar and anticipated loss of working relationships which were soon to be terminated created stress.
- Nurses were concerned that they did not know how much the patient and family had been told about the medical condition of the patient.
- All units indicated that the chaplains were a source of support for the patient, family, and themselves.
- There was a mixed response from the Clinical Coordinators. Some were present and participated, others covered the units so staff could attend and others were not present at all.
- During one session, one of the attending doctors walked by and stated, "Why don't you go and do nurse things instead of talking?" When he was informed the topic was death and dying, he stated that it did not happen, and when he was told the number of deaths for that month was fifty-three, he just kept walking. This was the same unit where one of the attending doctors had questioned one of the nurses about how observant she had been because a patient had coded and died during the night (the nurse had worked the day shift and the patient was stable when she had left the unit that afternoon).
- The stress in the pediatric unit was evident when it was observed that whole families were dying from AIDS and not just the children. An added stress was that a co-worker had just been admitted to the ICU.
- Supportive Sessions for the ICU and the AIDS Unit were identified by staff as most helpful to them in dealing with their high numbers of deaths.
- The AIDS Units of PS1 were not included in these sessions because sessions had been held with this group the year before and they have ongoing support groups as part of the AIDS Program.
- On one unit, when there was a very difficult impending death and a disturbed family, one of the nurses in the unit stayed with the patient and family on the day of the death, while the other nurses covered the rest of the unit. They were all comfortable with

this and said that it was important for the patient and family to do this.

- In one Critical Care Unit, staff could not identify patients by name but rather, only by bed number. There were at least fifteen deaths per month in this unit and most patients were unresponsive.
- The emergency room and the operating room shared an experience of a young woman who had been stabbed, and each unit indicated respect for the other's skills and support given to one another during this traumatic situation.
- One nurse, who chose not to attend, shared that she had blood from an AIDS patient splatter on her face and in her eyes. She had herself tested for AIDS and now wears clear, plain glasses to protect her eyes while at work.
- One unit, where the staff had been together for over five years, remembered a young cancer patient who was moved to another floor overnight in order that his room could be aired and cleaned. The patient stated that he would die that night if he was moved, and he did die. The staff stated that they have never asked for a patient to be transferred or moved again.
- When the interns were telling their professional death experiences, the pain was evident in their voices and faces as they stated that no one had ever taught or showed them what to do in these situations.
- Most staff asked, "What should we be doing for the dying patient and family?" Are there guidelines we could follow?
- The isolation of the dying patient was mentioned because of the cost of having a telephone or television in their room, particularly where the patient had limited resources or were elderly.

EDUCATIONAL INTERVENTION

Of the twenty-five units that received the two Educational Interventions, twelve units had a decrease in the TDA Scale, seven units remained the same, and six units had an increase in the TDA Scale.

LIMITATIONS

The limitations of this study were:

1. Not all staff attended both sessions due to vacation and staffing patterns. Handouts and materials were left in each unit or department for absent staff members.

2. Not all units had the same number of deaths so it was not possible to correlate the educational intervention with the documentation. The were four units out of twenty-five units with three or more deaths and each was in a different medical specialty.

3. The age, sex, years of experience, ethnic, religious, and cultural factors of the staff were not included which would influence their practice in the care of the dying and dealing with death.

IMPLICATIONS AND RECOMMENDATIONS

1. The findings of this study reveal a lack of communication about the dying and death process between patient, family, and staff. Apparently staff verbalize the importance of this communication but lack the comfort in documentation. Staff requested guidelines in documentation in order to improve patient care and met the Joint Commission on Accreditation Healthcare Office (JCAHO) standards.

2. Not all staff were aware of the resources in the hospital to meet the needs of the patient, family, and caregivers. These included: Chaplains, Social Services, Patient Relations, and Volunteer Departments.

3. Staff became more aware of the isolation of the dying patient either because of a lack of family or friends or because of economic limitations. Resources should continue to be explored to meet these needs.

4. As part of the total patient plan of care, guidelines should be developed to assist staff in meeting patient, family, and their own needs while caring for the dying patient.

5. A Learning Packet for in-service self-teaching would beneficial for the caregivers in meeting their needs in caring for the dying.

6. Each Department who has direct patient contact should have at least an annual in-service program on death and dying as it relates to their department.

7. A period review of the medical record of the patients who have died should be done as part of Quality Improvement using the Latimer Audit Tool.

8. All policies and procedures pertaining to dying and death should be reviewed to insure sensitivity to the patient and family. These may include notification of the death, opportunities for viewing the body, and follow-up care.

9. Institutions may want to extend visiting hours, and to allow the terminal patient to have children and pets visit.

10. Because medical and nursing education will vary, institutions should include in their mandates: total patient care and educational opportunities for staff to learn what is necessary for the care of the dying patient and family.

CONCLUSION

This study reviewed death in an acute care setting by medical record audit and an educational intervention on death awareness. Death anxiety can be reduced by an educational intervention and documentation increased. This study identified how and where death occurs in the acute care setting. It also identified staff issues and stresses that arise in caring for the dying patients, families, and themselves.

This study concurs with the Solomon Study which states that many physicians and nurses were disturbed by the degree to which technological solutions influence care during the final days of a terminal illness [46].

REFERENCES

1. *The Jerusalem Bible*, Ecc, 3:1-3, Doubleday & Co., New York, 1966.
2. W. Allen, *Without Feathers*, Warner Books, New York, p. 106, 1972.
3. C. L. Allen, *Medicine, Ethics by Committee, Insight in the News*, Lippincott, New York, p. 52-53, July 23, 1990.
4. A. Bowling, The Hospitalization of Death: Should More People Die at Home, *Journal of Medical Ethics*, 9, pp. 158-161, 1983.
5. V. Mor and W. Jeffrey, Determinants of Site of Death among Hospice Cancer Patients, *Journal of Health and Social Behaviour*, 24, pp. 375-385, 1983.
6. C. L. Thurow, *Perspectives on Health Care from the Economic Viewpoint*, presented at the 3rd annual leadership meeting of Allegany Health System, June 10, 1988.
7. R. Bayer, D. Callahan, J. Fletcher et al., The Care of the Terminally Ill: Mortality and Economics, *New England Journal of Medicine*, 309, pp. 1490-1494, 1983.
8. A. Scitovsky, The High Cost of Dying: What Do the Data Show?, *Milbank Memorial Fund Quarterly*, 62, pp. 591-608, 1989.
9. D. Callahan, *Setting Limits*, Simon and Schuster, New York, 1987.
10. D. Callahan, *What Kind of Life*, Simon and Schuster, New York, 1990.
11. A. D. Wiessman, *On Dying and Denying*, Behavioural Publications, New York, p. 4, 1972.
12. R. McCorkle, A Good Death, *Cancer Nursing*, 4, p. 247, 1981.
13. E. Stoller, Effect of Experience on Nurses' Responses to Dying and Death in Hospital Setting, *Nursing Research*, 28, pp. 35-39, 1980.

14. G. E. Dickinson, Death Education for Physicians, *Journal of Medical Ethics, 63*:5, p. 412, 1988.
15. C. Smith, Learning to Deal with Death, *Journal of the American Medical Association, 262*:21, p. 3073, 1989.
16. D. Morse, When to Touch, *Journal of the American Medical Association, 263*:16, p. 2225, 1990.
17. M. Katz, On Not Growing Accustomed to Death, *West Journal of Medicine, 149*, p. 488, 1988.
18. S. Wagner et al., The Physicians' Responsibility toward Hopelessly Ill Patients, *New England Journal of Medicine, 320*:13, pp. 844-849, 1989.
19. E. Seravalli, The Dying Patient, the Physician, and the Fear of Death, *New England Journal of Medicine, 319*:26, pp. 1728-1730, 1988.
20. E. Cassell, *Healer's Art*, Lippincott, New York, 1976.
21. J. Trevelyn, A Matter of Life and Death, *Nursing Times, 86*, pp. 36-37, 1990.
22. V. Wilson, How Can We Dignify Death in the ICU, *American Journal of Nursing, 38*, p. 42, May 1990.
23. C. Young, Afraid of Death, *Journal of Pediatric Nursing, 3*:5, p. 295, 1988.
24. D. Read-Sute, A Dream Dies, *American Journal of Maternal/Child Nursing*, p. 258, July/August 1990.
25. M. Nordbert, When Patients Die: Handling Grief in the Dialysis Unit, *Dialysis & Transplantation, 19*:4, pp. 164-168, 1990.
26. L. Degner and C. Gow, Evaluation of Death Education in Nursing, *Cancer Nursing, 11*:3, pp. 151-159, 1988.
27. L. Degner and C. Gow, Preparing Nurses for Care of the Dying, *Cancer Nursing, 11*:3, pp. 160-169, 1988.
28. M. Vachon, Losses and Gains: Issues and Topics, in *Cancer Nursing*, R. McCorkle and E. Hongladaron (eds.), Norwalk-Appleton-Century-Crofts, pp. 41-59, 1986.
29. M. Vachon, Staff Stress in the Care of the Terminally Ill, *Quality Review Bulletin*, pp. 13-17, May 1989.
30. R. Clark and E. LaBeff, Death Telling, Managing the Delivery of Bad News, *Journal of Health and Social Behaviour, 22*, pp. 366-380, 1982.
31. D. Price and P. Murphy, Emotional Depletion in Critical Care Staff, *American Association of Neuroscience Nurses, 17*:2, pp. 114-118, 1985.
32. P. Murphy, Reduction in Nurses' Death Anxiety Following a Death Awareness Workshop, *Journal of Continuing Education in Nursing, 17*:4, pp. 115-118, 1986.
33. J. Eddy and A. Wesley, *Death Education*, C. V. Mosby, St. Louis, 1983.
34. *Joint Commission on Accreditation of Healthcare Standard for Hospital*, Chicago, Illinois, p. 103, January 1992.
35. E. Latimer, Auditing the Hospital Care of Dying Patients, *Journal of Palliative Care, 7*:1, pp. 12-17, 1991.
36. D. J. Templer, The Construction and Validation of a Death Anxiety Scale, *Journal of General Psychology, 82*, pp. 165-177, 1970.

37. M. Amenta, Traits of Hospice Nurses Compared with Those Who Work in Traditional Settings, *Journal of Clinical Psychology*, *40*:2, pp. 414-420, 1984.

38. D. J. Templer, An MMPI Scale for Assessing Death Anxiety, *Psychological Reports*, *34*:1, pp. 238-243, 1974.

39. M. Vargo and F. W. Black, Attribution of Control and Fear of Death among First-Year Medical Students, *Journal of Clinical Psychology*, *40*:6, pp. 1525-1558, 1984.

40. H. Conte, M. Weimier, and R. Plutchik, Measuring Death Anxiety Conceptual, *Psychology, Journal of Personality and Social Psychology*, *43*:4, pp. 775-785, 1982.

41. J. Durlak, Using the Templer Scale to Assess "Death Anxiety," *Psychological Reports*, *50*:3, pp. 1257-1259, 1982.

42 R. Lonetto, S. Fleming, and G. Mercer, The Structure of Death Anxiety: A Factor Analytic Study, *Journal of Personality Assessments*, *43*:4, pp. 388-392, 1979.

43. W. McMordie, Concurrent Validity of the Templer and Templer/McMordie Death Anxiety Scale, *Psychological Reports*, *51*:1, pp. 265-266, 1982.

44. N. Waltman, Attitudes, Subjective Norms and Behavioral Intentions of Nurses toward Dying Patients and the Families, *Oncology Nursing Forum*, *17*:3, pp. 55-60, 1990.

45. R. Fulton, Anticipatory Grief, Stress and the Surrogate Griever, in *Cancer Stress and Death*, S. Day (ed.), Plenum Publishing, New York, pp. 169-180, 1986.

46. M. Solomon, L. O'Donnell et al., Decisions Near the End of Life, *American Journal of Public Health*, *83*, pp. 14-23, 1993.

CHAPTER 18

Medically Futile Treatment: Considering Lifting the Burden of Decision Making from Patients and Families

Connie Holden

It has been said that the 1970s was the decade of advancing patient rights, that the 1980s was the decade of unprecedented expansion of medical technology, and that the 1990s will be the decade of conflict and, hopefully, coalescence between the two. As exciting as life-prolonging medical advances are, they provide fodder and fertile ground for ethical conflicts and dilemmas. One of the debates that is raging loudly has to do with treatment that is felt to be medically futile; those interventions that, while *available*, are unlikely to improve the patient's condition or quality of life.

Today's ethics and laws give great primacy to patient autonomy; the right to accept or to make decisions about one's medical care. While it is most fitting that patients and families assume this control, should the process be altered when the patient is dying and the available therapies are unlikely to be of benefit? Is the physician obligated to offer or even discuss futile medical interventions with the patient or the family? In the spirit of patient autonomy, must the patient or family be given the opportunity to request, accept, or refuse futile therapies? Perhaps the term "therapy" is an oxymoron when applied to an intervention that has no likelihood of having a therapeutic effect. Schneiderman, Jecker, and Jonsen of the University of Washington, suggest that the "glare of autonomy" is blinding us and preventing rational thought about futile care [1]. While it is not the intent of this chapter to address issues of justice, the point should be made that the provision of futile interventions takes on a tone of urgency as the world struggles with runaway health care costs, a burgeoning population of elderly and uninsured and the proliferation of technologies and therapies that are capable of prolonging lives that are devoid of quality.

Returning to the question at hand, "Is it necessary for patients and families to participate in decision making about treatments that are felt to be futile?" Autonomy purists would say, "Yes, the patient has the right to direct all aspects of medical care." Others would suggest that asking for a decision about a treatment that is of no value to the patient, gives a seriously "mixed message," that, in fact, undermines the integrity of patient choice. I propose that it is not only unnecessary to involve patients and families in such decisions, but that it is inhumane and insensitive to do so. The burden of participating in a "non-decision" simply outweighs the benefits of being involved in the process. That perspective will be developed later in the chapter.

In ancient, as well as modern ethics, physicians have been absolved from providing care that is futile. In classical Greek medicine, the physician had an obligation *not* to treat incurable conditions. The Hippocratic corpus, as conveyed in "The Art," enjoins physicians to acknowledge when efforts will probably fail. Furthermore, Hippocrates stated that the physician who attempts futile treatments is "allied to madness." In Plato's *Republic,* he reports that Asclepian physicians did not practice the kind of medicine that "pampers the disease." He goes on to say that "for those whose bodies were always in a state of sickness he did not attempt to make their life a prolonged misery." Plato also said that the seriously ill should not be treated "even if they were richer than midas" [2]. And so, for centuries physicians have been exercising judgment when deciding when and what therapies are appropriate for the seriously ill person.

There is also contemporary support for physician judgment related to futile situations. The American Medical Association, the American Hospital Association, and several other professional organizations have issued formal policy statements related to futile care. In 1983 the U.S. government assembled a Commission made up of the finest medical ethics experts. The task was to produce policy statements and guidelines for addressing contemporary issues in health care ethics. Included in the vast work of the group was a paper entitled "Deciding to Forego Life-Sustaining Treatment: Ethical, Medical, and Legal Issues in Treatment Decisions" [3]. While the paper strongly promotes patient involvement in decision making, it also acknowledges the physician's responsibility in deciding which therapies are appropriate for a given situation. Even the notorious U.S. Baby Doe rulings allow for the withholding of treatments that are "futile in terms of survival of the infant" [4].

It is also important to note that contemporary Judeo-Christian doctrine addresses the idea of futile care. The Roman Catholic church has stated that the patient is not obligated to undergo "extraordinary treatment that would not offer a reasonable benefit to the patient" [5]. Additionally, Jewish moral law, which requires that the physician provide all available treatments to prolong life, makes an exception when the patient is in a state (*gesisah*) and treatment is deemed incapable of prolonging life for more than seventy-two hours [6]. Having established that the physician is not obligated to provide useless care, how can we explain the fact that intensive care units are filled with hopelessly ill and dying people who are being subjected to every available technology? A study published by Milderen Solomon and a group of researchers from the Hastings Center, suggests that health care professionals often lack understanding of national recommendations or guidelines [7]. Additionally, patients and families often request aggressive and life-prolonging care. Such requests are related to fear of death and the false belief that medical science will always prevail. Death had become foreign and institutionalized; to be avoided at all costs. Death had become the enemy; one that must be fought with all forces available.

Once again, an historical perspective illuminates current day practice. The last fifty years has been a time of phenomenal medical advances. The technique of intravenous fluid administration was developed in the early part of the century, but it was not until 1923 that pyrogens were discovered and it became possible to make sterile solutions. And it was not until 1940 that Karl Lansteiner and Alexander Weiner discovered the Rh factor, making transfusions a safe, life-saving therapy. Gastric feeding tubes were developed in the 1930s. Prior to the introduction of commercially-prepared solutions, feeding through a tube required tedious pureeing and liquefying of table food. Total parenteral nutrition was developed at the University of Pennsylvania in 1965 [8]. Another most important life-saving technology was the ventilator. The precursor to today's highly sophisticated ventilator was the iron lung or tank respirator, used to treat poliomyelitis in the 1940s and 1950s [9]. And last, but not the least problematic, in the moratorium against death, is cardiopulmonary resuscitation (CPR). This technique which was developed in 1960 was, and always has been, a technique intended to revive individuals who have experienced a sudden and unexpected cardiac arrest [10]. In a rather troubling departure from its intended use, it has become the practice, in the United States and Canada, to resuscitate anyone who suffers an arrest, regardless of age or underlying condition. CPR is initiated in all settings: the home, hospital, or nursing home. The only mechanism for circumventing this intervention is the order of a physician. Furthermore, it is commonly a requirement that the physician seek the permission of the patient or family member before writing an order to withhold this treatment. The cumbersomeness of this process results in thousands of terminally and seriously ill persons being subjected to futile resuscitative efforts.

There are a number of therapies that are of questionable value in the treatment of ill persons. These may include resuscitation, artificially-administered sustenance (TPN or gastric tube feeding), blood product administration, chemotherapy, radiation therapy, or dialysis. In the interest of offering hope and of assuring patient involvement in the decision-making process, some physicians find themselves half-heartedly offering these therapies, knowing they will not impede the progression of the disease. The physician's level of comfort with and expertise in discussing death, dying, and appropriate care affects the nature of treatments that are actually instituted.

Health care professionals must be prepared to enter into meaningful and helpful discussions related to end-of-life care. The manner in which these subjects are approached can mean the difference between an individual having a peaceful death and one that is made undignified and painful by unnecessary interventions. Judgment must be exercised in deciding what to offer. For example, it is widely agreed that one should not offer or consider radiation therapy for a patient who has heart disease—the patient simply would not benefit from the treatment. There is less comfort applying this reasoning to CPR for the end-stage patient. However, some American and Canadian hospitals have developed policies that allow physicians to write a Do Not Resuscitate (DNR) order based on medical judgment alone.

Resuscitation discussions and decision making are fraught with obstacles. The following observations have been gathered from years of practice in acute care settings:

1. While there is ample statistical data about the futility of resuscitation in persons who have terminal or chronic illness, it rarely gets incorporated into DNR discussions.
2. DNR discussions do not occur because the physician is uncomfortable talking about or unwilling to acknowledge the patient's impending death.
3. Patients and families have unrealistic expectation of CPR, in part, promulgated by the media.

4. Patients and families are not given complete and accurate information about resuscitation. They do not know that it includes defibrillation, intubation, and the possibility of further decision making related to discontinuation of ventilatory support.
5. There is fear that a DNR decision will result in the withholding of other comfort measures.
6. A DNR decision is not made because not all of the parties have "come to terms" with the impending death or because those involved do not want to appear to be "giving up."
7. Less functional families will have a high degree of "unfinished business" and guilt and may be bargaining for more time.
8. Some families have an exaggerated need to "do everything possible."
9. There can be a tremendous sense of responsibility on the part of the family members who are asked to make decisions related to withdrawing or withholding care.
10. In many families, end-of-life wishes have never been discussed.
11. Patients and families make a very reasonable assumption that if the physician posits CPR as a treatment option, then it must be of some benefit.

What can we as health care professionals do to foster appropriate non-burdensome decision-making related to futile resuscitation? Elizabeth Latimer of Henderson Hospital in Hamilton, Ontario, suggests that such discussions flow most naturally out of an ongoing relationship built over a series of contacts [11]. There are situations in which the patients or family's burden of making a decision is greater than the benefit of the proposed intervention. Acknowledging the risk of paternalism in these situations, it seems most humane that the physician *not* pose resuscitation as a treatment option. The discussion about the direction of care at this point in the patient's life is best handled by the physician in a gentle, yet directive manner. There is wisdom in focusing on the acronym AND (allowing a natural death) rather than DNR. This allows the decision to be related to what *is* going to be done (oxygen, pain management), rather than what is *not* going to be done (resuscitation). The end result is spared futile interventions.

REFERENCES

1. L. J. Schneiderman, N. S. Jecker, and A. R. Jonsen, Medical Futility; Its Meaning and Ethical Implications, *Annals of Internal Medicine, 112*:12, pp. 949-954, 1990.

2. D. W. Amundsen, The Physician's Obligation to Prolong Life: A Medical Duty without Classical Roots, *The Hasting's Center Report, 8*, pp. 24-29, 1973.
3. President's Commission for the Study of Ethical Problems in Medicine and Biomedical and Behavioral Research, *Deciding to Forego Life-Sustaining Treatment*, Government Printing Office, Washington, D.C., p. 219, 1983.
4. D. K. Stevenson, R. L. Ariagno, J. S. Kutner et al., The Baby Doe Rule, *JAMA, 255*, pp. 1909-1912, 1986.
5. G. Kelly, *Medico Moral Problems*, Catholic Hospital Association, St. Louis, p. 135, 1958.
6. D. M. Feldman, *Health and Medicine in the Jewish Tradition*, Crossroad Publishing Co., New York, 1986.
7. M. Solomon et al., Decisions Near the End of Life: Professionals Views on Life-Sustaining Treatments, *American Journal of Public Health, 83*:1, pp. 14-25, 1993.
8. A. L. Plumer, History of Intravenous Therapy, in *Principles and Practice of Intravenous Therapy* (4th Edition), Little Brown and Company, Boston, pp. 3-6, 1987.
9. J. F. Murray and J. A. Nadel, *Textbook of Respiratory Medicine*, W. B. Saunders, Philadelphia, pp. 1990-1993, 1988.
10. K. B. Kern and G. A. Ewy, Cardiopulmonary Resuscitation in Patients with Acute Myocardial Infarction, in *Modern Coronary Care*, Little Brown and Company, Boston, pp. 363-365, 1990.
11. E. Latimer, The Decision Not to Resuscitate: Talking with Patients and Families, *Canadian Medical Association Journal, 140*, pp. 133-135, 1989.

CHAPTER 19

Using Laughter as a Cathartic Process in Grief Counseling

Ben-Joshua Jaffee

This chapter is about a therapeutic process I came across a couple of years ago: the purposeful use of laughter in the helping process. This approach has been used by psychotherapist Annette Goodheart, now in Santa Barbara, for over twenty years with virtually all her patients, who consist mainly of incest survivors, the terminally ill (including AIDS patients), and substance abusers. I would like to share that approach with you as I understand it, as I observed and experienced it being used in a week-long training in laughter therapy,[1] and as I have just begun to incorporate it into my own private practice.

This last point is important. I am not writing as an expert, highly skilled in the use of this approach. I have only just begun to integrate it into my healing work with clients. Rather, I am here as a beginner in

---

[1] I wish to express my deep respect for, and acknowledge my great indebtedness to, Dr. Annette Goodheart as the inspiration for this chapter. It is based in large part upon her ideas and formulations as she presented them in a laughter training seminar in Santa Barbara in August 1989. The concepts and notions presented herein constitute a blend of both my own ideas, and my personal understanding, rendering, and interpretation of Dr. Goodheart's ideas. I derived them from my notes taken during the seminar, from my observations and participation in exercises and role plays during that week, and from handouts she distributed during the seminar. I have attempted throughout this chapter to attribute to her those specific ideas that are her own creations and those phrases that were presented in her own unique manner. However, because the content of this chapter is dependent upon my recollection, interpretation, and rendering of many of her notions and because I have adapted others and added my own, I cannot be completely certain in some instances how faithful I have actually conveyed Dr. Goodheart's ideas and intentions and how much of my own thinking I may have added to them. Consequently, I accept full responsibility for the soundness, credibility, and coherence of the material presented in the following pages.

its use and an informant, rather than as an advocate, to introduce and explore this approach with you; to say, "This is what I have discovered. It seems to me to have some promise. What do you think and feel about it? How does it fit you?"

Personally, I resonate with this approach. It appears to have real potential applicability as a therapeutic tool that can be used in conjunction with other approaches in grief counseling. When used at the appropriate time, in an appropriate way, by someone who is comfortable with it, I think that the purposeful use of laughter can be quite effective in helping clients cathartically release the sadness, anger, or fear they are feeling because of a loss they have experienced.

One prefatory remark. Throughout this chapter, when I refer to the grieving process following a loss, I refer to all the many kinds of loss we experience in our society. These include, but are not confined to, losses caused by physical death. So that, for example, the notions I am going to present are relevant also to the grieving people go through because of the loss of relationships, the loss of home or place, losses that come with aging, the loss of body parts, the loss of physical or mental capacities, loss of employment, the loss of hopes, dreams, expectations, etc.

THE GRIEVING PROCESS

Let me begin by providing a context for examining the relevance of this approach to the mourning process. For this purpose, I would like to use a paradigm that envisions that process as consisting of a number of tasks that need to be undertaken and completed if a person's grief work is to proceed successfully and if progress is to be made toward healing the trauma of the loss. This paradigm entails an active or proactive process that the griever needs to engage and participate in, as opposed to the idea of more passively just enduring or going through the various phases of grieving that I feel could possibly be implied in the grief cycle model. Thomas Attig cogently and convincingly spoke to this notion in his paper at the ADEC conference in New Orleans in 1990 when he referred to the grieving experience ". . . as an active coping process . . . permeated with choice" [1].

There are several different presentations of the "grieving tasks" notion in the literature. Some versions delineate three tasks, others four. They use similar concepts, which however are often worded quite differently. So, I have attempted to synthesize and integrate the conceptualization and workings of three prominent writers in the field, namely, Therese Rando, John Schneider, and William Worden, who seem to offer the most creative and compatible formulations of the tasks of the mourning process. The following section contains an amalgam of their writings [2-4].

TASKS OF THE GRIEVING/MOURNING PROCESS

There are four tasks to the grieving/mourning process: 1) recognizing and accepting the reality of the loss and understanding how it came about; 2) experiencing and going through the pain of the grief caused by the loss, i.e., reacting emotionally, physically and socially to the separation from that which was lost; 3) discovering what is left: adapting to a new life devoid of the lost person, object, situation or way of being, while not forgetting the old; and 4) discovering what is possible: reinvesting emotional energy in a new and different life—in relationship to a new person, object, situation, or way of being.

I now want to focus on the second task. It is perhaps the most difficult, the most feared and, therefore, the most resisted of the four tasks for a great many, if not all, grievers. That task is experiencing and working through expressing the very painful emotions of sadness, anger, and fear caused by the loss.

The reason these emotions are so painful is because they generate intense energy. In order for the pain to begin to be attenuated, this energy needs to be freed through a cathartic process. "Catharsis" is defined in the dictionary with words like "releasing," "purging," and "making pure." As an example, a cathartic for the intestinal tract cleanses, purges, and moves out the toxins trapped in the colon. In a similar way, in grief work, there is a need to release and move out the trapped emotions that are causing the pain. In other words, as Goodheart would say, we need an emotional movement, an *EM*, if you will.

BARRIERS TO CATHARSIS

In our society there are at least three major types of deterrents or barriers to a catharsis of the emotional and physical pain of the grieving that stems from the loss. The first of these barriers is our emotional defense mechanisms. The ego, the personality, attempts to protect itself against acknowledging and actually experiencing the full pain of the loss all at once. In addition, important parts of the physical body become contracted or constricted, trapping energy in the solar plexus and abdomen rather than allowing it to move freely and release. Of course, these are natural and, generally, healthy responses. The defense mechanisms prevent the personality from being inundated and overwhelmed by the impact of the loss, and allow the pain and the reality of the loss to be experienced and assimilated a little at a time. There is nothing dysfunctional about this unless it goes on for an inordinate period of time, thereby preventing the griever from dissipating the painful emotions, either enough or at all. Nevertheless, defense mechanisms do constitute one barrier to catharting the pain of the loss.

The second barrier to the cathartic purging of the pain of grieving is our personal belief systems. These are strongly held, emotionally based beliefs that we have grown up with that tell us that emotions need to be held down—kept under control, not expressed outwardly (especially for men)—and that if emotions are allowed to be expressed, they will engulf and overwhelm you.

The third barrier is our society's norms. These norms dictate, among other things, that we are to resist really feeling or honoring unpleasant, "bad" emotions; that if we do feel them, they should not be openly expressed; and that if they are expressed this is permissible only in the privacy of our homes or in certain designated settings. An example of this last norm, familiar to almost everyone in our society, is the strong social pressure not to cry in public and to apologize when one cannot help doing so.

We tend to be a pain-denying society. So when we are faced with really painful emotions, we tend to do one or more of three things: 1) we hide, deny, or repress them—we stuff them; 2) we divert them—we go on an eating binge or on a buying binge or we take that long-awaited trip to Fiji—anything to get away from and not feel the painful emotions; or 3) we drug them—either with legal drugs (alcohol or prescription drugs) or with illegal hard drugs. People who have direct experience with alcoholics or drug users know full well the great underlying emotional pain that these individuals are trying to dull or escape through their habit.

It is often quite difficult for many people to confront, to actually feel and express the intensely painful emotions of sadness, anger, depression, or fear that are generated by important losses in their lives. This is especially true of men who, for the most part, have been socialized to not be in touch with the so-called "soft" or "feminine" feelings of sadness and vulnerability. They are taught to be "tough" and "to be a man" like John Wayne, tall and stiff and not showing much affect. Therefore, men find it hard to do the crying or show the fear that so frequently accompanies grief. In contrast, women have been socialized to have much difficulty feeling and expressing anger and rage, emotions that often accompany the grieving process.

This is where laughter comes in. Laughter is also a way of cathartically releasing the energy of the painful emotions experienced by grievers. "Laughter?!" some of you may say incredulously. "Laughter in the face of grief?!" To many people this idea might seem downright "weird" or "sick," or at the very least grossly inappropriate, because laughter is not generally or readily associated with loss or grieving. Rather, it is regarded as trivial or inconsequential, whereas grief is serious, important, and heavy. Also, laughter is associated with humor, lightness, and happiness, not with the sadness, gloom, or pain of grief.

LAUGHTER AS CATHARSIS

However, not only is laughter not *in*appropriate; it can be very appropriate and exceedingly useful in grief work. This is because, according to Goodheart, all laughter is a cathartic response to some sort of tension or stress, whether that stress results from a negative experience such as the loss of a loved one or of a job or of a body part, or from a positive experience such as winning the lottery. If we were totally serene and peaceful, Goodheart contends, we would not laugh. We must experience some degree of emotional discomfort to be able to laugh. Or as an Indian guru is reputed to have commented, "Laughter is the excrement of the soul."

"But," you may protest, "I laugh when I am feeling happy and joyous!" However, according to Goodheart, joy and happiness are not emotions like sadness, anger, and fear whose energies need to be dissipated. Rather, joy and happiness are considered by her to be the basic, natural state for humans. A metaphor may make this notion clearer and more readily appreciated. Joy and happiness may be seen as the sun which is of course perpetually shining in the sky but which is often not visible due to the clouds which cover and hide its rays. The clouds are the various emotions which obscure the natural state of happiness and joy, and when these clouds/emotions move away, or are catharted, we can again experience the rays and warmth of the joy/happiness/sun which have always been there.

Looked at somewhat differently, when we laugh out of joy or happiness, usually that has been because there has been a release of some sort of positive tension or stress. For example, when we experience an unexpected pleasant surprise, the surprise response is the release of stress or tension. Or when we suddenly become aware that we are having a good time, that sudden awareness reaction brings tension release. Or when we finally achieve a long-sought goal, that sense of achievement results in a profound release of tension.

Now, because laughter is a cathartic process, it falls on an emotional continuum with crying, the venting of anger and other types of cathartic expression associated with grieving. It is not, as many erroneously believe, a qualitatively different phenomenon. We have all experienced this. When we laugh uproariously, the diaphragm convulses with the release of tension and stress, just as it does when we cry or lose our temper. Moreover, when we are in the middle of this convulsive laughter, tears stream down our face, and we cannot tell whether we are laughing or crying (where the laughter ends and the crying begins). Also, most of us are familiar with the story of Pagliacci, the clown who laughs on the outside while crying inwardly; and in the well-known aria from the opera of the same name, the laughter is heard to turn into sobbing.

For these reasons, when laughter is introduced appropriately and skillfully, it is capable of producing profound emotional and physical catharsis in people who are working through their grief. But let me be very clear about one thing: laughter is not a substitute for crying or for the cathartic expression of anger or fear. If one has to release any of these emotions, then one must ultimately cry or sob, yell or pound a pillow, or tremble with fear.

However, because laughter is a "lighter," less threatening form of emotional release than are these other kinds of catharsis, it tends to be more acceptable and, consequently, more readily accessible to many grievers of both genders. For this reason, it can help grievers access more easily, and thus lead to, the crying, the raging, or the trembling that many of them may need to do during the mourning process but that some of them may have difficulty readily and directly experiencing.

IMPEDIMENTS TO LAUGHTER

Individual, Personal Reasons

Almost everyone feels good after laughing. Yet, in our society, most of us do not laugh as much as we might, even though when we do, it does make us feel better. The following are some interesting and revealing questions we can ask of ourselves, the answers to which may help to shed light on this apparent inconsistency or paradox:

- What is our relationship with laughter? Are we friends with it, or do we hold it at arm's length? Are we easy and comfortable with it or awkward and hesitant?
- What do we appreciate about our laughter? and conversely, what have we heard about it that has been critical?
- Why is it that we do not laugh more than we do even though most of us would like to?

In response to this last question, I think that the reasons fall into two main categories. First, there are the personal, individual reasons that stem primarily from the role that laughter has played in our unique family backgrounds. For example:

- The degree to which laughter was or was not plentiful in our homes as we grew up can affect the frequency and ease with which we laugh as adults. Personally, in my own home there was not a great deal of laughter except when my father told some off-color jokes, but in my aunt and uncle's home laughter and the positive energy that accompanied it abounded. Consequently, I made every effort to visit their home as often as I could.
- The way that laughter was used in our homes can also influence our attitude toward, and our spontaneity in opening ourselves to, laughter. In some homes, laughter tends to be used constructively, enhancing the warmth and good humor among family members and increasing their sense of closeness and intimacy. In other homes, however it may tend to be used destructively to deride and poke fun at certain family members, to laugh *at* them, distancing them and making them feel denigrated, isolated, and alone.
- The extent to which laughter was or was not supported and encouraged in our homes can also affect and condition how much and how readily we resort to laughter as we grow up. Some families are quick to laugh, and children are supported, encouraged and even stimulated in their natural spontaneous laughter. In other homes, families are not comfortable with laughter, especially raucous laughter, and children are discouraged from laughing, either directly or indirectly.

Erroneous Belief Systems

A second category of reasons why we do not laugh as much as we would like to is society's myths about laughter—myths that keep us from being truly free to laugh unreservedly, especially the all-out guffaw kind of belly laughter. Here, of course, I am not using the word "myth" in the same sense that Joseph Campbell uses it [5]. Rather, I am referring to erroneous belief systems or erroneous conceptions. Consequently, I have coined a new term to cover this notion. I call them "myth-conceptions," erroneous conceptions about laughter that need to be dispelled. There are three such myth-conceptions that Goodheart thinks are important.

Myth-Conception 1: We must have a reason to laugh.

Not only do we need to have a reason; it has to be a good enough reason so that when someone asks "Why are you laughing? What's so funny?" and we explain it to them, they also will laugh. Have you ever noticed the way people ask that question? It is very often in an almost confrontational manner and in an accusatory tone of voice. (I will come back to this shortly and offer a possible explanation for such a reaction.)

However, laughter is a universal physiological response to tension or stress. As such, it is unreasonable, illogical, and irrational.

We are born as laughers. Infants begin to laugh as early as ten days old. When we see them lying in the crib laughing, it is most likely because they have just experienced some sort of stress or tension relief. Perhaps they have just been held or cuddled, and this has relieved the stress in their newly-formed nervous system. Or maybe they have just emptied their bowel or bladder, and that has momentarily dissipated the tension in their digestive system. Or perhaps they have just seen the familiar face of their mother and that has released the stress of feeling alone and isolated in their new strange world. So we are born as laughers, and we actually have to learn not to laugh as we grow up in our society.

Having a reason for doing something is one way of keeping control over that activity. So, far from needing to have a reason in order to laugh, looking for a reason for our laughter just controls it. All we have to do is ask ourselves (or someone else) why we or they are laughing, and that immediately stops the laughter.

Because laughter is a physiological response to tension or stress, by its very nature it causes loss of control—especially muscle control. When we are laughing all out, our head is thrown back, our arms and torso flail, we bend over and slap our thighs or pound the table. Many of us have had the experience of laughing so hard that we have fallen off a chair because of loss of muscle control. For the same reason, some of us have had the embarrassing experience of laughing so hard while eating that the food went spewing out all over the room or of being so consumed with laughter that we have lost sphincter control and wet our pants. We simply cannot keep muscle control when we are in the midst of uproarious laughter. Nor, for that matter, can we easily maintain rational control or control over other antithetical emotions. For example, we cannot be laughing fully and be afraid at the same time.

Moreover, as we all know, laughter is contagious. So we can start laughing for absolutely no rational reason other than that someone else is laughing. And this brings us back to the tone of voice, the emotion and the confrontational manner I referred to earlier with which people often challenge us with the question "Why are you laughing?!" Because laughter is contagious, if you are laughing, and I am afraid of losing control, then I will try to stop you from laughing so I will not have to laugh also and thus risk losing control myself.

The fact of the matter is that we do not need an external reason or stimulus—such as Jay Leno or Arsenio Hall or a sitcom—to start our laughing. Instead, as Goodheart puts it, we can become laughter independent, or as I prefer to say, laughter self-starters. "But how do you do that?," you ask. Goodheart has a very succinct and direct answer: "You just fake it till you make it!" In other words, you prime the laughter pump, so to speak, so that the natural spontaneous laughter can take hold.

There are two ways this can be done: the first way is to verbalize the problem you are dealing with or the emotional pain you are feeling (for example: "I feel overwhelmed by this sadness!") and then add a "tee-hee" at the end. The incongruity of the statement of your overwhelming sadness, followed by a "tee-hee" can start you chuckling or tittering, and there you are off on a true laughter spasm.

Sometimes "tee-hee" does not quite accomplish this. It tends to be located too high up in the body, in the head, and therefore it may be too light a stimulus to spark a chuckle or a giggle. In other words, it is not strong enough to correspond to the level of the emotion you are expressing. In that case, you can go down one level, to the throat area, and use "heh-heh" instead, to see if that will trigger a laughter spasm. If not, you can go even still lower, to the abdominal area, and use "ho-ho." You may have to play with these "laughter igniters" to see which one best matches the nature and intensity of the feeling you are experiencing (the overwhelming sadness in the previous example) and is therefore able to trip off the initial spontaneous, and often tentative, chuckle.

In doing this, it is essential to keep one thing in mind: when you add the "tee-hee" or "ho-ho," you are not minimizing, depreciating or trivializing your sadness; you are not laughing *at* your feelings. Quite the opposite: you are laughing *about* them (the proper preposition is crucial here!) You are honoring that is the way you feel, and you are laughing about the sadness.

A second way you can fake it till you make it is by just beginning to laugh artificially until the genuine laughter takes over. The diaphragm cannot distinguish between contrived and spontaneous laughter; once it starts convulsing, it will continue, as long as you persist in the fake laughter, until it turns into the real thing.

You might take a few minutes right now to experiment with one or both these methods of becoming a laughter self-starter, perhaps in a room where you can be alone so as to reduce any possible self-consciousness. If you can suspend or overcome any judgment about the strangeness of these techniques or any skepticism about their likely efficacy, and just open yourself to the process, I think you will find that they really do work well in stimulating your laughter in the absence of any customary outside stimulus. Then, when you have experienced this yourself and have become comfortable with the process, you will have a basis for trusting yourself to use it with clients *when it seems appropriate and after you have developed a solid relationship with them.*

Myth-Conception 2: We must have a sense of humor to laugh. Humor is the same as laughter.

It is true that in our society, laughter is associated with humor, but it is *not* the same thing. For example, when we see that infant lying it its crib laughing, do we exclaim "What a great sense of humor that baby has!" Of course not! Because a sense of humor is a cognitive, intellectual process. We are not born with it; we develop it as we grow up in our society.

In addition, there is no agreement about what is humorous. It is obvious to all of us that different people, as well as different cultures, have very different notions about what is funny. Moreover, having a sense of humor does not necessarily mean that one laughs. The most popular comedians do not laugh easily or often; they just manipulate our laughter. In this vein, whether true or not, Groucho Marx is reputed to have laughed just once in his life!

By contrast, laughter is *innate*—we are born as laughers. Laughter is *universal*—not culture-specific. We can laugh with anyone in the world, including people from very different cultures where neither we nor they can understand the other's language at all. I personally found this to be very true several years ago during the Goodwill Games in Seattle when I had the opportunity to spend some social time with a number of then-Soviet social scientists and with a group of Uzbek dancers. Neither they nor I could speak a common language; yet our meetings and our interaction resounded with laughter. Some say that we can even laugh with chimps and gorillas. To the degree that this may be so, I believe that it is because laughter is *physiological*, not a cognitive, phenomenon.

**Myth-Conception 3: The only time we can laugh is
when we are happy. We laugh because we are happy.**

If this were really true, it might help to explain why we do not laugh
as much as we would like to: we have to wait until we become happy!
And I think that many of us would agree that in today's world, achieving happiness is no easy accomplishment! As a matter of fact, the
reality is that the *opposite* of this myth-conception is just as true and
perhaps even more true. We are happy *because* we laugh. As we noted
earlier, laughter catharts tension and stress, and this of course makes
us feel better . . . and therefore happier.

Let's examine the dynamics of this process in a bit more detail.
When we are grimly concentrating all our attention and our energy on
a loss (or on any other problem, for that matter), it is as if we are
plastered up against the loss, as up against a huge rock. We cannot
easily see around it; therefore, we are unable to get a good and realistic
view of the relationship between the loss and the various other aspects
of our life. Consequently, we can not know how best to proceed or
function, i.e., how best to address the loss within the context of the
remainder of our life. However, when we can laugh *about* (not *at*) the
loss—when we can see it as a laughing matter—that in effect moves the
loss farther away, so to speak, and it begins to *seem* or appear *smaller*.
We are then able to see it in better perspective with respect to the rest
of our life and consequently to have a better idea of how to move in
relation to it, how better to address it. We are able to *play* with the pain
of loss, to be *light* (not heavy) with it. Consequently, we feel happier.

Goodheart believes that *all* issues or problems are open to these
positive effects of laughter, to being played with in this way, including,
and perhaps especially, the heaviest ones. I tend to agree with this;
laughter is neither trivial nor inconsequential!

Another reason we feel happier as a result of laughing is that
laughter engages and exercises every system in the body in a constructive way. This helps us function better physically, and therefore we feel
better and happier emotionally. For example:

* There seems to be at least some preliminary evidence that laughter
  may help re-balance the body's chemistry (the endocrine system),
  perhaps activating the body's natural painkillers (the beta-
  endorphins and the enkephalins), and triggering release of the
  hormones that increase the level of alertness (the catecholamines,
  epinephrine, norepinephrine, and dopamine).
* Laughter most certainly stimulates the cardiovascular system,
  dilating this system (e.g., our face gets red when we laugh hard);

oxygenating the blood; and alternately tensing and relaxing the entire cardiovascular system, making it more supple, more resilient, and more elastic.

- The diaphragm is convulsed when we laugh, and this jogs and massages all the nearby internal organs.
- Laughter also gives the respiratory system a major workout. With the help of the convulsing diaphragm, we gasp for breath when we laugh, and the lungs expel air out of the throat and mouth at a rate up to 70 miles per hour.
- As already noted, when we laugh, the musculature system undergoes a great deal of movement and activity—both toning and relaxing most of the body's muscles, including the facial muscles which usually don't get much exercise.
- Also, the two hemispheres of the brain become more synchronized when we laugh. This makes us feel more relaxed, peaceful, and able to function better; consequently we feel happier.
- Finally, socially sharing laughter with others results in feelings of togetherness and intimacy, and this also makes us feel happier. Victor Borge is quoted as having said: "The shortest distance between two people is laughter."

IMPLICATIONS FOR GRIEF COUNSELING

Now let's examine the specific value and the use of laughter in helping grievers with their mourning process. First, however, it will be helpful to recap what has been said about the major attributes of laughter for grief counseling:

- It is on a cathartic continuum with crying, the venting of anger and the expression of fear.
- It is a "lighter," less threatening form of emotional release than those other kinds of catharsis.
- For these reasons, laughter is able to help clients access the crying, anger, and fear that needs to be expressed and released as part of the second task of the grieving process.

Therefore, laughter can be *purposively introduced* into the grief counseling process as *one* therapeutic tool, to complement other therapeutic approaches. When, as counselors and therapists, we use laughter in this way, appropriately and skillfully, we can help initiate and facilitate in our clients the release of the more painful and more resisted emotional sequelae of loss. Working with laughter, we can help grievers come more gently and lightly into their deepest emotional storages. We can take them into their most painful emotions and memories of loss and help them experience their sadness, anger or fear *from the top, from above* so to speak, rather than from below, where the emotional storages are the most concentrated and the scariest and therefore evoke the greatest resistance.

As therapists or counselors, we know that it is not always helpful or constructive to go immediately and directly to the heart of a problem, i.e., into the deepest sadness, anger, or fear. That may be working too deeply too soon for certain clients and may cause them to pull back from dealing with their most painful feelings and memories of loss. Goodheart offers an earthy metaphor in this connection which I believe is very apt and powerful. She says that when we come head-on into the dark cave of our stored emotions, we come into our own shit—and we have to shovel and shovel it. That is very hard and very scary work! But just around the corner is the opening to the cave, and we can walk out into the sun, and then eventually all the shit will drop off. By using laughter, we can work on our shit in the sunlight, i.e., in a less threatening or overwhelming way, and through this process we can touch on and deal with some of our darkest storages.

As she has also commented, we need to take catharsis where it is available, and that can be through having clients start by laughing *about* the emotions stemming from losses in their lives. When we utilize this process in a therapeutically purposive and timely manner and in an appropriate way, we can help clients hold more lightly and *play* with their sadness and with the other emotions stemming from their losses. Charlie Chaplin once commented: "You must play with your pain, and then you can laugh." In this way, we can help grieving clients expedite their mourning process and in so doing, help promote the more rapid and more complete emotional, physical, and social healing of their losses.

Putting it differently and modifying another of Goodheart's trenchant comments: If you're going to be miserable and in pain as you complete the second grieving task, *you might as well enjoy it!*

REFERENCES

1. T. Attig, *The Importance of Conceiving of Grief as an Active Process*, paper delivered at the Association for Death Education and Counseling Conference in New Orleans, 1990 [unpublished].
2. T. A. Rando, *Grieving: How to Go On Living When Someone You Love Dies*, Lexington Books, Lexington, Massachusetts, pp. 226-240, 1988.

3. J. Schneider, The Transformational Power of Grief, *Noetic Sciences Review*, *Autumn*, pp. 26-31, 1989.
4. J. W. Worden, *Grief Counselling and Grief Therapy* (2nd Edition), Springer Publishing, New York, pp. 10-18, 1991.
5. J. Campbell with B. D. Moyers, *The Power of Myth*, Doubleday, New York, p. 5.

CHAPTER 20

Teaching Quality Care of the Dying Patient

Elizabeth J. Latimer

Palliative care is defined as the active and compassionate care of the sick person at a time when the goals of cure and prolongation of life are no longer most important to the patient and indeed, may not be physically possible due to the presence of advanced illness. The focus of palliative care is the provision of physical comfort (symptom control), psychological and spiritual care of the patient and family, and some provision for follow-up bereavement care for family after death has occurred. The philosophy of palliative care should extend to include the wider social community, because dying is seen as a life passage through which all persons in society will pass and therefore have a part to play [1, 2].

Because of the wide scope of needs of the patient and family, palliative care services are usually provided by an interdisciplinary team which includes: physicians, nurses, social workers, spiritual counselors, occupational therapists, pharmacists, physiotherapists, nutritionists, and volunteers. Volunteers have a particular role to play in supporting dying people. They are in a unique position to provide companionship and skilled friendship which can do much to enhance the quality of life for patients and families. The patient, their family, and friends themselves become a central part of the team in palliative care. The unit of care is the circle of caring people who share the patient's life.

A number of specialty services in hospice and palliative care have developed in Canada and other countries. The terms hospice and palliative care can be used interchangeably to describe care of a certain philosophy and nature. The word hospice may be used in different contexts, depending on the area or region where it is used, either to refer to a place (a hospice), or a community-based service program which cares for patients in their homes and often contains a large volunteer component. While specialty services will be available to care for some patients, it is likely that the majority of people who die will be cared for by primary care teams like family physicians, community nurses, and general hospital staff in acute or chronic care settings. This is not only appropriate given the large numbers of people who die, but it is also appropriate that dying not necessarily require "specialist" care unless the problems of the patient indicate that certain special expertise is required.

It is therefore necessary that all health professionals be given some opportunity to learn how to care for dying patients well. These professionals can then utilize the consultative expertise of specialized palliative care teams for assistance in matters of a more complex nature, like complex symptom control problems, and complex psychosocial situations.

Palliative care encompasses the following focus of intervention:

- assessing and meeting the emotional support needs of the patient;
- assessing the needs of families and working to support them;
- addressing the physical status and symptom control needs of the patient [3-5];
- ethical decision making and setting goals of care with the patient and family [6, 7];
- accompaniment of patient and family on the journey of illness toward death, providing support and attentive care all along the way; and
- bereavement support to patient in ongoing losses and to the family during the illness and after the death has occurred.

A health care professional, as a member of an interdisciplinary team, needs to develop a variety of skills and acquire a certain knowledge base in order to provide care. The level of skill required will depend on the role and mandate of the provider and the setting for care. For example, a physician working in an intensive care unit may wish and need to become most expert in gentle, clear, communication skills, and the ethical dimensions of life and death decision making with regard to cessation of life-prolonging treatment. A nurse on an oncology ward may require broader skills in support and care, as will a family physician. Social workers will require in-depth skills in family assessment and care, and a good knowledge of the resources in their setting and how to access them. Professionals who are going to work full-time in the field of palliative care require in-depth education and training in virtually all aspects of the care of the dying [3-5].

However, there is a skill and knowledge base that is fundamental to caring for the dying and that should be required of all providers. This includes:

- a certain familiarity and comfort with the issues of serious illness, loss, and death;
- a certain familiarity and comfort in the presence of the expression of strong emotions;
- some knowledge about interdisciplinary team work and an ability to work with team members of other disciplines;
- knowledge of symptom control, the depth of detail in knowledge being dictated by the professional discipline;
- values, beliefs, and attitudes that support the philosophy and ethics of palliative care [8];
- knowledge about the psychological, social, and emotional issues which confront seriously ill persons and their families;
- knowledge about the physical problems which can confront the individual or patient population under care and how to manage them (the depth of detail being dictated by the profession of the student, with physicians requiring quite specific knowledge in this area);
- a personal professionalism which encompasses caring and commitment and values good quality care;
- a degree of openness which will allow self-reflection;
- skills in interpersonal communication with colleagues, patients, and families
- skills in the physical care of the patient [3-5].

It can be seen that basic requirements include values and attitudes appropriate to the field, skills in interpersonal communication, skills in physical care, and a knowledge base that is relevant to palliative care and the setting of practice. Effective symptom control is a cornerstone of good palliative care and should be a part of all teaching programs. This chapter will describe some strategies for teaching and learning in palliative care which encompass values exploration and development, the acquisition of skills and knowledge, and the fostering of ways of being which are appropriate to caring for the dying.

TYPES OF EDUCATIONAL PROGRAMS

There are a number of educational programs which are appropriate and necessary in palliative care. Half- or full-day seminars are quite popular with practicing health professionals. These assume a level of previous professional preparation and clinical work experience and also a level of motivation to acquire specific knowledge in order to practice. Undergraduate education presents a greater challenge in that students may need to acquire a great deal of content and skills over a longer period of time. There are also a number of other course venues like professional rounds in hospitals and clinics where the audience can be introduced to specific aspects of palliative care content. The McMaster Continuing Education Program, with local palliative care experts, has developed a week-long interdisciplinary in-depth course in palliative care which brings practicing professionals together to learn.

THE LEARNERS

Before beginning to plan an educational program, it is essential to identify who the learners are. This is the most fundamental question to answer because out of this question flows the direction for teaching/ learning initiatives.

One would want to consider the profession of the students, the setting in which they will practice, their current educational level, their learning needs, their expectations of the outcome of the teaching/ learning experience.

THE EXPECTED OUTCOME OF THE
TEACHING/LEARNING EVENT OR PROGRAM

It is essential for planners to define what it is that they want learners to take out of the experience of learning and what they themselves as planners want to achieve. This relates to defining the objectives for the teaching/learning. Objectives should best be described in terms of the students. Some examples appropriate to a general introductory teaching program about palliative care applicable to interdisciplinary learners would be the following:

- "the student will have an opportunity to explore his/her potential feelings when caring for dying people";
- "the student will be able to describe the nature of 'total pain' of cancer and a basic approach to managing cancer pain";

- "the student will gain a greater understanding of the issues confronting dying patients and their families and be able to discuss
  these."

IDENTIFYING THE LEARNING NEEDS

This can be particularly difficult to do. The teacher can assume that
needs exist and simply teach what he/she feels the content to be and in
some settings and for some purposes this can be an efficient and
effective way of outlining and presenting the content which is encom-
passed by the subject. However, there are three current concepts in
teaching which are particularly relevant to palliative care teaching/
learning given the broad scope of the field and the multiple levels of
learning and skill development required. These are the notions of
1) self-assessment by the learner, 2) self-directed life-long learning,
and 3) the concept of problem-based learning [9, 10]. Using the
philosophy of problem-based learning, a learner can self-assess and
then self-direct under the guidance of a tutor or "teacher." These
philosophies encourage learners to focus on areas of greatest educational need and motivation. The concepts are particularly well-suited to
continuing education of the practicing professional, an area where
there is a great deal of teaching activity in palliative care at the present
time. However, they also work very well in undergraduate and
graduate education [9, 10].

Many types of palliative care teaching/learning projects can be
initiated by the presentation of a case-based problem, where students
can begin to identify issues to direct their research and study. If the
setting for learning is a clinical one, the best "cases" are the patients for
whom the student is presently caring. These patient problems are of
high relevance to trainees, because they are current, they clearly make
an impact on the student by virtue of their timeliness and the student's
acute awareness of the need to acquire knowledge and skills to care for
the person and manage in the situation. The student is highly motivated to learn and the learning will likely link into memory in a more
effective circuit because of the personal involvement of the student.

Paper problems, those which are developed by teachers to guide
learning, must be carefully written to illustrate the issues which the
student is meant to pursue for learning. They may include a companion
guide for the tutor wherein the issues to be pursued in the problem are
highlighted. Having identified the issues in a problem, the student does
some self-assessment of knowledge base and then determines where to
pursue knowledge in areas of need.

A self-directed learner requires considerable insight and intellectual honesty, and the ability to acknowledge what he or she does not know, as well as the drive and self-starting qualities to pursue the learning. Two sample "paper problems" are provided as an appendix to this chapter.

AN ATMOSPHERE FOR LEARNING—
THE CONCEPT OF "SOWING SEEDS"

The particular setting and atmosphere for learning must match the goals for the experience and foster the behaviors and attitudes which are espoused in the field.

In palliative care, a successful practitioner will listen well, will be open to other people and their ideas and viewpoints, and will be able to share feelings and thoughts. The subject matter, while comprised of "solid" factual content always carries a highly personal dimension. The setting for learning can foster the desired behaviors by its physical nature and the role modeling of the teachers and group leaders through the approaches they take. Therefore, opportunities for sharing ideas and thoughts, and strategies to encourage this, should be a central part of palliative teaching. Pauses for personal reflection can be introduced even to a large lecture format. However if values and attitudes are to be explored, a small group learning format is best. Teachers, presenters, and group leaders can role model by sharing their own vulnerabilities and questions.

Dying is a universal human event and thus any learning about caring for dying people is, in part, a philosophical journey. Because much of the teaching/learning involves subtle shifts in values and attitudes, the process is truly a lifelong event. While ideally teaching/learning will be planned for times when it is of high relevance for students, teachers and course planners can best be seen as those who "sow seeds" of awareness in their students or audience . . . seeds which may not come to fruition for some years after the actual teaching event or opportunity for heightened awareness has actually occurred. Fortunately, this notion matches the concept of lifelong learning in terms of the evolution of the self and of a knowledge base.

POTENTIAL VENUES FOR TEACHING AND
WHAT CAN BE ACHIEVED

There are a number of different settings in which teaching can be conducted. These will be divided into two broad areas—that of the classroom and the clinical setting.

Classroom Teaching/Learning

The lecture format is sometimes denigrated as a poor way for students to learn. However, there is still a place for a very good lecture, perhaps with the addition of some adaptations. In the field of palliative care, a lecture by an effective charismatic presenter can do much to inspire and motivate learners to want to pursue the subject further. Such subjects as the needs of dying patients and their families; the traditional and current treatment of dying people in our society; and the nature, philosophy, and scope of the palliative care field can be effectively conveyed by lecture format if the lecture is well-designed and is presented in an exciting and dynamic way. The basics of pain control and opioid analgesics can also be done by lecture, although a paper problem would probably be more effective.

Other methods can be introduced into the lecture format. Real patients and/or their families can be brought in to speak to students. Their messages are often very powerful and lasting and can motivate students to learn more. Alternatively, simulated patients who are well programmed to play a role can be interviewed by a teacher in a sort of drama, vignette, or "tableau" to illustrate certain issues and points or to demonstrate how to interview or take a pain history. Such interviews are usually best kept short to illustrate specific aspects of care. Fifteen or twenty minutes is about the length of time that the attention of the audience can be held before they will want to ask questions and be involved in discussion as to what has occurred.

Students can be asked to discuss certain questions with the person beside them in the lecture theater. I call this technique "duo dialogue," which not only helps students problem solve, but also encourages them to share thoughts and feelings, something which is sorely needed by the helping professions in the way of mutual staff support. It also gets students actively involved in the session and the issues. Questions such as: "If you were dying, what do you think your fears and concerns might be?" or "If someone had to give you some serious bad news, what circumstances would you like to exist around the sharing of this?" Students discuss in a dynamic way for five or seven minutes and then report to the presenter in the plenary format. An analogy can then be drawn to the fears and needs of actual dying patients [11, 12].

The intention of such "imagine that you are . . ." approaches is to encourage students to begin to identify with the position of the seriously ill and dying patient in order to understand their thoughts, feelings, and needs and the types of supportive interactions which might help them feel comforted. This identification helps students to bridge the potential gap they may perceive between themselves and the patients and families for whom they care and decrease their anxiety in the clinical situation.

Role Play

Role play as a teaching technique deserves some special comment. It is a powerful teaching tool both for those who play the parts and for those who watch the interaction. Role play can be short to illustrate a particular interaction, or longer to provide more content and flow. It can be stopped for comment and review or for students to identify what happened, and then continued. Parts can be re-played and students from the audience can be invited to come forward to try certain parts of the interview.

Those who play roles get to feel the part and this can be particularly powerful. For example, the student who has an opportunity to experience the feeling of having a doctor stand over them while talking and then feel the difference when the doctor sits down to talk will likely become a physician who will always strive to sit at the patient's level when speaking. While playing the patient and family can be very instructive, playing the interviewer can give students the chance to try different approaches to asking questions and giving information without the risk of hurting the "patient." The teacher or leader must provide an atmosphere of mutual support and permission to take risks in order for role play to be successful, effective, and fun for students. Role playing, while very effective, can be threatening unless there is a clear atmosphere of trust, something which group leaders must provide.

Small group sessions can be best for the exploration of values, attitudes, and beliefs. Again, role play can be effective, with students taking the parts in a play that illustrates different values, the clash of values, or how values can influence care. Students can exchange parts so that they get to "feel" the part of someone who holds values different from their own. Students can be encouraged to identify values, to reflect on the origins of the values they hold, and share these if they wish. Group trust is important and an atmosphere of mutual tolerance and respect is essential. Students must not be forced to share personal issues unless they wish to do so.

Self-study through reading or watching instructional videotapes and films are excellent ways to reinforce and consolidate information and ideas introduced in other formats. This is particularly important as the second step in problem-based learning after the issues in the problem have been identified and the student has formulated questions to which content answers are required.

TEACHING AND LEARNING IN THE
CLINICAL SETTING

The clinical setting provides an opportunity for students to practice what has been learned in the classroom and from their reading and to learn the assessment and interviewing skills necessary for care. There are several ways that this learning can occur.

Observation of a clinical interaction between the learner and a patient or family is a very direct way to assess skills and give feedback. This observation can occur with the teacher/supervisor in the same room, as might occur on a nursing unit or in a clinic, or from behind a two-way mirror when such facilities are available. The teacher's presence in the room may have an effect on the learner and the patient and their interaction, and this needs to be factored into the equation. Usually, the two-way mirror does not interfere a great deal, particularly once the student is accustomed to its use. Most learners find the direct observation anxiety-provoking at first and this should be discussed openly in an atmosphere of trust.

Audio or videotapes of actual clinical encounters are another way of directly assessing the student in the clinical situation. The patient's permission for the taping is required and the use of the tape should be explained. If the student is comfortable with the taping and if the equipment is as non-intrusive as possible, this can be an excellent way for the student to study interactions, body language, words chosen, and the reaction of the patient to these. The tape can be stopped and re-played so the student can actually see what has occurred and learn from it. Students can review tapes with the supervisor or on their own. Again, as self-directed learners, one would need to assume a fairly high degree of motivation on the part of the student.

Case discussion is one step removed from the actual clinical situation but can be very effective in attempting to assess how the student gathers data, evaluates it, and formulates an analysis of the patient's problems and an approach to managing them. The supervisor can ask direct content questions of the student and thereby assess knowledge base as well as its application. For example, in discussing the management of neuropathic pain, the supervisor can ask the student to outline the pathophysiology, the drugs used to treat this pain problem and their mechanism of action, side-effects, and other content questions.

The student can also review and reflect upon his/her feelings and reactions to the patient's situation and the interactions between them. Identifying and reviewing a particular encounter which was problematic may allow the student and clinical supervisor to re-play the interaction with each of them taking different roles in order to learn new ways of handling interviews. This also provides the opportunity for the student to "play" the part of the patient and to feel their feelings when certain things are said and done, for example, if he/she fails to pick up on certain cues from the patient, or is too brusque in answering questions.

Working with the clinical interdisciplinary team provides the learner the opportunity to develop interpersonal skills and a knowledge and respect for the roles of other team members. Communication skills are enhanced and the learner's own role is strengthened in relation to other roles and the experience of other viewpoints.

Review and discussion about feelings and reactions to patients and families provides an opportunity for the student to discover his/her own values and reactions. The student also has the opportunity to discover his/her personal reactions to death itself as it is confronted in the actual clinical reality. Such discussions are supportive of the student and also help to develop the insight and sensitivity necessary to care for dying patients well. Students also learn to support colleagues of their own and other disciplines.

ASSESSMENT AND EVALUATION

Traditional methods of evaluation can be used to assess content and knowledge base in palliative care. Instructors may choose to use case write-ups or develop multiple choice tests for students to assess knowledge. Case discussion also gives some sense of what he student knows in terms of content and its application. Clinical skills can be assessed by some of the methods described previously.

Problem-based learning is a good way to see how the student handles a situation. The student can be given a real patient to assess and then discuss it with the supervisor. The supervisor can ask about management and content by having the student describe assessment, approach to care, reasons for choosing a certain plan and therapies, and other relevant content like pharmacology and other therapeutics.

The self-directed learner is, indeed, learning for life and this is a continuous process based upon the student's ability to assess what he/she needs to learn. The ability to say "I don't know, but I will find out" is probably the most important skill to foster in learners. This requires insight and a degree of self-confidence and trust in an environment that makes it safe to be somewhat vulnerable.

CONCLUSION

Teaching quality care for the dying requires a definition of who the learners are, what they need to know, the setting in which they will practice, and the nature of their role there. The content of palliative care gives a good basis upon which to begin the teaching/learning process. Various aspects of this content will need to be emphasized more than others with particular groups. Problem-based learning is a learning method particularly well suited to palliative care.

APPENDIX I
Problem-Based Learning Case Scenarios

Case Number One

Ms. B. is a thirty-eight-year-old woman with endstage cancer of the rectum and metastases to her liver. She is being admitted to the hospital with problems of nausea and vomiting and a severe pain in her low back and radiating to her right leg. She has been taking morphine 75 mg. by mouth every four hours but finds it ineffective. Lately, she vomits after each dose. She is the mother of two children ages eleven and thirteen years. Her husband works shifts in a car manufacturing plant.

When Ms. B. arrives at the hospital, she tells you that she is happy to be coming in for care. She looks forward to getting her symptoms controlled. She is very upset as to why she is so sick. Her doctors had given her the impression that the cancer was all removed by surgery. "That's true, isn't it?", she asks. Her husband looks tense and tired. He leaves soon after you meet him.

Questions

1. Identify and discuss the issues presented in this problem.
2. Outline the action you would like to take to address each issue.
3. Describe in detail your approach to her symptom management and the rationale for your decisions.

Case Number Two

A seventy-five-year-old woman is brought to the Emergency Room by her family with severe shortness of breath. Your review of her old charts indicates that she has cancer of the lung which is advanced and there is no cure-oriented therapy which can be given to her. She deteriorates as you are assessing her and it looks like intubation and artificial ventilation will be required if she is to continue to live. Although ill, she remains oriented and can answer your questions. As you talk with her, it becomes apparent that she does not know she has cancer.

Her very large family are present and they confirm that they do not want her to be told how ill she is and they forbid you to talk with her about the respirator. At the same time, they ask you to do everything you can to keep her alive . . . they want "everything done."

Questions

1. Discuss the ethical and treatment issues presented by this problem.
2. Discuss your approach to management.
3. In the group setting, attempt some role-play approaches to talking with the family and the patient.

REFERENCES

1. *Palliative Care Services in Hospital Guidelines* (cat. no. H39-32), Health and Welfare Canada, Ottawa, 1987.
2. E. J. Latimer and H. Dawson, Palliative Care: Principles and Practice, *Canadian Medical Association Journal, 148*:6, pp. 933-934, 1993.
3. D. Doyle, G. W. C. Hanks, and N. MacDonald, *Oxford Textbook of Palliative Medicine,* Oxford University Press, Oxford, 1993.
4. The Canadian Palliative Care Curriculum, N. MacDonald (ed.) for the Canadian Committee on Palliative Care Education, *Pharmascience,* 1991.
5. S. L. Librach, *The Pain Manual. Principles & Issues in Cancer Pain Management,* Pegasus Healthcare, Montreal, 1991.
6. Ontario Medical Association, Committee on Hospitals, OMA Guidelines on Decision-Making in the Treatment and Care of the Terminally Ill, *Health Report,* pp. 1-17, April 1990.
7. E. J. Latimer, Ethical Decision-Making in the Care of the Dying and Its Applications to Clinical Practice, *Journal of Pain & Symptom Management, 6*:5, pp. 329-336, 1991.
8. E. J. Latimer, Caring for Seriously Ill and Dying Patients: The Philosophy and Ethics, *Canadian Medical Association Journal, 144*:7, pp. 859-864, 1991.
9. F. I. Burge and E. J. Latimer, Palliative Care in Medical Education at McMaster University, *Journal of Palliative Care, 5*:1, pp. 16-20, 1989.
10. V. R. Neufeld and H. S. Barrows, The "McMaster Philosophy": An Approach to Medical Education, *Journal of Medical Education, 49,* pp. 1040-1050, 1974.

11. B. M. Mount, Palliative Care of the Terminally Ill, *Annals of the Royal College of Physicians & Surgeons of Canada*, pp. 202-208, July 1978.
12. E. J. Latimer, The Pain of Cancer. Helping Patients & Families Part I & II, *Humane Medicine, 6*:2,3, pp. 95-100, 189-192, 1990.
13. E. L. Perez, J. Y. Gosselin, and A. Gagnon, Education on Death and Dying: A Survey of Canadian Medical Schools, *Journal of Medical Education, 55,* pp. 788-789, 1980.
14. M. D. Smith, M. McSweeney, and B. M. Katz, Characteristics of Death Education Curricula in American Medical Schools, *Journal of Medical Education, 55*, pp. 844-50, 1980.

PART V

Issues of
Religious Significance

The human person, being a rational animal, seeks meaning in the situations with which she/he is confronted. Through the course of human history, persons have found meaning in their religious traditions. While church or synagogue attendance may fluctuate, almost 80 percent of the human race identifies itself with a religious tradition. In this, the last section of the book, we examine how Judaism and Christianity influence ethical practice.

Rabbi Daniel Roberts holds that life was so precious in the eyes of the rabbis that every prohibition concerning the Sabbath, *kashrut*, or the holidays could be broken in order to save a life. For instance, although Jewish law traditionally forbids driving on the Sabbath, a Jew who refuses to drive a very sick person to the hospital on the Sabbath would violate Jewish law. The test of a people is how it behaves toward the old. It is easy to love children. Even tyrants and dictators make a point of being fond of children. But the affection and care for the old, the incurable, the helpless are the true gold mines of a culture. The aged live in fear of losing status. Regarding him/herself as a person who has outlived usefulness, she/he feels the necessity to apologize for being alive. The basic tenet of religion is to teach people how to cope, how to face life's tragedies, how to have hope in spite of a darkened vision of the world, and how to still treat others as human beings even as they lie on their death beds.

Douglas Graydon, Chaplain at Casey House hospice for persons with AIDS in Toronto, examines the spirituality of those living with that terrible disease. While his own background is Christian ministry, he believes the spirituality he sees transcends any particular orientation.

311

The threat of rejection due to AIDS' unacceptability continues to exacerbate the suffering of persons and families living with the illness. This is the most significant factor which contributes to retarding effective psycho/social/spiritual supportive counseling which might enhance the healing of this tremendous social health crisis. Graydon lists a few of the issues confronted by staff working with persons living with AIDS. They are: grief, isolation, judgment, role of lover or partner, age, guilt, abandonment, family dynamics, poverty, loss of control, anger, and spirituality.

Graydon makes a clear distinction between spirituality, faith, and religion. Spirituality is that which pertains to the soul, spirit, or incorporeal being as distinguished from the physical being or body. Spirituality can obviously be expressed within a religion, but is in no way limited by traditional religious observance. Faith is believing in that for which there is no empirical or objective evidence or proof. Faith is belief in a god or system of gods which are defined through dogmatic or creedal statements. Religion then becomes the expression of that faith; the how and when of faithful observance. The over-riding dynamic of spirituality is the ability it gives the individual to discern within her/himself "one's otherness." It is the ability to be conscious of something other than what is immediately in front of our eyes or at the tips of our fingers. Spirituality also includes the ability to ask and attempt to answer those questions we all reflect upon: Who am I? What am I? Do I have meaning? What is my role of life in this world?

Graydon holds that it is a cruel irony that the true spirit of HIV/AIDS, the grace that can assist the individual in overcoming the devastation of HIV/AIDS, lies deep within the pain caused by the disease itself. It is a paradox, or possibly more a mystery, that the purest spirit rises out of the deepest suffering. Almost all faith systems contain within themselves powerful symbols and stories of immense human suffering. Tests of pain form a crucible, from within which rises the human spirit shining bright, strong, and true. It is that ability of the human mind to rise above the limits of a dying body and still see the beauty and majesty of life which generates our quest for spirituality.

This realization that the human person can rise above the tragedies of life is the lesson we learn from death and bereavement and the lesson taught to us through AIDS. It is an important lesson and an appropriate way to end our reflections on some ethical issues of the dying and bereaved aged.

CHAPTER 21

Ask Your Ancestors and They Will Tell You*

Rabbi Daniel A. Roberts

The arguments of Dr. Jack Kevorkian, Derrick Humphery, and others have captivated the imagination and fear of the public. We have been sucked into believing that doctors and hospitals are conspiring to keep our loved ones alive in order to milk our pocketbooks and that to die with dignity we need "assisted suicide" or active euthanasia. Today, almost everyone who goes into a hospital or a nursing home is required to sign a "living will" indicating what level of care they would like to receive and at what point care should be stopped.

I, too, was one of those who was drawn into the idea that if I could no longer be a vibrant and active human being, my family should turn off the machines. I did not want my loved ones to keep me alive by artificial means. I feared becoming an economic burden to them, and I certainly detested the concept of lying in a hospital bed in a vegetative state. In fact, I once wrote my sons an impassioned plea requesting that should the time come that there was no chance of my returning to a full and active life, they should disconnect me from life-sustaining machines. I was an advocate and a devotee of this philosophy.

Of course, the questions I never answered for them were: When would that moment be? Which person or persons would decide that there was no chance of my returning to a full and active life? What did

---

*An exploration of Jewish texts from ancient to modern on the holiness of life, ethical dilemmas, and how life and death decisions are made.

being a full and active human being really mean to me? I left my loved ones to their own recognizance and definitions. Would I be kept alive longer than I should be because they had some kind of unrealistic hope that I would return to good health? Would they pull the plug too quickly because they were worried that my lingering would eat into their inheritance? Would they let me remain connected to machines because psychologically they could not handle my dying? Would they want me out of the way because they were angry that I was taking so long to die?

Like many others, I had fallen victim to the "new" and the "logical" without carefully investigating what ancient resources tell us about care of the dying. We are certainly not the first civilization to wrestle with assisted suicide and/or deciding when an individual is no longer economically viable to society. We know of communities whose norm was to send their aged out onto a mountain or an iceberg to die. Why did the writers of the Bible and the Talmud[1] choose to prohibit such actions? Why not allow those who were a liability to the community to go off into the wilderness to die? The answers to such questions are found in our ancestors' concepts of living and dying.

We start our journey at the beginning. The Book of Genesis tells us that in the beginning, when God created man, He did so "in His own image" [1]. The idea that every human being was created in God's image was as much a revolutionary idea as the oneness of God or resting on the Sabbath. A different ideology had begun in which taking another's life was a violation of God's command. Other civilizations sacrificed children to their gods, but in Genesis 22, when God restrains Abraham from sacrificing Isaac, we learn that God neither wants nor needs us to do this. We deduce from this story that *any* human sacrifice is prohibited.

"You shall be holy as I, the Lord your God am holy" [2] is mandated in the Book of Leviticus. That is, we are to live a life of holiness. Say the rabbis, "To save a single human life is to save the whole world. To destroy a life is to destroy the whole world" [3]. The object of life in the ancient world of the Bible was to strive for holiness by distinguishing between the holy and the profane. This was the ideology behind *kashrut* (kosher dietary laws): "to make a difference between the unclean and the clean,[2] and between the living things that may be eaten and the living things that may not be eaten" [4].

Life was so precious in the eyes of the rabbis that every prohibition concerning the Sabbath, *kashrut*, or the holidays could be broken in

[1] A commentary on the Bible.

[2] "Unclean and clean" are euphemisms for animals fit and forbidden for sacrifice.

order to save a life. For instance, although Jewish law traditionally forbids driving on the Sabbath, a Jew who refuses to drive a very sick person to the hospital on the Sabbath would violate Jewish law. It is interesting to note that prohibitions against murder, idolatry, or perverse sexuality are maintained—these exceptions reveal that although life *is* precious, the highest value is not always placed on it [5].

We read, "It is forbidden to strike another person, even if that person gives you permission to do so, because one has absolutely no authority over one's own body as to allow it to be struck" [6]. From this and other related sources it can be concluded that Jewish law would neither allow Shylock to collect the pound of flesh, nor Antonius to offer it, in as much as Antonius did not own his flesh in the first place. Our life and limb are entrusted to us by God, and we are forbidden to neglect or misappropriate them any more so than can we abuse any other property entrusted to us for safekeeping. It is because God, and God alone, can give us life and limb that God alone may take them.

The medieval Christian thinker, St. Thomas Aquinas, expresses a similar view in *Summa Theologica*:

> It is altogether unlawful to kill oneself, for three reasons:
>
> a) Because everything naturally loves itself, the result being that naturally everything keeps itself in being. . . Wherefore suicide is contrary to the inclination of nature.
> b) Because every man is part of a community and so, as such, he belongs to the community. Hence by killing himself, he injures the community.
> c) Because life is God's gift to man, and is subject to His power, Who kills and makes to live. Hence whoever takes his own life, sins against God, even as he who kills another's slave, sins against that slave's master. . . . For it belongs to God alone to pronounce sentence of death and life, according to Deuteronomy 32:39: "I will kill and I will make to live" (quoted in Cytron and Schwartz [6]).

The yardstick which the ancient Hebrews used to measure an action (including, of course, the treatment of the ill or infirm) was whether or not it promoted or profaned holiness. Rabbi Abraham Joshua Heschel writes:

> The test of a people is how it behaves toward the old. It is easy to love children. Even tyrants and dictators make a point of being fond of children. But the affection and care for the old, the incurable, the helpless are the true gold mines of a culture. . . .

In our own days, a new type of fear has evolved in the hearts of men: the fear of medical bills. In the spirit of the principle that reverence for the old takes precedence over reverence for God, we are compelled to confess that a nation should be ready to sell, if necessary, the treasures from its art collection and the sacred objects from its houses of worship in order to help one sick man.... Is there anything as holy, as urgent, as noble, as the effort of the whole nation to provide medical care for the old? ....

The aged may be described as a person *who does not dream anymore,* devoid of ambition, and living in fear of losing his status. Regarding himself as a person who has outlived his usefulness, he feels as if he had to apologize for being alive [7, pp. 72-73].

What do we wish to accomplish in the current debate over assisted suicides? In the future, will the sick and the infirm, once diagnosed with cancer, Alzheimer's disease, or some other "fatal" disease, feel the need to apologize for being alive? Will they be made to feel that it is *incumbent* upon them to instruct others not to take heroic measures to prolong their lives? Are we to suggest a new norm: that when people become economic burdens to their families or the medical community we should encourage them to engage in assisted suicide?

In the seventeenth century, Rabbi Gur Aryeh HaLevi wrote, "It is natural for old people to be despised by the general population when they can no longer function as they once did, but sit idle and have no purpose. The commandment, 'Honor your father and your mother,' was given specifically for such a situation" [8]. The reader will note that the command is not to love one's parents, only to honor them. According to the Talmud, "A father endows his son with blessings of beauty, strength, riches, wisdom and length of years... And just as the father endows the son with five things, so, too, is the son obliged in five things: to feed him and give drink, to clothe him, put on his shoes for him and lead him" [9]. The great philosopher, Maimonides further elaborates, "But if the condition of the parent has grown worse, and the son is no longer able to endure the strain, he may leave his father or mother, go elsewhere, and delegate others to give to the parents proper care" [10]. Thus, realizing that it would be impossible to command people to love their parents, the rabbis understood that they could preserve the dignity of parents by ensuring that their children were *respectful* through their responsibility to financially sustain their parents. We deduce that it would be a violation of the commandment to honor one's parents to suggest that the life-prolonging machines be disconnected in order to preserve the capital of a parent as an inheritance.

Ultimately, underlying all questions concerning assisted suicides and/or the removal of life support is the issue of what meaning can be derived from sustaining a person's life as long as we can. Then we must ask if there are other meanings to the concept of ending life with "dignity."

The Psalmist long ago gave us insight into the great fears of the elderly, or for that matter, anyone terminally ill, when he wrote, "Do not cast me off in old age; when my strength fails do not forsake me" [11]. The fears of dying alone, of being cast off—in pain, incapacitated, and warehoused—are so great these days that people are willing to leave this world early to avoid these fears. Suicides of older adults are on the rise. Everyone has heard of older couples who have made a pact to commit joint suicide, and members of their families who have found them in each others arms in the back seat of their car with the motor still running. Suicide among the elderly is a very serious problem and our society has not paid much attention to this phenomena.

Consider how many of the readers of this chapter have parents or grandparents who live in another city or state. As much as you feel torn and troubled about becoming ill and needing care, and are concerned about how your family will provide it, *your* parents equally feel isolated and alone and fret as to who will take care of them. In our individualistic society of individualism, parents worry about becoming an economic and psychological burden to their children. Assisted suicides and "pulling the plug" become more and more plausible options.

Another underlying fear rages within our souls. Within our psyche there is an innate will to live. I have watched cancer patients racked with pain continue to get up each day even though the opportunity to commit suicide is available to them. Why, I ask myself, do they fight every day for life? I would suggest that in part it is their innate desire to live and in part because they still have hope. The power of hope has kept many alive. Nietzsche suggests that "He who has a why to live can bear with almost any how" (quoted by Gordon Allport in Preface to Frankl [12, p. 12]). What greater fear could the dying have but that their heirs, either not wanting to bear the burdens of care any longer or anxious to acquire their estate, will allow them to die "before their time." The thought races through the mind of the dying that his/her guardians, under pressure to preserve estates, might not take the aggressive actions required to continue life. Leon Kass in his article, "Death with Dignity and the Sanctity of Life," reminds us:

> There is nothing of human dignity in the process of dying itself—only in the way we face it: At its best, death with complete dignity will always be compromised by the extinction of dignified

humanity; it is, I suspect, a death-denying culture's anger about dying and mortality that expresses itself in the partly oxymoronic and unreasonable demand for dignity in death. . . . insofar as we seek better health and longer life, insofar as we turn to doctors to help us get better, we necessarily and voluntarily compromise our dignity: Being a patient rather than an agent is, humanly speaking, undignified. All people, especially the old, willingly, if unknowingly, accept a whole stable of indignities simply by seeking medical assistance [13, p. 132].

The lesson to be learned from death is not that we should try to exit life as painlessly as possible; rather, dying is about how we cope with the knowledge that there is an end to life. The basic tenet of religion is to teach people how to cope, how to face life's tragedies, how to have hope in spite of a darkened vision of the world, and how to still treat others as human beings even as they lie on their death beds. Kass continues:

. . . a dignified human life is not just a lonely project against an inevitable death, but a life whose meaning is entwined in human relationships. We must stress again the importance for a death with dignity—as for a life with dignity—of dignified human intercourse with all those around us. Who we are to ourselves is largely inseparable from who we are to and for others; thus our own exercise of dignified humanity will depend crucially on continuing to receive respectful treatment from others. The manner in which we are addressed, what is said to us or in our presence, how our bodies are tended to or our feelings regarded—in all these ways, our dignity in dying can be nourished and sustained. Dying people are all too easily reduced ahead of time to "thinghood" by those who cannot bear to deal with the suffering or disability of those they love. Objectification and detachment are understandable defenses. Yet this withdrawal of contact, affection, and care is probably the greatest single cause of the dehumanization of dying. Death with dignity requires absolutely that the survivors treat the human being at all times as if full god-like-ness remains, up to the very end [13, p. 135].

Referring to the above in a footnote, Kass cites comments from New York attorney John F. Cannon:

If a person who is dying has ceased to be an agent and has been "attached to catheters, respirators, and suction tubes [that] hide the human countenance" or has "been swept off the stage and been abandoned by the rest of the cast," he can still respond virtuously to his awful predicament (in the former case, only if he is aware of it), and if he so responds, he can be said to have "lost" his dignity only in the sense that others have refused to grant it to him. He is no less "worthy" a person, but what he is "worthy of" has been withheld, or worse. Dignity, in other words, is something that is simultaneously earned and conferred.

From this perspective, to argue that assisted suicide or active euthanasia is a means to the end of "death with dignity" is to make the absurd claim that if I cannot maintain a "dignified attitude and conduct in the face of [my own] death," or if I manage to do that but it turns out to be too much to ask others to accord me the dignity my virtuous conduct deserves, killing me is somehow a way to let me die *with my dignity*; in the case of a loved one who is dying, it is to claim that if he is hopelessly racked by fear, pain and self-pity, or if the degree of courage he shows in the face of death merits more compassion and affection for him that I can bear to give, his *dignity*, and mine, will somehow be advanced by killing him [13, pp. 144-145].

Does asking others to participate in our death, or creating legal means for people to commit suicide, *really* advance human dignity? Is not dignity heightened more through people's actions on their death beds as they face death?

In defense of Kevorkian and others, some might cite Maimonides, who holds that one who ends the life of one whose disease is estimated by doctors to end in death within twelve months (a *terefah*) is not liable. Although this person cannot be tried by the courts, the rabbis assert that he will be tried by the heavenly tribunal. How could this be, especially when we will see further on that one is culpable if one even moves a person on his death bed? Rabbi Maurice Lamm, in a paper delivered at the First National Conference on Hospice for the Jewish Community explains, "It must be made clear, that the prohibition of fatally injuring a *terefah* is not a simple prohibition of murder, but a prohibition of fatal wounding through *chavalah*, a destructively-intended injury. If the fatality was a consequence of an injury for constructive purposes, such as healing or relieving, it would not be considered *chavalah*" [14].

Joseph Caro in his influential code of law entitled *Shulhan Aruch* ("A Set Table"), completed in approximately 1564, instructs us how we are to act in the presence of a person whose death appears to be imminent (a *goses*[3]):

---

[3] A time span of no longer than three days. This in contrast to a *terefah,* one whose disease is estimated by doctors to end in death within twelve months.

> A *goses* is to be considered alive in all respects. One does not tie his
> jaw, anoint him, purge him, stop up his orifices, remove his pillow,
> nor place him on sand, floor, or ground. One does not place a plate
> on his belly, nor a bit of salt. The announcement [of death] is not
> made, nor flute players and mourners hired. And one does not close
> his eyes until he has died. Anyone who closes another's eyes at the
> moment the *nefesh* (soul) is leaving has shed blood. One does not
> tear one's clothing, remove one's shoes, give a eulogy, or bring a
> casket into the house where the dying person is located until the
> person has died [15].

In other words, making plans for the funeral of a person while
she/he is on the death bed would be a violation of Jewish law, for
conceivably it could take away the dying's last vestige of hope. Bernie
Siegel, in *Love, Medicine and Miracles* [16] and *Peace, Love and Healing* [17], demonstrates that as long as people have hope, they can
extend the length and quality of their lives. What are the hopes that
we can give a person in his last moments? "One could hope for less
pain. . . . one could hope for the happiness of mate and children, for the
family's continuation of the values that one taught" [15].

Is it proper to remove obstacles impeding death? Moses Isserles in a
commentary to the *Shulhan Aruch* passage above, wrote:

> Thus, it is forbidden to accelerate a person's death. For example,
> one may not remove the pillow or mattress of a person who has
> been a *goses* for a long time and is unable to expire, on the grounds
> that some claim that the feathers of certain birds can be the cause
> of this condition. Likewise, such a person is not to be moved, and it
> is forbidden to put the keys to the house under the head of a person
> in this state in order to cause the person to expire. However, if
> something is present which is preventing the *nefesh* from leaving,
> e.g., the sound of pounding near the house as is made by a wood-
> cutter, for instance, or if there is salt on the person's tongue,[4] and
> these things are preventing the *nefesh* from leaving, it may be
> removed inasmuch as this does not constitute an act in and of itself
> beyond removal of the impediment [18].

As we can see from above, one prolongs living but not dying. There
is a fine line between actively causing another's death and the passive
euthanasia that allows us to comfort the dying and not aggressively

---

[4] "Salt on his tongue." A belief that salt on a dying person's tongue slowed down the
dying process probably originated in the observation that salt's power to preserve various
foods might also work to preserve life as well.

work to prevent their death. The distinction rests upon our own philosophy of dying. If we are comfortable allowing our beloved to slip peacefully into the next world then we can assist them in dying. That is, we can assure them that we will do everything to alleviate their fears: we will not allow them to die alone,[5] we will relieve their pain to the best of our abilities even if it means administering addictive drugs, and we will not cause their death before their time. Yet, neither will we do anything heroic that would delay their anguish. In addition, it would be important not only to tell them of our feelings for them, and that we will miss them, but that even while they are on their death bed, the manner in which they handle this sacred moment will be a learning experience for us as a model for our own dying moments. Victor Frankl, the famed logotherapist and author of *Man's Search for Meaning,* put it well:

> We must never forget that we may also find meaning in life even when confronted with a hopeless situation, when facing a fate that cannot be changed. . . . for what then matters is to bear witness to the uniquely human potential at its best, which is to transform a personal tragedy into a triumph [12].

Even on one's deathbed it is important and meaningful to know that one is having an impact on another's life. That is the true definition of dignity in death.

In the Talmud it is written, "Respect an old man who lost his learning: remember that the fragments of the tablets broken by Moses were preserved along side the new" [19]. It is our sacred trust to care for both the old and the new, to make both feel as if they were holy, for indeed from the very beginning both were created in God's image.

Norman Cousins summarizes the care we must give to the dying most eloquently in *The Anatomy of an Illness*:

> Death is not the ultimate tragedy of life. The ultimate tragedy is de-personalization—dying in an alien and sterile area, separated from the spiritual nourishment that comes from being able to reach out to a loving hand, separated from a desire to experience the things that make life worth living [20].

The concept of death with dignity must be conceived differently: as allowing our beloved to die with the knowledge that we will be with

---

[5] When a person is in his last moments one is to bring a *minyan* (a religious quorum) to his bedside so that he dies with people around him.

them, that we will minimize their pain, that we will not take heroic measures to extend their life beyond their alloted time, nor will we do anything to shorten it as long as there is hope. This would then truly be death with dignity and with love.

REFERENCES

1. *Genesis, 1*:27, 9:6.
2. *Leviticus, 19*:2.
3. *Sanhedrin, 37a*.
4. *Leviticus, 11*:47.
5. *Talmud*, Yoma, 85b.
6. B. Cytron and E. Schwartz, *When Life is in the Balance: Life and Death Decisions in the Light of the Jewish Tradition*, United Synagogue of America, Department of Youth Activities, New York, 1986.
7. A. J. Heschel, *The Insecurity of Freedom*, Schocken Books, New York, 1972.
8. G. A. HaLevi, (17th century), Commentary on the Fifth Commandment, in *Voices of Wisdom: Jewish Ideals and Ethics for Everyday Living*, F. Klagsbrun (ed.), Pantheon Books, New York, 1980.
9. *Talmud*, Mishna Eduyot, 2:9.
10. Maimonides, Laws Concerning Rebels, *Maimonides' Code*, Ch. 6, Section 10.
11. *Psalms 71*:9.
12. V. Frankl, *Man's Search for Meaning*, Washington Square Press, New York, 1969.
13. L. R. Kass, Death with Dignity and the Sanctity of Life, in *A Time to be Born and a Time to Die*, B. Kogan (ed.), Aldine de Gruyter, New York, 1991.
14. M. Lamm, *The Fundamental Jewishness of Jewish Hospice,* paper delivered at the First National Conference on Hospice for the Jewish Community, June 13, 1984.
15. J. Caro, *Shulhan Aruch, Yoreh De'ah* 339, 2, 1564.
16. B. Siegel, *Love, Medicine and Miracles*, Harper & Row, New York, 1986.
17. B. Siegel, *Peace, Love and Healing*, Harper & Row, New York, 1989.
18. M. Isserles, *Mapah to Shulhan Aruch, Yoreh De'ah* 339.
19. *Berakhot, 8b*.
20. N. Cousins, *Anatomy of an Illness*, Norton, New York, 1979.

ACKNOWLEDGMENTS

Reference 7. Excerpts from "To Grow in Wisdom" from *The Insecurity of Freedom*, by Abraham Joshua Heschel. Copyright © 1966 by Abraham Joshua Heschel. Reprinted by permission of Farrar, Straus & Giroux, Inc.

Reference 12. From: *Man's Search for Meaning*, by Viktor E. Frankl © 1959, 1962, 1984, 1992 by Viktor E. Frankl. Reprinted by permission of Beacon Press, Publisher.

CHAPTER 22

Casey House Hospice: Caring for the Person Living with HIV/AIDS

Reverend Douglas Graydon

Within this chapter I would like to briefly introduce Casey House Hospice and some of the psycho/social/spiritual dynamics of AIDS palliative care. This chapter will have three parts. The first is a very brief historical introduction to Casey House itself. The second part will focus upon some of the counseling dynamics experienced within the House, and the third section will consist of a discussion of spiritual issues that arise within the HIV/AIDS community. I will conclude with a reflection upon the spiritual experience of persons living with HIV/AIDS.

CASEY HOUSE HOSPICE

Casey House Hospice is a neo-gothic Victorian townhouse which was renovated into a hospice over eight years ago. The House was created because of the need in the AIDS community for a place where persons living with AIDS could die with dignity, autonomy, and honor. In its eight years of operation, over 500 people have lived and died at the hospice. The hospice is a thirteen-bed facility employing thirty full-time and forty part-time people. It works within what is called a primary care" model where a nurse, counselor, and physician coordinate care with the person living with AIDS. At Casey House, the patient or resident drives his/her care. It is the resident who, to the best of her/his abilities, determines the broad direction of their health care, identifying who the principle decision makers are and who constitutes her/his "family."

It is the responsibility of the nurse to coordinate the clinical care for the resident while the counselor coordinates the "psycho/social/

spiritual" care for the resident. The physician oversees the medical care. The counselor can be involved in a broad range of activities depending upon the needs of the resident. This could include facilitating family reconciliation, conducting individual or group therapy, or arranging funerals and wills.

Within the Casey House Hospice model, complementary therapies play a significant role. The Hospice has a full-time massage therapist and maintains a roster of other therapists including chiropractors, acupuncturists, aromatherapists, naturopathic and herbal doctors, physiotherapists, occupational therapists, and numerous other non-clinical specialists. This fulfills the mission of Casey House in providing a wide range of services and therapies which manage symptoms and attempt to alleviate pain. The overall goal is to enable persons living with AIDS to do just that: live with their disease until they die.

PSYCHO/SOCIAL PROFILE
OF A CASEY HOUSE RESIDENT

If there were a typical profile of a Casey House Hospice resident; it would be a single white gay male approximately thirty to thirty-five years of age living on social assistance and government funded disability pensions, no longer seeking active treatment but rather seeking comfort management in their latter stages of AIDS.

This gentleman (and increasingly woman) is surrounded by a small circle of friends and possibly a lover or partner. This grouping will have experienced multiple losses due to AIDS and so will be expressing the long-term emotional shock of seeing far too many friends die from AIDS. If there is a same-sex partner, they may be experiencing the pressure of a society which does not support same-sex relationships with any type of legal sanction or social approval. Many times these relationships, because of social stigma, collapse under the weight of the public scrutiny which results from the disclosure of an HIV positive status and AIDS diagnosis. Generally, these friends and/or partner are the principle source of emotional support for the person living with AIDS.

If there is a biological family involved, they have generally become disenfranchised from the person with AIDS due to the issue of sexual orientation. (It is not uncommon, even at the relatively late stage of admission to Casey House, for the family to learn of the HIV and AIDS diagnosis, approaching death, and sexual orientation of the child all at the same time.) It will therefore be this issue, if still unresolved, which will significantly hamper any positive healing during the dying process. The mother will often experience considerable stress due to feelings of guilt and shame. Her normal support groupings of friends and extended family may be unavailable to her as she tends to her dying child because of her fear of sharing the nature of her child's illness. Besides this stigma of AIDS, she will be experiencing the trauma of a child's premature death—something very much contrary to the natural order of life as we experience it in North America.

The father will also be struggling with these same issues. However, he may be paralyzed in communicating his feelings to his child because of the issue of sexual orientation. Within the father/son relationship especially, the issue of sexual orientation may cause feelings of guilt and remorse, if not rejection, even at the bedside of the dying child. The reality of homosexuality may prove too threatening for North American males who have enough difficulty expressing feelings of love for one another even at the best of times, even between father and son. It is likely then that fathers may be profoundly absent from the closing days of their son's life. The counselor can be presented with a considerable challenge in attempting to get fathers and sons communicating honestly and lovingly with each other. Brothers and sisters are generally more comfortable with issues of sexual orientation and so can be more emotionally supportive. However, they too will feel the additional stress of stigmatization and isolation of AIDS as they will be fearful of sharing this news with friends.

The threat of rejection due to the unacceptability of AIDS continues to exaggerate and exacerbate the suffering of persons and families living with the illness. This is the most significant factor which contributes to retarding effective psycho/social/spiritual supportive counseling which might enhance the healing of this tremendous social health crisis.

PSYCHO/SOCIAL ISSUES
FACING A PERSON LIVING WITH AIDS

Listed here are a few of the psycho/social issues confronted by Casey House counseling staff working with persons living with AIDS. Also identified are a few of the programs developed by the hospice to meet the needs of the resident and her/his family.

- grief
- judgment
- age
- abandonment
- poverty
- anger
- isolation
- role of lover or partner
- guilt
- family dynamics
- loss of control
- spirituality

Casey House Hospice programs which attempt to address the above include:

- peer support groups
- preplanning of funerals
- legal services—power of attorney, medical power of attorney
- counseling services—individual, group, and family counselling
- development of rituals which facilitate or mark grief/death
- bereavement services

Through a wide range of supportive counseling approaches Casey House attempts to soften the dying process. The person living with AIDS is experiencing tremendous loss, grief, isolation, and even total abandonment from family and friends. Casey House attempts to maintain the dignity and autonomy of the resident through its programs which are geared toward respecting the residents right to choose, and supporting the residents' friendships and same-sex partners even if this goes contrary to the wishes of the biological next of kin.

The issues listed above do not differ significantly from those of any person facing a life threatening disease at an early stage. However, with HIV/AIDS there is considerable suffering imposed upon the sick and dying due to the judgment and moral condemnation which accompanies a socially unacceptable sexuality or lifestyle. There is profound physical and psychological suffering in HIV/AIDS. The tragedy is that most of this suffering can be eliminated if the stigma surrounding this disease were eradicated.

SPIRITUALITY AND THE PERSON LIVING WITH AIDS

The issue of spirituality is at times more complex or at least unfocused. Within HIV/AIDS, it is important to make a clear distinction between spirituality, faith, and religion. Spirituality is that which pertains to the soul, spirit, or incorporeal being as distinguished from the physical being or body. Spirituality can obviously be expressed within a religion, but is in no way limited by what we may call traditional North American religious observance [1, p. 53].

Faith is believing in that for which there is no empirical or objective evidence or proof. Faith is belief in a god or system of gods which are defined through dogmatic or creedal statements. Religion then becomes the expression of that faith; the how and when of faithful observance.

Descriptors of religion would include:

A) a belief in a god or series of gods;
B) a distinction between sacred and profound objects;

C) ritual acts which are focused around certain objects;
D) an observed and identifiable moral code and creedal statements;
E) shared feelings of awe, mystery, guilt, joy, etc;.
F) a feeling of community and shared responsibility;
G) the use of prayer and other forms of ritual communication;
H) a sense of world view or cosmic order in which members invest meaning, purpose, and fulfilment.

The overriding dynamic of spirituality is the ability it gives the individual to discern within her/himself "one's otherness." It is the ability to be conscious of something other than what is immediately in front of our eyes or at the tips of our fingers. It is to be conscious not only of ourselves or "myself" but to be conscious of others around us as well. To be aware of the membership we share in that which is known as "community" whether that be social or religious.

Spirituality also includes the ability to ask and attempt to answer those questions we all reflect upon:

• Who am I?
• What am I?
• Do I have meaning?
• What is my role of life in this world?

In a hospice setting, when confronted with issues of personal mortality, this spiritual dynamic takes on a more focused search for an interior life which might promote enhanced feelings of wholeness, passing beyond the boundaries of our physical bodies.

Within a hospice, good pain management can eliminate almost all physical pain and yet people can experience considerable emotional and spiritual distress. And so the types of questions which might focus upon interior healing and begin accessing spiritual energies would include:

• Can I, or will I, take an active role in my healing?
• What is my attitude toward life?
• Is it a positive attitude?
• Is it negative or apathetic?

I believe many of us who work within the hospice movement often witness people who have a positive attitude regarding life which enables them to maintain a higher quality of living than those instilled with negative or apathetic thoughts. We have also experienced the person who cannot, it seems, rise above those negative thoughts regardless of encouragement by others and who suffers more deeply living a life void of hope and pleasure.

The questions which can unlock our spiritual path and lead us to greater harmony and life fulfilment include:

- What does healing mean to me at this point in my life?
- What is my attitude toward my death?
- Can I forgive others in my life? Can I forgive myself?
- Is there any way that I might be able to enjoy a sense of inner peace?
- Can I sense within myself any kind of inner strength?
- Do I accept and love myself?
- Can I perceive myself as being loved by others? [2]

Within AIDS palliative care, and within Casey House Hospice, these questions take on greater importance as this disease, with all its oppressive stigma, rips away human self-worth and dignity.

Spiritual thoughts and feelings are, I believe, intensely private feelings. We keep them hidden because society does not generally know how to nurture and support such feelings except within the very highly ritualized faith expression of the organized religion. Many individual spiritual feelings fall outside of those rituals and are seen as strange, or are simply not understood.

Studies from hospice settings show how caregivers within the hospice environment value the issues of spirituality within the care that they deliver. Over 90 percent of professional caregivers consider spirituality very important to good health care delivery and yet less than 50 percent actually sustain or nurture conversations around spirituality, attempt to assist persons in articulating their unique sense of spirituality, or unlock the spiritual resources within a person who is experiencing the dying process [1].

One of the challenges, as Chaplain at Casey House, is to consider how to best support alternative spiritual expressions. We are far more comfortable as a society talking about sex than we are talking about and sharing our spirituality. I believe it is because we lack the tools. I believe we are a spiritually illiterate society. Spirituality is so inter-twined with feelings of self-worth and self-image that when expressed it opens profound and powerful avenues of self-discovery that travel to the very core of a person's being and as a result leaves that person tremendously vulnerable. If we nurture that person's unique spirituality, then the sense of self is strengthened and inner healing can take place. To judge or value a person's sense of spirituality can retard, hinder, and even destroy feelings of self-worth, dignity, and acceptance.

For example, when a person with HIV/AIDS opens up to you and articulates feelings of how they are loved by a greater being for who and what they are, and you respond by saying, "that's nice to hear, but you are a gay man and so you are not acceptable in the eyes of God," you have destroyed a fundamental part of that person's identity. Great care must be exercised when someone opens up spiritually. Our role as caregivers is to facilitate the individuals self-assessment of their own spirituality.

Casey House supports this process through what I call traditional and non-traditional ways of accessing spirituality. Traditional ones are most familiar: Judeo-Christian prayer and meditation, sacraments, and ritual. However, the majority of my experience rests within that which I call non-traditional. Two examples of non-traditional ways of accessing spirituality are dream work and dialogue with images.

Dream work occurs when the counselor listens to the resident's dream and assists the resident to understand and interpret the dream for her/himself. What do the symbols, images mean? What is the meaning of the story? And how might this inform the resident's sense of "otherness" or spirituality?

Dialogue with images is when the resident creates an image through some medium of the expressive arts therapeutic process and then simply "dialogues" with that image. By allowing the image to "speak" to the resident, a safe environment may be created which allows the resident to travel inward and discern a deeper sense of self and spirit.

Both of these approaches are really nothing more than simple tools which assist the resident in focusing his/her mind toward accessing their spirituality. They are similar to the more commonly experienced religious forms of worship which are only, in a more sophisticated way, tools of once again accessing individual spirituality.

TOOLS AND METHODS
FOR ACCESSING SPIRITUALITY

TRADITIONAL
- prayer
- meditation
- Judeo-Christian ritual
- "God talk"
- clergy
- prayer groups

NON-TRADITIONAL
- dream work
- meditation
- other types and forms of ritual
- guided memory
- dialogue with images
- peer support

All of these approaches listed above function as nothing more than an access point which facilitates tapping that resource or consciousness within us known as spirituality. I continue to believe that the most effective way of expressing spirituality is simply through the learned art of listening and sharing with another. It is the simple act of witnessing in a gentle, supportive, nurturing, and respectful way.

SPIRITUALITY AND AIDS[1]

Within the disease known as HIV/AIDS, many people have difficulty perceiving any type of spirituality or divine presence. If there is a greater power, divinity, God, or whatever title you choose to use, it is difficult, if not impossible, to discern this type of a presence within the trauma of HIV/AIDS. This disease slowly strips away the human form. Through the myriads of viral and bacterial infections, HIV/AIDS destroys the body, the mind, and it seems at times the soul as well. For a society which prides itself at dominating, controlling, and even eradicating disease, HIV/AIDS seems the ultimate joke. Mother Nature's latest laugh at humanity's attempt to achieve health, happiness, and the ideal family life.

There is extreme suffering in HIV/AIDS. Anyone who is experiencing this disease, either infected or affected, knows this. The isolation, the abandonment, the sheer terror of watching yourself or a loved one deteriorate both in mind and body all speak of how difficult it is to reach out either to others, or within oneself to tap that resource known as spirituality. How can a God ordain such an illness? How can anyone believe that there is a divine love working within the chaos of HIV/AIDS? Where is spirituality within HIV/AIDS?

It seems at first a cruel irony that the true spirit of HIV/AIDS, the grace that can assist the individual in overcoming the devastation of HIV/AIDS lies deep within the pain caused by the disease itself. It is a paradox, or possibly more a mystery, that the purest spirit rises out of the deepest suffering. Almost all faith systems contain within themselves powerful symbols and stories of immense human suffering. Tests of pain form a crucible, which rises from within the human spirit shining bright, strong, and true.

It seems we are at our best when we face our greatest challenge. Whether it is war, famine, or disease, or when confronted by the truths

---

[1] This part of the chapter was originally written in 1992 as a reflection paper on HIV/AIDS and spirituality.

of our age, the truth of life and death, and love, we rise above the mundane parameters of our daily life and live a spirituality which enables us to savour every sunbeam, treasure every moment of life, and celebrate every expression of love.

James Woodward in his book, *Embracing the Chaos; A Theological Response to AIDS*, explores the mystery that when we live on the edge of life and death, when we are rejected by mainstream society or suffer the loss of loved ones, we experience God most clearly [3]. That is where we live the pain of this finite world most deeply and so therefore utilize our spirituality as a tool vital to our very existence. It is that ability of the human mind to rise above the limits of a dying body and still see the beauty and majesty of life which generates our quest for spirituality. Our conscious mind demands that we make sense of this madness. That there is a purpose, a reason, a plan which can accommodate in some form the suffering we experience so that we as individuals and as members of a family can learn and grow in spite of the illness. In other words, we search within HIV/AIDS for that awareness, that inner spirit, which can say to us, "I still have meaning, regardless of my disability, my disfigurement, my feeble mind. I have worth as a human being and so am loved."

As the physical body is lost to this disease, it becomes necessary to search deeper within the soul for energy and understanding to simply cope day to day. For those who manage to accomplish this, what they find is an apparent bottomless well of energy. An energy which assists in sustaining and at times even nurturing the quality of living. And it is in the quality that we find meaning. So that even a life which seems bleak and harsh for one can have tremendous depth and substance for another.

The spirit that lives in each of us cries out for nothing more than to be loved and valued for simply what that spirit is. A human being. A being of fears and joys, muscle and sinew, hopes realized and dreams as yet unfulfilled. And the spirituality of HIV/AIDS is nothing more complex or mysterious than simply that. The value of loving without question, without judgment, without qualification. And if that loving can be realized by both the person infected and those affected around him or her, then the spiritual energy released can be considered nothing less than divine. And yet there is no objective or empirical proof of this spirituality. It can only be validated through the experience of those who choose to risk. Those who risk loving and giving and striving for meaning in life.

As a chaplain I encounter people who seem to see more clearly, feel more deeply, and love more honestly because they have managed to tap that universal spirituality which assists in liberating them from the confines of their illness. People who experience intense pain and yet also experience an inner peace. People rejected by families and their communities who meet each new stranger with love and acceptance. People who have lost many loves to HIV/AIDS and yet who can still love anew with passion and hope.

I remember a man who was so at peace with himself and his impending death from AIDS, he caused his caregivers great anxiety because there was nothing required except basic physical care. When asked how he achieved such a state of peace, he simply replied that he knew he was loved. This man came from a dysfunctional family. His brother never visited and his mother came to see him only after months of disinterest. So how did he know that he was loved? He knew deep within himself that he was loved and valued by something greater than himself or his family. He chose to call this love God. For him, this love was the source of his strength and dignity.

Another man who spent months as a resident of Casey House learned of this same spirituality a different way. He distanced himself from his family years ago because of his homosexuality, then fled to Vancouver when he discovered that he was HIV positive. Finally, destitute, he called upon this same family who welcomed him home, paid off his debts, and loved him till he died. Over the last few months of his life, a love filled with both the joy of reunion and the pain of approaching separation surrounded him. That love allowed him to blossom as a human being, claiming his dignity and integrity. That man was able to reach a state of spirituality based upon that love which allowed him to face his death with a quality of living which was joyful to witness. It was a tragic loss of a young life. His family suffered deeply. But this man was able to return home to his family both physically and emotionally and so for him spiritually, his life had purpose, meaning, and completion.

Finally, I remember a mother and child. The mother was dying from AIDS and she was desperate to secure the well-being of her child. She had left abusive parents years before and was fearful to contact them. Only through the loving acceptance of her friends and caregivers did she reclaim her self-worth and confidence to finally reach out to her mother. She called her mother to visit and the mother responded quickly. But upon arrival, the mother continued to live out old abusive patterns. Soon the daughter was anguishing in the guilt of imposed sinfulness and punishment. She could not sustain her sense of self-worth under the pressure of her mother's negative influence. She had neither the physical strength nor the spiritual strength to combat her mother's destructive loving. It reached such a pitch that the mother was asked to leave and her daughter was only barely able to reclaim her sense of self-worth and secure the safety of her child under the guardianship of a friend before dying.

These three experiences have taught me that forces divine, sometimes called God, rarely work outside or independent of the human spirit. God does not "make" people love themselves or each other. It is only when we choose to love, and love without question or qualification, that we can tap that universal love we call divine and "see" the spirituality that does exist within HIV/AIDS.

It is often said within the Christian tradition that the Holy Spirit moves through people. But only through those who choose to make themselves available to that spirit. In more secular terms, people can only tap their spiritual energy if they choose to make themselves available to that energy. And it seems that spiritual energy within each of us is found more quickly if we are loved and valued by others for simply who we are.

Is there spirituality with HIV/AIDS? Most definitely. It is found within the lives of those who choose to love without question or judgment. It is found in the lives of those who know that they are valued greatly as people regardless of how limited or debilitated their lives may be. There is extraordinary spirituality within the life of the bed-ridden wife when she knows and experiences love. There is profound spirituality within the life of the man who knows he is rejected by his family but accepted by his God.

For the spirituality of HIV/AIDS is the same as the spirituality of any true tragedy. The spirituality of HIV/AIDS is found within the human spirit that continues to love against all obstacles, even that of illness and death. And that love will always be divine, will always be of God.

CONCLUSION

At best, the only role a caregiver can fulfill is that of being present to the person who is dying. We can attempt to alleviate pain and enhance comfort, but the reality is that it is the dying person who must travel this road alone and resolve issues within themselves with their own resources and energy. If healing happens, it is a human journey which unfolds with mystery, awe, and beauty. The following words are testimony of just such a journey. Not all of us bear such an eloquent witness to this process. All of us, however, have already embarked upon such a journey:

Before I came here, life was not worth living.
Since being here, I have regained my sense of self,

I have regained the love of my daughter who was lost to me.
She accepts me now for who I am.
Despite the loss of my body, my muscles, my senses,
I am happy in a way I have never been happy before.
I have a sense of spirit I have never had before.
I have the love of my daughter and my family.
I am happy with myself.
I am ready to face death because I am myself.

— Casey House Hospice resident

REFERENCES

1. M. Millison and J. R. Dudley, Providing Spiritual Support: A Job for All Hospice Professionals, *The Hospice Journal*, 8:4, pp. 49-66, 1992.
2. R. Doran, *AIDS: A Praxis for Hope*, lecture address, Regis College, Toronto, 1992 (with permission of author).
3. J. Woodward, *Embracing the Chaos; A Theological Response to AIDS*, SPCK, London, England, 1990.

Contributors

Stephen R. Connor, Ph.D. is a licensed clinical psychologist who has worked in the field of hospice care since 1975. He has done research on use of denial by the terminally ill, the impact of bereavement intervention on use of health care services, and on factors affecting anticipatory grief. He has chaired the psychosocial work group of the International Work Group on Death, Dying, and Bereavement and currently chairs the National Hospice Organizations Standards and Accreditation Committee. Connor has published on a variety of hospice-related topics and is a frequent presenter at national meetings on psychosocial and management issues in hospice care. He is currently in private practice and is the Executive Director of the Hospice of Central Kentucky in Elizabethtown.

Esther Magrethe Gjertsen has been an advisor in the Norwegian Cancer Society for seven years. She is also an Associate Professor at the Department of Social Medicine, University of Oslo. Research interests include chronically ill and elderly peoples' life situation, "quality of life" issues, and functional capacity studies.

Rev. Douglas Graydon, B.Tech. (Arch. Sci.), M. Div. has been the pastoral counselor of Casey House Hospice for over five years. Rev. Graydon has been active within the HIV/AIDS field for almost ten years. Besides being the author of numerous articles and papers, Rev. Graydon facilitates seminars and workshops on HIV/AIDS palliative care and spirituality.

Mary Guerriero Austrom, Ph.D. is an Assistant Professor in the Department of Psychiatry, Indiana University School of Medicine and Director of the Education and Information Transfer Core at the Indiana Alzheimer Disease Center. Her clinical and research interests include the grief and stress experienced by family caregivers of Alzheimer disease patients. She has written several articles and chapters on these issues. In addition, she is interested in the training and education of both family and professional caregivers of the elderly and has developed numerous educational programs as well. Dr. Guerriero Austrom is actively involved with various organizations locally and nationally devoted to issues affecting the elderly.

Hugh C. Hendrie, M.B. Ch.B. is Albert E. Sterne Professor of Psychiatry and Chairman of the Department of Psychiatry, Indiana University School of Medicine. In addition, Dr. Hendrie is the Co-Director of the Indiana University Center for Alzheimer's Disease and Related Neuropsychiatric Disorders. Dr. Hendrie received his M.B. Ch.B. at the Faculty of Medicine, University of Glasgow; a Diploma in Psychiatry from the University of Manitoba; and an M.S. from Wayne State University. Dr. Hendrie is internationally known for his work and contributions to the field of psychiatry. He has written over 100 articles, book chapters, and abstracts on various topics in psychiatry, including psychogeriatrics. Dr. Hendrie has received numerous federal grants for his research efforts in biological psychiatry and the epidemiology of Alzheimer's disease and has spoken to groups, both nationally and internationally, discussing the nature of his research.

Reverend Peter Hill, spent four years of training in the New South Wales Baptist Theological College. Subsequently, thirteen years were spent in parish ministry. During the past fifteen years he has worked as Chaplain in hospitals in the regional city of Lismore, New South Wales. During this time he completed counseling training in the fields of marriage and family as well as that of loss and grief. He has visited major Palliative Care institutions and hospices in the United Kingdom and North America and presented papers in 1989 and 1993 at the King's College Conference on Death and Bereavement in London, Ontario, Canada.

Connie Holden, R.N., M.S.N. is a graduate of the University of Wisconsin-Madison with a Master of Science in Nursing. She has fourteen years of both clinical and administrative experience in hospice and is currently the Executive Director of Boulder County Hospice in Boulder, Colorado. She serves on the following ethics committees: National Hospice Organization, Hospice Nurses Association, and Boulder Community Hospital. She also serves on the Colorado Governor's Commission on Life, and the Law-Physician-Assisted Suicide Subcommittee.

Ben-Joshua Jaffee received his doctorate from Columbia University School of Social Work and has been a professor at the University of Washington School of Social Work for the past twenty-nine years. Since 1985, he has taught both Masters-level and continuing education courses on a variety of topics concerning loss, grief, and death. In 1991, he offered the first two courses in loss and grief ever to become part of the School's main curriculum, courses he has continued to teach each year since then on an ongoing basis. He has been a volunteer in a home hospice program and has served on the Steering Committees for both the 1991 and 1996 World Gathering on Bereavement, the 1994 annual conference of The Compassionate Friends, and the Children Grieve, Too program, all in Seattle. He has presented papers on the topic "Using Laughter as a Cathartic Process in Grief Counseling" at the World Gathering on Bereavement, at the 14th Annual Association for Death Education and Counseling Conference in 1992 and at the 1993 King's College Conference on Death and Bereavement. At this latter conference in 1995, he presented a paper on the topic "Educating Graduate Social Work Students in the Principles and Practice Application of the Grieving Process."

Dennis Klass is Professor and Department Chair of Religion at Webster University, St. Louis, Missouri. A Psychologist of Religion (Ph.D., University of Chicago), Klass has been active in the area of death, dying, and bereavement since 1968 when he was a graduate assistant in the famous Death and Dying Seminar at the University of Chicago Hospitals. Since 1979, Klass has focused his attention on parental bereavement in a long-term ethnographic study of a local chapter of The Compassionate Friends. He was given the Compassionate Friends National Board's Appreciation Award in 1992 for his work. Klass wrote *Parental Grief: Resolution and Solace* (Springer, 1988) and co-authored *They Need to Know: How to Teach Children About Death* (Prentice-Hall, 1979). He has written over forty articles or book chapters on death and grief and on the psychology of religious leadership. He is on the editorial boards of *Omega, Journal of Death and Dying* and *Death Studies*. A licensed psychologist, Klass maintains a small clinical practice with difficult and complex bereavements.

Pearl E. Langer M.S.W., C.S.W. is an experienced family therapist, educator, and consultant in staff training. She has a unique specialization in the field of aging especially as this pertains to family dynamics. Pearl also specializes in loss and bereavement and lectures at the University of Toronto on this subject and on intergenerational relations. She continues to conduct numerous training programs for professionals and is a member of the Ontario Association of Professional Social Workers, the Ontario College of Certified Social Workers, the Canadian Association on Gerontology, the American Society on Aging, and the Ontario Network for the prevention of Elder Abuse.

Elizabeth I. Latimer, M.D., F.C.F.P., C.C.F.P. is presently Professor in the Department of Family Medicine, McMaster University, Hamilton, Ontario and Director of the Palliative Care Program of the Hamilton Civic Hospitals. In addition, she is the Co-ordinator of the Regional Palliative Care Program of the Hamilton-Wentworth District Health Council, and Past Founding Chairman of the Section of Palliative Care, Ontario Medical Association. Dr. Latimer is a Fellow of the College of Family Physicians of Canada.

Dr. Dorothy C. H. Ley was concerned that hospice care not lose touch with its basic philosophy. In direct compassionate languages she reminds us of what has always been most important: providing people who have a terminal or life-threatening illness with the physical, emotional, spiritual, and supportive care they need in their last months of life. She had a unique vision of hospice care as a doctor with a pioneering career in cancer treatment, as a family member, and as a patient with a terminal illness herself. Her leadership roles in promoting and teaching palliative care have dramatically changed how people with a terminal or life-threatening illness are treated in Canada and internationally. Dr. Ley's example and her advice can be the foundation upon which we develop hospice care into the twenty-first century.

Flora MacDonald served sixteen years (1972-1988) as Member of Parliament for Kingston and the Islands during which time she held three Cabinet positions: Secretary of State for External Affairs (1979-1980), Minister of Employment and Immigration (1984-1986), and Minister of Communications (1986-1988). During her time as an Opposition Member of Parliament, she held the critic's post for Indian Affairs and Northern Development, Federal-Provincial Relations, External Affairs and Status of Women. Born and educated in North Sydney, Nova Scotia, she is a graduate of Empire Business College and the National Defence College one-year course in Canadian and International Studies. She holds honourary degrees from a number of universities in Canada, the United States, and the United Kingdom (the University of Maine, Orono; Queen's University, Kingston; McMaster University, Hamilton; Mount Saint Vincent University, Rockingham, Nova Scotia; Acadia University, Wolfville, Nova Scotia; the State University of New York, Potsdam; York University, Toronto; Royal

Military College, Kingston; and the University of Edinburgh). Miss MacDonald served as executive director of the Progressive Conservative National Headquarters from 1957 to 1966. She spent the next six years as an administrative officer and tutor in the Department of Political Studies at Queen's University. From 1966 to 1969, she was also National Secretary of the Progressive Conservative Association of Canada. She was Visiting Fellow at the Centre for Canadian Studies of the University of Edinburgh from September to December 1989, and Special Adviser to the Vancouver-based Commonwealth of Learning from August 1990 to October 1991. From 1990 to 1994, she was appointed Chairperson of the International Development Research Centre (IDRC). Flora MacDonald is currently Director of the following companies and organizations: Canada Trust Company; Canadian Crafts Council; CARE Canada; Carnegie Commission Re Preventing Deadly Conflict; Centre for Refugee Studies, York University; Friends of the National Library; Queen's University Council; Refugee Policy Group, Washington, D.C.; Shastri Indo-Canada Institute. She is Patron of the Commonwealth Human Rights Initiative and Honourary Patron for Canada of the National Museums of Scotland. From 1990 to 1994, she was chairperson of the Capital Fundraising Campaign, Mount St. Vincent University, Halifax. In 1989, she was appointed by the Secretary-General of the United Nations as Member Eminent Person's group to study Trans-National Corporations in South Africa. Miss MacDonald was named an Officer of the Order of Canada in April 1993 and the Order of Ontario in May 1995.

Victor W. Marshall, Ph.D., is Director of the Centre for Studies of Aging, and Professor of Behavioral Science, at The University of Toronto. He also serves as Network Director of CARNET: The Canadian Aging Research Network, a federally-funded Network of Centres of Excellence. Born in Calgary, he was educated at The University of Alberta, Calgary, and Princeton University. In addition to authoring several books and articles in the aging area, he served as Editor-in-Chief of *The Canadian Journal on Aging* for five years. He is an Associate Editor of the *Handbook of Aging and the Social Sciences,* and serves on the Executive Advisory Board of the *Encyclopedia of Gerontology.* His interests in aging and dying began with his doctoral dissertation research in the late 1960s. His writings have also dealt with aging in relation to the family, long-term care, and health policy. His current research focuses on social theory of aging, independence and aging, and aging and the labor force. He directs a multidisciplinary research program in the latter area funded by the Innovations Fund of Human Resources Development Canada.

John D. Morgan is Professor of Philosophy and Director of the Centre for Education about Death and Bereavement at King's College of the University of Western Ontario, London, Canada. Dr. Morgan has been teaching courses about death and bereavement since 1968 and has coordinated the King's College International Conferences on Death and Bereavement since 1982. Dr. Morgan is author of twenty-seven articles or chapters dealing with death and bereavement and has edited or co-edited nine books. Dr. Morgan's research interests focus on issues of cultural attitudes related to death and bereavement.

Sidney Z. Moss, L.S.W., B.C.D., is a clinical and research social worker. He is a Family Therapist and Certified Grief Counselor in private practice who has specialized in issues of separation and grief. He has published widely about family losses over the life cycle including remarriage after widowhood, death of adult siblings, and death of the very old. He is currently working at the Philadelphia Geriatric Center on a study of the meaning of the death of an elderly parent for a middle-age child.

Miriam S. Moss, M.A., is a Senior Research Sociologist at the Philadelphia Geriatric Center where she has been engaged in a range of gerontological research since 1970. Her work has focused on family and social relationships, caregiving for elderly persons, the characteristics of the last year of life, and death and dying. She and her husband, Sidney, have written together extensively, and they were joint recipients of the Richard Kalish Award of the Gerontological Society of America. She is currently co-principal investigator in a study of death of an elderly parent.

Patrice O'Connor, R.N., M.A., C.N.A. has been the administrator of a Hospice/Palliative Care Program for fourteen years. Ms. O'Connor has lectured nationally and internationally and published on palliative care issues. Patrice O'Connor is the Palliative Care Consultant at St Lukes/Roosevelt Hospital Center.

Phyllis Palgi, Ph.D. is Past Head of the Department of Behavioral Sciences, Sackler School of Medicine, Tel Aviv University. She was born in South Africa and immigrated to Israel in 1947. She has a Ph.D. in Anthropology having studied in Capetown University and Columbia University. She served as the first government anthropologist and introduced the academic teaching of anthropology into Medical School and Nursing Schools in Israel. She pioneered death studies and applied ethno-psychology in Israel and published extensively on the subject.

Colin Murray Parkes is consultant psychiatrist to St. Christopher's Hospice, Sydenham and St. Joseph's Hospice, Hackney. He is President of Cruse: Bereavement Care, author of *Bereavement: Studies of Grief in Adult Life* (Routledge, London and New York) and numerous other publications on death and bereavement and has lectured widely on these subjects.

Cand Polit is with the Norwegian Cancer Association.

Rabbi Daniel A. Roberts, D.D., has lectured several times at the King's College International Conference on Death and Bereavement in London, Ontario, and is an acknowledged expert on spirituality, dying, and teenage suicide. Rabbi Roberts has also written three chapters in published books, including "Ask Your Ancestors and They Will Tell You" in a forthcoming book edited by John Morgan. He has produced a multimedia presentation on teenage suicide prevention, "Inside, I Ache," which is used in schools all over the country. Currently, Rabbi Roberts is pursuing a D.Min. from Pittsburgh Theological Seminary and is writing a thesis about comforting the mourner. He has been the spiritual leader of Temple Emanu El since 1972.

Margaret A. Somerville holds professorships in both the Faculty of Medicine and the Faculty of Law at McGill University, Montreal. She is Gale Professor of Law and the Founding Director of the McGill Centre for Medicine, Ethics and Law. She is the recipient of many honors and awards, including the Distinguished Service Award of the American Society of Law and Medicine (1985), the *Pax Orbis ex Jure* Gold Medal, for support and dedication to the cause of world peace through law (1985), and the Order of Australia (1989), in recognition of her international contribution to law and bioethics. Professor Somerville has an extensive publishing and speaking record. She is currently the Chairperson of the National Research Council of Canada Ethics Committee, a member of the Board of Directors of the Canadian Anti-Doping Council and of the American Society of Law, Medicine and Ethics. She is also active in the clinical sphere, serving on clinical and research ethics committees and consulting for Teaching Hospitals. She plays an active role in the worldwide development of bioethics and the study of the wider legal and ethical aspects of medicine and science.

Eric C. Tappenden, M.S.W. is the President of Canadian Memorial Services, a non-profit service organization which administers *The Simple Alternative* as an option to dealing with commercial funeral homes in the greater Toronto area. As an executive with the Ontario

Government in the 1980s, Mr. Tappenden directed the overhaul of the *Funeral Directors and Establishments Act* and the *Cemeteries Act*. From 1990-1993 he was Vice President of Public Services for Commemorative Services of Ontario, a non-profit cemetery organization. Mr. Tappenden is active in volunteer work with his church, the Canadian Mental Health Association, a local hospice, and the Bereavement Ontario Network. In 1993 he was the recipient of the University of Toronto Arbor Award for excellence in volunteer service.

Neil Thompson, Ph.D. is a senior lecturer in social work at North East Wales Institute, Wales, United Kingdom. He has previously worked as a social work practitioner, manager, and training officer. He is the author of a number of books, including *Anti-Discriminatory Practice* (Macmillan).

Judith van Heerden M.B. Ch.B. Before joining the Unit of Family Practice/Primary Care as a lecturer in 1988, her full-time career was devoted first to Pediatrics and later to Radiotherapy. While working with cancer patients she was instrumental in establishing terminal care services in Port Elizabeth. Allied to this interest, an AIDS Training Course for student interns was launched at UCT in 1991. At present she is involved in research on health care for prisoners, which has increased her awareness of medical ethics and patients' human rights.

Index